ST. PAUL.

MINNESOTA

AND

ITS RESOURCES

BY

J. W. BOND

FALLS OF ST. ANTHONY

REDFIELD
110 & 112 NASSAU STREET
NEW YORK.
1853.

LITH. OF SARONY & Co NEWYORK.

MINNESOTA

AND

ITS RESOURCES

TO WHICH ARE APPENDED

CAMP-FIRE SKETCHES

OR

NOTES OF A TRIP FROM ST. PAUL TO PEMBINA AND SELKIRK SETTLEMENT ON THE RED RIVER OF THE NORTH

BY J. WESLEY BOND

REDFIELD,
110 AND 112 NASSAU STREET, NEW YORK.
1853.

STEREOTYPED BY C. C. SAVAGE,
13 Chambers Street, N. Y.

TO

THE CITIZENS OF MINNESOTA,

This Work is respectfully Dedicated

AS A TOKEN OF APPRECIATION FOR THEIR ENTERPRISE, INTELLIGENCE, AND MORAL WORTH, BY THEIR FELLOW-CITIZEN,

THE AUTHOR.

PREFACE

This work is offered as a brief general view of Minnesota, as it existed prior to its organization as a territorial government in 1849, and "as it is" at the present time. As a guide to the immigrant, and the tourist in search of general information and pleasure, it is believed to contain much valuable and interesting knowledge.

The facts and statements contained in this work will be found particularly correct, and it is thought will meet the desire of the community throughout the states—at least that part of it intending to remove hither, who wish a reliable work for reference and information concerning the many interesting topics pertaining to this territory.

The style, though somewhat glowing, is not in the least overdrawn. Those familiar with the country will admit, on a perusal, that the half has not been told. To present a plain and truthful picture has been my only aim; and if, in any instance, I have erred, an absorbing interest in the cause of Minnesota must offer sufficient atonement for such error.

The matter contained in the "Camp-Fire Sketches," and several other chapters, is entirely original. I have also made valuable selections from the writings of David Dale Owen, United States geologist; Rev. E. D. Neill, of St. Paul; ex-Governor Ramsey, and several others of considerable repute.

A reference to the "Appendix" will show some important matters unavoidably omitted in the body of the work, to a careful perusal of which the reader is respectfully invited.

I particularly acknowledge my indebtedness to the St. Paul press, and to my friend Major J. J. NOAH, whose valuable assistance in compiling and superintending this publication has contributed much to its merit. I therefore present this work as partly original and partly made up of compilations from other paragraphists, who have incidentally preceded me upon the subject. It will, perhaps, prove altogether more valuable on that account.

J. WESLEY BOND.

ST. PAUL, MINNESOTA, *September* 1, 1853.

CONTENTS.

MINNESOTA AND ITS RESOURCES.

CHAPTER I.

THE EARLY HISTORY OF MINNESOTA.

A VERY few years ago, and the present territory of Minnesota was a waste of woodland and of prairie, uninhabited save by the different hordes of savage tribes from time immemorial scattered through its expanse, with of later years a few white traders only intermingled. At intervals a zealous missionary of the cross, or adventurous traveller, by turns found their way to the Great Falls of St. Anthony, and even to the source of the Father of Waters himself—and with awe filling their souls at the grandeur and sublimity of the works of nature, and with swelling hearts lifted "from nature up to nature's God," have returned to the bosom of society in the great world then far, far away to the south and east, and recounted there the wonders seen, the dangers encountered, the uncultivated and wasted paradise they explored, the legends and character of the Red Men among whom almost alone they mingled.

Minnesota has indeed been "the home of many a traveller and the theme of many a traveller's story." Here, indeed, alone and solitary was seen to glide the canoe of the dark-browed Indian over his own loved lakes; and from the rocky bluff, where stand the churches now dedicated to God, and raising their tall spires heavenward, only arose the smoke of the wigwam and the council-fire, while the whoop of the savage resounded over the flowing stream below—across whose still, smooth waters, the soft, sweet sound of the organ's tones, the sonorous tolling of the church-going bell, and the busy hum of commerce, now reverberate. The scenes and sights then witnessed have disappeared across the river to the westward, and soon will be transferred still further from our gaze, and the home, the hunting-grounds, and even the very graves of the Indians will be obliterated for ever.

The two fierce tribes which now inhabit our territory, the Chippewas of the old Algonquin stock, and their inveterate and hereditary enemies, the equally fierce and more numerous Sioux, have for ages waged an exterminating warfare—one which is well-known spares neither age, sex, nor condition. Our fair land has been the scene of many a Thermopylæ though on a smaller scale, and the fierce clangor of the hand-to-hand combat has resounded far and wide. Here thousands of the brave sons of the forest have met death uncomplainingly and sung their last wail of despair and agony amid untold horrors. Their smoking blood has enriched many a now fertile field—as, like that of Lancaster, it sunk into the ground, when it should have mounted and cried aloud for vengeance. That vengeance has been meted out from time to time by either party, and many an ensanguined story could be told of more than Roman heroism—of more than Spartan valor.

This feud, so bitter, has descended to our own times, and of its continued strifes many of us have been reluctant witnesses, while of its horrors, all have heard repeatedly. We live and move upon more than classic ground—ground consecrated by the outpoured blood of many a poor untutored victim—"who if they were the children of the forest, still heard the voice of their God in the morning breeze—they beheld him in the dark cloud that rose in wrath from the west—they acknowledged his universal beneficence in the setting sun as he sank to his burning bed. Here they lived and loved."

In Europe, near two hundred years ago, as in America, at this day Minnesota, or what is now Minnesota, was a land toward which many an eye was turned, and in regard to which fact and fancy wove a wondrous tale of interest and romance.

In consequence of this, from the time when Father Menard, the devoted Jesuit missionary, was lost in the forest in 1658 while crossing *Kee-wee-nah* Peninsula, and his sad fate conjectured only from his cassock and breviary, long afterward found preserved as "Medicine" charms, among the wild Dakotas of our territory, down to the time when Schoolcraft, in 1832, traced our giant Mississippi—a giant more wonderful than the hundred-armed Briareus—to its origin in the gushing fountains of Itasca lake, Minnesota has continued a favorite field of reserch.

Here Hennepin in 1680, was first to break the silence of these northern wilds with a white man's voice, in giving to the foaming waters of St. Anthony's falls, their baptismal name in honor of his patron saint. Here was the scene of his captivity among the M'day-wah-kaun-twan Dakotas, and here he experienced the compassion and protection of *Wah-zee-koo-tay*, the great Nahdawessy chief.

Here too, not very long afterward, Baron La-Hontan, journeyed; and in this territory, that romance of geography, his *La Longue Riviere*, had its location and due western course—the creature of La-Hontan's imagination, or rather of truth and fable curiously interwoven and intermingled.

More reliable than either, the gallant Le Sueur, a brave, enterprising, and truthful spirit, in 1700 explored the *sky-colored water* of the St. Peter's to its Blue Earth tributary, and in the vicinity of his log fort L'Hullier, on the banks of the *Mahn-kahto*, first broke the virgin soil of our territory with the spade and pick-axe, in delving for copper ore, tons of which, or a green earth supposed to be the ore of that metal, he had conveyed to his native France. He it was, also, who appears to have been the first white man or trader, that supplied the "Sioux" and "Aiavvis" (Ioways) with fire-arms and other products of civilized labor; and to his truthful and generally accurate Journal, we are likewise indebted for the best statistics we possess of the early history of the Dakota race, which then, fully a century and a half ago, as now, occupied the greater portion of our territory.

Following Le Sueur, after a considerable interval, came Captain *Jonathan Carver* in 1776, and however extravagant we may regard some of his statements, and however discreditable we may deem his efforts to engross millions of acres, including nearly all the inhabited portion of Minnesota, and the very land upon which Saint Paul now stands, by a pretended deed of gift from the Indians, still we must concede him to have been an adventurer of no mean courage and enterprise, and his narrative a valuable link in the chain of our early annals.

Still later, and within the present century, Cass and Schoolcraft, Nicollet and Fremont, Long and Keating, have visited and explored our land; and Pike, too, the heroic Zebulon Pike, who, in 1802, during the "Expedition to the Upper Mississippi," of which he has presented so admirable a narrative, gave promise of that fortitude, courage, and determination, which marked him throughout a glorious career, until his mangled body surrendered up his noble spirit, happy in the triumph of his country's flag, on the plains of Canada.

These are our records—these in part, our historiographers. Their works form stepping-stones, across at least that portion of the river of time, which, in this region, for about two hundred years, has rolled its tide occasionally within view of the white race. The gaps between, it is not unfitly our duty to lessen and to close up.

The materials for this purpose are not scarce, though somewhat difficult to embody in a tangible or reliable form. Not a foot of ground that we tread, but has been trod by nations before us. Wild tribes of men have marched their armies over the sites of our towns and fields—fierce battles have been fought, where ere long churches may rear their spires—our ploughshares may turn furrows amidst the graves of buried races, and our children play perhaps, where generations of children have played centuries before them. Dakota and Ojibway, Shiann and Ausinabwaun, Winnebago and Ioway, Ozaukie and Musquakie, each, in turn or together, dwelt in the land, hunted and warred through it, migrated to and from it. When the first Jesuit missionary, one hundred and ninety years ago, visited Lake Superior, he found the Chippewas and Sioux engaged in that war, which has continued with but little intermission nearly to the present time. How long before—for how many centuries previous—this contest was waged, we know not—the records are dim, the traditions vague and uncertain. But we do know that, from the St. Croix to the Mille Lacs, the ancient home of the M'day-wah-kauntwaun Sioux, whose rich maple bottoms are a Golgotha of hostile bones, through all the midland hunting-grounds to Lake Superior, and northwest by wild rice-shallows to the fertile lands of Red lake (whose waters have so often drunk blood from battles on its shores as to have gained the ensanguined cognomen which we mildly translate "Red"), we can trace the terrible results of this warfare of the Algonquin and Dakota races—a warfare which in its results completed that general disruption of all the old geographical relations of the various tribes of Minnesota, which the Dakotas, perhaps, were the first to disarrange, when they located on the Upper Mississippi.

The incidents of this war—the battles, where fought—the victories, where and by whom won—the councils held, and alliances formed—the advances, the retreats, and the final conquests—are among the inquiries not unworthy of instituting. The character of this work prevents, at this stage, a further commentary on these inquiries; therefore I close this chapter with a brief review of Minnesota since its first settlement and organization.

Previous to the admission of Wisconsin as a state, all that part of the territory east of the Mississippi was a part of Wisconsin territory. After the admission of Wisconsin as a state, there was a considerable population here without any government. Hon. John Catlin, secretary of the territory of Wisconsin, came up here, believing that this was then the territory of Wisconsin, and that the duties of governor devolved upon him (the governor of the old territory having accepted an office under the new state of Wisconsin), and issued a proclamation ordering an election for delegate to the house of representatives of the United States. This election was held October 30, 1848. Henry H. Sibley and Henry M. Rice—two of the most prominent men in the territory—were the candidates. Mr. Sibley was elected. He went on to Washington city, and, after some little difficulty, was allowed to take his seat, and to attend to the interests of the people of the territory.

On the third day of March, 1849, the last day of the session of Congress, the territory of Minnesota was organized. On the next day General Taylor's presidential term commenced, and a few days thereafter he appointed the following officers for the territory: Alexander Ramsey, governor; C. K. Smith, secretary; A. Goodrich, chief-justice; and B. B. Meeker and David Cooper, associate justices of the supreme court of Minnesota; H. L. Moss, United States district attorney; and Joshua L. Taylor, United States marshal. Mr. Taylor declined the appointment, and A. M. Mitchell was appointed marshal. Governor Ramsey arrived soon after his appointment, the other officers shortly after, and on the first day of June, 1849, the governor proclaimed the organization of the territorial government. He also ordered an election of members of the legislative assembly, and a delegate to Congress. Mr. Sibley was elected to Congress without opposition.

An election was held in November of that year (1849) for county officers created by the assembly, which had just adjourned; but the next regular election for all officers, including a delegate to Congress, was held on the first Monday of September, 1850. A. M. Mitchell and Henry H. Sibley were the candidates for Congress. Mr. Sibley was successful, and Colonel Mitchell resigning, Henry L. Tilden, Esq. (now deceased), was his successor. Mr. Tilden was removed in the fall of 1851, and Joseph W. Furber, speaker of the first house of representatives, was appointed in his place. A. Van Voorhies and N. Greene Wilcox, filling the offices of register and receiver of the land-office at Stillwater, were removed by the administration that appointed them in the summer of 1852, when Allen Pierse and Jonathan E. M'Kusick were appointed their successors.

Charles K. Smith, the first secretary of the territory, was removed by the same administration in the fall of 1851, and Alexander Wilkin received the vacant office. Chief-Justice Aaron Goodrich was likewise superseded about the same time by the appointment of Jerome Fuller, Esq., editor of the *Albany Register;* but the United States senate of 1852 rejecting his confirmation, Henry Z. Hayner, Esq., of Troy, New York, received the "ermine," which he wore until removed by the incoming administration of General Pierce.

Prior to the organization of the territory, Major Murphy filled the station of agent for the Dakota or Sioux Indians, Dr. Livermore for the Chippewas, and General Fletcher for the Winnebagoes, all of whom were subsequently superseded by General Taylor; and Nathaniel M'Lean as Sioux agent, J. S. Watrous as Chippewa agent, and A. M. Fridley as Winnebago agent, were the successive incumbents. A new land-office having been established by Congress in Benton county, in 1852, Reuben W. Richardson and Charles Christmas were appointed receiver and register thereof. Charles J. Henniss and Charles Cavileer were appointed collectors of United States customs, the first at Saint Paul, the latter at Pembina, on the Red river of the North, the boundary-line between the United States and British North America.

The first legislative assembly convened in 1849 held its session at the Central house, on the second day of September, and David Olmsted, Esq., was chosen president of the council, and J. W. Furber, Esq., speaker of the house. The second session commenced on the 7th of January, 1851, in the brick building now known as the "Rice House," and continued in session ninety days in order to form a code of laws. The councillors, being elected for two years, of course held over; but the house, being new members, elected M. E. Ames, Esq., speaker, while the council chose David B. Loomis, Esq., president. The code was formed chiefly from the present practising code of New York.

The third session convened in a brick building belonging to Judge Goodrich, on the first Wednesday in January, 1852, and Hon. W. H. Forbes was chosen president of the council, and Hon. John D. Ludden speaker of the house, both of whom were members of the former legislative assembly, re-elected. The fourth session convened on the fifth day of January, 1853, and Hon. Martin M'Leod was chosen president of the council, and Hon. David Day speaker of the house, both of whom were old members re-elected. The most important feature of this assembly was the formation of eleven new counties from the land recently acquired by treaty from the Sioux.

The details of this and other treaties will be found hereafter; but from the date of the consummation of the Sioux treaty in 1852, the limits of the territory were extended beyond the Mississippi river into a region as fair as that of the far-famed Nile, lying invitingly and blooming before us. This event closes the history, so far as historical matters may be presumed, up to the present time, all the past forming but a preface to this great work.

In closing this imperfect sketch of the dim and shadowy past, an allusion perhaps ought to be made to the organization of the Minnesota Historical Society—an important event in the early history of the territory, and one which has contributed much to make it widely and favorably known throughout the Union.

"It may seem a strange thing, even to some among our own citizens, and still stranger to people elsewhere, that an *historical society* should have been formed in this territory, less than a year after its organization, when its history was apparently but a few months old; when the wilderness was, as it is yet, around us; when the smoke of Indian lodges still intercepted our view of the horizon; when our very name was so new, that men disputed as to its orthography, and formed parties in contesting its literal meaning.

"An *historical* society in a land of yesterday! Such an announcement would indeed naturally excite, at the first glance, incredulity and wonder in the general mind. Well might it be exclaimed, 'The country which has *no past*, can have no history;' with force could it be asked, '*Where* are your *records?*' and if we even had them, it would not be surprising if it were still demanded, 'What those records could possibly record? what negotiations, what legislation, what progress in arts or intellect could they possibly exhibit?'—'Canst thou gather figs from thorns, or grapes from thistles?'

"True, pertinent as such queries might seem, yet nevertheless they would be dictated by error—they would be founded in great misapprehension: for Minnesota has a history, and that not altogether an unwritten one, which can unravel many a page of deep, engrossing interest; which is rich in tales of daring enterprise, of faithful endurances, of high hopes; which is marked by the early traveller's footprints, and by the ancient explorer's pencil; which is glowing with the myths and traditions of our aboriginal race, sprinkled over with their battle-fields, with the sites of their ancient villages, and with the *wah-kaun* stones of their teeming mythology."

The society was organized by act of legislature in 1849, and holds its meetings in January of each year. Among its members are some of the leading minds of this country, as well as every influential citizen of the territory. Through the unremitting labors of the Rev. E. D. Neill, the secretary of the society, much useful and interesting information and collections have been obtained. The annals of the society are published each year, comprising all the papers written for the uses of historical research. Four of these valuable publications have been issued already at the expense of the association.

The object of the society is "the collection and preservation of a library, mineralogical and geological specimens, Indian curiosities, and other matters and things connected with, and calculated to illustrate and perpetuate the history and settlement of, the territory;" and the secretary is required "to keep a register of each donation, stating from whom obtained, on what conditions, and other items of interest connected therewith; and shall report the condition of the library and cabinet at each annual meeting."

"It is a mark of wisdom thus to write up the history of a country from the titlepage, that in after-times, when 'childish things are put away,' and 'by St. Paul the work' of civilization 'goes bravely on,' the growth of that new empire upon western waters may be all mapped out beneath the eye of posterity, from its infant-like creepings upon the greensward of St. Anthony, to the stately steppings wherewith it approached the door of the Union, and demanded admittance as a state."

Its present officers are, Hon. Alexander Ramsey, president; Hon. Martin M'Leod and Hon. David Olmsted, vice-presidents; and Rev. E. D. Neill, secretary. Any person taking interest in the historical affairs of our country can become a member by forwarding one dollar to the secretary at Saint Paul, for which he will receive a copy of the annals, and all the privileges of contribution of papers, &c.

CHAPTER II.

COMPRISING A GENERAL GEOGRAPHICAL AND DESCRIPTIVE VIEW OF THE TERRITORY, GENERAL FEATURES, ETC.

THE territory of Minnesota, as organized by the act of Congress of March 3, 1849, is an extensive region, being about four times as large as the state of Ohio, and is six hundred and seventy-five miles in extent from its southeastern to its northwestern border. It extends from the Mississippi and St. Croix rivers and the western extremity of Lake Superior on the east, to the Missouri and White-Earth rivers on the west, a distance of over four hundred miles; and from the Iowa line (latitude 43° 30′) on the south, to the British line (latitude 49°) on the north, also a distance of over four hundred miles—the whole comprising an area of 166,000 square miles, or 106,000,000 acres. At one point along the northern boundary, viz., Lake of the Woods, the line extends to latitude 50°—a fact not generally known—while on the southwestern part it extends for seventy miles below the Iowa line, to the junction of the Missouri and Sioux rivers, in latitude 42° 30′; thus running through seven and a half degrees of latitude, or a distance due north of five hundred and twenty-five miles.

Almost the whole of this is a fine rolling prairie of rich soil, a sandy loam, adapted to the short summers of the climate, and which produce bounteously, nay luxuriantly. The surface of the country, excepting the Missouri plains, is interspersed with numerous beautiful lakes of fresh water—all abounding in the finest fish, and their banks covered with a fine growth of woodland. The land is about equally divided between oak-openings and prairies, the whole well watered by numerous streams navigable for steamers.

In the eastern part, viz., on the head-waters of the Mississippi, Rum river, and the St. Croix, are extensive pine and hard-wood forests, apparently inexhaustible for centuries; while from the mouth of Crow-wing river, a tributary of the Mississippi, an extensive forest of hard-wood timber, fifty miles in width, extends southwesterly into the country watered by the Blue-Earth river, a tributary of the Minnesota river, emptying into it one hundred and fifty miles above its mouth. The latter stream, rising near Lac Traverse, flows southeasterly a distance of four hundred and fifty miles, and empties into the Mississippi at Fort Snelling, seven miles above St. Paul, and the same distance below St. Anthony. This is one of the finest streams in the valley of the Mississippi, and the country through which it flows is not excelled for salubrity of climate and fertility of soil by any part of the United States. In a good stage of water, steamboats can ascend it almost to its source. A portage of a mile or two then connects it from Big-Stone lake with Lac Traverse; and the outlet of the latter, the Sioux Wood river (all of which are thirty miles in length), with the famous Red river of the North. This stream is navigable at all seasons for steamboats from the Bois de Sioux to Pembina, on the British line—to Selkirk settlements, one hundred miles beyond—and even to Lake Winnipeg. The whole trade of these extensive regions will eventually seek this channel to a market, following down the Minnesota to the Mississippi at St. Paul, and thence to the states below. A railroad connection will eventually be made from the mouth of the Bois de Sioux to Fond du Lac; also from the same point to St. Anthony and St. Paul via Sauk rapids and the Mississippi. Another will connect the same point with Lac qui Parle, on account of the portage at Big-Stone lake; thence down to the mouth of Blue Earth; thence southeasterly through Iowa to some point, say Prairie du Chien or Dubuque, on the Lower Mississippi. Let not the credulous reader smile at this: I have been through a principal portion of the regions here described, and, without enthusiasm, write from a survey of the country and a knowledge of its capacities and resources when once brought out. Let no one think the great tide of immigration will confine itself to the banks of the Mississippi and Minnesota rivers; on the contrary, the whole interior to the north and west of these two streams will soon be peopled, and thickly peopled too.

The only interruption to the navigation of the Lower Minnesota river in dry seasons is what are called the "Rapids," some forty miles above its mouth. This is a ledge of sandstone rock, extending across the stream, and will soon be removed.

The Mississippi above St. Anthony is navigable an almost indefinite distance to the north; and the steamer "Governor Ramsey" has already been running in the trade above the falls for four years, as far as the Sauk rapids (eighty miles), which, with the Little falls (forty miles beyond), are the main obstacles in a navigation of over four hundred miles from St. Anthony to the falls of the Pokegama. St. Croix lake and river are navigable to the falls, sixty miles above the junction of the lake and Mississippi; and the St. Louis river is navigable from Lake Superior twenty miles to Fond du Lac. Numerous other streams are navigable for light-draught steamers and flat-boats from fifty to one hundred miles, penetrating into the interior to the pineries, and giving easy access into the country in all directions. These are the Blue-Earth, Rum, Elk, Sauk, Crow, Crow-wing, Vermilion, Cannon, and others.

On the northeastern border of the territory is Lake Superior, with its valuable fisheries and its shores abounding in inexhaustible mines of copper, coal, iron, &c., besides affording us the facility of that vast inland sea for immigration and commerce.

The Great Father of Waters too—the mighty Mississippi—after rising in Itasca lake, in the northern portion of the territory, flows by a devious course for some eight hundred miles through the eastern part, and below the mouth of the St. Croix forms the dividing line between us and Wisconsin for some two hundred more to the Iowa line. This mighty river gives us the whole lower valley to the gulf of Mexico for a never-ceasing market for our agricultural produce, our lumber, and our manufactures; for, with the unlimited water-power at numerous points, it were idle to argue that we are not destined to become a manufacturing as well as an agricultural community, and that the whole of the lower Mississippi valley will not be dependent in a measure on the Minnesota, of which we are all so justly proud.

As to our being too far north for comfort or convenience, or for future greatness as a state, I have not patience to even speak of it; I am not writing for the edification of people so very silly as to believe any such humbuggery. We can grow all the cereal grains—winter wheat and corn among the rest; and as a grazing country it can scarcely be equalled. Cattle and sheep, and all kinds of live stock, are more healthy here, and can be produced in as fine a degree of perfection, as in the states. The evidence of farmers who have turned their attention to this branch of farming industry fully proved this by their past experience in the states, contrasted with their great success while here.

The inhabitants now number twenty thousand. One year more, at the present rapid rate of immigration, will see it doubled. There is not an instance in the whole history of the great Northwest, or of frontier life and civilization, in which a territory, *immediately after its organization*, has been settled with such rapidity, and in which thriving, busy, bustling towns have sprung up almost as it were at the touch of some enchanter's wand. The whole history of this territory is only eclipsed by that of California, and that only in the sudden accession of numbers which *gold* (the *God* of nine tenths of the human family) has drawn together, like some huge maelstrom—the most discordant materials from the four quarters of the globe. In real agricultural wealth, in comforts, and the happy and contented character of an intelligent population—in short, in all the elements which go to elevate the character of a people, and constitute the real greatness of the state—California is far, very far, in the background.

Our progress is indeed onward, and the end not even the most sanguine can divine. The wildest day-dreamer may wake up to morrow and find his schemes, air-castles, and anticipations, in a fair train for speedy realization; and others, more vast, gigantic, and unthought of, treading rapidly on their heels! He lives in a railroad, nay, in an electric age, where action follows thought, and the conception of designs vast and mighty, and their speedy prosecution and completion, are almost simultaneous.

Minnesota has just entered upon the fifth year of her political existence. So far as business prosperity is concerned, it promises to be a bright one — brighter than any that has preceded it. Navigation has opened, and boats from below have appeared within our borders and at the wharves of St. Paul a week earlier than the usual time, taking one year with another. Our merchants and business men have been east and south for their spring and summer supplies, and are returning with stocks much larger than have heretofore been brought to the territory. Our mills, from the St. Croix to the Blue-Earth, and for scores of miles north and south along the former stream and the Mississippi, maintain their ceaseless noise and motion day and night, converting the products of our rich pine-forests into building materials for markets below and improvements at home. In the towns and villages, along the roads and highways and byways of the older settlements, and out upon the broad prairies, and by the shores of the broad streams and margins of the clear lakes of the "Sioux Purchase," the sound of the hammer and the axe is heard, busy at improvement. All is life, all is hurry, all is energy, all is onward, all is *hope*. The boats from below come swarming with hardy adventurers from other portions of our common country, and from other lands, to mingle with those now here — to settle and live among us — to be part and parcel of us — to make common cause and bide common destiny here with those who have prepared the way for the future advent of a mighty and prosperous commonwealth into the great American Union.

Minnesota at this time partakes to a large degree of the general prosperity now so happily and manifestly apparent throughout the country. I can see nothing within her, or upon the surface, indicative of a reverse of this agreeable and promising state of affairs. Her business people have not over-traded, and are consequently not dangerously in debt. Let them be equally cautious at present and in the future, and all is safe with them and with the reputation of the territory. Her farmers, and mechanics, and laboring men generally, are enterprising and industrious. *Their* energy, frugality, and perseverance, after all, are the leading element and surest guaranty of her future greatness and prosperity. Upon them depends not only a great deal, but very nearly all. That they will continue to address themselves manfully to the great task before them, of giving life and progress to the new land of their adoption, we have an assurance in the past. I speak in no boastful or vainglorious theme when I say there is largely more *character* in Minnesota than was found at the same age in any of the older western members of our republican family. I know the fact from the experience of candid men, who have lived on other frontiers, and now bear testimony in favor of Minnesota. Croakers and grumblers we may ever expect to find among us—drones and loafers; but the great family of the hive works together steadily and harmoniously. They, and those who are to come after them, will reap their reward in a glorious, happy, and enviable future.

The following items and categorical description of Minnesota are from the pen of the late and deeply-lamented Colonel James M. Goodhue, editor of the *Minnesota Pioneer*, an obituary notice of whom will be found during the progress of this work:—

"*Minnesota*" is spelled with a letter *n* at the end of the first syllable, and a letter *n* also at the beginning of the second syllable; and the *i* in the first syllable is pronounced short, as in *pin*.

St. Paul is named for the old apostle of the Gentiles himself, and for him alone; and is therefore neither in the possessive case, signifying that that respectable apostle either is or was the proprietor of the town, nor is it in the plural, signifying that there is more than one town of St. Paul; and therefore it should be spelled without an apostrophe and without an at the end of the word.

The St. Peter river is the Minnesota river, and has been for more than a year. The latter, which is the Indian name, is agreed upon universally as the appropriate name for it, the word signifying *sky-tinted water;* wherefore it is clearly proper to name it the Minnesota, aside from the fact that we need to save what few names in the calendar of saints that are not appropriated, for the brood of next-year villages; and St. Peter will be wanted to christen a town to rival St. Paul.

Minnesota comprises a vast area—certainly large enough for a state—extending through more than six degrees of latitude, and in width from the Missouri on the west to the St. Croix on the east—that is, it extends east of the Mississippi river. The portion lying east of the Mississippi, or between Wisconsin and the Mississippi, is a comparatively narrow segment; but of the part even on the east side, all the northern portion still belongs to the Chippewa Indians, and embraces immense forests of hard wood and of pine, through which the Mississippi and its tributaries roll their dark, solitary waters.

In the north is Red river, a sluggish, deep river, navigable for batteaux, Durham boats, and steamboats. It rises in Minnesota, and flows northeast, that river and the Mississippi flowing off in opposite directions, and the portages between their waters being very short.

The Missouri river is not navigable for steamboats as far up as the Minnesota line, ordinarily, without the removal of obstructions.

The Mississippi river is navigable always, when open, to Fort Snelling, which is six miles southwest of St. Paul, and yet *up* the river! At Fort Snelling the Minnesota pours in its deep, quiet volume, being a stream about the same size as the Mississippi, which comes hurrying down from the falls of St. Anthony, nine miles above, to join it below the promontory on which sits Fort Snelling like a lazy old sentinel.

The Minnesota river is navigable ordinarily to Traverse des Sioux, one hundred miles, and extraordinarily another hundred miles and more. It seems about the same thing as far up as you choose to run a boat—generally deep, rather narrow, rather sluggish, and *very* crooked; suitable only for short boats in any stage of water, and very likely in low water

2

not navigable at all, without improvement, above the rapids, forty miles above its mouth.

The St. Louis river, emptying into the west end of Lake Superior, is navigable to the falls, twenty miles, for large vessels.

The St. Croix is navigable from its mouth nearly to the falls of St. Croix, sixty miles, but is shallow above Stillwater. Boats such as now navigate the Mississippi, therefore, seldom go above Stillwater. A small boat ran all last season from Stillwater to the falls.

Minnesota abounds in lakes. Between the St. Croix and the Mississippi they seem to be innumerable, and they are also frequent west of the Mississippi. Their shores are chiefly of gravel or pebbles, and usually one or the other side of the lake is covered with a growth of timber. The water is rather shallow, clear, cool, and entirely destitute of the qualities of the boggy marshes and sloughs of the south. Many of the lakes are covered with wild rice, and are alive with waterfowl. Frequently the lake opens at one end into a tamarac swamp, filled with young tamaracs (a tree resembling the spruce) as thick as they can stand. Through this swamp the water then passes out into another basin, a little less elevated, which it fills, and makes another lake; and thus there is often formed a succession of lakes, connected by a spring-stream that runs through them all.

Near Lake Superior there is an elevation of land, that approaches the dignity of a mountain; but the nearest approach to mountains elsewhere is in the towering bluffs along the shores of the Mississippi, and from Dubuque to St. Paul these bluffs are really the grandest feature of western scenery. Except these bluffs, and the dense forests of the great woods, there is no portion of this vast territory where a loaded wagon may not be driven, provided the streams can be crossed.

Viewed from a distance, the ranges of bluffs in Minnesota have the irregular outline of mountains seen in other states. But the very apex of the highest of them may always be reached on one side by an easy, gradual slope. We do want mountain scenery here, as well as everywhere in the valley of the Mississippi river; and have often thought we could afford to give away one of our smooth, fertile counties for one of the White hills, to be planted down in the middle of Minnesota.

At Rock island, and east of Rock island, for hundreds of miles, and probably west also, there is a ridge in the shell of the earth (making the rapids of the Mississippi and Rock rivers there), which divides the region north and south of it, by an isothermal line, that varies very sensibly the climate and temperature, as you proceed north or south of it, making a change much greater than is indicated by the parallels of latitude—the slope south of the ridge, presenting a plain of vast extent, which is very slightly convex, north and south, and upon all which the rays of the sun fall about equally vertical, while north of the ridge is another slope extending as far north as Sauk rapids, with a more northern inclination, but upon the whole expanse of which the rays of the sun fall nearly equally vertical. At Sauk rapids, crops out another ridge or backbone of granite, extending east and west, north of which extends another wide plain, very slightly convex north and south; but *how* far north, we have not been there to observe, probably to the high lands dividing the sources of the Mississippi and the Red river of the North. Hence we universally observe that they have winter and sleighing weeks earlier, at and above Sauk rapids, than between Sauk rapids and Rock island; and weeks earlier between Rock island and Sauk rapids, than in the great slope below Rock island. These ridges upon the globe, east and west, may be compared to the ridges sometimes observed upon an egg, and, in our opinion, make an important feature, in explaining the phenomena of climate, which has not been heretofore observed or commented upon by geologists, as it deserves to be. As a proof of the correctness of this view, drawn from our own observation, we invite the attention of travellers upon the Mississippi to this fact—that a marked change in the development of forest foliage in the spring, is observable in passing both the ridges referred to: that at Rock island and that at Sauk rapids. The seasons, therefore, are about the same, through the whole extent of country, from Sauk rapids down to Rock island, below which, passing immediately into a more southern slope, the seasons are about the same throughout the whole extent of country for hundreds of miles south of Rock island. The difference of climate between Galena and Muscatine, would be very marked, while the difference of climate between Muscatine and Burlington would not be perceptible.

The whole world can not produce a climate more salubrious than that of Minnesota. We have never yet known a case of fever and ague in it, nor any unwholesome water, either in wells, springs, lakes, or streams. *It is for our cool, healthful climate that braces up the human frame for vigorous exertion, physical and mental,* that we regard Minnesota incomparably superior to any other new state or territory in North America. They may raise more corn in Illinois, more wool in Ohio, more pork in Iowa, more cotton in Mississippi; but Minnesota can beat them all at raising *men.* In our coldest weather, when the mercury congeals, men perform as much labor out of doors as at any time in the year. The air is then still as death—the smoke from the chimneys falls to the ground—every human body creates around itself an atmosphere of warmth. The stillness and dryness of the atmosphere, and the vigorous health we enjoy, account for the comfortable enjoyment here, of a degree of cold that would be intolerable in St. Louis. In summer, we have a few days intensely hot; but frequent showers, from spring until harvest, and most of them in the short nights. At midsummer, the sun seems scarcely to go down in the west to lave his golden axle in the Pacific, before we again behold his blazing chariot in the east. At nine o'clock in the evening, it is then scarcely too dark for your wives and daughters to be sewing. Our frequent showers multiply mosquitoes. These insects, which at first were a terrible annoyance, have about ceased to be troublesome in St. Paul; we made no use of mosquito bars last season. Autumn, indeed often until the middle of December, is a season of delightful sunny days, rising by degrees into the rigor of winter; and winter in Minnesota is the most social, comfortable season of the year. We experience no chilling winds, and shivering, drizzling rain-storms, usually. It is very uncommon to have a winter as open as the past has been. Sleighing generally continues good here through all the winter months. The river generally closes about the fifteenth of November, and opens the last of March, and a boat may generally be expected early in April; but before it closes, supplies are brought up for the semi-annual payment to the Sioux, Chippewa, and Winnebago annuities. All these Indians are paid in Minnesota. The aggregate amount of annuities paid them in cash and goods, including what the Sioux will receive under the treaties recently ratified, and the cost of transportation, amounts to several hundred thousand dollars. These payments, and the supplies furnished to Fort Ripley and Fort Snelling, and the goods and provisions furnished by the traders to the Indians, constitute much the largest share of the business heretofore done by steamboats, at the port of St. Paul.

The Indian trade is carried on chiefly by factors or agents of a few large establishments, which have their outfits or dépôts at St. Paul; these agents are at different points in the Indian country, but mostly near where the payments are made. They buy furs and peltry; but their chief business is to sell goods to the Indians, at a profit, in anticipation of payments. An Indian hunter requires his outfit of ammunition, blankets, guns, and a variety of necessaries for himself and his family. When he returns from his hunt, he generally sells his furs to the outfit that furnished him. If any balance remains due to the outfit, he does not pay it, but it is expected to stand as a charge against the annuity, if there be an annuity; or if not, then against the contingency of an annuity, to be paid as a part of the public debt of the tribe, out of the ultimate proceeds of the sale of their lands. This has been the established mode of procedure for many years; and there never has been a time when the trader with the Sioux Indians could discontinue and refuse to extend these credits, without an absolute certainty of forfeiting all former balances due to him, for the supplies of previous years.

We might say something of the admirable oaks and rock

maples, and black walnuts, found in the Big woods, which for various purposes of manufacture, will be of immense value to the trade of Minnesota; but we will now write only of pine lumber. Formerly, we had our doubts as to the great extent of our pineries. Now we have no doubt. As yet, our lumbermen only go up the St. Croix and its tributaries, and Rum river, a tributary of the Mississippi, but a few miles above St. Anthony, lying between the Mississippi, and the St. Croix. From that region comes merely the pine of the St. Croix, and of the Mississippi. But far above Rum river, are other tributaries of the Mississippi, and eighty miles of solid pine timber on the shores of the Mississippi itself, below Pokegamon falls, in the Chippewa country, and many unexplored tributaries, besides, properly in the pine region; so that *centuries* will hardly exhaust the pineries above us. We are ashamed that we ever distrusted Providence, or suspected that our munificent Maker could have left two thousand miles of fertile prairies down the river, without an adequate supply of pine lumber at the sources of the river, to make those plains habitable.

There are many saw-mills on the St. Croix; eight saws at St. Anthony propelled by water, and four at St. Paul propelled by steam. Sawing is far the best business doing in St. Paul. The logs delivered here cost less than mere stumpage in Maine; and yet lumber sells very high, and much beyond what our mills can supply, is rafted or hauled from St. Anthony. It would pay well to put up forty good steam saw-mills, now, in St. Paul. If any surplus of lumber were made, it could be taken to a market below, in the form of shingles, lathing, planed flooring and siding. We want, here, a patent wooden ware factory, large enough to supply the trade of the whole river down to New Orleans. Come what may, lumbering can not fail, unless the government foolishly undertake to cut off building and fencing, and immigration throughout the valley of the Mississippi river.

We also have more and better inducements for agriculture than any other country can boast.

1st: A better climate—in which the labor of one man will

produce more, will yield a larger surplus above his own necessities, than any other western state or territory can boast of. We have none of the languor and debility and agues, that turn men into feeble women, in the harvest-field, as they have south of us. Labor, here, stands up firmly on its legs, the year round, and drives things through.

2d: We have as good land—it is useless to say better—but as good as there is in the world. For fertility, Cottage Grove prairie, or the whole valley of the Minnesota river, or the valley of the Red river of the North, can not be beaten; yes, we undertake to say that at Pembina, in latitude 49° north, they can raise as sound corn, and as much to the acre, as can be raised anywhere on the Wabash. Now, if our readers are not going to believe us, let them stop short here; for we are prepared to make a wager, that we will raise larger and better crops in Minnesota, acre for acre, of any or all crops ever cultivated in that state, than can be raised in Illinois. We will name our farmer, living here, for our champion, and will back him up with our money. There is time enough. May is soon enough here. We will give Illinois May the start, and Minnesota shall come out ahead. Don't care what the crop is—any grain, any root—anything from a castor bean, or an apple or pear tree, or a pumpkin, to a sweet potatoe or a tobacco plant. Why, sucker, do you know you have frosts about two weeks earlier in Illinois, than we do here? It is a fact! We will show these people *sights*, who come up here in May, and go shivering back home, saying that Minnesota is "too cold for *craps*." We can beat them, too, at stock-growing, can raise hardier cattle and sheep, and thicker meated, sweeter beef, than they can anywhere down South. We feed stock a fortnight longer—but what of that? Our cattle are healthier, our grass is sweeter and more luxuriant, and our water better for stock; and we can make more at raising stock here at the same prices. But we have higher prices here for meat and for all produce—and always must have, having soldiers, lumbermen, and Indians, to feed, and make us a home market. The cost of shipping produce from below, operates as a perpetual tariff to protect our farmer. He gets the same price he could below, and the cost of freight and the charges beside.

Wild game, except water-fowl, we do not consider abundant in these parts; but we have the fattest ducks and geese feeding upon the rice lakes, and the most of them, that you ever saw or heard of. As for fish, it is no exaggeration to say that Minnesota—her rivers and streams, but especially lakes—are alive with them. We will warrant all fishermen in all parts of the world, an abundance of sport and of success in fishing. You can catch just as many bass and pickerel as you want. In the river, we catch not only the catfish (none of your slimy, muddy cats, either), but also the wall-eyed pike, a most delicious fish. In many streams the speckled trout abounds, varying in size from five inches to two pounds. But it is idle for a novice to try to catch trout. It is as ticklish a business as fortune-hunting.

On the west shore of the river, are the Sioux Indians. They are daily on the east side, begging some, trading a little, and some of them stealing. They never speak English, even if they do know a few words of it. They are civil men, women, and boys. At night they generally paddle (that is, the squaws paddle) their canoes home, across the river. In a residence of three years, we have not seen three drunken Indians in St. Paul, of any age, male or female. We state this as an astonishing fact, creditable to the character of our liquors, but still more so to the Sioux Indians. They are under better moral influence than any other Indians, perhaps, on this continent. The Sioux treaties having been ratified, these Indians will be removed before next winter, to their reservation on the head waters of the Minnesota river. A great many people, hundreds, are living now in the Indian country, making all sorts of improvements, including expensive mills. Settlers are pouring in there every day, and will continue to do so; for the government could not, if it would, shut out the swarming millions of our countrymen, for a distance of many hundred miles, of country treated for, of which the river is the boundary.

It is hard to answer the question, "What is your population

composed of?" The people who constituted Minnesota when it was organized were a majority of them Canadians, *voyageurs* and their families, and half, and quarter, and eighth, and sixteenth breed Indians, running through the whole gamut of colors, from the dusky Indian to the fair Scotchman; and these people are still in Minnesota—quiet, good people, though not all as intelligent and energetic as the scheming Yankee. They are living all over the territory, on both sides of the river, where our organic act found them, and gave them the political rights they so highly enjoy. Such is their attachment to our flag and our government, that nowhere could volunteers be more readily raised than among them to fight its battles. Since the date of the organic act, settlers from all parts have come in, from the east, the middle, and the south. However divided upon other questions, there is not and will not be in Minnesota any disposition to suffer any infringement whatever upon the rights of any and all the states of the Union to manage their own domestic affairs.

The Mississippi river is just as navigable all the way up to St. Paul, when the upper or lower rapids do not interrupt, as a river can well be; although there have been times, and may again be, when the sandbars interrupt the passage of boats of the usual draught. The boats running here are of the same class that run from St. Louis to Rock island and Galena. There are always two if not three boats regularly running between St. Louis and St. Paul. There will be a daily line of boats the coming season between St. Paul and Galena, a town with which we have a large and growing trade—most of our trade, in fact, upon the river, above St. Louis. Dubuque, however, is now struggling for a share of our trade, and may eventually succeed to some extent when the railroad shall be completed to the Mississippi opposite that town. If the town of Dubuque had the "go-aheaditiveness" that may be found in Galena, she would long since have secured the Mississippi trade. There will be a boat or two, and probably more, running regularly from St. Paul to points on the Minnesota river during the coming season. There is no doubt but there will be two boats land at our wharves every day during the coming season. For safety, elegance of accommodations, regularity, and all that constitutes good boating, these boats and boatmen in the St. Paul trade can not be surpassed. The "Greek Slave" is owned and commanded by Louis Roberts, Esq. She will run on the Minnesota immediately after the opening of navigation, but we presume will eventually take her place in the St. Paul and Galena trade. Thus it will be seen that the traveller and the immigrant at St. Louis, or the traveller coming from Chicago to Rockford by railroad, and from Rockford to Galena by stage, can hardly miss a good boat any day to St. Paul; and we learn that the fare will be very low. There are no snags in the river above Galena—no risk—never a steamboat accident—no cholera—nothing to prevent you coming cheaply, agreeably, and comfortably through, at least to see Minnesota, and look at St. Anthony and Stillwater, and at our own extensive town of St. Paul, which is fast tumbling up into the rank of cities.

If a traveller comes here, and has any sort of curiosity, he will take a stage to St. Anthony, eight miles, look at the falls and as pretty a town-site as the Almighty ever fashioned, and take the little steamboat "Governor Ramsey," above the falls, to Sauk rapids, about eighty miles; and if he does not say he sees the most delightful, the most charming land and river scenery all the way up—as far as he chooses to travel—that ever lay out of doors, then we have no sense or judgment. Or, if he wants to see what the practical farmer can do in Minnesota, let him ride down to Cottage Grove. This is upon the tongue of land extending down between the confluence of the St. Croix and the Mississippi. The farmers there raise more oats, roots, everything that is good to eat, than they have any use for, and they sell a handsome surplus every year to St. Paul and Stillwater. It is on the east side of the river, too—no trouble about Indians, and some of the best land that ever was, not yet taken up. From Cottage Grove you may proceed to Point Douglass, a place of much promise, and surrounded with choice land. Thence you will pass through a charming country, thirty miles, along the west shore of Lake St. Croix, to Stillwater.

Stillwater is the headquarters of the outfit and lumbering done above it, on the St. Croix, and has a more substantial, reliable business, for the extent of it, and more capital, and less pecuniary embarrassment, than any other town in Minnesota. There the penitentiary has been erected, and there has been located one of the land-offices in Minnesota — another is in Benton county. There come the steamboats, either on their way up or down the Mississippi; and although you might go across in a stage from Stillwater to St. Paul by land, you will probably prefer to go around in the boat. But first you must go up the St. Croix, and see the busy sawmills at the Marine, Oceola, Taylor's falls,. and the falls of St. Croix. These places are all actively engaged in lumbering. Being back at St. Paul, you will of course go up, four or five miles, to Mendota and Fort Snelling. Southwardly from St. Paul, about six miles *up* the Mississippi river, on a high, smooth promontory, standing upon white sandrock, is the fort, below which unite the Minnesota from the southwest and the Mississippi from the northwest; but an island extends down for half a mile, and keeps the channels of the two streams separate, except a narrow slough or cut-off that connects them just below the fort. About half way down the island, on the Sioux or west side, sitting on the shore of the Minnesota river, is Mendota, which has been incorporated by our legislature, and is destined to a rapid improvement. The tenacity with which the war department hung to the large tract of country embraced within the old military reserve at Fort Snelling, has been the only obstacle to the improvement of Mendota heretofore.

Hurrying back to St. Paul (and the boat is there before you think of it), you take the stage to St. Anthony, passing through as pretty a specimen of Minnesota on your way as need be; and you are soon there, although you might go in half the time if that railroad that *is* to be were completed. You will find St. Anthony a right smart village, very neatly built along the east bank of the river, and on a bench a little back from the river, that overlooks the falls and a fine region west of the river. You may be disappointed in the grandeur of the falls, as you certainly will be in the size of the river, but not in the unsurpassed beauty of both, or the charming beauty of the whole scene that surrounds you. The mills, eight saws, you will find actively employed, and water enough (if the throat of the channel through which it is supplied, between the island and the shore, were sufficiently deepened) to drive all the sawmills in the world! Less than half a mile below the milldam (which confines all the water passing down on the east side of the island, while on the west side the water leaps unrestrained down the falls) there is an eddy, to which lumber is hauled from the mills to be rafted down to St. Paul, distant by the river some thirteen or fourteen miles. Look upon the map, and you will see that St. Anthony is only about two miles north of St. Paul. A railroad of eight miles, therefore, or a plank-road, would be of great service to both towns. That steamboats, fit to navigate the river below St. Paul, never can if they would, and never would if they could, make a difficult trip of fourteen miles for the sake of getting two miles nearer to Lake Superior and to the north pole than they are at St. Paul, in competition with a plank-road or railroad eight miles long, is evident from the fact that they can not and do not do it in competition with *common* roads. An extension of a railroad in the proper and natural direction (northerly up the Mississippi river toward Lake Superior) would not touch St. Anthony, but would leave it several miles west of the line. We should, however, favor the construction of a road by St. Anthony, a place where all travellers will desire to visit, where there will be much manufacturing, especially of pine lumber, the university of Minnesota, and a place, in fact, which will ultimately be one of much importance, as a beautiful retreat, and a place of quiet and repose.

St. Anthony is said to contain fifteen hundred inhabitants; but what they do for a living, beyond the few engaged in lumbering, we are unable to say. In our opinion, the ultimate hope of that town for a large population rests upon that class of retired people of substance, as well as invalids and people of fortune, desiring literary privileges in a retired, beautiful town, who will certainly be more strongly attracted there than to any place we know of in the Great Valley. They have there a newspaper, the *St. Anthony Express*, which is really the most valuable institution they possess. Whatever we could do to attract the attention of the world to such advantages as St. Anthony really does possess, we have cheerfully done and written.

All-Saints, or Hennepin, is on the west side of the river, opposite St. Anthony. Here is the old government mill, and a new saw-mill, and many other buildings have been recently erected. This is the county-seat of Hennepin county, which, since the reserve has been taken off, and Lake Minnetonka has been *discovered*, has increased in population very rapidly. This county has been organized for judicial purposes at the last session of the legislature, and is destined to be one of the most wealthy agricultural counties in the territory. All Saints, or Hennepin, or Minnehaha (what a pity they can not find a name for the place), is in all respects as pleasantly situated as St. Anthony for mill purposes, and will soon be a flourishing village. A few miles below on the way to Fort Snelling, is Little Falls, where a small stream from Lake Minnetonka, passing through Lake Calhoun, leaps down a perpendicular ledge, some seventy feet, in a way to stir up a great many stupid stanzas and swelling odes, and sublime distiches. A few miles, three or four back, is Lake Calhoun, which it seems to be generally admitted must be considered our classic lake; and all the little poetasters of the Union, when they go into that region, are compelled to affect, if they do not feel, poetic fervor; they catch the *cacoethes scribendi;* and soon they break out in couplets, sonnets, distiches, odes, descriptions, sketches, and various other phenomena of disordered imaginations. From All-Saints, you might take a pony and ride a hundred miles up the Minnesota river, through a varied landscape of rich prairie and heavy timber, and rich bottoms, like those of the Illinois, the grass so high that you could not look out from the top of your pony—or through the Big woods, or across mill-streams, past newly-erected dwellings, large fields recently ploughed and fenced, preparatory to receiving a crop the coming spring—on across rolling prairies of rich luxuriance, sloping away in the wide, blue dreamy-looking basin of the Minnesota, the loveliest view of broad, fair voluptuous Nature, in all her unconcealed beauty, that ever flashed upon mortal vision, to Henderson. It is a town recently laid out on the Minnesota river, at its most westerly bend below the Blue Earth, and on a direct line between Old Village lake, on the Cannon river, to the new fort and Indian agency, which have been located on the Upper Minnesota. There has been about a thousand cords of wood cut here during the past winter, to be boated down to St. Paul. A saw-mill and various other improvements are now being constructed. The proprietors contemplate opening a road the present spring to Cannon river, a distance of from twenty to twenty-five miles, which will afford facilities for the immigrants by land to reach the country west of the Minnesota, by the best and shortest route. Although some thirty miles by the river, below the Traverse des Sioux, it is about ten miles nearer to the fort and agency by land, owing to the course of the river being south of east from the fort to Blue Earth, and thence west of north to Henderson. A heavy growth of timber, of sugar maple principally, extends west about five miles, where it is met by a clean, smooth, rich, and fertile prairie, extending to the New fort, and beyond that to sundown. A road has been opened through the woods to the prairie, and supplies have been hauled to the new fort the past winter. The road passes by several beautiful lakes, well timbered, and presenting many facilities for the agriculturist, being well watered, well timbered, superior prairie-land, and convenient to a *Western* market.

Travelling a little north of west, at the distance of thirty-five miles from Henderson, where the river comes from a point *east* of *south*, you again strike the Minnesota at Little Rock, near the point selected for the new fort; which is on a beautiful plateau, in view of the Minnesota stretching off for miles nearly southeast and northwest. Near this point is the Little Rock river, the lower line of the Indian reserve; and some twelve or fifteen miles up the Minnesota is the new location of the Sioux agency, near the mouth of the Red wood on the south, and the Beaver river on the north. Both those streams are susceptible of being made to drive machinery for the manufacture of flour, sawing lumber, &c. Near this point a large farm is contemplated for the use of the Indians, and contracts have been taken for ploughing six hundred acres of land, and making twenty-four thousand rails, the coming season. At this agency the Sioux will receive annually, hereafter, forty thousand dollars worth of provisions, and eighty thousand dollars in cash annuities, besides the goods, iron, salt, &c., &c., provided by the treaties.

Here will be located the agent, interpreters, blacksmiths, farmers, and other employees of the Indian department.

If you wish to come down the crooked river in a canoe, after passing the Big and Little Cotton-Wood rivers, you can land at Mankato city, just below the mouth of the Blue Earth river. Here there is much improvement, and this point may be termed the head of steamboat navigation, even in high water. Above this point, after passing the Cotton woods, the river becomes so narrow, so very crooked and shallow, and many boulders being in the channel, that steamboats in any ordinary stage of water could not get up, nor turn in the river if they did get up. This point is about thirty miles, by land, from the New fort, and is surrounded by valuable agricultural land. Water power in abundance may be found on the Blue Earth and its tributaries. Descending from the Blue Earth some twelve miles, we land at Babcock's Mills, located on the east bank of the Minnesota, and surrounded by a vast supply of excellent walnut, maple, basswood, and other valuable timber. Eight or ten miles by water, still further down the river is Traverse des Sioux, where the Upper treaty was made; and for many weeks, hundreds of Dakota lodges stood everywhere scattered about on the sloping hillside, shaped like loaves of sugar, taken possession of by the ants, that hurry in and out, and seem busy to no purpose. At Traverse des Sioux (the crossing of the Sioux), there has always been, and still is, a well-worn trail, crossing from the east to the west side, connecting Lake Pepin on the Mississippi, and all that region, with Lac qui Parle, and the regions watered by the head waters of the Minnesota, and the high lands in which rise and flow off to different seas, all the principal rivers west of the chain of great lakes. Twenty miles by water below the Traverse, is Le Sueur, on the south side of the river, a place which the energy, capital, and enterprise of some of the merchants in St. Paul, have already made an attractive point on the river. Le Sueur is on a slope rising from the shore gradually, like the site of Peoria, Illinois. It is not only in the midst of one of the richest and most inviting regions for all sorts of human enterprise and industry, but east of it, within a day's drive across a region of groves and prairies which Nature has already made a road over, lies the rich valley of Cannon river (the River La Longue of La Hontan), which will have its easiest and most natural avenue of river trade, through Le Sueur and down the Minnesota river to St. Paul.

This is the hub round which the northwest, from Lac qui Parle to the Missouri, from the Missouri to the Red river of the North, and from Red river to Lake Superior, and from Lake Superior to the Mississippi, does and will revolve, turn it as you may—the capital of the territory, which from a half dozen huts and a hundred and fifty inhabitants, and a little log catholic chapel, in the spring of 1849, now numbers hundreds of new buildings, many of them elegant; half a dozen superb churches, with bells in their steeples; inhabitants numbered by thousands, surpassed by none in shrewd foresight and activity, and business talent; with a corporation, such as it is; streets being graded; a mile and a half of new sidewalk, extending the whole length of the town, sawed, built, and paid for, by voluntary contribution, in little more than one week—churches filled on Sunday—two new churches to be erected (another presbyterian, and a German methodist)—two hotels built, and two more very large ones now building, one at each end of the town—saw-mills, foundries, and all sorts of enterprises put in operation in a twinkling—an academy of the highest grade for young ladies, projected this season, and the thing now actually commenced—a steamboat business and a trade now actually greater than that of any other town but Galena, above St. Louis. These are only some of the changes in the fortunes of this vigorous town, which we have witnessed, since we landed in St. Paul, on the eighteenth of April, 1849, from the old "Senator," the prompt, honest, faithful, old "Senator," Captain Orrin Smith, who now runs the "Nominee," and whose insides—engine and boilers—are good enough to wear out half a dozen new bodies.

The projectors of this town appear to have had but the smallest possible ideas of the growth and importance that awaited St. Paul, not anticipating that it would be either a commercial centre or a political centre—nor that it would be the capital of a new territory, nor the centre of the largest pine lumber operations on the continent; nor the seat of a new surveyor-general's office, for the government surveys of these wide regions; nor the point of trade and supplies, of outfits and steamboat operations above it to the sources of the Minnesota and Mississippi rivers. The original plat was laid off in very good imitation of the old French part of St. Louis, with crooked lanes for streets, irregular blocks, and little skewdangular lots, about as large as a stingy card of gingerbread, broke in two diagonally, without a reservation fit to be called a public square—without a margin between the town and the river—without preserving a tree for shade of all the majestic ones that occupied its site, the ugly stumps of which now disfigure the town—and without permanent evidence of boundaries made by the survey. In fact, it was a survey without measurement, a plan without method, a volunteer crop of buildings—a sort of militia muster of tenements. So much for the old plat. Then came in Rice and Irvine's addition, up the river, commencing at Mr. Neill's church, and embracing the upper landing. This is laid out but little, if any, better. In fact, the two plats appear to have taken a running jump at each other, like two rival steamboats; which having inextricably run into each other, the passengers and crews have concluded to knock down the railings and run along together, as one craft. Then came in Smith and Whitney's addition, next below the old plat. This is about as irregular, being laid off upon a contracted scale also. Hoyt's addition came in behind Smith and Whitney's, bearing a strong family resemblance to the older additions. Leach's addition comes in above Rice and Irvine's, extending far up town. Then came in the Kittson addition, below the old plat of Smith and Whitney's addition. Kittson's is laid off in smaller lots than any of the other additions; and its streets make no sort of coincidence with other streets in town. It would save immense cost, and prove an eternal blessing to St. Paul, if the whole site of the town could be now thrown into one common field, and platted as it ought to be, with large reservations of public ground, with straight, wide, regular streets, and blocks and lots of uniform size.

Near St. Paul, above and below, are two fine mill-streams; and from springs, rising from the terrace in the rear of the town is a smaller stream, of pure water, which passes down to the river across Rice and Irvine's addition. This stream formerly passed down back of where St. Paul is, and emptied through the ravine in Fourth street, into the river at the lower landing. It is sufficient to supply a large city with water; and the corporation intend to conduct it down through an aqueduct, to furnish the town. The sooner it is done, the better.

There are two steamboat landings in St. Paul, the lower and the upper. Some expenditure is needed to make either of them complete for business purposes in all stages of water. At the lower landing there is wanted an embankment down Sibley street, from the foot of Fourth street to the river; and a levee along the shore—all which can be done easily, and some progress has already been made in that work. The levee has also been much improved, but yet requires further improvement. A want of space on the levee is very apparent, and it will by no means afford the necessary facilities for the business of the summer. At the upper landing a bridge has been built above high-water mark from the mainland across the slough to the river bank. Between the two landings is a precipitous bluff, one hundred feet high, which might be graded down so as to make a good levée, and perhaps at some time it will be. Besides these two landings, there is in Kittson's addition, half a mile below the old lower landing, a new landing being made, which is to be connected with the bluff in the rear of it by a plank-road upon an embankment across the marsh to the new hotel there being erected—the "Kittson House."

The *geology* of Minnesota is a subject to which we have paid but little attention. The portion of the territory, however, south of a line extending east and west through Sauk rapids of the Mississippi river and Patterson rapids of the Minnesota river, appears to be of the usual limestone and sandstone formation of the valley of the Mississippi below; while above that line the granite crops out, and the formation is chiefly of the primitive rock. This formation must be much modified, however, as you approach Lake Superior, which has been the theatre of the most gigantic volcanic movements that Nature ever exhibited—to which we are indebted for our rich copper regions. They are west of Lake Superior, where chaos seems tumbled into worse confusion, amid gorges, and hills, and chasms, which art alone can make passable or even jackassable. The mines are situated in the land of the Chippewas, and are yet unwrought to any extent, but known to be as rich as the richest of those mines that are wrought farther east, along the southern shore of Lake Superior.

Relying perhaps too much on the dogmas of geologists, we were for a long time incredulous about the existence of coal in Minnesota; but we can doubt it no longer. We have in our possession specimens of the finest quality of bituminous coal, free from sulphur, and burning with far less cinder than the coal of Rock island, which we *know* was found within a day's drive above St. Paul. We can no longer doubt that the coal-fields of Iowa, passing along far up the valley of the Des Moines, cross over and make deposites in the valley of the Blue-Earth and the Minnesota.

We can not present a more lively picture of the region above us, to Sauk rapids, than the following account of "a trip from St. Paul to Sauk rapids," copied from the *Pioneer* of June 12, 1851, which will be new to some of our readers:—

"Two lines of convenient stages make each two trips a day from St. Paul to St. Anthony and back. We left on Thursday morning; and were delighted to see farming operations progressing—ploughing, fencing, planting—everywhere on that charming prairie, which is spread out between the two towns, a distance of eight miles. This alone inspired us with fresh hope, to see so great a change wrought in so short a time—so many hundreds of acres under tillage, which were covered last year only with wild grass and flowers of the prairie.

"A mile before we reached St. Anthony, we saw its bright, fresh-painted houses, shining among the distant trees, and saw the waterfall glistening in the sunshine, and seeming more like a picture than the original of a picture; but as we approach nearer, and listen to its sullen roar, and see the spray, and examine more closely the material of the exhibition, the cataract becomes a grand reality, filling the beholder with mingled emotions of beauty and of sublimity, the proportions of which depend upon the constitution of his own mind. Far away, down the steep, rocky channel, below the falls, sweeps the angry current. But now we begin to see the pleasant, fresh-painted houses of the villagers on the right hand: here a cottage, and there a substantial two-story house, and there again a cheap building, without cornice or ornament, peculiar to the west—a building which is neither a one-story nor a two-story house (detestable style of architecture)—and away upon the sloping hillside various houses in the process of erection; and piles of fresh-sawed lumber away off among the tall prairie-grass of last year's growth, betokening that buildings will soon be there, and streets of St. Anthony, now known only by reference to the town plat.

"Here are stores—new law-offices—more new houses—more piles of fresh-sawed lumber—new cellars commenced; and now we come to the sawmills, active as ever, shingle-machines, lath-factory, lathes, and the bustling industry of men and teams in and around the mills, like a big heart sending its active pulsations of business all over town and into the neighboring country, and far off into the pineries. Here is a company of gentlemen, officers, from Fort Snelling, taking a survey of the village and the waterfall, from the terrace back of Main street. They think, and truly think, that St. Anthony is destined to be a famous and fashionable watering-place—

that neither Saratoga, nor Newport, nor Niagara, can offer equal inducements for a summer residence to invalids and people of leisure. Now we pass along Main street, and here seems to be an unimproved space intervening between the upper and lower part of the town—to the upper town, which certainly shines with prosperity, everything looking new and clean. Here we come to the St. Charles hotel, a fine, spacious building, full of strangers. What a contrast within a few months! What a change since a year ago, when the stranger who visited St. Anthony could not obtain a dinner, unless through the compassion of some citizen he were invited to dine at some private house!

"After dinner at the St. Charles, the whistle of the steamboat is heard, and we must hurry down to the 'Governor Ramsey.' This boat, the first that ever rode in the waters of the Mississippi above the falls, was built by Captain Rollins and others, who for enterprise deserve the lasting gratitude of Minnesota. In the hands of such men a comparatively small sum of money would be so expended as to open the navigation of the river many hundreds of miles farther. This boat differs from all other boats, in having locomotive boilers, consisting of a great number of small cylinders, all of which, coming in contact with fire, present a large extent of boiler-surface within a small compass, for the generation of steam. Contrary to the predictions of many, the boilers do not become crusted with lime, but are kept, with proper care, entirely clean. The engines are also different from any that we see elsewhere in the west, and are very perfect in their way; so is their management by the engineers, for the stern paddle-wheel responds to their touch quick as thought.

"The boat being small, of course does not afford very complete arrangements for passengers. There is a small cabin which sleeps perhaps a dozen, and a still smaller cabin for ladies. The freight, of course, is a very important part of the business of this boat, and especially the transportation of Indian and garrison supplies. Among the passengers are the Rev. M. Chase, of Natchez, Miss., and several gentlemen and ladies from the state of New York—three ladies, all in the bloom of health, and particularly fine-looking women, who stand in the relation to each other of grandmother, daughter, and grand-daughter. Now the boat, with some difficulty, passes out between two islands into the main channel, and heads up stream, the water swift, oh how swift! being just at the head of the falls. A feeble boat could not stem the current. Fire up, boys! Dry wood this season; last season they had to burn green wood. It takes half a cord an hour to run the boat.

"For a long distance on our right extends a boom, parallel to the shore, by which mill-logs from above are turned down between the island and the east shore into the millpond. The river looks much smaller than at St. Paul, and seems to be lifted up out of the chasm through which it runs below the falls, to the level with the shores; or rather, which is the fact, there is no chasm until the river finds one after breaking over the apron of rock at St. Anthony. As to the shores of the Upper Mississippi, there are none of the abrupt bluffs, such as are seen down the river; but the land comes down, by an easy, gradual slope, to the very edge of the water; and as you look away far back, and see the smooth land now covered with green, gradually rising as the view now recedes from the river, far, far away, the remotest object is a swelling ridge of prairie-land, or of oak-openings, on the right hand; and on the left a forest—nothing short of a dense forest of vigorous young trees, as far as can be seen; and in the channel, islands, some of them large, covered invariably with a heavy growth of elm, hackberry, maple, and cottonwood; and whenever, as an exception to the general appearance of the shores, there is anything assuming the form of an abrupt bluff, it is crowded with pine-trees. Occasionally a spot of universal beauty bursts upon the view: such is the landscape at the mouth of Rice creek, or Itasca prairie, or the eastern shore near Swan river. The land is evidently very rich. At Itasca we noticed the formation to be a bed of gravel, upon which rested a body of marl, supporting a rich, sandy loam, not less than eighteen inches or two feet deep. At various points we saw extensive fields under cultivation—crops of oats, potatoes, everything that had been sowed or planted, giving rich promise, and all with whom we conversed bearing full testimony to the excellence of every kind of crop that has been tried there. The land, fields, the crops, speak for themselves, and there is no room for argument about it. There is *no better land, in the whole valley of the Mississippi*, than the whole region extending from the falls of St. Anthony to Sauk rapids, above which we have not been. We are informed that the land is much the same above Sauk rapids, which place is northwest of St. Paul nearly one hundred miles, and north less than forty miles. At a distance of from three to fifteen miles from the east shore of the river, extends a tamarac swamp for an immense distance between St. Anthony and Sauk rapids, designed by Nature it would seem expressly to furnish farmers with rails without splitting them—a hint from Providence which the settlers up there are not slow to comprehend.

"At various intervals along the river the trees, &c., in this tamarac-swamp are visible far in the background, picturesque as a forest of tapering masts. What lies east beyond that swamp we do not know; but Benton county may well be content with the vast extent of fine arable lands that are in sight of the river, sufficient for ten thousand farmers, and as yet unclaimed. The soil is exactly like that of Rock river—quite as little waste land—much more timber; and with a landscape which we can recollect nothing down the river to compare with, unless it be the shores of the Mississippi at the lower rapids, including the background of Nauvoo and Montrose. The first night we passed on board the boat, at the mouth of Elk river. (The 'Governor Ramsey' does not run at night.) The next morning we moved onward, every mile attracting our attention to new beauties of scenery. All seemed surprised—we certainly were—at the vast extent of forests on the west bank of the river. Every few rods we met a canoeful of Winnebagoes, returning with their goods from 'the payment.' There, in a huge bark-canoe, filled with squaws, and papooses, and bales of goods, comes their head-chief, Winnishik, himself sitting in the stern and steering.

"Most of the canoes, on the approach of the steamboat, slide out into some little nook or eddy, near the shore, until our boat has passed. At short intervals we find farms, some of them large, and all giving good promise.

"The 'Thousand islands' is an exaggeration; but then the islands are so many and so large, that they seem to have taken resolute possession of the channel, as if to drive the stream back—which, however, swiftly glides between them, giving the boat good warm exercise to brave the current. We come to the granite formation at the foot of the rapids, striking out boldly across the river, to bar the channel. Useless. What obstacle will not the power of steam overcome? The boat dashes across through ripple and eddy, then tacking suddenly takes another course, buffeting the stream, escaping the rocks, and riding in triumph above and beyond the chain of rock. Good, old, primitive granite, how familiar you look!—the very material of those cragged mountains among which we were born. How like the familiar faces of the old men does it seem, who tottered to the church where we worshipped in infancy!

"We are at Sauk rapids, and here the boat lies panting and cooling herself in the swift water like a weary beast. Let her rest, while we walk along the shore of the rapids, about three miles, to the head thereof. We leave the boat and warehouse, and the few teams that are busy there with freight and passengers. How wide the river is, spreading out over a vast expanse of granite fragments!—swift, but nowhere precipitous, and evidently impassable for steamboats. But what a chance for building a canal on the east bank, by simply constructing a wall of granite, laid in cement, without excavating and without any expense but a wall and three or four locks! And what an excellent water-power all along the rapids, without need of so much as a dam, unless perhaps a short wing-dam! The Indian trade is now mostly concentrated at Watab, which is on a delightful prairie three or four miles farther up the river.

"But here is Russell's, at the head of the rapids. Here is a good, comfortable house, stables, oxen, fat swine, large enclosures, fields of oats, and everything to indicate thrift and good living. Here reside the judge and the clerk of the court, and courts *must* and *will* have things comfortable. The next morning (Saturday) returned to the boat, which cast off her ropes at eight o'clock, and we swept swiftly back through the enchanting scene which we have above hastily sketched—reached St. Anthony at 4, P. M.; took stage back to our own delightful St. Paul and the labors of the press, highly delighted, and more confident than ever of the glorious destiny of Minnesota."

The *geography* of the Mississippi between St. Paul and St. Anthony may be thus illustrated: Sit at a table, with your face westward, and lay your left arm horizontally upon the table, bending it at an angle of forty-five degrees. Your shoulder will represent the location of St. Paul, your elbow the location of Fort Snelling (the junction of the Mississippi and Minnesota rivers), and your hand the location of St. Anthony.

In the *forearm*, from the *elbow* to the *hand*, the falls have produced a *paralysis*. That portion of the river is not navigable. Therefore, as the *shoulder* is nearer the *head* than the *elbow*, and nearer the head than a paralyzed forearm *can* be that has no power of *motion*, we say, with the utmost truth and reason, that St. Paul is at the *head of navigation* for such steamboats as can afford to run in the trade up the river from St. Louis and Galena.

As regards temperance, this territory is well adapted to the wants of the temperate and the intemperate. The legislature at its recent session refused to pass the restrictive law: consequently on the *east* of the Mississippi the spirits are manifest, when, how, and where they please. On the *west* of the Missis-sippi, by a wise provision in the treaties by which the Indian title was extinguished, the trade and intercourse law is in operation, and spirituous liquors of all kinds are prohibited under the severest penalties. This fact is noticed particularly, because it is very important that every immigraut should understand the matter, that he may locate to suit his propensities. Those whose liberty is not confined in bottles, casks, and decanters, will suffer far less inconvenience by making their homes in the country west of the Mississippi; while all

3

who believe that potato-whiskey is the staff of life, are at perfect liberty to remain east of the "big river."

In these random remarks about Minnesota, in the hurried sketch of the territory above written—truthful, but rough and without method—we have omitted to mention many facts, which, however disconnected, ought to appear in a general view of the territory. Among these may be mentioned the country extending from the Mississippi, below the Minnesota, south to the Iowa line.

The valley of the Cannon river now contains many settlements, and is a fertile agricultural region, well watered and well timbered. Many towns have sprung into existence lately on the Mississippi, within the new purchase. Little Crow, Hastings, Red Wing, Wabashaw, Winona, Minnesota City, Minneowah, Mount Vernon, Brownsville, and many other towns and villages, have surprised us by the apparently magical manner of their springing into existence. In many places, where one year ago the whoop of the Indian alone disturbed the quiet, may now be heard the hammer, the saw, or the puffing of steam-mills, while the eye beholds all the improvements necessary to the comfort of a large and rapidly-increasing population. The distance by the river has gradually diminished from Galena and St. Louis to St. Paul. River distances at first are always exaggerated. It is less than nine hundred miles from St. Louis to St. Paul, and less than four hundred from Galena to St. Paul. The course from Galena to St. Paul is more west than north. The fare between St. Louis and St. Paul, with elegant cabin accommodations and fare, has usually varied from eight to twelve dollars; and, from Galena to St. Paul, from three to six dollars. It will be very low this season. When the traveller comes up, he will reach Minnesota on the west bank of the river long before he reaches it on the east bank. You pass twenty or thirty miles through Lake Pepin, with odd-looking peaks, and crags, and cliffs, overlooking you. This lake is a mere widening of the Mississippi. All is Wisconsin on the east side until you come to the St. Croix. Entering that, if the boat first goes to Stillwater, you find that also widened into a lake, up which you proceed thirty miles to Stillwater, Wisconsin still being at your right hand. But Wisconsin extends no farther than the St. Croix, up the Mississippi river. The boat stops an hour at Stillwater; touches at Willow river, on the east side of the lake; stops at Prescott or Point Douglas again, at the mouth, and then proceeds up the Mississippi again. From the mouth of the St. Croix to St. Paul is thirty miles. You pass Cottage Grove and Red Rock; and here, three miles below St. Paul, is Little Crow Village, on the west bank. Going on, you pass around a great bend that takes the boat southwest, and in the curve of this great bend in the river you see St. Paul, high and far, all around, under and upon the bluff, and upon terrace after terrace beyond and behind the bluff—the giant outlines of the most vigorous town in the northwest. At St. Paul you will find stages waiting to take you to St. Anthony. If you stop in St. Paul, you will find good hotels, and can get fair board at three dollars per week. If you conclude to stay with us, you may buy a lot, and put up a small house in ten days. For green dimension lumber you will pay twelve dollars per thousand feet at the St. Paul mills, or nine dollars at St. Anthony, which is quite as cheap, or a shade lower. For shingles you will pay two dollars to two and a half per thousand. You will buy nails, glass, putty, provisions, everything you want, in St. Paul, about as cheap as in Galena or St. Louis. If you are a farmer, love liquor, and want land on the east side of the river —good land, if not the very best—you can have it. Or you can go over to the west side, where good farms may be had for the improvement, and government will not ask to be paid for them for years. Talk of California or Australia as you may, there is no country in the world which affords an equal prospect of growing rich with Minnesota; and while gaining wealth, you can enjoy the blessings of health and the comfort of a vigorous family growing up around you. No country affords better facilities for schools or for places of worship than the settled portion of Minnesota.

CHAPTER III.

GENERAL REMARKS AND REFLECTIONS — AGRICULTURAL ADVANTAGES — A TALK WITH FARMERS, CAPITALISTS, MECHANICS, LABORERS, TOURISTS, AND ALL OTHERS.

The Reverend E. D. Neill, in a "Thanksgiving" discourse, delivered on the 26th December, 1850, the first thanksgiving day appointed by the governor of the territory, after speaking of the hardships of the early pioneers of the other portions of the United States, says: "No such distresses have been felt by us, the early colonists of Minnesota. Uninterrupted general health has prevailed throughout the land. The country so far has been as near an El Dorado as any ever found beneath the skies, and its fountains are as renovating as any that are not fountains of eternal life. While the cities in the valley below were filled with gloom by the reappearance of that mysterious scourge, the Asiatic cholera — while the ploughs were left to rust in the field, and the crops to remain unharvested — we were permitted to pursue our callings with alacrity. Not an authenticated case of the death of one of our citizens by that epidemic can be discovered.

"In addition to general health, we have been free from the hardships of emigrant life, and have possessed all the necessaries of existence. Though not far from a thousand miles by the usual route of travel, northwest of the city of St. Louis, and though there are no roads to our settlements from Lake Superior, or the capitols of Wisconsin and Iowa, our territory has been easy of access. Instead of being weeks upon the way, toiling with oxen through swamps and pathless forests, camping out by night with scarcely any covering but the firmament studded with stars, and with no lamps but those hung in heaven, our immigrants have been speedily transported hither in noble and convenient steamers, and with but little expenditure of their means, and with no bitter thought that they had been obliged to leave some of their family upon the boundless prairies, a feast for the wolf and the bear. Nor have any of our inhabitants been destitute of the necessaries of life. 'Tradition declares that at one time the colonists of Plymouth were reduced to a pint of corn, which being parched and distributed gave to each individual only five kernels.' The new settler in this territory has always had an abundance. The farmer has added to his gains; and it especially becomes him to observe this day, and with gratitude to praise the God of the harvest. It also becomes us to give thanks to-day, that we are at peace with the Indian tribes within our borders.

"The poetesses of New England have sung our praises. Authors have called us the 'New-England of the West,' and her inhabitants would love to see us adopt their social and ecclesiastical forms. The public presses of the middle and southern states have viewed us with a kindly eye. No scenes like those enacted at Alton, Nauvoo, or Vicksburg, have been perpetrated here. To go to Texas was once synonymous with fleeing from justice; on the contrary, to emigrate to Minnesota implies a disposition to be active, intelligent, industrious, and virtuous, and there has never been any stigma attached to the act.

"Though this reputation we enjoy is to a great degree undeserved, let us see that we do not lose it. If the words are true—

> "'He that filches from me my good name,
> Robs me of that which not enriches him,
> And makes me poor indeed,'

it is proper for Minnesota to frown upon all who by their conduct disgust strangers and residents. They are her robbers. They impoverish the territory, without enriching themselves.

"Finally, we should give thanks to God for our fair prospects. It was a common belief of the early explorers, that one of the great thoroughfares of nations, from Europe to

China, would pass through this district of America. Hennepin, La Salle, and Carver, were confident that there would be a short route to the Pacific by the head waters of the Upper Mississippi. The latter looked forward to the time when a communication would be opened between New York and the remotest West. View the map of the United States, and you will readily perceive that we occupy the geographical centre, and that St. Paul is in the same latitude as Oregon city. Is there not a prospect that in half a century, the Indian lodges that now surround us will be far removed; that the shores of Lake Pepin will be the abode of many a maiden as constant to her first love as Winona, and in addition strengthened and ennobled by the religion of Christ; that the steam-engine, either in boat or car, will move from Montreal to the rapids of St. Mary, and stop at the roaring waters of St. Anthony; that a populous city will be the capital of a state, and a dépôt like Damascus, or Petra, or Babylon, in olden time, for the productions of the south, the furs of the north, the manufactures of the east, and the gold, or, what is better, the golden grains, of the west; that the gates of the Rocky mountains will be thrown open, and the locomotive groaning and rumbling from Oregon city, will stop here with its heavy train of, perhaps, Asiatic produce, on its way to Dubuque, or some other point; that the mission stations of Remnica and Lac qui Parle will be supplanted by the white schoolhouse, the church-spire, and higher seminary of learning! Is it not true, even now, that—

"'Behind the scared squaw's birch canoe,
The steamer smokes and raves,
And city lots are staked for sale
Above old Indian graves.'

Do we not

"'——— hear the tread of pioneers
Of nations yet to be;
The first low wash of waves where soon
Shall roll a human sea?

"'Each rude and jostling fragment soon
Are plastic yet and warm;
The chaos of a mighty world
Is rounding into form.

"'The rudiments of empire here
Its fitting place shall find;
The raw material of a state—
Its muscle and its mind.'"

For the benefit of the farmers, capitalists, mechanics, tourists, and all others now arriving, I give such facts, practical suggestions, and sound advice, as a long residence, and an intimate acquaintance with the advantages and capacities of Minnesota have thrown within our reach.

Farmers have been told repeatedly that no more productive land than this is to be found, and also of the amount and quality of the crops; the immense size and rapid growth of all kinds of garden vegetables; the superiority of the bottom lands for grazing purposes; and, also, that no business can possibly pay better for the amount of capital invested, than the establishment of at least a hundred dairies, on a large scale, the manufacture of butter and cheese for exportation, and the raising of cattle, sheep, hogs, poultry, &c., for home consumption.

I suppose that all men will now take this for granted; it is too late in the day to argue the question with anybody; in fact, the knowing ones are already rushing in upon us much faster than accommodations can be found for them.

I will, however, not get into any glow of enthusiasm about it, nor allow my personal interests or predilections in favor of any one portion of the territory over all others—the Minnesota river country for instance—the usual hobby of almost all our writers—to influence me in a fair and impartial review of the merits of the whole territory.

I say, then, that all the land on both sides of the river, which is at all adapted to farming purposes *is* good, and that all objections as to the soil being too light and sandy, are not based on a proper knowledge of the adaptation of soils and climates to each other. The heavy, wet, black soils, underlaid by the cold clay-beds of Illinois and Iowa, would no more suit the climate of Minnesota, than would those of the tropics suit the climate of the frozen regions.

The summers of Minnesota are short, and require a warm

sandy soil to produce good crops, which consequently never fail. Add to this our late autumnal season, which lingers into the lap of winter, in November, the absence of frosts weeks later than in the states just south of us, and the refreshing, copious thunder-showers, which occur so frequently to moisten and replenish the bounteous earth, all tend to facilitate the growth and maturity of *such* crops as must be seen to be credited.

Excluding the tamarac swamps, and some rather rough and barren spots of broken ground, interspersed among them to the east of the Mississippi, and on its head waters — the land is as good as any farmer need desire, and will produce all kinds of crops grown in the states below. The only choice for a farmer to exercise, is as to where his particular location shall be made, and this each one will soon determine for himself.

I advise him to visit the valley of the Minnesota river, where he will find land, wood, and water, prairie, and timber combined, and forming as rich a country as can be found in the west. Several steamboats are now running from St. Paul to the settlements on the Minnesota river, and are crowded every trip with freight and passengers.

By going over into the Sioux country, he will have the advantage of being able to open up as good a farm as on the eastern side, and in not being required to pay for it for several years, as the lands are not surveyed, and will not be for some time yet. Or he can go up the Mississippi river, and locate at any point between St. Anthony and Crow Wing, where there is a good home market, for all that he can raise, at his own door.

The Chippewa and Winnebago tribes of Indians, and Fort Ripley, are located in this direction; while the main pine region of the territory, viz., on the head waters of the Mississippi, Leaf, and Crow Wing rivers, yet remain to be opened. Farming produce will find a quick and steady market in years to come in this particular section, when it will be a *perfect drug* from over abundance, and no consumers in the shape of lumbermen and manufacturing operatives in other quarters.

I want every farmer to locate with reference to the future.

when farming, not speculation, will be the business of the territory.

The soil of the delta, between St. Paul, Point Douglas, and Stillwater, resting upon a bed of limestone, is well adapted to the growth of winter wheat, and will soon fill up with a large farming population.

The land is finely situated, and, from its contiguity to the above-named points, and the easy access to both rivers, affords many desirable and valuable locations. Cottage-Grove Prairie is well known.

The Brophy settlement is within a few miles of St. Paul and St. Anthony, and is situated amid many beautiful lakes, while the soil is good, the timber plentiful, and markets close at hand.

Lake Minnetonka, which is situated twelve miles west of St. Anthony, is in another fine farming region, and many immigrants have located there; also the most of a pioneer association from Northampton, Massachusetts. The country along the river farther north, and near Hastings and Red Wing to the south, is also of the very best quality, and—now that we are prepared to exhibit Minnesota, even at the World's Fair, if we could get her there—will gladden a farmer's heart to behold.

Before you choose, then, look around you, and visit any or all of these places immediately.

If you do not find a claim to suit you—one combining all the requisites of soil, wood, and water, with a frontage on the river, and a mill-stream running through it (and the most of these are already taken)—then buy out some one already located, or take the next best that you can find; make a claim somewhere, and improve it; do not remain around the town a single day, but go to work with a stout heart, and a determination to overcome all obstacles. Do not be discouraged by bad weather, or the selfishness or indifference of any that you may apply to for advice or aid in effecting your first settlement. Any aid that can be given in advising the immigrant as to the proper course to pursue in selecting a favorable point for location, openings for the investment of capital, and situations for young business men, that I may be aware of, will be cheerfully afforded by myself.

Push ahead, then, I say, with a hopeful heart, and remember that it takes energy, invincible determination, and a large expenditure of toil, and sweat, and muscle, with a rigid economy, to achieve success, even in Minnesota.

Capitalists will here find a wider field for the profitable investment of their funds than can possibly be found elsewhere. If they *will* speculate in lands, we have a hundred town-sites at a hundred available points, where lots can be bought cheap, with a prospect of a rapid advance, if a liberal policy be pursued; if not, ninety of them will always remain in embryo, and exist as at present upon a sheet of rolled-up paper. I would advise town proprietors to offer very liberal inducements, and to give at least every alternate lot to any man who will improve by building and making it his permanent residence. They will find their advantage in the rapid augmentation in value of the remaining portions. But we want men to come here with money to invest in producing something, in steam and water, saw and grist mills, which are now much wanted in all directions. A hundred mills would pay well now, if they could be at once located at St. Paul, St. Anthony, and the Sauk rapids, the St. Croix, Lake Pepin, Lake Minnetonka, and more especially on the Minnesota river, as there is but one now there.

We also want a manufactory of wooden ware, some tanneries, glass-works (gas also in a year or two), foundries, furnaces, boatyards, &c., &c.; everything, in short, from a steamboat to a jackplane, from a ploughshare to a locomotive-engine to run on the St. Anthony aud St. Paul railroad, *which is to be surveyed this summer and built the next.* Mark that, stranger, as you go along, for it *will* be done!

Mechanics and laborers will find work everywhere, in town and country. There is a demand for both, and high wages ready. Mechanics get all kinds of prices, according to the trade and skill of the man. Two dollars per day is the medium price. Common laborers get from one dollar to one dollar and a quarter per day.

Those who can not find work in the towns, will be sure to do so on the farms, or on the government roads now in process of construction. There are twenty miles of road to build at the falls of the St. Croix, which will occupy all this season, seventeen miles at Sauk rapids, ten at Swan river and at La Belle Prairie, and ten miles on the Long Prairie road. These last-named points are from seventy-five to one hundred miles up the Mississippi above St. Paul. A portion of the Mendota and Wabashaw road and bridges is also under contract at the foot of Lake Pepin. A United States military road is to be surveyed this summer from Mendota to the Missouri river. Ten thousand dollars have been appropriated, and a large party will be required; the men, horses, and provisions, will be collected there.

If you should not find work immediately, make a good claim at once, strike out for yourself a while, put up your shanty, and if you can not hire a few acres broke in time for a crop in the spring, *dig up an acre*, and plant potatoes, corn, and vegetables, enough to last you through the next winter. Work afterward, at anything you may find for your hand to do, and pay for the breaking up next fall (if you can not do it yourself) of at least ten acres, fence it, and as much more as you can next winter; and by this time, 1855, you will have a homestead of your own—a good crop of oats, corn, and potatoes, in the ground—and, if you are a lucky fellow, a wife and children in the shanty, yourself as independent as a lord, and a thousand times more happy.

If you are a bachelor, get married as soon as you have enough in the house for two to eat. The territory *must* be peopled, and even the very rapid immigration from outside does not do it fast enough. Don't waste time, either, by going east for a wife. *You* want a whole-souled, strong, wholesome Minnesota woman; somebody to make butter and cheese, to spin and weave your *homespun* coats and breeches. Look to it, young man, and while you raise brag crops and cattle, and take the premium at your annual county agricultural exhibition, raise also a set of rollicking boys and girls, which, if sent on to the next World's Fair, to be held in 1856, will take the highest premium there as perfect specimens of humanity.

The tourist in search of pleasure, exciting scenes, good health, or information of this region, and the gentleman of elegant ease and leisure, will now find ample accommodations of the very best character, go where he may. For beauty and sublimity of scenery, fine climate, bracing and invigorating, good water (and liquors, too, if wanted), fine fishing and hunting, from a prairie-hen to a buffalo bull, we just set up Minnesota *against the rest of the world and all the other planets,* and coolly offer to back her with any odds you may choose to offer. To the tourist who desires to see the territory, and who is not willing to sit down here and think St. Paul is the whole of it, as many do, we will point out the route of an excursion which can not fail to please, and add vastly to his stock of knowledge, and which no one—having the time and means—should fail to take.

Arriving here by steamboat, take the stage for St. Anthony, and then the steamboat for Sauk rapids. Along the river for one hundred miles is to be found the most enchanting scenery that you have ever seen, and at Sauk rapids is the finest water-power in the territory, excepting at St. Anthony. By stage you can then go north to Crow Wing, Fort Ripley, and the Chippewa and Fort Ripley Indian agencies, at Gull lake, and on Long-Prairie river. Returning to St. Anthony, strike west to Lake Minnetonka, where you will find the prettiest country lying wild that the world can boast of—got up with the greatest care and effort by old Dame Nature, ten thousand years or more ago, and which she has been improving ever since. Go there, stranger, but don't go into ecstasies nor "go off" until you can make your mark. Select the very best claim you can find, and settle down; for be assured that this luxurious spot promises untold wealth to you in future.

Now drive to Fort Snelling, and return to St. Paul. Look at all this country, at the claims, the houses, farms, &c., of the pioneers located there; at the Little falls or Minne-ha-ha, the fort, and take a peep from the summit of Pilot Knob, above Mendota, and if you do not return enthusiastic in your praise, you are a stoic, a stone, and as cold and inhospitable as an iceberg. It would be easier to kindle fire from snow than to raise a single ray of warmth within *your* heart.

Next take the stage for Stillwater, stopping to fish a day or two at the celebrated "Half-Way House" of John Morgan. Then go to the St. Croix falls, where you will see the finest little bit of scenery on this continent; visit Cottage-Grove prairie, Point Douglas, Red-Wing, Vermillion, and Cannon rivers, Hastings, &c., and so return.

Lastly, take one of the half-dozen steamboats now running up the Minnesota river, and you will then have made the grand tour, unless you wish to take a trip to Pembina and Selkirk's settlement, on the Red river of the North, in latitude forty-nine and fifty degrees, or take a buffalo-hunt away out toward the Missouri plains.

You can go by steamboat as high up the Minnesota as the new government fort and Indian agency, above Red-Wood river; passing by a host of embryotic towns, already located, surveyed, and half sold off, and "that too in this portion of embryotic Minnesota." Of these, Shakopee, Le Sueur, Traverse des Sioux, Kasota, and Mankato at the mouth of the Blue-Earth, are the most prominent at present, and are probably all good-enough points.

We consider the mouth of the Blue-Earth as the main point on the Minnesota river, situated at its extreme southern bend, and on a line west from the foot of Lake Pepin. A territorial road of one hundred and twelve miles has been laid out from Lake Pepin to St. Paul, and it is also at the head of good steamboat navigation, even at high water, as the river above is as crooked as the twistings of a politician trying to carry water on both shoulders. Some of this stamp among us should go up above Blue-Earth, and see their past and present tortuous course mapped out. It is here that the railroad from Iowa, following up the Des Moines, and thence down the valley of the Blue-Earth, will eventually cross the Minnesota, to connect in the valley of the Red river of the North with the great Atlantic and Pacific railroad, the route for which is now being surveyed from St. Paul to Puget sound.

Return now to St. Paul, and you can justly claim to have seen a little of Minnesota, and to have been all along the civilized lines of travel and settlement, which, like the spokes of a wheel, diverge from the central point, and shed as so many sunbeams, rays of light, and thought, and intelligence, throughout the pagan land of yesterday. You will have seen the spot where, ere long, the combined forces of energy, enterprise, and wealth, will have erected one of the noblest fabrics yet reared by the hard-toiling, strong-fisted, and sinewy sons of this republic.

CHAPTER IV.

REVIEW OF THE WEATHER OF MINNESOTA—ADAPTATION OF THE SOIL AND CLIMATE.

I REGRET that my observations have not extended regularly through a space of time which would enable me to give full and reliable results of the climatic changes of this latitude. Owing to frequent changes of residence, and the demands of business, I have not as yet been able to give that strict attention to the meteorology of our territory which is due to a subject so replete with interest and importance; and I now present this imperfect sketch in the hope that some one having the inclination for the pursuit, and at the same time a more elegant leisure than I have had, will yet do what I have but partially done—or rather failed to do.

For the time that my observations were carried on, viz., from December, 1850, until July, 1851, inclusive, I have an accurately kept register, together with a series of monthly tables, in which all the details of the weather for that period are minutely given. For the remainder of the year 1851, the monthly tables intended to accompany this review were kept at Fort Snelling; and although not so full in detail, are yet quite valuable.* The mean temperatures of the months of August, September, October, November, and December, 1851, as given in the Meteorological Register for that year, I obtained of Dr. J. Frazier Head, of Fort Ripley, in latitude 46° 10′ N. So that the yearly mean is made up from observations taken at St. Paul, during the months of January, February, March, and April; at Sauk rapids, during May, June, and July; and at Fort Ripley, during the remainder of the year. The distance between Fort Snelling and Fort Ripley is a little over 1° north.

These results show a uniformity in the weather of Minne-

* See Annals of the Minnesota Historical Society, for 1854.

sota that is seldom met with elsewhere. When sudden changes do occur, it is to be remarked that they are always low extremes—that is from below the freezing point to far below zero, and consequently do not injuriously affect the system as in those latitudes where a continual elemental war is constantly kept up, and the alternate rising and falling of the barometer and thermometer are as sudden and irregular as the turnings of a weathercock amidst a tempest. From a residence of over two years in Minnesota, I can safely say that the atmosphere is more pure, pleasant, and healthful, than that of any other I have ever breathed on the continent of North or South America. This is particularly the case in winter, the most buoyant, elastic, and vigorous portion of the year. As regards the healthfulness of this region at all times, and more especially in winter, I would add, in the language of a former report upon the weather, that "with proper care and no unnecessary exposure, it may be safely said that coughs, colds, and that scourge of the Eastern states, consumption, would be almost entirely unknown. When either is unfortunately contracted, no climate is better adapted for its speedy eradication. It is all a mistake to send a consumptive patient to the south—a mistake just becoming apparent to the faculty. Those whose lungs are diseased and weak, should come to the north. I have tried both extremes, and can speak *feelingly*, the best of all evidences, and I confidently assert that they will stand far more chances of recovery in this particular latitude than anywhere in the enervating south, even if it be the most salubrious of the West Indies."

It is true that a fever, which in some instances has proved fatal in its effects, has raged within our midst during the past fall and winter; but it has, I believe, been altogether local, or peculiar to St. Anthony and St. Paul, and is owing to causes which it is not probable will soon occur again. The principal of these is believed to have been the unprecedented drought of the preceding summer, by which the river bottoms, the ponds, and the marshes, became exposed, and threw into our usually pure air a poisonous malaria.

The drought of 1852 was a striking feature in the meteorology of this territory. The summers are usually very moist, large quantities of rain fall, and heavy thunder-storms are very common. In this instance, with the exception of a storm of wind and rain on the fourth day of July, no rain fell from the time of the great cataract of water, which deluged us in May, until the following September, and but very little fell until October. The air, generally so full of electricity at all seasons, seemed then utterly void of it, and, for five months, no sound of thunder broke upon its stillness. Droughts are of frequent occurrence in various other parts of the country, and depend upon atmospheric causes not yet fully understood. As it has been satisfactorily ascertained that an equal amount of moisture falls in every climate, in a given space of time, say a year; so with ours in the case of which I speak. More than sufficient snow has already fallen, during the past winter, to make amends for the lack of moisture of the preceding summer, and as its drought was unprecedented in our memories, so is the quantity and depth of the frozen vapor which now covers the earth around us.* The fall of snow throughout all the country to the north and west, and toward Lake Superior, has been at least five feet. The roads were, for a portion of the time during the early part of the winter, almost impassable, and even rendered travelling upon snowshoes difficult. The amount of snow that generally falls is much less than would be supposed in so high a latitude, being really much less than falls in many places further south. Two feet is a large quantity, and more than the average, there having been a winter or two of late years, when not enough has fallen for common sledding purposes, the ground scarcely being covered, though these are remarkable exception. A portion, however, always remains till spring, and the ground is generally covered from November till March.

This is extremely favorable to the preservation of winter wheat, which has not been tried to much extent; still I am satisfied it will succeed, and the crop become a more certain

* The amount of snow in the winter of 1842–'43, was almost equal to that of the past season. A large quantity also fell in the spring of 1843.—*Note by an Old Settler.*

one than in the states, from the fact that the snow will prevent its freezing out, and that it will also be less subject to attacks of rust, the fly, and all the diseases incidental to it elsewhere. I am very certain that Minnesota will in time become one of the very best wheat-growing states in the whole Union, and that she will take the place of Illinois and other states where it can no longer be depended upon with any certainty. When sown at an early period, say September, it has already succeeded well, as far north as La Belle Prairie, in latitude forty-six degrees. Those who are in doubt on the subject, can read Mr. Philander Prescott's letter on the agricultural resources of Minnesota, published in the Patent Office Reports for 1849–'50. Spring wheat also produces well, even at Red Lake and Selkirk settlement, in latitude forty-eight and fifty degrees, as bountifully as in other places farther south.

The most remarkable characteristic of the winter of Minnesota, is its great dryness—there being an almost total absence of rain or moisture. Not more than one heavy rain-storm has occurred within its limits during the last ten years. A slight sprinkling of rain, however, *does* sometimes happen. A heavy thaw also takes place in January, and sometimes lasts a week or two, accompanied by mild southerly winds. Such a thaw occurred in February, 1853. The weather is generally very clear and bracing, mostly calm, though uproarious winds occur occasionally. The prevailing winds are from the west-northwest and north, and always bring clear weather; they prevail about two thirds of the winter. East, north, and southeast winds from the great lakes bring snow-storms, and are always damp, chilling, and unpleasant. The mercury, though almost always below the freezing point, is seldom far below zero; on three or four occasions it sinks to from twenty to thirty-five degrees below, though this weather never continues more than three or four days. The coldest day of the past winter was February 8, when the mercury fell to twenty-five degrees below zero. At these periods there is but little wind, and the cold is felt much less than any one not accustomed to the climate would imagine. Very heavy *hoar frosts* frequently occur, when the whole air seems filled with little icy crystals, which sparkle in the morning sunlight like millions of precious gems. The surrounding forests being encased in glittering frost and ice, present a most magnificent appearance.

The Mississippi generally closes early in December, and opens the latter part of March. The winter continues for about four months; though we often have cold, rough weather for an additional month or two. In summing up its merits, I would add that, owing to its even temperature, and hence allowing out of door exercises and employments for a greater number of days than that of most other countries, it is highly conducive to health, longevity, and social intercourse and advancement.

The spring is usually boisterous and cold. There is then more wind and dampness than in the winter. That there are exceptions to this however, the spring of last year, and the month of March, 1851, may be evidenced. The prevailing winds are similar to those of winter, viz., from west-northwest to north. The season continues cold and backward until early in May, when a sudden change takes place, and all nature is soon robed in the cheerful liveries of this gay portion of the year. The frost usually leaves the ground in April. The latter part of May and early in June is the usual seeding-time.

The summer is very cool and pleasant, with a fine breeze at all times, blowing mostly from the west, southwest, and south. This mitigates and makes endurable the extreme heat of the sun, which, beaming through the clear and brilliant atmosphere, rivals that of the tropics in intensity. This great heat is of but short duration, rarely continuing longer than a week at most. The nights are always cool and bracing, and the sleep obtained is sound, refreshing, and sweet. Thunderstorms are very frequent, usually occurring in the afternoon and evening, and sometimes continuing all the night. Those at night are always much the heaviest, and of the longest duration. A remarkable thunder-storm occurred at Sauk rapids on the 12th and 13th of July, 1851, which continued uninterruptedly for some thirty hours; the rain falling at intervals in torrents. It was accompanied by a hurricane of wind from the southeast, which prostrated forest-trees, tearing them up by the roots like twigs, and snapping others off like pipe-stems. It created considerable havoc along the western bank of the Mississippi above Crow river, and extended some distance in a northwest direction. Its breadth I never ascertained. Heavy hail-storms sometimes occur. The most remarkable one which I have noticed is thus described in a letter to the *Minnesota Pioneer*, dated Benton city (Sauk rapids*), June 18, 1851:—

"The most terrific rain and hail storm that I ever remember, occurred here last night, from ten P. M., until after midnight. It came up suddenly from the west, and for several hours the heavens were a perfect glare of light, most painful to the eye to witness; while the thunder was truly deafening at first, and most terrific. The rain fell in perfect sheets of water, and the hail descended like a shower of bullets, crushing through the windows and flying across the room with violence; while the house creaked and shook and rocked like a ship at sea, and I verily expected it to come tumbling about my ears each moment. The hailstones, unlike ordinary ones, were rough and jagged, as though a storm of the splinters and shivers of an iceberg had been hurled over this embryo city; which, owing to the meager number of houses, suffered but little. Ere long the rattle and clatter of their falling, drowned the thunder completely. By the glare of the lightning, I could see the rain-drops and hailstones driven by the gale, skim along the ground, and striking, bound several feet into the air, in a dense sheet of mingled ice and water, like waves of hail rising and rolling on before the storm. I could hear the clash and roar of the successive waves as they struck the house or a fence in their course, like regular discharges of firearms. The largest stones were about one inch in diameter, and fell upon the roof like grape-shot. The surrounding trees are well stripped of limbs and leaves, which were cut and split in shreds, and dashed off in large quantities. Altogether, it was a well-grown hail-storm for a new country, and as a meteorological

* Sauk rapids is situated on the Mississippi, seventy-six miles northwest of St. Paul.

phenomenon, I have thought a hasty description worthy of record."

The summer season is short—warm weather seldom sets in before July, although there are at times exceptions. Very hot weather occurred last year in May. What is lost in this respect is more than fully made up in autumn, which is here the most lovely portion of the year. Frosts seldom occur before October, while a beautiful Indian summer lasts till the middle of November, when winter soon after sets in suddenly. As a general thing, there are no gentle gradations of heat and cold between the change from spring to summer, and from fall to winter. That season usually lingers in the lap of spring, until he can no longer hold his sway, when he gently yields his long supremacy, and retreats to northern climes, without evincing any disposition to protract his stay. No crops are nipped, nor buds or blossoms perish from a renewal of his icy breath, in the shape of chilling, killing frosts. He melts away before the soft murmurings of the southern gales, and leaves no trace behind. He yields at once, and with a grace which does credit to the rude, rough, storm-king—and immediately a marked change takes place. No "elemental war" from heat to cold, from wet to dry—each striving for the mastery during an intervening month or two, as in the states, occur. On the contrary, the soft breath of early summer comes breathing along the southern vales, like the wellings up from a full and gushing heart—throbbing forth its warm pulsations, and giving life and vigor to every living thing beneath its touch. The unclouded sun pours forth his genial beams, revivifying the face of nature, and causing it to bloom and blossom. But anon, each day almost, a change comes over the spirit of his dream, and the storm-clouds gather in the western sky; then heaven's artillery is heard pealing forth its echoes from sky to earth, from plain to plain, and the refreshing rain descends in copious, grateful showers.

The bountiful earth, thus nourished and replenished, produces plenteously; and soon the ripened grain is waving in the breeze, the golden corn is glistening in the morning sun, the ripe and luscious melons dot the rich, smooth soil. 'Tis true there are no fruit-trees bending beneath the rosy peach, the pear, the plum, the cherry, and the apple, to gladden the eyes of the pomologist and cause the mouth to water in anticipation of the luxurious feast. Yet this is altogether owing to the newness of the country, and the want of time, as yet, to plant and produce those fruits; not, forsooth, that we are too far north, or that it is too cold to ripen them in perfection; nor that the inclemency of our winters, will destroy them by freezing. There can be no more certain criterion of the climate of any country than its vegetable production, and it may be stated here generally, that while all the grains and vegetable productions of the Middle and Western States, have been produced within the bounds of Minnesota, with almost every variety of wild tree, shrub, flower, and herb — and while all the tame grasses and most of the fruits *can be produced* within her limits, with the exception of the peach (which has failed at Galena and Dubuque), every objection to its being too far north is futile and ridiculous. Mr. Oakes, the father of C. H. Oakes, Esq., of St. Paul, has raised, successfully, all the above fruits, and others (except the peach), at Lapointe, on Lake Superior, in latitude a little south of forty-seven degrees; which is nearly two degrees northward of St. Paul. They can also be cultivated here; the soil being adapted to their culture, as also to that of melons, of corn, and sweet potatoes. All men should understand at this late day, that soils and climate are adapted to each other; and that parallels of latitude are a very unsafe rule to go by in judging altogether of the climate of a country; as it is always greatly modified by local causes. The geography of a country has much to do with its climate; its topography, its elevation, its lakes, its rivers, hills, and valleys, its soil, forests, prevailing winds, moisture and dryness, more or less affect its temperature.

The warm, loose, sandy soil of Minnesota, with the long, late autumnal season, will mature the cereal grains and fruits, almost as perfectly as that of far more southern climates. But "the world is indeed a slow coach after all," and progresses in the acquisition of knowledge at a snail's pate, at best. Truth is always outstripped by error, and falsehood spreads itself with the fleetness of the wind. The world delights to be humbugged, and all seem to act upon the principle that they must either humbug somebody, or be humbugged themselves. Men delight in being deceived; nay, in deceiving themselves against the dictates of reason, facts, and common-sense. Hence we may still expect to hear the oft-repeated cry of "You can't raise a *cawn crap* in Minnesota—you can't live away up there," &c., &c. We expect to find men for twenty years to come, who will persist in believing that the flame of a blazing fire here becomes congealed into spears of solid, icy flame, and that we are obliged to wrap blankets around our fires to keep them warm. Anything else that can be said, though equally ridiculous, will, of course, find multitudes of believers.

I come now to speak of the autumn; that quiet, sedate and melancholy portion of the year, which is here, as I have before remarked, its most lovely period. The atmosphere is warm and dry throughout the main portion of the day, and cool and bracing in the evening and early in the morning. Little rain falls and but few frosts occur. The thick, peculiar haze so common to the Indian Summer everywhere, here is as drowsy in its appearance as though it were endeavoring too soon to lull the day to sleep; as it rests over the quiet landscape, the craggy bluffs, the peaceful lakes, and flowing streams, and sometimes almost hides the rich and variegated face of nature, as imperceptibly it wanes and falls into the sere and yellow leaf. The prairies then become ignited, and blaze forth their mimic fires, which revel in their wildness. With an aurora borealis lighting up the northern heavens, and the vast buffalo ranges away to the Missouri, a perfect sea of roaring flame—the night if not turned into day, certainly eclipses its glorious beauties. Auroras are very common, and occur quite frequently in winter. The following is a description of the most brilliant one which I have noticed. It occurred on the night of the 6th of September, 1851, and was witnessed from the valley of the Red River of the North, in latitude forty-eight degrees:—

"The finest exhibition of the aurora borealis I ever witnessed, occurred to-night, beginning at 9 o'clock. No description—

not even the most vivid and wild imagination—can do it justice. It consisted of bright masses of light, in some directions illuminating large portions of the heavens—at others, and nearly over the whole surface of the sky, bright rays shot upwards, beginning not from the horizon, but at an elevation of about 45° and extending far south of the zenith. The rays, in fact, appeared to shoot upward all around the upper portion of the heavens, uniting at the zenith, and producing one of the finest effects that was ever produced by Nature in her wildest freak or grandest effort. To the north and south of the zenith, the rays assumed many variegated tints, among which the most beautiful pink and green and various indescribable shades were the most prominent. These were constantly changing color and the rays their forms; sometimes like moving columns of light, which the Indians poetically call 'the dance of the dead,' the bright white and colored rays or columns moving and darting past each other in an erect position, and of which a giant's causeway, if brilliantly illuminated and put in rapid motion, would afford a faint idea.

"The whole mass of light would then cover the northern heavens and encircle around the zenith; assuming the varied shapes of the most beautiful drapery; the lower edges being tinged with a bright pink, intermixed with green above, while at the apex the light was white and so brilliant as almost to dazzle. Then it would again shift and spread rapidly across the heavens in a curved belt or zone, like an eagle's plume, as though the hand of the God of the heavens and the earth was about to appear and make a record on the clear moonlit sky below, and then anon the rays and clouds of variegated light would gather into most beautiful and fantastic shapes, picturesque and wild in the extreme; and so quickly, too, that the eye could scarcely trace their motions; occasionally darting down their fringed edges which waved to and fro like canvass fluttering in the storm, resembling a tempest in the heavens, consisting of dancing beams of brilliant light for lightning; and the falling clouds, rays and coruscations of pink and green, with every conceivable variety of colored halo for the accompanying rain. It continued equally beautiful till long past midnight, and was watched with admiration and awe by all our party. Auroras, mirages, and other meteorological phenomena, are very frequent along the northern boundary of Minnesota, and thence north to Hudson's Bay. Charles Cavileer, Esq., U. S. collector of customs at Pembina, in latitude forty-nine degrees north, longitude ninety-seven degrees, ten minutes, west, has furnished me with the following particulars relating to the meteorology of that distant region, for the winter of 1852–'3. Mr. Cavileer says :—

"During December, there were but five entire clear days, and seven generally clear; seven cloudy, and four mostly cloudy. The rest variable. There was but one day of perfect calm, between sunrise and sunset, but calm generally prevailed at night; and such nights, too, the most beautiful imaginable. The prevailing winds were from the northwest and southeast; the most disagreeable ones are from the northeast, east, and south, and are damp and chilly. The northwesters are cold and dry, while those from the west are pleasant, and bring fine warm weather. But seven or eight inches of snow fell, with a sprinkle or two of rain, and one sleet. The 1st and 28th were the warmest days, the mercury stood at two P. M., thirty-four degrees above zero, and at sunrise on the 15th, at thirty-eight below. There were seven auroras, and are classed from the tables of the Smithsonian Institution. But two of them were in any way striking. The peculiarity of that of the 22d being in the east and northeast, brightest due east, light red and fiery. That on the 29th was a very pretty affair, commencing at seven, P.M. The sky was clear, with a silver moon and bright star-light. Its first appearance was in the northwest, like that of the moon before she shows her face; then rapidly assumed class five, and extended from the northwest horizon to the northeast; the arch a bright white, and segment very dark. But the fantastics of the outsiders constituted the main beauty of the scene—sometimes taking the form of the rainbow, and, numbering from one to three above the arch, showed most grandly; then rays, beams, and patches of light, would flash up to the northeast, running west almost as quickly as the eye. The outsiders made their exit about ten, but the arch continued till eleven. December 12, at eight o'clock, P. M., I observed a large and splendid meteor slowly traversing the north-east sky from east to west. It appeared like a large ball or globe of fire; a very bright, white light, travelling very slowly, and leaving no wake or light in its track. It was in sight a minute, and then exploded without leaving a spark.

"The first *mirage* of the season was on the evening of the 22d, at sunset, and showed plainly the whole course of the river Maurais, the timber on its banks appearing but a few miles distant. The houses on the north, that can hardly be seen through a common atmosphere, were raised high up, showing them plainly, and even things lying about on the ground. The second and last of the month was on the morning of the 29th, from sunrise till ten o'clock, A. M., and was a most grand natural exhibition. Not only the whole course of the Maurais could be traced, but Oak island, forty-five miles distant, was clear to the view; and Pembina mountain, thirty miles off, was dimly seen in the distance. These were the first *mirages* I ever witnessed, and it is certainly a very novel thing to be thus butted in the face by things you know to be so many miles distant. In January, 1853, there were ten auroras and eight *mirages*.

"The *mirage* of the 24th was the most grand of all. It commenced before sunrise and continued till ten, A. M. Just at sunrise, the view was truly magnificent; in all quarters of the compass, as far as the eye could reach, the country appeared to rise as if we were standing in the centre of a basin. The Pembina mountain, to the west, loomed up grandly; different distant points on Red river, to the north and south, were counted and named; while the rivers Maurais, Prune, and Gratiara, were in plain sight; and I really believe that, with a good glass, we might have seen Fort Garry, seventy miles below us to the north, so very clear was the atmosphere. About ten minutes after sunrise the mountain was invisible; at eight o'clock, fog to the north, half part of mountain again in view, and at ten, A. M., all had gradually disappeared. The sky at sunrise was about half-clouded; the clouds lying all round the horizon, with a few light ones overhead, and maintained the same situation throughout the phenomenon. The aurora, the *mirages*, the beautiful frosting of the trees and vegetation, with the change of the atmosphere, &c., will more than pay for wintering in the climate; and, if for nothing else, I shall never regret having spent two winters on the forty-ninth degree of north latitude, amid these northern wilds."

I know of no point in Uncle Sam's domains better situated for a meteorological and astronomical observatory than this. It being on his most northern boundary, nearly midway between the Atlantic and Pacific oceans, and in the range of the great plains that extend from the north pole in a southerly direction along the base of the Rocky mountains, and thence southerly through Minnesota, Wisconsin, and Illinois, perfectly free from the influence of winds from the oceans or northern lakes, we are surrounded by an atmosphere purely our own.

CHAPTER V.

THE ST. LOUIS RIVER OF LAKE SUPERIOR, LA POINTE, FOND DU LAC, ST. CROIX PINERIES, ETC.

The head of Lake Superior is about five miles wide, the shore forming nearly a regular semicircle. The St. Louis river enters the lake near the middle of this bend. The entrance from the lake is about west, forty or fifty rods, when the river bends suddenly to the north, keeping its course parallel with the lake shore about half a mile, when the course is again changed to the southwest. Here the river widens out into a bay about six miles long, and, in places, two miles wide; having several small islands in it. The bend of the river, near the mouth, forms a peninsula between its north bank and the lake, about a mile long, and averaging about a quarter of a mile in width. It is a body of sand, producing only some small evergreen underbrush, and a beautiful grove of tall, straight, limbless, yellow pines. On the south side of the river there is a tract of several hundred acres of low land, a portion of which is similar to that on the north side, but much of it is swampy. The American Fur Company, previous to 1840, had a trading post here, about half a mile from the lake, but it was subsequently removed to Fond du Lac, at the foot of the falls.

The river at its mouth is less than a quarter of a mile wide, and obstructed by a sandbar, holding countless snags; but on passing this a few rods, it brings the boat beyond the bend, into calm, deep water, in any weather. At the head of the bay the traveller is in want of a pilot. From that point to the falls, the river is full of islands and fields of wild rice, around and through which there are numerous channels. The inexperienced may row several miles, and find himself at the head of a bay or cove, and be under the necessity of returning to seek the true channel. From the lake to the falls, called twenty miles, the northern shore is bold and rugged, except in a few places where it falls back, forming a small plat of table-land between it and the river, or gives vent to a small mountain stream. The bluffs on the south side are similar to those on the north, for several miles below the falls; they there disappear. The Fond du Lac river, from the southwest, enters the lake about two miles south of the outlet of the St. Louis, and the valleys of the two rivers are merged in one some six or seven miles from the lake.

A few rods below the falls, a creek of pure, never-failing water from the north, forms a junction with the river. The west side of the valley formed by this creek is occupied by the American Fur Company, and the east by the missionary establishment of the Methodist Episcopal Church. The whole valley does not afford above eighty acres of arable land.

About three miles north of Fond du Lac, a peak of one of the mountains towers far above all others. The only ascent is on the north side, and is tolerably easy for a footman. The south side is a perpendicular rock of several hundred feet in height. The summit is a level bare rock. The stone forming this peak is unlike anything else seen in the country. It is of a dark gray color, and so close in texture, that the united strength of myself and interpreter could not break a piece of it by hurling it against the mass on which we stood. The beholder can scarcely resist the impression, that he stands on a pyramid, in the midst of an immense basin, whose outer rim is the limit of human vision. Lake Superior, though twenty miles distant, appears as if lying at his feet, and stretching itself away to the east, until sight loses it in the distance; and the river, with its islands, channels, and rice-fields, is all in full view from the falls to its mouth. The writer has never seen another spot where such a comprehensive view of the vastness of creation could be obtained.

The falls of the St. Louis river are nothing more than a succession of rapids for the distance of about fifteen miles, except at the head of "Knife Portage." At that point the water falls about ten feet perpendicularly. Above that point, to the mouth of Savannah river, eighty miles from the lake, there are few banks seen in high water. The bottoms are several miles wide in places, indeed most of the way, and often overflown. But, from Fond du Lac to the above-named falls, the water rushes through a narrow gorge, the banks in several places being from fifty to one hundred feet high, and always crumbling in. In several places within two miles of Fond du Lac, they are composed of shale, sand, and boulders; the slaty shale lying in regular strata, dipping several degrees westward on the south side, and equally eastward on the north side. Just above these banks, on the north side of the river, an acre or more of trap rock mixed with copper, precisely like that below Lapointe, is exposed to view in low water. It has the appearance of having once been covered with a bank similar to those above described, which has washed away; and it was the opinion of the writer, that the same formation might be found under many of the hills around the falls. Up the creek before mentioned, a mile from the river, the same mixture of shale and sand may be seen in many places. The Indians considered this metallic substance in the trap rock valuable, and in the treaty made at Lapointe, in 1842, they reserved this spot, stipulating that the trader's store, one mile below, should be the corner of that session. The head chief often told the writer, that he expected to take out a great amount of wealth from the river, at that spot, as soon as he should get the means.

The first portage on these falls is about eight miles long, on the north side of the river. It is over a very rough country, through several very swampy places, and is generally impracticable for horses, or anything that can not walk a pole. At the head of this portage canoes are used again, for two miles, and there the "Knife portage" is made on the south side of the river, three miles, to the grand falls above alluded to. In high water, both of these portages are longer. On both sides of the river at the Knife portage, much of the surface of the ground is covered with masses of slate equal to any hone for edged tools. They have the appearance of being thrown up by some internal revolution, there being nothing like order or regularity in their position, and the intervening ground being even.

Europeans who have seen this slate allege that it is equal to that used in England for tiling. The supply, even on the surface of the ground, is inexhaustible.

There can scarcely be a limit to the amount of fish, pickerel chiefly, that may be taken on the rapids during about three weeks of the spring. In the spring of 1843, a two-fathom canoe filled in one hour in the morning, by two men, one steering and the other using a dip-net. Both work the canoe up the rapids sufficiently far, when one stands in the bow with a net, while the other backs the canoe with his might in addition to the rapidity of the current. From twenty to fifty large fishes are frequently thus taken in passing about twenty rods of the rapids.

From Fond du Lac, a trading post situated eleven miles inland on the St. Louis river, eastward, for perhaps fifty miles, the margin of the lake is a flat strip of land, reaching back to a rocky ridge about eleven miles off. The soil of this flat land is a rich red clay. The wood is white cedar and pine, and of the most magnificent growth. The American line is beyond the mouth of the St. Louis, as far northeast as Pigeon river, one hundred miles. A mountain extends all the way between the St. Louis and Pigeon rivers. It evidently abounds in copper, iron, and silver. The terrestrial compass can not be used there, so strong is the attraction to the earth. The needle rears and plunges "like mad." Points of survey have to be fixed by the solar compass.

The Indian and half-breed packmen have astonishing strength. One Indian, who is described by the others as being as large as two men, carried for a company of eleven men provisions for ten days, viz., one barrel of flour, half barrel of pork and something else, besides the utensils. *Mirage* is a common phenomenon in spring and summer. For the bays not opening so soon as the main lake, or not cooling so early, an object out on the lake is viewed from the shore, through a dense medium of air and a thin medium. Hence is a refraction of rays, which gives so many wonderful sights that the Chippewas call that the spirit or enchanted land. Sail vessels which are really thirty miles off, are seen flapping and bellying about almost within touch. Turreted islands look heady and toppling towards the zenith. Forests seem to leap from their stems, and go a soaring like thistles for the very sport of it.

The ice does not leave some of the bays till the 10th of June. The fish are delicious, especially the salmon trout. But little land game. We calculate on wonderful enterprises in that country after the opening of the Saut canal.

Lapointe is a town on the lake, situated at the head of a bay some twenty-five miles from the high lake, and secluded from the lake by several islands. There is a warehouse three hundred feet long, built of tamarac poles, and roofed with bark. This building is very much warped by the pressure of age; it is entered by a wooden railway. The town is dingy and dreary. A luxurious garden contains a variety of fruit-trees and shrubs, planted by Charles H. Oakes, Esq., now a resident of St. Paul.

The following narration of a trip from Lapointe to Stillwater, *via* Lake Superior, Brule and St. Croix rivers, will be found interesting :—

"It was a beautiful bright afternoon in August, that, with two hired half-breed voyageurs, in a birch-canoe provisioned for eighteen days, we left Lapointe, and struck out into the clear, smooth, deep waters of Lake Superior. The coast scenery, that from Saut St. Marie to this point had been very dull and monotonous, now suddenly changed, reaching through all the degrees of beauty, from gentle slopes, rolling hills, to widely romantic, broken mountains. It is here that the Porcupine mountains set in towards the shore, and in places come out boldly, as if in the act of crossing the lake, but were suddenly split down vertically, forming a mural escarpment, perpendicular from the water's edge, hundreds of feet high, as smooth and solid as the masonry of a vast fortress. The strata are of the old red sandstone, of a fine compact texture, and never in the world can quarries of handsomer stone be found than those. Blocks from ten to fifteen feet long, the outer surface smooth as pressed brick, lay disjointed ready for shipment.

"Many of these bold mountain masses project over the water from sixteen to twenty feet, supported at the outer edge by perfectly-formed columns, worn so by long action of the waves. These columns are of very curious workmanship indeed. We passed under many of these rocky arches, like majestic gateways, and examined more than a dozen columns of various diameters and heights, and all appearing as if drawn after more well-proportioned architectural models.

"The journey now before us was about three hundred and fifty miles, ninety of which lay along this coast, up to the mouth of Brule river. Fortunately for the voyageur at this season, there is scarcely the shadow of a night upon the lake. At ten o'clock we could still read distinctly, and at twelve there were soft crimson pencilings upon the western horizon of that gorgeous twilight which makes the summer evenings here so enchanting. I have seen night here so transcendently beautiful, with its bright stars and silvery moon—its atmosphere so transparent—that the arch of heaven looked more serene and heavenly, more like the abode of spiritual beings, and the clear blue ether more like the drapery that garnishes a poetic or imaginary, than a real world. As we glided along in the stillness of the night, our canoe moving so lightly as not to ruffle the polished surface, the scenic picture was all that the most enthusiastic novelist could desire. On one side, some miles distant, lay a long string of conical islands, thickly covered with green forest-trees; and on the main shore, at an equal distance, wrapped in a shadowy gloom, lay green slopes, or in sullen grandeur hung bold peaks or cliffs of mountains. Not a sound was heard, except for a time the stunning noise of a cataract that came leaping from the top of the heights, dashing down from rock to rock, its bright spray dancing upon the moonbeams and enveloping the dwarfed pines in an eternal sheet of mist. We had left far behind us all traces of civilization, and were traversing a spot as primitive in its features as when the "stars sang together, and all the sons of God shouted for joy" at the new creation. The scenery is grand at all times; but in the stillness of night, lighted up by a Lake Superior moon, it is magnificently picturesque beyond description.

"It was a dangerous though fortunate gale, on the second day, that carried us about ten miles an hour for eight hours to the mouth of the river we designed to ascend. We reached the delta, formed by sand and driftwood, at dusk, and encamped. The next morning the canoe was well pitched, the freight uniformly disposed along the bottom—my place being on a pile of coats and blankets amidships—when old Charon and assistant took their position, denuded of all clothing except their breechcloth and shirt fore and aft. The Brule is a narrow, wild, roaring, rocky stream. Looking up the mouth, it comes rushing down a woody, mountainous gorge, leaping over huge trap and granite boulders, apparently defying all forms of navigation. This tumultuous, whirling current we ascended one hundred miles, averaging twenty-five miles per day, in a light bark canoe, twenty-seven feet long by five midships, tapering sharp at the ends, turning up like a Chinese junk, freighted with about twelve hundred pounds. The boat is set up the rapids by poles; and where the rocky walls encroach upon the bed of the river, crowding it into a narrow channel, and this further interrupted by reefs and boulders, the passage is attended with great difficulty and danger. The boatmen are naked, that, should they miss a stroke with the pole, like a flash they dart into the stream, holding firmly the canoe, towing it to shoal water, otherwise it would be instantly dashed to pieces by the force of the current against the rocks. No one who has not travelled with these fellows can form any idea of their expertness in managing a boat among the rapids. I take time to speak of the mode and danger of ascending this stream, as romantic persons have signified a determination to make the trip next summer, and should they fail to get good, experienced voyageurs, they will stand a fair chance of being left in the wilderness some hundreds of miles from any white settlement, with the pleasing prospect of a long groping through one of the most impenetrable forests in the world. Men who have been in the service of the American Fur Company understand the streams and rapids the best.

"The country reaching south from the lake one hundred miles is rough, cheerless, covered with pines, elms, tamarac, cedars, &c. The rocks, of igneous origin, which form the mineral region in Michigan, extend across Wisconsin, and reach Minnesota, by what appears a singular dislocation, throwing them nearly two hundred miles south. Copper is found on the Brule in Wisconsin; and when I reached the falls of St. Croix, specimens were exhibited, coming from the trap range which here makes its appearance.

"The Brule in olden times was great trapping ground. We saw the remains of large beaver-dams, and well-beaten paths, which the trappers call *portages*. They are across long, sharp points, where the river makes a sudden bend. It was through this stream that the numerous trapping posts on the St. Croix and tributaries, the St. Peter and other tributaries of the Upper Mississippi, were supplied from the large fur-company post at Lapointe. There are now no longer beaver or otter found here; but rats are numerous, and some martin.

"After passing the ridge of highlands, on the third day, the country is level, marshy, and numerous lakes are covered with ducks, and are alive with speckled trout, of a good size and delicious flavor. There are several hard portages, in places where the rapids are too dangerous; and when, on the fourth evening, we reached Le Grand Portage, at the head of the Brule, we hailed it with joyful delight. This was the portage across the ridge which divides the south from the north running streams—from the Brule to the headquarters of the St. Croix. From toilsome, up-hill poling, we would now descend smoothly with the current, under sail, or with light oars.

"I had often listened to what I considered extravagant stories of the feat and strength of 'pack-men;' and now I witnessed what, as I attempt to relate, I can scarcely credit. The portage now to make was three miles, up and down hill, over a hot, sunburnt, barren heath. The afternoon was sweltering, the dry sands reflecting a scorching, suffocating heat, and the thick forest which hemmed in the trail cut off every motion of the air. The canoe was taken ashore, and the freight made up into packages. A strong leather strap, about four yards along, four inches wide in the centre, tapering gradually to the ends, is used, by lashing the long ends around the packages, the broad centre forming a loop which is placed against the forehead, the burden lying upon the shoulders. My trunk was large, crammed to overflowing, weighing about one hundred pounds. The strap went round this, upon which was placed four large, heavy blankets, cotton tent, three overcoats, bag of flour (eighty pounds), iron-bound keg with liquor (twenty pounds), when 'Hercules' squatted, slipped the noose over his head, rose up, then seizing his hands full of camp-kettles, pans, &c., started off as erect as a soldier, and kept me blowing, sweating, and panting, to keep pace with him across the portage. The other, old Sowyerain, seventy years of age, was loaded equally heavy!

"We were now upon the St. Croix, or rather at the boiling spring, which sends a portion of its waters to the south to seek the gulf of Mexico, and another north to the gulf of St. Lawrence. At this small point, in this beautiful crystal basin, two rivers take their rise. One mile below this the St. Croix is half a mile wide, forming a deep lake, three miles long, perfectly alive with amphibia and fish. Oh, how awfully wild, lonely, and still, are these places! We know that we are hundreds of miles from all civilization. White men have been here, but left no traces behind. We move down to a small, open spot, and camp for the night on the margin of the lake. There is not a ripple on the water, and the dark shadows of the heavy trees on the opposite side are reaching over; for the red, hot sun is now low in the west; and oh, what a solitary stillness, as if the wheels of Time stood still, and Nature paused in breathless suspense!

"The descent of this river was very irksome and tedious, requiring four days. The stream is tortuous, and has but little current; is bordered by an almost continuous succession of marshes, wild-rice fields, and large cranberry-patches. On the third day the country changed, and large natural-grass meadows spread out from the shores for miles. The grass was about six feet high, and would yield at the rate of many tons to the acre.

"At Le Grand Portage, and some other places, we passed the remains of ancient Chippewa towns. I could not avoid a feeling of sadness when passing them, and in places I rambled over these forlorn, sad spots. In one open, beautiful spot, some twelve decayed frames remain, and the marks of camp-fires, kindled here perhaps for centuries, but now deserted, and still as death. All the old home associations—the familiar forests, the haunts of the deer, wolf, and bear—the mausoleums of the dead—all, all are left behind, as the imperative command of the white says to the red man, 'Onward, onward, to the wild, snowy mountains of the west!' America crowds them upon Mexico and the mountains: Mexico and the sterile mountains crowd them back. In one spot we met a few squalid, miserably-poor, half-starved men, squaws, and dogs, who had wandered a long way back from the main tribe. They were living upon whortleberries and what fish they could spear in the river."

THE ST. CROIX PINERIES, ETC.

The following article is from the pen of John P. Owens, Esq., editor of *The Minnesotian*, the organ of the whig party in St. Paul. It will prove worthy of an attentive perusal:—

"Since our residence in Minnesota, it has happened a hundred times, to others as well as ourselves, to be 'chucked' down under the high bluff among our pleasant friends of Stillwater, with no manner of way or convenience for leaving there, except at California expenses, unless you chose to take the back track to St. Paul, wait for a steamboat going down the lake, or paddle a batteau up against the swift current of the St. Croix. The interesting and valuable region comprising the valley of that river has been neglected by strangers, as well as citizens of other parts of the territory, mainly because it happened to be destitute of good roads, and off from the beaten track of general travel. Added to this, the inhabitants of that region are an entirely different class from those who dwell over this way. They have not among them any speculators or town-builders, to answer the purpose of conspicuous advertisements in the columns of daily newspapers, by keeping the great and unprecedented advantages of their several locations prominently before the people about the streets, and at the hotels, and upon the steamboats. Their vocation is the active and laborious one of getting pine-logs out of the interminable forests up toward the sources of the river, converting them into building materials, or running them whole in 'ten-acre rafts' to the markets below. A man, to follow this business successfully, has very few spare hours throughout the year for running about the country. In July and August, he cuts his hay, near where his winter's operations are to take place; in September, October, and November, he gets up his supplies; from then until April he is 'in the woods,' with no chance to get out of them, and no disposition to get out even to 'crow,' until the spring freshets unlock the chains of winter, and sweep his logs into the booms; and then till July and haying-time comes round again, the months are occupied by the most important and interesting of the whole year's transactions—getting his property to market, and receiving his well-earned cash therefor.

"But, thanks to the good-natured responses of our dear Uncle Sam to the St. Croix people's petition for a good road through their country, and Mr. Sibley's faithful attention to their interests in seeing the ways and means put through to consummate the measure, the important region of country to which we allude is about to be placed in easy and accessible communication with its neighbors residing in other parts of the territory, as well as 'the rest of mankind.'"

(The author of this work spent the most of the year 1852, with a force of over fifty men, in opening a United States road from Stillwater to within seven miles of the falls of St. Croix. It is now completed to Sunrise, a distance of sixteen miles above the falls.)

"In addition, some adventurous genius on a small scale, down about Oquaka, Illinois, last year conceived the good idea of procuring a steamboat suitable to perform the duties of a tri-weekly packet between Stillwater and Taylor's falls, the extreme point of steam navigation up the St. Croix. It is true he did not appear to have a very correct idea of the kind of craft the people really wanted and would well support in that trade; but, such as he thought and planned, he late last season brought forth. . . . Indeed, the little Humboldt' is a great accommodation to the people of the St. Croix. She stops anywhere along the river, to do any and all kinds of business that may offer, and will give passengers a longer ride, so far as *time* is concerned, for a dollar, than any other craft we ever travelled upon. She is also, to outward appearances, a temperance boat, and carries no cooking or table utensils. She stops at the 'Marine,' going and returning, to allow the people aboard to feed upon a good, substantial dinner; and the passengers are allowed, if they feel so disposed, to carry 'bars' in their side-pockets and 'bricks' in their hats. A very accommodating craft is the 'Humboldt,' and a convenience that is already set down on the St. Croix as one indispensable.

"We happened on the St. Croix at a time peculiarly adapted for observing what is going on in that quarter. Over here about St. Paul, people are too apt to imagine they are doing the entire business of the territory. The difference between us and the St. Croix folks at this time is very striking, so far as regards the great essential particular of buying and selling. We are buying — they are selling. We, of the Mississippi, have now going out of our river a small quantity comparatively of logs and lumber. But we have by every boat from below *coming in*, dollars in amount of articles for consumption, to where the exports are cents in the shape of products of our forests going out. We are aware this state of things will not continue long, as our country is rapidly filling up with farmers; but it is so just at this time, On the other hand, our neighbors of the St. Croix, with a population on both sides of the river, from Point Douglas to the farthest point toward its source of lumbering operations, not equal by several hundred souls to that of St. Paul, will send to market this season sixty million feet of sawed lumber and logs, provided the streams continue at their present stage a few weeks longer. Some weeks ago we made an estimate, placing the entire amount of logs in the territory at a much less figure than this. We were hugely mistaken. Circumstances have greatly favored the St. Croix lumbermen this season. For two years past, the low stage of the water has prevented them from clearing the upper streams of logs: now they are getting them all out, old and new. The present season opened with quite a freshet, owing to the heavy falls of snow last winter. The boom was early filled, and many millions have already reached the markets below. But the 'June rise,' caused by the steady rains for the past three weeks, has probably done the business thoroughly for them. From Stillwater to the Boom, six miles below Taylor's falls, you are scarcely out of sight of rafts and strings of logs. The whole way up, and about the boom, it requires no great stretch of fancy to imagine one's self passing through a country in military possession of Queen Victoria, so often do we pass detachments of stout, hardy men, dressed in red.

"The lumbermen of the St. Croix, during the sessions of the Wisconsin and Minnesota legislatures of 1850–51, procured the incorporation of the 'St. Croix Boom Company,' with a capital of $10,000. This work was considered absolutely necessary, to facilitate the business of driving, assorting, and rafting logs. The stock was speedily taken; and by the following season the boom was built and ready for service. The work is substantial and permanent. Piers of immense size are sunk at proper distances, from the Minnesota shore to the foot of a large island near the centre of the stream, and again from the head of the island to the Wisconsin shore. The boom timbers are hung from pier to pier; and the whole river is entirely commanded, with no possibility of scarcely a single log escaping. The charter of the company compels them, however, to give free passage to all boats, rafts, &c., ascending or descending the river. This duty is rather difficult to perform at certain times, particularly when the logs are running into the boom briskly, and hands are not to be had to raft and run them out. This was the case once this season. The Asia came up with a heavy freight, which she had signed to deliver at Taylor's falls. When she reached the boom, a barrier of three or four miles of logs compactly intervened upon the water's surface, and forbade her further progress. The company had been unable to procure laborers to clear out the logs, but were nevertheless clearly liable to damages for obstructing navigation. They chose the only remedy at hand, which was to receive the freight, and pay its transportation up to the falls in Mackinaw boats. With a full complement of men, the boom can always be kept clear at the point where it crosses the main channel of the river. But owing to the unusual demand for labor, this has been a difficult matter the present season.

" This boom is undoubtedly the most complete and expensive work of the kind in the northwest. It is the business resort of all the lumbermen on the river, and those who wish to have any transactions with them, during the season of rafting and running. It is to them precisely what 'Change is to the merchants of a large city. Mill proprietors, dealers, pilots, loggers, and raftsmen, here do congregate daily, to talk over their affairs and transact their business. If you wish, at this season, to see a man residing in that section of country, you will be more apt to find him at the boom, some day during the week, than at home or anywhere else. Every man's logs on the river are compelled to pass through the boom, and during the process they are assorted and rafted, and delivered to him or his pilots immediately below. So much per thousand is allowed the company by law for this labor, which, by-the-by, we understand has never yet been sufficient to pay. It is thought, however, that the present season will show a different result, owing to the large increase of business.

" It is a curiosity to see the huge size of some of the rafts from this boom. Two noted St. Croix pilots passed Stillwater with a fleet of three million feet under their command. We believe that this is the largest lot of logs that ever went out of the St. Croix in one body.

" The first mill reached in descending the St. Croix from Taylor's falls, is the Osceola, on the Wisconsin side. Its water power is a spring branch from the neighboring bluffs, similar to the Marine and other mills below the falls, and is said to be the best on the river. This mill has been in operation since 1845. It is now owned and managed by the Messrs. Kent, Mr. Mahoney, who had been identified with the establishment since its inception, having retired last fall. With proper improvements, Osceola can be made one of the most extensive manufacturing establishments on the river.

"Marine Mills is next in order. This is a place on the St. Croix, noted for its extensive manufacturing facilities. The Marine Company erected last season an extensive new mill, which is now running. There is sufficient water power to drive two saws, but the new mill has been erected with a view of using steam machinery. It speaks well for the prosperity of the Marine Company, and the lumbering business, to see in operation such elegant and complete mills as this. The workmanship and machinery are not excelled by any in the territory.

"The establishment of Mr. Mower, the Arcola, is six miles above Stillwater. Here has also been erected, within the past year, a new mill, which is operated by steam—the only mill of the kind as yet in operation on the St. Croix. Mr. Mower also continues his old water-mill, and appears to be driving an extensive business.

"Passing on to the upper edge of Stillwater, we come to the ruins of the extensive steam-mill of Messrs. Sawyer, Heaton & Setzer, which was destroyed by fire a few months since. But the determined proprietors have no notion of giving it up so. We noticed men at work removing the rubbish, preparatory to rebuilding.

"The M'Kusick mill, at Stillwater, is still ripping away after the old fashion. His establishment is noted for the excellent and neat manner in which he prepares his lumber for market.

"We visited the new steam-mill below Stillwater, belonging to Messrs. Churchill & Nelson, Carlton, Loomis, and others. It is not yet quite ready for motion, but will start off full rigged next month. If we are any judge of such matters, this mill, in many respects, 'takes them all.' It has the same power as the Oakes establishment of St. Paul, and will drive the same amount of saws and machinery, but is more spacious, convenient, and eligibly situated for doing business. The engine was built in Detroit.

"On the Minnesota side of the lake, opposite Hudson, Mr. M. Perrin is erecting a steam saw-mill, which will be in operation soon. In the vicinity of Hudson are the mills of Messrs. Mears and Bowron. Then at the mouth of the lake is the mill of Messrs. Stevens & Co. This completes the list, making, when Messrs. Sawyer, Heaton & Setzer's new establishment is completed, eleven mills in the valley, with, in the aggregate, over twenty upright saws, and the usual amount of circulars attached. This amount of machinery should be able to cut two hundred and fifty thousand feet of lumber every twenty-four hours — worth, in the St. Louis market, fourteen dollars per thousand. We think we have heard it remarked that Minnesota has no resources!

"While people are going crazy about the valley of the Minnesota and other portions west of the Mississippi, they should recollect there are *old* locations worth looking at, with a high market at the door of every farmer for the next hundred years, or as long as the pineries last. Going by land from Stillwater to Taylor's Falls, you pass over the same character of country as lies between St. Paul and Stillwater, with the exception that the land is of a much better quality generally. West of the road lies Cornelian lake, a large and beautiful sheet of water. Immediately back of Marine is another large lake. Marine is situated upon the line of the open and timber country. Immediately north of that point commences the heavy 'hard wood' growth, consisting of oak of the largest size, sugar maple — which predominates — bass wood, ash, white walnut, &c. This extensive forest runs north some thirty miles to the mouth of Sunrise river. The heavy timber continues the whole distance, the western border being within twenty miles of St. Paul. The land is of the very best quality, rolling but not broken, and the heavy timber so thick that the rays of the sun can scarcely reach the ground. The timber, soil, and character of the country, through this forest and around Lake Chisago, is precisely similar to what we see about Lake Minnetonka. Lake Chisago has about forty miles of coast. Around its shores are settled several families of Swedes, who are beginning to farm in a small way. There is also a settlement of these people in the vicinity of Marine.

"Sunrise river, or creek, takes its rise about four miles north and six miles west of Marine, and about six miles north, bearing east, of White Bear lake. It runs in a northerly direction, and empties itself into the St. Croix sixteen miles above Taylor's falls. The valley of this stream is unsurpassed as an agricultural country. But very little land along it is yet taken up, which is also the case with the entire timber country we have spoken of east of it. It is proper also to mention, that the source of Sunrise is in the same township as that of Rice creek, a tributary of the Mississippi sixteen miles above St. Paul. Toward the mouth of Sunrise, northwest of Taylor's falls, and traversing the banks of the stream, is one of the most fertile and beautiful of prairies, extending eight or ten miles north and south, and from two to three east and west. Only about two sections of this delightful farming paradise is yet claimed. What renders this tract so very valuable is, that it is immedately adjacent to the immense hardwood timber country we have alluded to, and close on up toward the pine region.

"The country northeast of us is an impassable region of lakes and swamps. The facts are just as we have stated, although it is true the country is exceedingly well-watered with spring branches and clear lakes. A very large proportion of these lands are marked 'number one' in the field notes of the surveyors, while, according to the same authority, there is no land of this high character (or at least scarcely any) immediately about St. Paul.

"As has been published to the world a thousand times, this is the most northern point of continuous steamboat navigation from below on the water of the Mississippi, or its tributaries. The celebrated falls of St. Croix are half a mile above, but boats can not ascend over Taylor's falls; although there is no precipitous fall at the latter place, only swift rapids. The scenery and character of this bold and romantic locality has been so often described by able pens, that we will not hazard all we could do — a bare attempt to go over the ground successfully. The picture is graphically and truly delineated in Mrs. Ellet's 'Summer Rambles in the West,' to which we invite the attention of those of our readers who have never visited this noted spot. Suffice it to say, that those who visit Minnesota, and go away without seeing 'Rock island,' the 'Delles,' 'Taylor's Falls,' and the 'Falls of St. Croix,' leave out of the note-book of their observations a section of country and scenery that is worth going three times the distance to behold. There is nothing like it anywhere else in this part of the world. No conception can be formed of the character of its boldness and grandeur by viewing the falls of St. Anthony. It is altogether a piece of architecture and workmanship of an entirely different style, as much so as a Corinthian palace is different from a Gothic cathedral.

"The geologists have told us all about the formations of this region. The dark green trap rock — known by the common name of 'green stone' — similar in texture and general appearance to the more grayish copper-bearing rock of Lake Superior, is thrown up here in immense masses, lying all over the surface so thick that a team can not be driven over it with safety. This upheaving process has only been carried on in the immediate vicinity of the falls. Half a mile back on the Minnesota side it entirely disappears. This is also a copper-bearing rock, and it is not uncommon to find large boulders of pure copper in excavating wells and cellars. We have one now on our table, taken from a well immediately in the village of Taylor's Falls a few weeks since, which weighs about one pound, and is over ninety per cent. of pure copper. There is no doubt that this metal exists in large quantities in this trap range; but at the present time the citizens of the Falls have a more certain, if not a more profitable occupation than prospecting for copper.

"Taylor's Falls is really one of the oldest places in Minnesota, although the neat and pleasant village of thirty or forty houses — all tastefully built and cleanly painted — which one sees there now, has sprung into existence during the past two years. The 'claim' upon which this thriving village stands, was made by Jesse Taylor, Esq., a well-known citizen of Stillwater. He afterward entered into partnership with Mr. Baker, an Indian trader, remembered by all our older settlers as the gentleman who built the large stone house on the Mississippi, above Fort Snelling, now owned by Kenneth M'Kenzie, Esq., of St. Louis. Messrs. Baker, Taylor, and others, proceeded here to erect the first mill ever commenced on the St. Croix. Mr. Baker died before it was completed, and the frame was afterward removed to Osceola, six miles below on the Wisconsin side, where it was re-erected and still stands, doing good service for its present owners. Jesse Taylor subsequently sold his claim to Joshua L. Taylor, the gentleman first appointed marshal of Minnesota, by President Taylor, in 1849, who still owns a portion of the old claim. Another of the Taylor family a brother of J. L., and a well-known and influential citizen of the St. Croix Valley, in partnership with Mr. Fox, at this time carries on trade in the old 'claim cabin' erected by Jesse in 1837; so it will be seen there is no sense in calling the place anything else than Taylor's Falls. Mr. W. H. C. Folsom holds forth on the opposite corner in the same business—that of general merchandise—which two establishments complete the stock of mercantile transactions at Taylor's Falls. He is engaged in a very extensive trade with the lumbermen, and is one of the master spirits of the Upper St. Croix.

"There is no mistaking the fact, that Taylor's Falls is already a place—quite a place—and is bound to be a still greater one. There are two good hotels already finished; and the one at which we stopped, the Chisago house, is *better furnished*, and as well kept—barring the inconvenience of having no meat and vegetable market at hand—as any house in St. Paul, St. Anthony, or Stillwater. Some of the finest trout and other fishing, as well as hunting, to be found in this northwestern region, is about these falls. A great many improvements in the way of building, are in progress at Taylor's Falls, with men at the helm, such as we might name as leading citizens of the place—situated so as to command the trade of the increasing lumbering region to the north—being at the extreme head of navigation, and with an unequalled farming country back, there can be no retrograde movement to Taylor's Falls.

"Lest we might excite feelings in the minds of some that would afterward be doomed to disappointments, we will state the fact, that no lots are for sale at Taylor's Falls, except to those who wish to build. The proprietors have determined the property shall not fall into the hands of speculators who will let it remain idle.

"The evening we arrived was that of the first day of court, being the first court held by his honor Chief-Justice Welch, since his appointment to the bench. Chisago is a new county, containing, comparatively, not a great number of inhabitants, and those neighborly and peaceably disposed toward each other. So there was not much business on the docket, and rather dry picking for the eight or ten lawyers present. Perhaps they didn't appear there for the purposes of legitimate practice. Lawyers *will* be found hovering about county courts, whether they have business or not, particularly when important election days are approaching.

"The old milling site of St. Croix Falls, which it would take all the courts in Christendom, and all the Philadelphia lawyers, with their number multiplied by ten thousand, to decide to whom it rightfully belongs, is now wearing greater signs of active prosperity, than it has since the famous 'Boston company' laid the withering curse of their hands upon it. It always appeared to us a burning shame, and a disgrace to the country, that so great and glorious a water privilege, planted by the hand of Nature directly within striking distance of one of the most inexhaustible pine regions in the world, should be suffered to lay waste from year to year, or be used at ruinous sacrifices to every man who touched it. These results have not been from natural causes, but from man's selfishness and cupidity, and a desire to override and crush his fellow-man. We do not wish to be understood as giving any opinion as to which of the parties litigant are in the right; but certain it is, Mr. Hungerford, who now has possession, is making the Falls look vastly more like a business place than it has for years. The mill has been refitted with new machinery the past winter, and is now driving ahead rapidly, day and night, running four saws, with the remaining two almost in readiness to start. Things about the village wear a prosperous appearance; and if the property were only out of law, there would be no more thriving, driving, go-ahead village in the state of Wisconsin than St. Croix Falls.

"If a suit in a Wisconsin chancery court should eventually prove a thing less enduring than the trap rocks which form the St. Croix falls—a matter we think extremely doubtful—there are yet hopes that this immense water-power will result in some great and profitable benefit to some member or members of the human family.

"Here also is the battle-ground of the great legal contest, carried on by a 'Boston company,' with the Honorable Caleb Cushing at their head, on one side, and Mr. Hungerford on the other. The water-power is of immense force and value, and can be turned to account with but little expense. The rocky reef which forms the falls forms thus a natural dam, and on the shore below are the seats for extensive mills. The Boston company laid out a town here, built a number of cottages; but when the contention commenced, all business was suspended—the lumbering mills thrown idle; but now that Mr. Hungerford has taken possession, the activity and enterprise of the place will continue. The lumbering business on this river in a few years will be immense. The first signs of civilized life we met were at the falls, but above this the river is filled with logs for fifty miles."

CHAPTER VI.

THE MINNESOTA RIVER COUNTRY—THE UNDINE REGION OF NICOLLET, ETC.—COAL, ETC.

WITH the exception of the "Big Woods," the whole country may be considered as prairie, the streams only being skirted with wood. On the whole there is a want of timber for ordinary farming purposes in a thickly-inhabited district; but if the growth of timber be encouraged, as the population gradually increases, a deficiency may never be experienced.

Throughout the greater part of this region, the traveller is surprised and charmed with the everchanging variety and beauty of the scenery.

The alluvial land bordering upon the river, varies in width from a quarter of a mile to a mile or more. The greater portion of this constitutes numerous natural meadows, covered annually with a luxuriant growth of grass. A small proportion of these alluvial lands is covered with ash, elm, sugar and white maple, butternut, white walnut, lime, linden, box elder, cotton-wood and hickory. A considerable portion of these flats, being subject to annual overflow, are wet and marshy.

A remarkable feature of this country consists in the small lakes and ponds scattered over it. Many of these are beautiful sheets of water, having the appearance of artificial basins, which greatly enhance the beauty of the country, especially when skirted, as they sometimes are, by groves of trees, and frequented by water fowl, which tend to animate and relieve the otherwise almost deathlike silence which so pervades the prairie.

For about fifty miles above its confluence with the Mississippi, the Minnesota has a sluggish current, and is slightly whitish—hence the Dakota name of "Minnesota" or water "tinted like the sky."

Coal beds are believed by many to exist on the head waters of the Mankator or Blue Earth river, and other tributaries of the upper Minnesota. Pieces of Cannel coal have been found from time to time, though not in such abundance, nor are the indications at any point so strongly marked as to induce us to believe that any very extensive beds will be found in those localities. David Dale Owen, United States geologist, in his report of a geological survey of Wisconsin, Iowa, and Minnesota, in 1848-'9, says:—"On the Mankato, and its branches, several pieces of lignite were picked up from the beds and banks of the streams. Some of this lignite approaches in its character to Cannel coal; but most of it has a brown color, and exhibits distinctly the ligneous fibre, and other structure of the wood from which it has been derived. Diligent search was made to endeavor to trace this mineralized wood to its source, and discover the beds where report had located an extensive and valuable coal field. At one point, a fragment was found seventy feet above the level of the river, projecting from the drift; but no regular bed could be detected anywhere, even in places where sections of the drift were exposed down to the magnesian lime stone. The conclusion at which those who were appointed to investigate the matter arrived, was, that the pieces occasionally found throughout the Minnesota country, are only isolated fragments disseminated in the drift, but that no regular bed exists within the limits of the district.

As regards salubrity, soil, timber, and water, we doubt whether any portion of the west presents greater inducements for immigration than the charming valley of the Minnesota river. The eye is delighted with a succession of rural landscapes of unsurpassed and varied beauty. The scenery is not bold and craggy like that of the Mississippi, and upper St. Croix, but picturesque, and homelike. The wide-spreading prairies, studded with oak groves, terminating in sloping banks, and fringed with meadows, which bound the right bank of the Minnesota at its entrance; and the rolling prairies which make a gentle declivity down to the winding stream on the left, excite, upon first entering the mouth of the Minnesota, an expression of admiration from every person of natural or cultivated taste. How much more beautiful the scene when adorned by the handiwork of civilization, as it soon will be. The bottom lands are generally from a quarter of a mile to a half mile wide, and afford natural hay meadows that can not be surpassed. The topography of the valley as seen from the river, is more picturesque than that of any other river we have seen. The banks, which are rarely more than fifteen or less than ten feet high, above the bottoms, are sometimes concealed from the steamboat traveller by heavy timber growing down to the river bed. But generally, except through the *Bois Franc*, or great woods, the green banks and rolling prairies are in full view. Oak groves resembling cultivated orchards, and a back ground of apparently dense timber, complete the beauty of the view; and there is scarcely a quarter section of land presented to the eye of the traveller, but suggests the most beautful sites for farmhouses and improvements. The natural scenery can not fail to cultivate among the future settlers of the valley, a refined taste in rural architecture. Although there is similarity, there is nothing monotonous in the diorama which feasts, but does not pall, the sight of the voyageur. Not a spot but seems to await with impatience the adorning hand of civilization; not an acre but appears ready for the axe, the plough, or the scythe. It is a common remark, that the whole country looks as if it had been suddenly deserted by a civilized people—the fences and buildings removed, and the orchards left standing.

Farms can be made in this valley at a trifling expense; nature has almost finished the work.

There are many beautiful sites for towns along the river. Little Rapids will probably be a place of importance, as steamboats that can go as high as Mendota, will find no obstruction below that point. The river is narrow—from sixty to eighty yards wide, and very crooked.

There is plenty of hard-wood timber on the river, sufficient to supply the country below. It consists of hard and soft maple, oak, ash, elm, white and black walnut, hickory, cherry, cottonwood, &c. For the distance of thirty-six miles, the river winds through the *Bois Franc*, a dense forest which crosses the river, and is from fifteen to forty miles wide, and one hundred long.

In a few years, many steamboats will be running with freight and passengers between the bustling city of St. Paul and the thriving towns and settlements of the Minnesota river—but that is looking to the future. For the present and the next four or five years, there will be sites for farms, as cheap—as good land—as healthy, and nearer to markets—convenient to the great Mississippi above and below the falls, where sagacious farmers will locate and improve in preference to going farther off, for the mere gratification of fancy.

In pointing out the most favored portions of our territory for agricultural settlements we are guided more by the travels of scientific and experienced men than by practical knowledge. Excepting the farming done on the east side of the river, there has been but little land broken in the territory. The strip of land lying between the St. Croix and the Mississippi, while it proves abundantly productive of leguminous plants, grass, oats, &c., does not appear so well adapted in body and depth of soil for the more weighty cereals, as the lands to the southwest of the Mississippi, toward the sources of the Cannon, Vermillion, and Blue-Earth rivers.

Seventy-nine years before the survey of Nicollet, the country was explored by the English traveller Carver, in 1766. He records, as follows: "The river St. Peter, which runs through the territories of the Naudowessies, flows through a most delightful country, abounding with all the necessaries of life, that grow spontaneously; and with a little cultivation it might be made to produce even the luxuries of life. Wild rice grows here in great abundance; and every part is filled with trees bending under their loads of fruits, such as plums, grapes, and apples; the meadows are covered with hops and many sorts of vegetables; while the ground is stored with useful roots—with angelica, spikenard, and ground-nuts as large as hens' eggs. At a little distance from the river are eminences, from which you have views that can not be exceeded

even by the most beautiful of those I have already described. Amidst these are delightful groves, and such amazing quantities of maples, that they would produce sugar sufficient for any number of individuals. This country" (near Mankato city) "likewise abounds with a milk-white clay, out of which china-ware might be made equal in goodness to the Asiatic; and also with a blue clay, which serves the Indians for paint."

This language will undoubtedly sound very strong when read in the far east, yet it is corroborated by the more extensive and minute observation of the past few years. Within the last three years, every mile of this country has been traversed, and recently much of it claimed; and, like a really good thing, the more we see and hear of it, the better we like it.

G. W. Featherstonhaugh, F. R. S., ascended the St. Peter's on an exploring tour in 1835. In his work he says: "The channel [at the confluence of the Mankato with the St. Peter's] is one hundred yards wide, and the country extremely beautiful; the prairie occasionally coming down to the water's edge, while at other times bold bluffs arise with well-wooded slopes, interspersed with graceful clumps of trees.

"About half-past five, P. M., I landed for the night at one of the loveliest encampments I had yet met with; charming slopes, with pretty dells intersecting them, studded with trees as gracefully as if they had been planted with the most refined taste; everything indeed around us was interesting. I could not but think what a splendid private estate could be contrived out of so beautiful a territory. A mansion, built on one of these gentle slopes, backed by thousands of well-formed trees, decked in their autumnal colors; thousands of acres of the most fertile level land, with the river in front, and a world of prairie in the rear, abounding with grouse."

I take pleasure in quoting these two disinterested English authorities; the one writing in 1766, the other in 1835, followed by M. Nicollet in 1845. What they say borders apparently so closely upon poetic exaggeration, that it is only by considering their entire disinterestedness in the matter that a stranger who has not visited the country will be disposed to give full credence to what they conjointly record. Carver was a very close and practical observer, and made strenuous efforts to secure the country to himself and heirs, by a pretended or real grant from the Indians. Nicollet, as an engineer, is eminently scientific and practical. Featherstonhaugh, a distinguished geologist, while he surveyed the rocky strata with scientific earnestness, indulged his poetic fancy in admiring the picturesque landscapes—the wide-spread lawns, rolling waters, rocks, dells, and grottoes, fringed with trees—so gracefully formed and disposed, as if directed by the highest artistic skill. He evidently left the country, then an uninhabited wilderness, with feelings of regret. He longed for a splendid private estate that could be contrived out of so beautiful a territory—a mansion with a rolling lawn sweeping down to the river in front; on either side thousands of acres of level, fertile land, with a prairie in the rear abounding with grouse.

About one year since, the Indian title to the lands west of the Mississippi, in Minnesota, was extinguished. In a short time, these same Indians will be removed and shut up in the wilderness behind the new fort, now in course of construction. In anticipation, however, of the tardy movements of the government, and before the savage occupants leave, or any steps taken to bring the land into market, the restless surge of immigration is flowing rapidly onward, inundating the entire country. Already every eligible site for a town upon the Mississippi, from the Iowa line to St. Anthony, is claimed, and improvements in rapid progress. Nor is the condition of the Minnesota essentially different. Perhaps the enterprising aspirants here even excel the Mississippians. The Minnesota penetrates the very heart of the new purchase, and is navigable as long as the Mississippi remains open in the fall. The eye of practical sagacity has already discovered to thousands the inestimable value of this country and its river-towns.

Ascending the Minnesota for three hundred miles, thence projecting a line south to the Iowa boundary, following this east to the Mississippi, thence up the river to the starting-point, we enclose a tract of immense size probably unequalled in agricultural value, all things considered, by any public lands now held by the government. Two sides of this beautiful plateau are washed by broad, sweeping rivers alive with steamers; numerous smaller rivers and streams course through the interior, affording abundant water-power, while lakes of fresh water are dotted over the surface, as though Nature, in a moment of extreme prodigality, had determined to make this the most favored of all pastoral countries.

Of the fertility and productiveness of the soil, it is now superfluous to speak; and it is also generally well known that, while there is an abundance of open land for farming or grazing, there is an ample supply of heavy timber for all needful purposes. So some of the advantages possessed by the country are—

1. A most congenial and salutary climate.

2. Fertile and productive soil.

3. Open prairies, interspersed with belts of heavy timber (basswood, hickory, white oak, white ash, black walnut, sugar-maple, &c., &c.).

4. Rivers, streams, and lakes, watering every fractional portion of the country.

5. Navigable streams, already the highway of an immense business—the number of steamers increasing yearly.

6. A direct steam communication with the great markets and railroads of the south.

7. Land open for settlement without any other expense than to locate upon it; nor will any tax, or even the minimum government price, be demanded till the survey is completed, which may not be for two or three years.

8. The towns on the Mississippi, Red-Wing at the south edge of the Undine region, St. Paul at the central edge, and St. Anthony above, are ready to supply all the wants of the farmer, and purchase his surplus provisions in return.

9. The country is generally level, the soil a decomposed mould, easily worked, and in its natural state covered with a luxuriant growth of grass, averaging from eighteen inches to three feet in height. For years neither hay nor pasture can be an item of expense.

10. From experience, we know that all the grains of the

middle states thrive here to the greatest perfection, and the superiority of leguminous plants is a matter of common consent.

11. In the vicinity of Mankato city, brick-clay of a very fine quality is found in abundance, while quarries of building-stone are found along the rivers and streams in many different localities.

The above statements are so fully endorsed, that the writer has no apprehensions of being charged with drawing upon his own fancy. M. Nicollet, in his report of the "Hydrographic Basin of the Upper Mississippi," says:—

"I shall now proceed to give a short account of some of the regions of country adjoining the *Coteau des Prairies.* Among these, that which appeared to me the most favorable, is the one watered by the 'Bold Mankato' or Blue-Earth river, and to which I have given the name of 'Undine Region.'

"The great number of navigable tributaries of the Mankato, spreading themselves out in the shape of a fan; the group of lakes, surrounded by well-wooded hills; some wide-spreading prairies with a fertile soil; others apparently less favored, but open to improvement—the whole together bestow upon this region a most picturesque appearance. It was while on a visit to the beautiful lakes *Okamanpidam* and *Tchanhassan* that it occurred to me to give the name I have adopted, derived from an interesting and romantic German tale."

Mankato city is the name of a newly-surveyed site of a future city in the very heart and centre of this elegant country. It is near the junction of the "Bold Mankato" with the Minnesota river, and at the extreme south bend of this latter stream, nearly a hundred miles in a southwesterly direction from St. Paul. Here it is upon the glittering banks of two silvery streams of spacious capacity, with fertile prairies opening to the warm, sunny south, sweeping off for miles and miles till the closing vista is bounded by fringes of forests, while in the rear, close to the south bank of the river, stands heavy timber, ready to the builders' hands, to be converted into domicils of comfort or elegance, that Mankato city is located.

The town-plat has been laid out, and is owned by Henry

M'Kenty, a man of activity, enterprise, and perseverance, who, in securing this choice spot and expending upon it his funds, has done so after a mature and careful consideration of its commercial relations with the Undine country, with the Minnesota river, and the southern outlet by way of the Mississippi, after crossing the country a hundred and thirteen miles to the foot of Lake Pepin, with heavy wagons over a good natural road.

It is almost physically impossible to tap the Undine region with a railroad and escape this point. When it is reached, it stands in the very centre and heart of the richest country, much of the most available land lying still west, stretching out into the Wahpeton country, and toward the sources of the Blue Earth and tributaries. These streams are navigable for large barges to within a few miles of their rise. For the present, communication may be made by steamers up the Minnesota, or over land, following the Cannon river valley, or Legrange river, striking the Mississippi at Red Wing. For those coming up from below, bringing stock, wagons, &c., the point of debarkation will be at some place near the foot or head of Lake Pepin.

A new town called "Gorman," is being laid out on the Cannon river, midway from Mankato and Lake Pepin, on the territorial road; and in as good a locality for a town as any yet started in the territory. The land in the vicinity of the Cannon is as good as any in Minnesota, and is rapidly filling up with hardy farmers from New England. The proprietors are Messrs. Robert Kennedy and A. J. Morgan. Mr. K. has superintended the surveying and laying out the town-site into lots. Success to the enterprise. The town is called Gorman, after Hon. Willis A. Gorman, the present governor of Minnesota.

A description of the country between Lake Pepin and Mankato city is of some importance: "The extreme length of the road is one hundred and thirteen miles. A tangent would make it about one hundred and five, thus being eight miles in avoiding swamps, &c.

"The country near the lake is very broken, being cut up by

ravines descending from the highlands to the lake. In many of these ravines may be found some of the richest farming lands in Minnesota. Hardly a ravine but has its "trout brook" shaded with a luxuriant grove of all kinds of timber. At your near approach to the highlands, you continually encounter springs; and it is not an unfrequent occurrence to find at the *very* height of some ridge, a spring of limpid water. I made it a point to search the highest lands for water.

"After you leave the lake, say five or six miles back, you will find a different country, the soil of which would be hard to analyze. It is what I would call poor, or rather none of the best, being sand intermixed with numerous small flints. Timber is scarce, and what there is, is scrubby burr oak of the leanest kind. But remember we are on the dividing ridge between the Cannon, on the north, and the Waze Ozu, on the south, so that while barrenness presents itself in your immediate vicinity, an hour's travel either to the right or left brings you to Eden-like valleys. When some eighteen or twenty miles back, again there is a sudden change from sterility to rich prairies, abounding in water and groves of fine timber; such a country as would make a farmer's eyes water, and if covetous, would make him wish to own all that *joined* his farm. The soil is a loam, slightly sandy, abounding in small hazel-brush. The greatest enemy the farmer will find here is the gopher; the ground is literally ploughed by them, so much so, that in many places their excavations made it difficult to proceed on horseback, as we were constantly breaking through, even where the ground appeared smoothest. I travelled about forty miles over this undulating prairie, when I struck the woods that skirt the Cannon near its head, on the east side—consisting of the largest kind of oak, ash, walnut, elm, sugar maple, &c., many trees of which were four and five feet in diameter, sixy feet to a limb, and straight as a reed. The woods are from two to five miles wide, and extend in length, I know not how far.

"When you reach the Cannon, which here runs north, you will find yourself in one of the loveliest of countries. The Cannon is some eighty feet wide and about a foot deep, with fall enough for an immense water-power. It does not overflow its banks at this point, rising only some five or six feet. This may be attributed to several large lakes above, which act as reservoirs. On the west side is a prairie which extends some four miles back, to Lake Tepe-Tonka; so level is it that a good sized dog might be seen on any part of it.

"Lake Tepe-Tonka, more properly Tetonka, is a beautiful sheet of water, some four miles long and two wide. Along its pebbly shores may be found wagon-loads of fish carcases, portending abundance of the 'live article' in the lake. From this lake flows a branch of the Cannon, thus bounding the above-mentioned water. The country west of this point is good, bad, and indifferent, being alternately prairie, swamp, and marshes."

I append also a description of "Mille Lacs," which, though east of the Mississippi, is of some interest to those ignorant of its localities: "Mille Lacs is the largest body of water in the territory southwest of Lake Superior, being about eighteen miles from north to south, and fifteen miles from east to west. On the east side, about one third the distance down from the north shore, is a point projecting into the lake composed of large boulders. The land along the east shore is well timbered with oak, maple, ash, elm, birch, and aspen. The shore is from four to twelve feet high, and walled with a line of boulders, some of which are remarkably large. The lake is shallow for a long distance from the shores, and the bottom entirely covered with boulders. Southwest of the point named above, is a tamarac swamp, the level of which is lower than that of the lake; the lake being walled in by a bank ten or twelve feet high, composed of boulders and soil. This heaping up of boulders so as to form barriers higher than the surrounding country occurs also at many other points. At one place the boulders form an inclined plain ten or eleven feet high, for a long distance; while the general level of the country is not over seven or eight feet above the waters of the lake.

"In the southeasterly portion of the lake are several small islands, composed entirely of boulders, filled up sometimes as high as twenty feet. Around one of these islands is a wall of boulders several feet higher than the centre, the formation of which, as well as of the lake barriers, I attribute to the action of ice. On the west side of the lake, near its outlet, is a projecting point, bearing northeast, and in that direction corresponds with the point mentioned on the east shore, and marks, probably, the course of a granite ridge concealed beneath the drift. Near the point is the largest island in the lake, and the only one covered with a good soil; on it the Indians have gardens. The ridge forming the point is covered with pines.

"Rum river is about twenty feet wide at the outlet of Mille Lacs; in less than a mile it expands into Rice lake, about three miles long, and a quarter of a mile wide. The country at the lower end of the lake is from twenty-five to thirty feet above the level of the water. Two other lakes occur in the distance of about five miles, both filled with rice. The last one is about two miles long, and three quarters of a mile wide.

CHAPTER VII.

THE PRINCIPAL TOWNS — ST. PAUL, AND MATTERS CONNECTED WITH THAT NORTHWESTERN METROPOLIS — THE PRESS, CHURCHES, ETC. — OBITUARY NOTICE OF JAMES M. GOODHUE.

St. Paul — latitude 44° 52′ 46″, longitude 93° 4′ 54″ — is a port of entry, the county-seat of Ramsey county, and the seat of government of the territory of Minnesota. It is pleasantly situated on the east bank of the Mississippi river, eight miles from the falls of St. Anthony, and five miles from Fort Snelling; about two thousand and seventy miles from the mouth of the Mississippi river, and near its confluence with the Minnesota river, and is elevated about eight hundred feet above the gulf of Mexico. It is near the geographical centre of the continent of North America, in the north temperate zone, and must eventually become a central nucleus for the business of one of the best watered, timbered, and most fertile and healthy countries on the globe. It is surrounded in the rear by a semicircular plateau, elevated about forty feet above the town, of easy grade, and commanding a magnificent view of the river above and below. Nature never planned a spot better adapted to build up a showy and delightful display of architecture and gardening, than that natural terrace of hills. The town has sprung up, like Minerva full armed from the head of Jupiter, and now contains five thousand inhabitants; its whole history of four years forming an instance of western enterprise, and determined energy and resolution, hitherto unsurpassed in the history of any frontier settlement.

Whatever direction we take among the localities of Minnesota, we find subjects of interest, whether in awaking the spirits of the dusky past, or alighting upon the improvements of our own times. There is scarcely a section of the world newer than this; and we may add, there is no section which has started upon the horizon of civilized life more suddenly.

St. Paul occupies perhaps the most eligible and commanding, and also one of the most beautiful locations on the upper Mississippi. Commercially, it is the key to all the vast region north of it, and, by the Minnesota river, to the immense valley drained through that important tributary to the Father of Waters. The approach to it by the river from below is grand and imposing. The traveller, after leaving Dubuque, more than three hundred miles below, sees nothing to remind him of a city, or even a prosperous business town, until he rounds the bend in the river below St. Paul, and her tall spires, substantial business houses, and neat dwellings, burst upon his view.

By the general course of the river, St. Paul is situated upon the east bank of the Mississippi. The *local* course of the river, however, at this particular point is from southwest to northeast. This circumstance often confuses strangers in casting about for the points of the compass. The site of the town is elevated, and stands partly on the alluvium on the margin of the river, and partly on the elevated table-rock some hundreds of feet above. Thus conspicuously perched up, it glistens and shines with white paint and red brick, like a piece of new cabinet-ware just from the shop. Five years ago, when the territory was organized, there was not the sign of a village in the country. The organization was completed; law and order secured: and white adventurers flocked in, and huddled together for company and protection, thus laying the foundation of a city which already numbers thousands. The main street is fully a mile in length, with buildings running from shanties to five-story bricks. The "seven" churches with lofty spires, show that the aspirations of the St.-Pauleans are upward, and, though in the wilderness, they make the welkin ring. A travelling friend observed he had, in Constantinople, where they have five sabbaths a week, heard the Turkish Salims, the catholic and protestant, the Greek, Armenian, and Jew, each sending forth their summons for prayer to the faithful: but judging of piety by bell-ringing in St. Paul, it would put the eastern devotee to shame.

From the lower landing of St. Paul, we rise upon a bench some seventy-five feet above the river, and come upon the site of the lower town, which — with the extension up the river as far as the upper landing, a distance of three fourths of a mile, where is a most vigorous young town of later growth — completes St. Paul, the capital of Minnesota. Retiring from the lower town, about half a mile northerly, across a plain which appears to have once been the basin of a lake, for it is nearly walled in by a bluff fifteen feet high, we suddenly rise upon a third bluff nearly two hundred feet high, and some three hundred feet above the Mississippi. This ascent is wooded, and so is the region beyond for perhaps twenty miles. From this point we overlook St. Paul; extending the vision down the river some twenty miles, we take within the compass of the eye a wide stretch of the late Sioux lands and bluish hills, far away up the Minnesota in the west.

To the north, although the grounds descend from the bluff for some three miles, there are but few objects of distinct outline. After viewing a small lake, lying about a mile to the northwest, as a setting to a border of oak-openings, we proceed through a constantly alternating succession of oak-covered knolls, marshy dells, and around the margins of small tamarac swamps. These swamps, though dismal, for their size, are the most curious objects to the eye of the stranger which this region presents. The trees grow so thick, that they choke each other out of the chance for a subsistence, or else they die a natural death after a certain age, so that they resemble a scene of shipping in a seaport most strikingly. It is easy, when in a dreamy mood of mind, to fancy these bare poles as the masts of some diluvian squadrons, which had lost their reckoning, and finally, getting discouraged, moored in the mud.

There are no guide-boards on this road, and the angler or sportsman, who can't *parlez français* with the French residents whose cabins nestle in some of the sly retreats along the path, may thank the stars if he does not get lost over night.

The region is spotted all over, at distances of one to three miles, with bright and cool little lakes, that abound in fish; among which is the real White Mountain trout.

The scene over the bluff in the rear of the upper town of St. Paul, is the delightful prairie which extends off about six miles toward St. Anthony falls.

The true quality of the soil of the comparatively chaotic lands in the rear of St. Paul, is, after all, better than that of the lands of Western New York. It has less of the black alluvion than our lands generally, yet it is highly productive; and so far as experience has tested its capabilities, it does not depreciate at all by cropping. It is strongly impregnated with lime, and possesses, in a high degree, the active principle imparted by a variety of mineral substances.

This soil can be made, by the application of manure, of which an abundance can be had for the trouble of carting from town, more productive than the best river bottoms. For the purpose of gardening, I am inclined to prefer it to the latter; and if I was to make a claim, I would "take up" the lands I could find unoccupied, nearest the town.

A stranger is generally somewhat astonished and not unfrequently very much amused at the scene presented for contemplation on his first arrival at the St. Paul landing. In short, his first impressions with regard to the state of society here are altogether unfavorable. He is welcomed by an unusual and motley group of human beings, gathered from all parts of the Union, the Canadas, the Indian lands, and Pembina, besides the curiously-mixed-up race of natives. This is indeed a most peculiar feature of the capital of Minnesota, which in respect to its inhabitants differs materially from any place I have visited in the west. Being an old settlement of French and half-breeds, and the present seat of government for the territory, situated near the head of navigation and contiguous to the Dakota land, a strange spectacle is often presented, or strange indeed to the uninitiated. All the different classes, however, mingle together, forming a singular mass, variously habited, speaking different languages, and distinguished by a variety of complexions, features, and manners.

Yet all this appears quite common, and excites no curiosity among those who have resided here but a few months.

But how different the spectacle appears to the stranger and visiter. Chained, as it were, by a spell of astonishment, he pauses a moment to view the scene, before setting foot on shore, to mingle in the promiscuous multitude. A variety of persons attract his attention. Merchants in search of newly-arrived goods; editors, anxious for the latest news; citizens, receiving their long-expected friends from the east or south; carmen and coachmen with their teams, all indeed join in the tumultuous strife and enjoy the excitement. A little removed from the crowd may be seen another class, which by the way is too numerous, for so small a community as that of St. Paul. This is composed of a host of lawyers, politicians, office-holders, and office-seekers, whom we may perhaps call refugees from other states, though actuated by the hope of gaining some honorable position and a share of the public spoils. They are discussing very boldly, perhaps, a subject pertaining to the territorial government, or the late doings of Congress.

Amid the busy crowd may be seen the courteous and sociable governor, conversing freely with his fellow-citizens, or politely receiving General A., Colonel B., or some other distinguished personage just arrived. Close by the side of his excellency a Dakota, Winnebago, or Chippewa warrior strides along as boldly and quite as independent as the greatest monarch on earth. He is attired in a red or white blanket, with his leggins and mocassins fantastically ornamented with ribands, feathers, beads, &c., while his long braided hair is adorned with a number of ribands and quills, his face is painted with a variety of colors, giving him a most frightful appearance. In his hands he carries a gun, hatchet, and pipe. As the noble fellow moves along, so erect, so tall and athletic in his form, a feeling of admiration involuntarily fills the stranger's mind—he pronounces the Indian warrior the lion of the multitude, and is forced to respect his savage nature. The eye follows him along till he joins, perhaps, a company of his own tribe, some of whom are quietly regaling themselves at the end of a long Tchandahoopah, others gazing at the white man's big canoe. Now the astonished gazer beholds a group of dark-eyed squaws, some carrying their heavy burdens, others with papooses on their backs, with their bare heads sticking above a dirty blanket. The little things may be sleeping and as the mothers walk carelessly along. their heads dangle about as though their necks would break at every step. They sleep on, however, nor heed the scorching rays of the sun shining in their faces.

The stranger having become satisfied with the contemplation of such and similar scenes, at length concludes to debark, and soon he too becomes one of the promiscuous multitude. He soon forgets the oddities that so much excited his curiosity among us. Though he finds a great multitude of French half-breeds and Dakotas; yet the character is decidedly eastern. The red men who are now so numerous, will ere long flee away before the influence of civilization, while the native French, half-breeds, &c., will be absorbed by an eastern society. In short, everything is fast partaking of a Yankee spirit, and yielding before the influence of Yankee enterprise.

Another writer thus impartially describes St. Paul:—

"The town site is high and conspicuous, being elevated from seventy to eighty feet above the water at common stages. The central part embraces an extensive level plateau, terminating along the Mississippi, in a precipitous bluff. This bluff after running for some distance recedes from the river on the east and west, and by assuming a gradual ascent, forms two commodious landings, called the upper and lower town, meeting upon the elevated plateau of the central part. As a natural consequence there is a good deal of strife between the two sections for the ascendency in commercial matters particularly. The site upon which the lower town is mostly built, is several feet below the central and upper parts, and has quite a sandy soil, while the higher portions are on a limestone formation, lying above the sandstone.

"The latter formation in many places is so soft that the swallows make their nests in the rock, as in ordinary sand-banks. Much of the sandstone is nearly as white as loaf-sugar, and is said to be of a superior quality for the manufacturing of glass. These high rocks passing up far above the water, and displaying their snow-white sides to view, form a peculiar and exceedingly beautiful feature in the scenery of the Upper Mississippi.

"In the rear of St Paul, or on the north, rises another bluff, or line of hills, which encircles the town site, in the shape of an amphitheatre, bending gradually until they approach quite near the river again toward Fort Snelling on the southwest, and toward Lake Pepin on the southeast. These smooth and beautiful hills extending from one half a mile to upward of two miles from the town, afford many most delightful situations for country-seats and farms. From these elevations, an extensive view is afforded of the surrounding country, particularly of the town below, and land of the Dakotas beyond the Mississippi. Far away to the south and southeast, the Father of Waters is seen rolling his silent tide majestically along, guarded on either side by rock-bound bluffs and hills. Indeed we seem to behold even now, through the dim vista of future years, the glittering mansions of St. Paul's merchant-princes rising up in every direction, on these hills now in the state of nature or rudely adorned by the humble *chaumiere* of the French and half-breeds, or the simple lodges of the noble Sioux.

"There is one serious objection to the back-grounds of St. Paul, at present, though in time, it will doubtless form a great blessing. A great many springs of 'pure cold water' are continually gushing from the base of the above-mentioned hills, forming several bad marshes, and rendering an access to many of the choice situations rather difficult. Good roads will soon be constructed over these wet places, while the water supplied by the living fountains, can easily be brought in town. There are also several small lakes in the vicinity supplied by springs, and situated much higher than St. Paul, which can be made to supply a large city with excellent water. In short the place has many natural advantages for a great town."

Every day makes it clearer, that St. Paul is destined to more importance as a city than the most sanguine have dared to anticipate. Not only has our town already become, in the four short years of its existence, the emporium of trade for all that vast area of country above us, extending from the shore of Lake Superior to the head waters of the Missouri — a trade yet limited, to be sure, by reason of the sparseness of the population, but hourly increasing, and which must soon become incalculably great; but there will be soon a fresh impulse given it, by the settlement of those matchless lands inhabited by the Sioux Indians, lands of vast extent as well as fertility, watered by the Minnesota river and its tributaries. Standing at the steamboat head of the Mississippi, the main artery, nay the *only* artery, north and south, through the continent of North America, it can have no rival, no competitor for the business of those regions of which it is already the focus. Our line of business is essentially with the north and the south, the east and the west, turning, as it were upon a pivot, on this, the head of steamboat navigation; and from this point there will in time radiate railroads, to connect here with steamboats, in various directions. But there is a probability, nay more than a probability, that a plan of internal improvements will be executed by the British government, which will hasten the development and growth of St. Paul beyond all parallel. I refer to the contemplated construction of a line of railroad from Halifax, in Nova Scotia, to the Pacific ocean, north of Lake Superior. The construction of that road would immediately require the construction of a railroad from St. Paul to intersect it. The chain of lakes would prevent its intersection east of us, besides that here the steamboat approximates nearest to it — the valley of the Mississippi being, on every account, the proper line of connection with it. The whole of the intercourse of the southern and western states with Oregon, nay, with California, would take this route; all the emigration and immigration, probably all the trade of those states with China, Japan, and the East Indies in short, would take this route; and there would not be a busier transhipment city than St. Paul on this continent. If, already, it has come to be known that this very route to the Pacific is not only shorter, cheaper, healthier, and far better than any one south of it — if, as we know, St. Paul has already become a place of outfit for companies migrating to Oregon, without railroads — what may we expect to see when the traveller from New Orleans, who lands here, may be whirled here upon a continuous railroad, through the high, healthful, romantic ranges of the buffalo, along the northern verge of the temperate zone, to the blue Pacific!

The route from Halifax to Fuca straits, opposite to Vancouver's island, has been ascertained to be quite as feasible as the route proposed from Lake Michigan to Puget's sound, and a very large part of the country is the finest wheat country in the world. The distance would vary but little from that of our route — while from London to China it would be considerably less than ours. By measuring a globe, it will be seen that Lake Huron is less distant from London than New York from London; and as Lake Superior is but six hundred and fifty feet elevation above the Atlantic, a railroad from Halifax to Lake Superior might be constructed on almost a dead level. This would enable England to transport all the produce of the Mississippi basin to Halifax, at a much less cost than to any Atlantic city. Besides, Halifax is much nearer to Europe, and would avoid the storms and dangers of navigation between Halifax and New York. An examination of this subject will show that, should England build the road, she will not only have a great advantage over us, but would control us and the world: for it is her commerce with Asia, and not ours, which must sustain the road.

The route for such railroad-connection would be nearly or quite due north from St. Paul, following the chain of small lakes on the east side of the Mississippi, touching the western shores of Mille Lac and Sandy lake, a route not only practicable, but highly favorable for a railroad, nearly level, and requiring less grading than almost any other route that could be found on this continent; and the whole distance from St. Paul to the dividing ridge north of Lake Superior, along which the British railroad will be extended, between Halifax and Puget's sound, is less than four hundred miles. It will by no means be necessary that the road from St. Paul should be extended to Pembina, which is much too far west, and a much more distant point for connection, although the face of the country to Pembina is entirely practicable for the construction of a railroad.

That the northern route to Oregon will soon be *the* route for all northern emigration (railroad or no railroad), is a certain event ; and the very next season will make St. Paul an important point for outfits to the Pacific.

The railroad survey by the United States government, from St. Paul to Puget's sound, is treated of hereafter. Whether our government constructs that road or not, I consider it certain that England will complete the one described above ere many years, and St. Paul thus be *the thoroughfare* from our eastern cities to the Pacific.

Without going so far back as the early part of 1847, to note the few rude trading cabins or tamarac logs, which marked the present site of St. Paul (then flourishing under the unpoetic *soubriquet* of "Pig's Eye"), I will commence picking up "incidents" about the middle of that year. Then it was that the "squatters" upon the public lands which mark the site of St. Paul proper, conceived the idea of laying out a town thereupon. The names of those who were then sole "proprietors," barring Uncle Sam's prior lien, are: Vetal Guerin, Alex. R. M'Leod, Henry Jackson, Hartshorn & Randall, Louis Roberts, Benjamin Gervais, David Farribault, A. L. Larpenteur, J. W. Simpson, and J. Demarrais. These worthy pioneers are all yet living—living in exemplification of the old truism, that the first settlers of a new country generally live and die the poorest men in it. One or two of them, who appear likely to escape this apparently predestined fate, only stand as monuments of exception to prove the verity of the rule. All had an unequal interest in that portion of the present capital of Minnesota, embraced in the area extending from about half way between Sibley and Jackson streets, up to St. Peter's street, and from the river back to Eighth street. This they employed Ira B. Brunson, of Prairie du Chien, to lay off into town lots, during the month of July, 1847—little dreaming that in less than five years it would prove the nucleus, around which would concentrate the future commercial and political metropolis of a mighty commonwealth—the heart of that northwestern emporium, which is to give pulsation and life-blood to the northern giant of the Mississippi valley.

"St. Paul" it was named, from the parish name of the catholic church which had been organized six years previous. No visible signs of its future greatness became manifest during that or the succeeding year, if we except the land sales at the falls of St. Croix, in August of 1848, at which time the proprietors proved up their pre-emptions, and procured titles from the government. This year the old warehouse at the lower landing, now occupied by Constans & Burbank, was erected, and the building at the corner of Jackson and Third, lately occupied by George Wells, remodelled from a rude cabin into what was then considered a spacious and commodious hotel. Mr. Bass made the improvement, and was the first landlord. Mr. Larpenteur's dwelling-house, on the opposite corner, was built the same year; also Mr. Hopkins's store, on the southwest corner of the same streets.

John R. Irvine held and entered the "claim" on the river immediately above the town plot. He had not thought much of it—merely occupying it as a residence, with a few acres adjacent to his dwelling under cultivation, which supplied the wants of his family. The keen, speculative eye of Henry M. Rice, first conceived the idea of laying off the extensive plateau embraced in the claim of Irvine, and immediately adjacent to St. Paul, into an "addition" thereto. Rice "bought in" with Irvine; and in the winter of 1848–'49—just *before* the passage of the act by Congress organizing the territory—their addition was divided into lots. The mere fact, that a man of the known energy and enterprise of Rice had taken hold of St. Paul, infused new life into the place, and it soon had a *name*, even beyond the limits of the neighboring regions. This name was sent far and wide over the country when, through the patriotic perseverance and devoted zeal of Henry H. Sibley, the organic act, naming St. Paul as the temporary capital, passed both houses of Congress, and was approved by the president on the third of March, 1849.

Other "additions" rapidly multiplied. Smith and Whitney's (Hon. Robert Smith, of Alton, Illinois, and Cornelius S. Whitney, at the time land-office receiver at St. Croix Falls) was laid off in April of the same year, and Hoyt's in May. Samuel Leech, land-office register at St. Croix Falls, not to be outdone by his fellow-officer, had laid off, in August of that year, the "addition" which bears his name. In 1850, Guerin and Bazil's, Randall and Roberts's, and Patterson's additions, were laid off. The following year came Winslow's, Kittson's, Willes', and Irvine's enlargement. In 1852, we had Bass's, Brunson's, Baker's, and Winslow's (No. 2). And now the compass is upon a strip of land between Selby's and Rice's farms, making town lots under the title of "Irvine and Ramsey's new addition." There are other small additions, perhaps, which have been made at various times, not noted, because of their insignificance. All alluded to are important parts of St. Paul as it now is.

In June, 1853, John Esaias Warren, Esq., recently of Troy, New York, bought out the half of Winslow's addition in the lower town, and it is now known as "Warren and Winslow's cottage addition." Its location is admirably adapted for building nice, comfortable residences in the shape of cottages *ornée*, with all the romance of scenery, &c.

Perhaps, now that her fate is decided, and her high destiny as the great commercial, social, religious, educational, and political emporium of the northwest unalterably fixed, it would matter little whether St. Paul remained the capital or not. But it *did* matter, and very essentially too, at the time the infant struggle took place to secure this advantage. Without it she would never have been able to hold the confidence of those who had labored most for her, or attract the attention of people then far away, who have since become part and parcel of her most active bones and sinews.

Until the contest for the capital, and consequent centre of political power, was decided in favor of St. Paul, shrewd and calculating men looked upon her as no "sure thing." It is true her advantages of position commercially would always have made her a place of considerable note. It is this latter, *added to* the former, which has made her what she is, and secured to her that which she is destined to be. Neither could have accomplished the work separately. To name one fatal disadvantage, had there been no capital here, St. Paul would have been deprived of the immense benefits of her newspaper press, those main arteries of her present healthful life. At least, not more than one would have been able to live here, and that in a condition so weakly and sickly that its wheezing and consumptive echoes would have fallen far short of sending forth her just meed of praise and advantage in the full and clear-toned clarion-notes which have been borne on every breeze throughout the land. But the moment it was decided that St. Paul was to be the political as well as the commercial centre of Minnesota, new life and energy were infused into every limb and muscle of her body. She arose and robed herself in the habiliments of strong, determined, youthful vigor, and started fairly and fully upon her march to future greatness. She had passed the ordeal. From that hour she was to go forward—never look back. Property immediately advanced more than two hundred per cent. Those who had stood back, fearful to invest, came into the front ranks, and gave their means to the improvement and building up of St. Paul. Persons from abroad flocked in and invested liberally; and there was never any more doubt as to the future. No one, from that day to this, has felt any fears of the result.

Nothing will better partially illustrate the steady and healthy advance of St. Paul as an important mart of trade and commerce, than the increase in the number of steamboat arrivals from year to year. The number of arrivals, in 1848, was 47; in 1849, 73; in 1850, 104; in 1851, 119; in 1852, 171. But, as remarked, although this is a good illustration of our steady increase commercially, it is only a partial one. Were there any means of getting at the comparative increase in the amount of *freight* which has been shipped to this port from below during the past five years, I could find therein more nearly correct data. This I have not. I will therefore state some observations and incidents unsupported by figures.

In the month of May, 1849, the mercantile business consisted of—L. Roberts's store, at the lower landing; Freeman, Larpenteur, & Co.'s, same place; Henry Jackson, just closing out, in his old house at the top of the bluff; W. H. Forbes, St. Paul outfit, Bench, between Jackson and Roberts streets; J. W. Simpson, next door; and the small Indian trading establishment of Olmsted & Rhodes, on Third street, in the old cabin which was recently removed to give place to the handsome new store of Mr. Chamblin. This completed the lower town. Then you travelled over an extensive corn and potato field to a little clump of shanties and balloon-frames in the neighborhood of the "American house." Here was Levi Sloan, upon his present site, with a small stock; and next above the American were the Messrs. Fuller, with a somewhat larger assortment. This was all. The capital invested in merchandise in the entire town could not have amounted to over forty thousand dollars.

The Fur Company did a very limited business here at that time. Their centre was at Mendota, where both Mr. Sibley and Mr. Rice—the then prominent members of the Chouteau firm in this part of the country—resided and did business. The frame of the "American house" was just up. In a few weeks the room in the extreme east end of the building was finished off for a store, and was stocked and opened by Mr. Rice, who had charge of that branch of the Fur Company's business known as the "Winnebago and Chippewa outfits." During the summer Mr. Rice erected the then extensive store and warehouse near the upper landing, now occupied by the Messrs. Fuller. When he opened (in the month of August), his shelves presented much the largest stock ever previously seen in St. Paul. Many people prophesied that there were more goods in that establishment than would be sold in St. Paul in five years.

Late in the fall, the Messrs. Elfelt arrived from Philadelphia, with a very heavy stock of goods, and opened in the place vacated by Mr. Rice. They were another exemplification of extreme verdancy in the minds of immoveable croakers. Other smaller establishments had risen into existence during the summer and fall; and, at the close of navigation, perhaps there were sixty thousand dollars invested in legitimate mercantile trade in St. Paul.

This, be it remembered, was three years and six months ago. I have endeavored to compile an estimate, as accurately as time and circumstances would admit, of the present amount of capital invested in merchandise in our go-ahead young city (1853). I include in the calculation goods to arrive early after the opening of navigation:—

Dry goods	$100,000
Groceries	83,000
Assorted merchandise	100,000
Clothing, including hats, caps, &c.	30,000
Boots and shoes	10,000
Hardware	5,000
Farming implements	8,000
Books and stationery	12,000
Drugs, paints, oils, glass, &c.	12,000
Iron and nails	20,000
Miscellaneous	10,000
	$390,000
Add capital invested in Indian trade, government contracts, &c., the centre of which is at St. Paul	400,000
	$790,000

This is not far from the mark. Added to this, lumber, manufactured at other places than St. Paul, to the value of about forty thousand dollars, has been disposed of at this point the past year. The amount of provisions, grain, and country produce generally, raised in the territory, and disposed of in the St. Paul market the past year, there are no means of arriving at. If our merchants would pay attention to this matter, and keep accurate statistics in relation thereto, that the same might be published from time to time, they would do themselves as well as the country a great benefit.

A large share of the trade of St. Paul is already a wholesale business. Our merchants the past winter have supplied many of the traders in the smaller towns, who have heretofore purchased at Galena. They also have supplied Benton county and the numerous settlements and towns springing up in the valley of the Minnesota. This is a branch of business that is hereafter bound to increase with great rapidity as the country above and west of us fills up.

The extent of both branches of mechanics and manufactures

is hard to get at accurately in so new and rapidly-changing a place as this. Carpenters and joiners are, of course, the most numerous branches of mechanics. Of these, there are from one hundred and fifty to two hundred, all most of the time actively employed at their business. Bricklayers and plasterers, painters and glaziers, and all the various branches incident to the great leading business of building, enter largely into our population, and bear equal proportion to the departments first named. Let us get at nearly the extent of our manufacturing capital:—

Three steam sawmills, with an investment in machinery and stock	$100,000
One flouring-mill	12,000
One sash, door, and blind manufactory, planing-machine attached	10,000
One iron-foundry and machine-shop	3,000
Three stove and tin-ware establishments	8,000
One plough and farming-implement manufactory	3,000
Four wagon and carriage manufactories	8,000
Blacksmith-shops, not enumerated, say	5,000
Cabinet-ware and furniture, two	9,000
Boot and shoe manufactories, say	5,000
Saddles and harness	5,000
Bakers and confectioners, four	4,000
Miscellaneous	5,000
	$177,000

It will thus be seen that we have in this rising frontier metropolis, containing only, at the outside, a population of five thousand, investments in mercantile and manufacturing transactions to the amount of nearly one million dollars! This is, of course, all outside the value of real estate, buildings, public and private, personal property, &c. Some of these manufactories are quite extensive, particularly our sawmills, which will readily be perceived by the amount of capital it requires to carry them on. The lower mill, owned by Messrs. Oakes & Co., is a model of its kind, as well as a good indicator of our rise and continued progress in the way of manufacturing. "It will make any man think more of St. Paul to take a 'look' through this mill." It now runs two upright saws, one circular, one cross-cut circular, and three lath saws. A shingle-saw and planing-machine will be attached upon the opening of navigation. There is also a turning-lathe attached. This mill is capable of cutting twenty thousand feet of lumber and ten thousand lath in twenty-four hours. The mill near the upper landing runs one upright and one circular saw. It is an excellent little "machine," and turns out ten thousand feet in twenty-four hours. In the same neighborhood is the mill of John R. Irvine, having the same number and character of saws, with shingle and lath machines added. It does about an equal amount of business in the way of cutting lumber. A fourth saw-mill is in process of erection at Dayton's bluff, by Messrs. Ames & Co. I have not included the investment of capital in this new mill in our estimate.

Next in importance in the way of manufactories is the sash, door, and blind establishment of Wise and Gise, situated on the second bench, near the catholic church. It is also driven by steam. They have all the late improvements in this branch of manufactures; and, with planing-mill attached, they convert rough pine boards into beautiful and substantial doors, sash, and blinds, with remarkable rapidity, and, of course, at much cheaper rates than these articles can be made by hand. In the lower department of their establishment they have extensive machinery for grinding and polishing plough mould-boards and shares, hoes, axes, and other articles of agricultural cutlery. It would make any one think still more of St. Paul to take a look through this establishment.

The St. Paul iron foundry and machine shop, situated in the vicinity of the lower saw-mill, is a new branch of manufacturing among us, having gone into operation during the past winter. It is the first establishment of the kind above Galena. All descriptions of castings, for machinery or other purposes, are now turned out. The business is yet in its infancy, but will be increased as rapidly as custom and facilities afford.

The number of buildings at present in St. Paul is about six hundred (exclusive of stables and other out-houses), which may be classed as follows:—

Dwellings, offices, and shops	517
Manufactories and business houses	70

Churches	6
Hotels	4
Schoolhouses, public and private	4
Courthouse and jail	2
Capitol	1
Amount	604

There is not included in this count any building now in process of erection that is not ready for the roof. The number not of this class—those already commenced and those contemplated—would swell the aggregate at least forty. Among the better class soon to be erected, is the second presbyterian church, and the Baldwin school edifice. The former is to be the largest and most imposing church edifice yet built in St. Paul. It will be of brick, with a lofty spire, and is to stand on the elevation a short distance east of the capitol. The old "public square," originally platted in Rice and Irvine's addition, situated in the vicinity of the methodist church, is about to be vacated by the town as a site for the Baldwin school. This school is to be a female academy of a high order, and takes its name from a munificent endowment by a gentleman of Philadelphia. An act incorporating the institution and appointing a board of trustees, was passed during the late session of our legislative assembly. I have seen a proposed plan of the building, which, if adopted, will raise up an edifice that, aside from its great prospective usefulness, will be a beautiful and highly imposing ornament to our city.

The new hotel, at the corner of Eagle and Fort streets, the foundation of which is already laid, may be noted as one of the most important and elegant buildings that will beautify and improve the exterior of St. Paul this season. But for unfortuitous circumstances, this building would have been erected and finished last season. The delay has, perhaps, been all for the better. The building will now be much larger than was originally contemplated, and of brick.

During the past two years, a large proportion of the buildings erected have been of brick. The disposition to indulge in cultivating this good taste is rapidly on the increase. Those who are able and ready to build, are beginning to find there is economy in erecting, at the outset, safe, permanent, comfortable, and tasteful dwellings and storehouses. There is about the city numerous piles of brick and sand, which will shortly rise into stately walls, to add materially to the substantial business appearance of the place, and to relieve the eye from the monotonous lines of pine weather-boarding, daubed with white lead.

From the outset, the means of grace have been abundant in St. Paul. If she should ever go down to a degraded end, through sin and infamy, it will not be the fault of the various religious institutions and denominations of our common country, or the want of faithful and zealous ministers sent here to instruct her. The catholic church was the first to organize here. The first organization took place in 1841, and shortly after the log house of worship yet standing on Bench, between Minnesota and Cedar streets, was erected. The older society at Mendota being called the church of St. Peter, the one here took the name in contradistinction of the great apostle of the Gentiles — St. Paul. This gave name to the town; and it is but an act of simple justice to state, that to the good taste of the catholic clergy are we indebted for the excommunication of the outrageous cognomen of "Pig's Eye," which in its flight from our high and salubrious bluffs, found no resting-place until it reached an entanglement of sloughs, marshes, and mosquito dens, some miles below. In May, 1849, a large and devout congregation worshipped in the log church, under the care of the Rev. Mr. Ravoux, a faithful and zealous man. The following year, Minnesota was set off as a bishopric, with the seat at St. Paul; Father Cretin, of Dubuque, was ordained bishop, and arrived here in the spring of 1851. During that year the brick building, at present used as a church edifice, was erected. It was originally designed for a college, and will be so used after the erection of the contemplated cathedral. This latter building will be upon a magnificent scale. Funds are now being raised for its commencement. The catholic church of St. Paul now numbers about eight hundred communicants, mostly of Canadian, French, and Irish extraction.

The first protestant church organization in St. Paul was the methodist episcopal. It was organized on the 31st of December, 1848, by Rev. B. Close, now of Oregon, and numbered at the time eight members. The following summer, the present brick church edifice of this congregation was erected. It was the first brick church in the territory—Rev. Mr. Neill's dwelling being the first brick building of any kind. There are now seventy-three members in communion, and the church is well attended on the sabbath-day. Rev. Messrs. Stevens, Dickens, and Fullerton, have at different periods officiated as ministers in charge. Rev. Chancey Hobart has been the presiding elder of this district from the time the territory was organized, and still holds the position, much beloved and respected by Christians of all denominations, as well as his neighbors outside the church.

Rev. E. D. Neill, missionary of the presbyterian church, N. S., arrived here in April, 1849, he having been assigned this post by the general assembly of his church. He instantly set about his work with that commendable and earnest zeal which characterizes him in everything he undertakes. He labored upon each sabbath-day in the (then) only schoolhouse in the village, until he could build, mostly at his own expense, a temporary place of worship near his dwelling. In this, the first presbyterian congregation was organized on the 1st January, 1850. It consisted of only seven members, including the pastor, all of whom are yet living, save one. April following, the building, a slight frame one, was destroyed by fire. This accident gave zest to the contemplated erection of the present elegant brick edifice, at the corner of St. Peter and Bench streets, which is the best-finished, appointed, and most commodious church in St. Paul. Worship was first had in it during the early part of the following winter. The building is now thoroughly finished, and last summer a superb organ was added to the choir. The number of communicants connected with this church is small in comparison to the number in attendance each sabbath-day. They comprise about forty out of a regular congregation of rising two hundred. Aside from his rigid attendance to his ministerial and other religious duties, Mr. Neill is almost an *indispensable* in the way of a good citizen. His labors as secretary of the Minnesota Historical Society, in collecting and writing our history "as we go along," and his zeal in the cause of popular education, are truly commendable. In fact, all of our clergymen take a deep and laborious interest in this latter great and commendable work.

The scattered members of the baptist flock were also collected in 1849, by the the late Rev. Mr. Parsons. He died on his way home from the East, in November, 1851, just after the completion of the church edifice on Fifth street, which he had worked hard to finish and pay for. His funeral sermon was the first ever preached in the house. The present pastor, Rev. T. E. Cressey, was called during the summer of 1852, to take charge of this congregation. It has about twenty-five communicants.

The Home Missionary Society of the protestant episcopal church, established a mission in St. Paul in the summer of 1850. Rev. Messrs. Breck, Wilcoxon, and Merrick, were placed in charge. Under their superintendence, the present neat church edifice, on Cedar street, was erected the ensuing summer. On the 12th of April, 1851, Right Rev. Bishop Kemper preached the dedication sermon, at which time the parish was organized. Rev. Mr. Wilcoxon is rector.

The methodist episcopal church established a mission among the Germans of this place in the spring of 1851. Rev. Jacob Haas was called to labor in this vineyard. By his devotion and industry, a respectable congregation was soon collected, and a church organized. They worshipped in the lower schoolhouse until last August, when they had completed a small but comfortable church building, situated upon the lower extreme of Smith and Whitney's addition. This organization numbers about forty members, and is at present under charge of Rev. Mr. Korfhag—Mr. Haas having been called to Dubuque last fall.

In the fall of '51, by the constituted authorities of the presbyterian church, O. S., Rev. J. G. Riheldaffer was sent among us to build up a church. He was well received, and immediately went about his work. He has now a church numbering fourteen members, and preaches every sabbath to an intelligent congregation at the courthouse. The organization of this church took place during February, 1852. It is yet in its infancy, and has no permanent place of worship. From the high estimation in which Mr. R. is so deservedly held by all our citizens, through respect to his many good qualities as a man and citizen, as well as his ability and zeal as a Christian minister, there will be ample means provided to complete this substantial and elegant structure at an early day.

One excellent and commendable trait has characterized the bearing and conduct of our ministers connected with the several denominations of the protestant church. With scarcely an exception, they have exercised a truly Christian charity and forbearance toward each other, and avoided all sectarian contentions. They have labored unitedly, not only for the spiritual, but also for the temporal welfare of this people.

All of our church edifices have excellent and fine-toned bells attached to them; and their music upon a sabbath morning never fails to carry the migrated citizen back to his native city or village in the "old settlements," and remind him of the green valleys and sun-clad hills of his "boyhood's home."

There are two "catholic" temperance societies, Irish and Canadian, which hold regular meetings.

The first masonic lodge was instituted in St. Paul during October, 1849. The work was commenced under a dispensation from the grand lodge of Ohio. The lodge now numbers about one hundred members. A grand lodge for the territory, has also been organized and holds its meetings in St. Paul. This body was incorporated by act of the legislature during the late session. St. Paul lodge, and all the other lodges of the territory, now work under the jurisdiction and authority of the grand lodge of Minnesota. A second lodge is about to be instituted here. The order is in a prosperous and highly flourishing condition—daily dispensing its fraternal deeds of charity and material good among the brethren.

The first lodge of the independent order of odd-fellows was instituted in St. Paul, May 3, 1850, by John G. Potts, Esq., of Galena, D. D. G. S. for Minnesota—a charter having previously been obtained for this purpose from the grand lodge of the United States. It took the name of "St. Paul Lodge, No. 2"—"Minnesota Lodge," at Stillwater, being the senior organization of the territory. St. Paul lodge has been in a flourishing and highly prosperous condition since its organization. There were only nine charter members. It now numbers eighty members, among which are six P. Gs.

"Hennepin Lodge, No. 4," was instituted June 2, 1852, with five charter members. It now numbers about forty, of which five are P. Gs. This lodge is also in fine condition. The utmost harmony and good feeling exist among the members of the two lodges and between the brethren individually. Their work is carefully done, and would be highly creditable to what are usually termed "country lodges" anywhere. About twenty-five ladies have taken the degree of Rebekah from the two lodges.

"Minnesota Encampment of Patriarchs, No. 1," was instituted during September, 1851. It is the only encampment yet in the territory, and numbers twenty-eight or thirty members. It is well-officered, and is rapidly increasing. A commendable interest is taken here in the advancement and prosperity of this too-often-neglected branch of the order. Upon the whole, odd-fellowship is doing much good in St. Paul, and the order is daily rising in popularity.

During the present year (1853), a grand lodge of this order, under the style of the "grand lodge of Minnesota," has been instituted at St. Paul—a charter for that purpose having been obtained at the last annual meeting of the G. L. U. S.

This view of our city would be incomplete without such brief history and notice of our public and private schools as shall enable the immigrant and reader to judge of the opportunities for education.

Miss Harriet E. Bishop has the honor of opening the first school taught in St. Paul, July 23, 1847, in an old log shanty with loose floor and bark roof, that stood near the site of the first presbyterian church. The first day, she had nine scholars in attendance, of whom two only were whites. At the end of her first session of three months, her school numbered thirty scholars, a majority of whom were not very distantly related to the aborigines of the country.

1848.—During the summer of this year a schoolhouse was built in the upper town, and a school commenced therein by Miss Bishop in November, which was continued during the winter, with an average attendance of thirty scholars.

1849.—A schoolhouse was built in the lower town, and two schools were taught during the fall by Miss Bishop and Miss Mary A. Scofield respectively. These schools were continued during the winter, and the Rev. Mr. Hobart also opened and taught a school for a short time in the methodist church. The number of scholars in attendance during this winter was one hundred and twenty.

1850.—Misses Bishop and Scofield united their schools and taught the fore part of the summer sixty scholars. During their July vacation D. A. J. Baker commenced a school, which drew off part of their scholars, and the school was afterward conducted by Miss Bishop. The free public schools were organized in the fall of 1850, and Mr. Baker was employed to teach the lower school, and Mr. Henry Doolittle the upper. A school was also started at the episcopal mission, numbering about fifteen pupils. The whole number of scholars attending school this year was nearly two hundred.

1851.—The summer schools of 1851 were four in number—two public and two private. Effect was given to the school law during this year by the appointment of a superintendent in November, who, in conformity with the law, selected and recommended a uniform series of books for the use of the public schools throughout the territory. This and other measures of the superintendent gave economy and increased efficiency to the public schools of our city, and they have since progressed rapidly both in increase of numbers and attainments of the scholars. The recommendations of the superintendent having been unanimously adopted throughout the city, the public schools went into operation under the charge of Mr. George H. Spencer, assisted by Miss Bass, and the late Mr. B. B. Ford, assisted by Miss Brewster. The mission school and the private school of Miss Bishop were continued with increased patronage, and two catholic schools were opened—one in the basement of the church, for boys; and the other by the sisters of charity. The number of scholars in attendance at all of these schools was not far from three hundred.

1852.—During the past year, and especially the past winter, we have had occasion to visit some of the public schools of our city, and have uniformly admired the efficiency of the teachers and the scholarship of the pupils. A grammar-school, which was formed by the union of the first and second districts, was successfully conducted by George H. Spencer, who had an average attendance of seventy pupils. Our primary schools have been equally well attended and as successfully conducted. Jackson street school, No 1, was taught by Miss Bishop; No. 2, by Miss Sorin. Walnut street school, No. 1, was taught by Miss Merrill; No. 2, by Miss Esson. The catholic and episcopal schools were continued as usual, and the whole number of scholars in attendance at all the schools was over four hundred. Let no emigrant hesitate to come to Minnesota on account of the education of his family. The disposition of the people to secure educational privileges, is best expressed by the maxim they have adopted: "The property of the people shall educate the children of the people." The liberality of the general government has appropriated two thirty-sixths of the entire territory for public free schools, and donated forty-nine thousand acres to endow a state university. It will be but a few years until as good a practical education as can be had anywhere, may be had at St. Paul; and when the endowments of the state university at St. Anthony, and the Baldwin school at St. Paul, are available, will also offer unequaled advantages of education. The citizens of St. Paul may justly feel proud of their public free schools.

There are in St. Paul twenty-five practising attorneys-at-law and ten physicians. Most of these gentlemen are worthy members of their professions, and occupy prominent spheres in the ranks of citizenship. Our bar, in point of talent and legal acumen, would not discredit much older communities. However, there is a sufficient number of legal gentlemen already on hand to answer all the ends of justice for the next ten years. We would not recommend a further increase by immigration.

It is true we have very little sickness here; but when one is ill, it is the greatest of consolations as well as the surest means of safety, to have a physician worthy of trust and confidence. Our doctors generally possess these qualifications in an eminent degree. The small number of deaths, even in comparison to the number of cases of sickness, attest the truth of this. The same remark made in regard to the number of lawyers, will also apply to physicians. The country is, as one of them remarked the other day, so "wretchedly healthy," that those already here are put to their utmost exertions to "make a living." We would not advise any further ingress.

The *first* preparatory steps to commence the publication of a newspaper here, were taken in August, 1848, by Prof. A. Randall, then an *attaché* of Dr. Owen's geological corps, engaged in a survey of this region by order of government. The project grew out of the celebrated "Stillwater convention" of that year. It was this which first suggested to the mind of Mr. Randall, that if there was to be a territorial organization here—whether it be a *new* territory, or be harnessed up by John Catlin in the old cast-off gear of Wisconsin—it would necessarily follow there must be a newspaper. Having the capacity and means necessary to undertake the enterprise, he set about it. The leading men of the territory—Mr. Sibley and others—guarantied their countenance and liberal aid; and during the early part of the fall, the arrangements were so far consummated, that Mr. Randall proceeded to Cincinnati—his then home—to purchase press and materials. Winter setting in unusually early, he was not able to return before the close of navigation. Meanwhile he awaited the issue of the bill to organize the territory, then pending before Congress. It did not pass until the last day of the session. By this time, Randall had concluded to set up his office in Cincinnati, and there print the first number of his paper. A partnership had been formed between him and the present senior editor of the "Minnesotian." The first number of the "Minnesota Register" was accordingly issued—*printed* in Cincinnati, it is true, but *dated* at "St. Paul, April 27, 1849"—one day before the first number of the "Pioneer." Messrs. Sibley and Rice had passed through Cincinnati, on their way home from Washington, and liberal contributions from their pens were found in the first number of the Register. These, added to Mr. Randall's extensive knowledge of the country, made one of the most interesting *local* sheets for Minnesota that has ever been issued. The mere fact of its not having been *printed* here makes no particular difference. It was a Minnesota newspaper—a *St. Paul* newspaper, and the *first* one ever published.

Randall, being a man of unsettled purpose and roving disposition, caught the California fever just at this juncture, and sold out the Register to Major M'Lean, late Indian agent at Fort Snelling, who had determined to migrate hither, and resume the business of printing, to which he had been bred, but had not followed for thirty years. Randall's arrangement was continued by M'Lean, under the style of "M'Lean & Owens." The press and materials were shipped to St. Paul, and the junior editor made his way hither in the month of May. M'Lean remained behind, owing mainly to the breaking out of the cholera, and did not arrive till late in August. This circumstance was a serious blow to the success of the Register. The Pioneer had shot far ahead; the "Chronicle" had been established by James Hughes about the first of June; and the little Register appeared to be "nowhere."

It became evident, however, that both it and the Chronicle could not live separately: so about the time M'Lean came on in August, the two were united, under the title of the "Chronicle and Register"—Hughes selling out and retiring, and his foreman, Quay, taking an interest with M'Lean & Owens. Quay continued two or three weeks, and, becoming dissatisfied, quit the concern and the country.

The Chronicle and Register was continued by M'Lean & Owens, with growing prospects of success, until July following. It was the acknowledged whig sheet of the territory, and possessed the confidence of the friends of the administration almost unanimously. At this time M'Lean, having some months previously been appointed Indian agent, became unwilling to continue the business longer. The establishment was sold to David Olmsted, a democrat. Owens went out with M'Lean; and during the few months which Olmsted owned the establishment, the paper had different editors at different periods. Part of the time it edited itself.

In November, D. A. Robertson arrived with his press, and early the following month issued the first number of the "Minnesota Democrat." About this time C. J. Henniss, formerly of Philadelphia, became the owner of the Chronicle and Register. The printing was divided between the Pioneer and a *new whig office*, to be established the following spring. Out of this latter establishment grew the "Minnesotian." The Chronicle and Register went down—the presses and materials passing into the hands of Robertson.

The first number of the Minnesotian was issued September 17, 1851. Its publication was commenced by a committee —J. P. Owens having charge of the editorial, and J. C. Terry the mechanical department. The 6th of January following, the establishment passed into the hands of Owens & Moore, where it still continues.

The Pioneer continued in the hands of its original proprietor till the day of his death, last August. His name still remains at his head, although the establishment has ceased to belong to his estate.

The people of Minnesota are remarkable for the liberality with which they support their local newspapers. The three establishments of St. Paul all appear to be doing a prosperous business. The aggregate investment in printing-offices in this place, we presume amounts to twelve thousand dollars. Of the influence of the press, and its energy and usefulness in developing the resources and advantages of Minnesota, too much can not be said.

One of the best criterions at hand by which to judge of our sure and steady advance in business importance, is the rise in the value of real estate. A number of lots situated on the river below Sibley street, which less than six years ago cost Capt. L. Roberts not more than *five dollars*, were sold by him to a company of our oldest citizens for four thousand dollars!

The purchasers know the value of property as well as any men among us. They consider that they have secured *a great bargain*. Others stood ready, with money in hand, to grab this property, and were greatly disappointed that they did not secure it. Last fall a lot on St. Anthony street, a square below the American house, which Mr. Rice *gave* to one of our attorneys in 1849, and paid him a dollar for making out the deed, was sold by said attorney for eighteen hundred dollars. Lots in that neighborhood now command a thousand dollars or more. In 1849, I could have purchased a quarter of a block, one lot of which the Pioneer office now stands upon, for two hundred dollars; now the same property is worth three thousand dollars, without the improvements. Lots upon Third street which, at that time, could have been purchased at from seventy-five to one hundred and fifty dollars, are now worth from twelve to fifteen hundred. No sort of a lot, even in the outer additions, can now be bought for a hundred dollars.

But what has been is nothing to that which *will be*. There is plenty of chances yet—and better ones than ever—for "making money" here by investing in real estate. No one need be afraid to take hold at present prices. The advance is rapid and continual; and, with the advantages which will accrue by the opening of the vast and fertile country beyond us, there can be no reverse movement.

Lumber averages about twelve dollars per thousand; shingles, three dollars; bricks, six dollars per thousand at the yard.

Common foundation-stone, seventy-five cents per perch, at the quarry; cut-stone for windows, sills, &c., fifty cents per foot.

Lime, one dollar and twenty-five to one dollar and thirty cents per barrel. Sand, twelve and a half cents per load at bank. Two horses and wagon, from three to five dollars per day—generally four dollars. Lathing, and plastering with two rough coats, and furnishing all the materials, from thirty to thirty-two cents per yard. Journeymen carpenters receive from one dollar and seventy-five cents to two dollars per day. Stone-work, cellar-walls laid in mortar, one dollar and seventy-five cents to two dollars per perch.

Vacant houses are hard to find, and consequently rents are very high. A small shop or office, fifteen by twenty feet square, on any of the improved streets, will rent readily at from six to ten dollars per month. A one-story building, situated in any part of the town, containing four rooms, each say twelve feet square, with or without a cellar, pump, or cistern, will rent for from twelve to sixteen dollars per month. As a general rule, the rent of a small dwelling for two years will pay all the cost of its building. Rents can not fall until the supply more nearly approximates the increasing demand for tenements. The lumber and building-material market is much better stocked than some time ago, so that the pressing demand for buildings will be more readily supplied. Buildings are erected in St. Paul with telegraphic rapidity. If one makes a trip to the country on a fishing or hunting excursion, he is astonished on his return at the number of buildings and shanties commenced and completed during his absence.

Many economical persons, with families, knock together, as soon as they land, a rude shanty, in which they live quite comfortably, until a better building can be erected, and thus avoid the expense of high rent.

Eligibly-situated property in St. Paul has more than doubled in value each year for the past four years, and we have no doubt but much of it will continue to advance at a similar rate for the next two years. It may reasonably be estimated that our population and improvements have increased sixty per cent. during the present year.

About five years ago, the land upon which this city is located was purchased at the land-office for one dollar and a quarter per acre. Before that, it was held by no other title than squatters' claims.

A number of town-lots have changed hands since the opening of navigation at prices ranging from one hundred to twelve hundred and fifty dollars. The lots are usually fifty feet front by one hundred and fifty deep. Those sold for one hundred dollars each are located in the additions to the original town-plat. On the squares around the capitol owners are asking from two to five hundred dollars per lot.

The following sales have lately been made: A lot on Fourth street, opposite the courthouse, for five hundred and twenty-five dollars; a lot on Third, above Minnesota street, for twelve hundred and fifty dollars; two lots on Fourth street (corner of St. Peter's and next lot), with improvement worth two hundred and fifty dollars, for eleven hundred and seventy-five dollars; one lot on Third, below Wabashaw street, for one thousand dollars. Numerous other sales have been made recently for cash, but the above will suffice to show at what rates lots have been selling this season. The sales quoted are of property located in the central part of the town, which, however, is not so closely built up as the thickly-settled parts of either "up town" or "down town."

In approaching the conclusion of this rough and imperfectly-sketched picture of St. Paul, we must arrive at the further but consistent conclusion that a high and glorious position among the commercial and manufacturing marts of the great western valley is rapidly approaching her. In fact, it may be said to be already upon her.

I have endeavored to present St. Paul as it now is. The historical reminiscences thrown into the background are generally derived from personal observation—*most* "of which we saw and part of which we were." The statistical results arrived at have chiefly been furnished by reliable citizens, and will be found correct in the main. Some inaccuracies will be found embodied in this sketch, but there are none of any great or material magnitude.

The chief object has been to make the stranger acquainted with the history, rise, progress, and prospects, present and future, of St. Paul. I wish the immigrant, when he arrives, to know where he is—among whom he is—and what prospects of success await him by remaining with us. Also the compilation of historical and statistical data, as the foundation of future notations and speculations in regard to the onward progress of this predestined emporium of the northwest. If what is here written and compiled should never be of future use to ourselves, perhaps it may be of some slight aid to those who are to come after us. I thus take leave of St. Paul at the opening of the business season of the year 1853. "There she stands!"

One of the most interesting places in Minnesota, and one that most who have come into the territory have seen and admired, lies between St. Paul and St. Anthony. It is composed for the most part of prairie and openings; and, after a tedious journey of several days by the river, a ride over this region is delightful indeed, especially when one has become weary of the monotonous succession of bluffs and densely-timbered river bottoms that have bounded the vision for several hundred miles. The wayworn traveller longs for a change in the scene by the time he lands at St. Paul; and if he will but step into one of the fine "Concord coaches" always in readiness on the arrival of a boat, to carry him to the great falls of the Father of Waters, he will soon be gratified. In a few minutes he will be out upon the beautiful prairie, that commences about one mile from St. Paul, and extends nearly half way to St. Anthony and several miles northward. How invigorating the air feels that comes over the flowery plain, or the large fields of grain and corn! The new-comer here seems to breathe with fresh delight, and he feels better and stronger than ever before. Here and there a little gem of a lake meets the view. Cultivated fields and improved farms now appear quite numerous, among which is one owned by ex-Governor Ramsey, containing some two hundred and forty acres under improvement.

The prairie is soon crossed, and the openings commence and extend nearly to St. Anthony city. Farms now appear more numerous, while most of the land on either side of the road is under improvement. In a cluster of trees, just as we enter the beautiful opening, stands a neat, newly-erected building, which plainly tells that the "schoolmaster is abroad" in Minnesota. Many of the farms in this neighborhood are quite small, after the New England fashion, and the land is held at high prices. Gardening is carried on quite extensively by many, and great quantities of vegetables, melons, &c., are raised for the St. Paul and St. Anthony markets. The soil and situation of this place are both remarkably well adapted to horticultural pursuits. The quantity and quality of melons and tomatoes raised here are quite surprising to persons from the east.

A nursery, the first in Minnesota, has been established in this place by Mr. L. M. Ford; and, in connection with the Scott nursery at Davenport, Iowa, he is prepared to furnish trees and plants to any who wish to plant orchards or embellish their grounds. Fruit-trees grown in this territory I think will be in demand for planting some distance south of this, as the soil and climate are calculated to produce very hardy trees.

Most of the country lying between St. Paul and St. Anthony is known by the name of "Groveland," which is quite an appropriate name, though a part of the prairie is included within the settlements.

In connection with this history of St. Paul and its newspaper press, I present the following article from the annals of the Minnesota Historical Society for 1853, prepared by the secretary, the Rev. E. D. Neill:—

OBITUARY NOTICE OF JAMES M. GOODHUE, LATE EDITOR OF THE "MINNESOTA PIONEER."

"The body that once encased the mind of James M. Goodhue is no longer visible, but dwells in a narrow house, the silent and dreary grave. Until he ceased to breathe, his value to the community was not fully known. In life, he was viewed chiefly in the aspect of an individual battling for his own interests. In death, it is discovered that he was the individual, above all others, who had promoted the general welfare of Minnesota, and especially that of the capital.

"In April, 1849, he found St. Paul nothing more than a frontier Indian-trading settlement, known by the savages as the place where they could obtain *minne-wakon*, or whiskey, and wholly unknown to the civilized world. When he died, with the sword of his pen he had carved a name and reputation for St. Paul, and he lived long enough to hear men think aloud and say that the day was coming when schoolboys would learn from their geography that the third city in commercial importance, on the banks of the mighty Mississippi, was St. Paul. His most bitter opponents were convinced, whatever might be his conduct toward them, that he loved Minnesota with all his heart, all his mind, and all his might.

"The editor of the 'Pioneer' was unlike other men. Every action, and every line he wrote marked great individuality. He could imitate no man in his manners nor in his style, neither could any man imitate him. Attempts were sometimes made, but the failure was always very great. Impetuous as the whirlwind, with perceptive powers that gave to his mind the eye of a lynx, with a vivid imagination that made the very stones of Minnesota speak her praise, with an intellect as vigorous and elastic as a Damascene blade, he penned editorials which the people of this territory can never blot out from memory.

"His wit, when it was chastened, caused ascetics to laugh. His sarcasm upon the foibles of society was paralyzing and unequalled by Macaulay in his review of the life of Barrere. His imagination produced a tale of fiction called 'Striking a Lead,' which has already become a part of the light literature of the west. When, in the heat of partisan warfare, all the qualities of his mind were combined to defeat certain measures, the columns of his paper were like a terrific storm in midsummer amid the Alps. One sentence would be like the dazzling, arrowy lightning, peeling in a moment the mountain-oak, and riving from the topmost branch to the deepest root; the next like a crash of awful thunder; and the next like the stunning roar of a torrent of many waters. To employ the remark made in a discourse at his funeral—'With the ingenuity of Vulcan, he would hammer out thunderbolts on the anvil of his mind, and hurl them with the power and dexterity of Jove!'

"The contrarieties of his character often increased his force. Imagining his foes to be Cossacks, he often dashed among them with all the recklessness of Murat. The fantastic magnificence of his pen, when in those moods, was as appalling in its temerity as the white ostrich-feather and glittering gold band of Napoleon's famed marshal.

"His prejudice was inveterate against sham and clap-trap.

He refused to publish many of the miserable advertisements of those quacks who seek to palm off their nostrums upon young men diseased through their own vices. When a 'stroller' for a living, or a self-dubbed professor, came to town, he sported with him as the Philistines with blind Samson. By sarcasm and ridicule, 'Jarley with his wax-works' was made to decamp.

"When he was unjustifiably harsh, his apology was that in the 'Medea' of Euripides:—

> 'Manthano men hoia dran mello kaka
> Thumos de kreissona tone emone bouleumatone.'

He was not hypocritical; he never wore a mask. His editorials showed all he felt at the hour they were dashed from his pen. When untrammelled by self-interest or party-ties, his sentiments proved that he was a man that was often ready to exclaim:—

> 'Video meliora proboque
> Deteriora sequor.'

"As a paragraphist, he was equalled by few living men. His sentences so leaped with life, that when the distant reader perused his sheet, he seemed to hear the purling brooks and see the agate pavements and crystal waters of the lakes of Minnesota; and he longed to leave the sluggish stream, the deadly malaria, and wornout farms, and begin life anew in the territory of the sky-tinted waters. When the immigrant from week to week was disposed to despond, and give way to the distress of homesickness, the hopeful sentences of his paper in relation to the prosperous future, chased that dismal feeling away.

"The deceased was born in Hebron, New Hampshire, March 31, 1810. His parents possessed the strong faith and stern virtue of the puritans, and felt that an education was the greatest treasure they could give their children. After passing through preparatory studies, he entered Amherst college, where he listened to the lectures of the distinguished geologist Hitchcock and other devout men of science. In the year 1832 he received a diploma from that institution. It was his desire to have attended a meeting of his surviving classmates in the halls of his 'Alma Mater,' but another summons came, to take 'his chamber in the silent halls of Death.'

"Having studied law, he entered upon the practice of the profession. He became an editor unexpectedly to himself. Having been invited to take the oversight of a press in the lead region of Wisconsin, during the temporary absence of its conductor, he discovered that he increased the interest of the readers in the paper. From that time he began to pay less attention to the legal profession, and was soon known among the citizens of the mines as the editor of the *Grant County Herald*, published at Lancaster, Wisconsin. While residing at this place, he became interested in the territory 'of sky-tinted waters' (Minnesota). With the independence and temerity of one Benjamin Franklin, he left Lancaster as suddenly as the ostensible editor of the *New England Courant* left Boston, and he arrived at the landing of what is now the capital of Minnesota, with little more money and few more friends than the young printer who landed at Market-street wharf, in the capital of the then youthful territory of Pennsylvania. This part of his life he has described with some minuteness in the *Pioneer* of April 18, 1852, in connection with a life-like picture of

"'THE FIRST DAYS OF THE TOWN OF ST. PAUL.

"'The 18th day of April, 1849, was a raw, cloudy day. The steamboat "Senator," Captain Smith, landed at Randall's warehouse, lower landing, the only building then there, except Roberts's old store. Of the people on shore, we recognised but one person as an acquaintance. Took our press, types, and printing apparatus, all ashore. Went with our men to the house of Mr. Bass, corner of Third and Jackson streets. He kept the only public house in St. Paul; and it was crowded full from cellar to garret. Mr. Bass was very obliging, and did everything possible for our encouragement. The next thing was a printing-office; and that it seemed impossible to obtain. Made the acquaintance of C. P. V. Lull, and his partner, Gilbert. They furnished us, gratuitously, the lower story of their building, for an office—the only vacant room in town; being the building on Third street, since finished off and now occupied as a saloon by Mr. Calder. The weather was cold and stormy, and our office was as open as a corn-rick; however, we picked our types up and made ready for the issue of the first paper ever printed in Minnesota or within many hundreds of miles of it; but upon search we found our news-chase was left behind. William Nobles, blacksmith, made us a very good one, after a delay of two or three days. The paper was to be named "The Epistle of St. Paul," as announced in our prospectus, published in the February preceding; but we found so many little saints in the territory, jealous of St. Paul, that we determined to call our paper "The Minnesota Pioneer." One hinderance after another delayed our first issue to the 28th of April—ten days. Meantime, Rev. Mr. Neill arrived. It was encouraging to find a young man of education ready to enlist all that he had or hoped on earth, in the fortunes of our town. Stillwater and St. Paul were then running neck and neck, as rival towns. Not a foot of pine lumber could be had nearer than Stillwater. But about this time one of the mills at St. Anthony was put in operation; but there were then only a few buildings at the falls of St. Anthony. We looked about St. Paul to buy a lot. Mr. Larpenteur's house was built; also, French's house and shop (now a tin shop), and the little shop, then the drug-store of Dewey & Cavileer, recently Major J. J. Noah's office, next door west of Calder's (then our printing-office); also the office of Judge Pierse (then the fur store of Olmsted and Rhodes). Mr. Lambert's house was partly finished. As you go up Third and Bench streets, the next buildings were two old tamarac log-houses, a little east of where Mr. Neill's church is; then passing the schoolhouse, there were two more of the same sort in the street, in front of the houses now occupied by Mr. Benson and Mr. Hollinshead near the junction of St. Anthony, Bench, and Hill streets. Beyond, was the house John R. Irvine lives in, and nothing else but the symptoms of two or three balloon frames. The Fullers were at work putting up a small store with their own hands. Returning, on the right, was the old underground dead-fall, in the ground opposite John R. Irvine's house; then at the junction of Third and Bench streets, was Vetal Guerin's log-house (now Le Duc's); then the building in which Mr. Curran lives, at that time unfinished; then the old bakery next door east; then Mr. Hopkins's at the corner; turning the corner to the head of Randall's stairs (not then built), was the old building, still there (now belonging to F. Steele), which Henry Jackson used to own, where he kept a grocery, postoffice, and a tavern, free for all the world and the world's wife. Up along the bank of the river stood, and yet stands, the building occupied as a store by William H. Forbes, the St. Paul outfit; next was a little log building, the nucleus of the "Central House;" next the old log catholic church, where the Rev. Mr. Ravoux faithfully labored, and sometimes saw miraculous visions during the time of Lent; then the log-house belonging to Mr. Laroux, which is now being metamorphosed into a neat building. This brings us back to Vetal's the junction of Third and Bench streets. Half a dozen other buildings along Roberts street, and Mr. Hoyt's neighborhood, in addition to the above, constituted St. Paul. But let it be remembered that the fashionable drinking-place then, was that little log-house next east of Goodrich's brick store. Mr. Bass was busy in hurrying up a new saloon, the building lately occupied as the clerk's office, on the spot where the Minnesota outfit stands. The ground west of Roberts's, and north of Third streets, was covered with any quantity of hewed timber stripped from the forest opposite town. We looked about for a lot; and saw that the two ends of the town must soon unite in the middle. Along the lower end of Third street, owners of lots had the coolness to ask from one hundred to two hundred dollars a lot. Between Lambert's and where the Sligo iron store is, on Third street, the price was seventy-five, and soon after ninety dollars. We bought a fractional lot with Dr. Dewey; and on our half of it, built the middle section of the building where the *Pioneer* office is, for a dwelling-house, and lived in it through the next year, without having it lathed or plastered.

"'But to return a little. We were at length prepared to issue our first number. We had no subscribers; for then there were but a handful of people in the whole territory; and the majority of those were Canadians and half-breeds. Not a territorial officer had yet arrived. We remember present, at the date of our first issue, Mr. Lull, Mr. Cavileer, Mr. Neill, and perhaps Major Murphy. The people wanted no politics, and we gave them none; they wanted information of all sorts about Minnesota; and that is what we furnished them with. We advocated Minnesota, morality, and religion, from the beginning. William B. Brown built a shell of a building (being the south end of the Sligo iron store now), which Mr. Neill occupied for a meetinghouse. It was half filled with hearers on Sundays; for Sunday was like any other day, or perhaps rather more so.

"'This town grew rapidly. The boats came up loaded with immigrants; but then, as now, a great many feeble, weak-hearted folks, were frozen out and went back down the river, not being made of the right stuff. Mr. Owens came up with the "Register" press, from Cincinnati, one number of that journal having been printed in that city. Colonel James Hughes also came from Ohio with the "Chronicle," which was issued soon after, from the building where "The Minnesotian" is now published. Soon after the Register, by M'Lean & Owens, was issued from the building that is now the law-office of Simons & Masterson, St. Anthony street. After a few months, the Chronicle and Register were united in the old Chronicle office, under the firm, name, and style of Owens & M'Lean and Hughes & Quay. Mr. Quay soon left the office; and soon after Colonel Hughes sold out, and Mr. M'Lean became sole proprietor of both offices, and Owens editor; Major M'Lean being appointed Sioux agent at Fort Snelling.'"

A short period before the deceased was confined to his room he fell from his ferry-boat into the river, and had to use great exertion to keep from drowning; this, in connection with a mind oppressed by the cares of one so active in life, is supposed to have shortened his days on earth. Not long after he was on a bed of sickness, there seemed to be the presentiment that his heart might have commenced "beating its funeral march to the grave."

"Some days before he died, with great calmness and clearness of mind, he conversed with the minister, whose services he attended when in health. In looking back upon his life, he saw much to regret. He acknowledged his unworthiness in the sight of Heaven, and hoped that he had placed his trust in his Redeemer. He was desirous to live in order that he might show to the world that he had determined to act upon new resolutions. To the last, he felt an interest in Minnesota. During his sickness he was patient, and freely forgave all his enemies.

"His spirit left his body on Friday evening, August 27, 1852, at half past eight o'clock. His funeral took place on Sunday afternoon. A discourse was delivered in the presbyterian church, to the largest assembly ever convened upon a similar occasion in Minnesota.

"The legislative assembly of 1853 very properly recognised his services in bringing Minnesota into notice, by giving his name to one of the new counties formed out of the recently-ceded Dakota lands."

CHAPTER VIII.

PRINCIPAL TOWNS CONTINUED — ST. ANTHONY'S FALLS — POINT DOUGLASS, STILLWATER, MENDOTA, ETC.

A RIDE of an hour from St. Paul, over fine country, brings us to the celebrated falls of St. Anthony, a place of great resort for visiters from the east and sunny south. In the way of cataracts, it is decidedly the glory of our west and northwest. The pulse of the traveller seems to beat quicker as he feels himself approaching the scene, where Father Hennepin, of old, was so carried away with admiration as to call the red man's falls after his patron-saint. The name has indeed a kind of sacred halo about it, yet we love the more sonorous and far more appropriate appellation of the Indians. (The Dakotas call the falls " Rara," from *irara*, to laugh.)

Long before coming in sight of the grand scene, the ear is greeted by the deep, solemn roar, that truly resembles the " sound of many waters." It seems, indeed, as though some mighty strife were going on amid the elements of nature. A strange and indescribable feeling steals over the senses — a feeling that awakens a spirit of admiration for the Almighty's handiwork. The falls at length burst upon the enraptured view — the noble falls of St. Anthony. We are immediately impressed with the peculiar appropriateness of the Indian's name, as he gazes on the " laughing waters." One is not here so completely overwhelmed at the incomparable Niagara, with the great height of the water's fall, their deafening roar, or the lofty character of the scenery. St. Anthony is more within the grasp of the human comprehension, and is therefore looked upon with more real pleasure. Niagara appears to wear a kind of threatening frown, while the former greets you with a more winning and complacent smile. Yet on account of the vast body of water continually rushing over the rocky mass in the river's bed, the scene is one of great sublimity, as well as one of beauty and loveliness. As we gaze on the scene, and listen to the warring elements, how forcibly are we impressed with the truth of Brainard's beautiful lines: —

> "And what are we,
> That hear the question of that voice sublime?
> O, what are all the notes that ever rung
> From war's vain trumpet, by thy thundering side?
> Yes, what is all the riot man can make
> In his short life, to thine unceasing roar?
> And yet, bold babbler, what art thou to Him
> Who drowned the world, and heaped the waters far
> Above its loftiest mountain? A light wave
> That breaks and whispers at its Maker's might!"

The Rev. Albert Barnes, in a sermon preached in 1849, uses this language in relation to the falls: —

"I visited the falls of St. Anthony. I know not how other men feel when standing there, nor how men will feel a century hence, when standing there — then, not in the *west*, but almost in the centre of our great nation. But when I stood there, and reflected on the distance between that and the place of my birth and my home; on the prairies over which I had passed; and the stream — the 'Father of Rivers' — up which I had sailed some five hundred miles, into a new and unsettled land — where the children of the forest still live and roam — I had views of the greatness of my country, such as I have never had in the crowded capitals and the smiling villages of the east. Far in the distance did they then seem to be, and there came over the soul the idea of greatness and vastness, which no figures, no description, had ever conveyed to my mind. To an inexperienced traveller, too, how strange is the appearance of all that land! Those boundless prairies seem as if they had been cleared by the patient labor of another race of men, removing all the forests, and roots, and stumps, and brambles, and smoothing them down as if with mighty rollers, and sowing them with grass and flowers; a race which then passed away, having built no houses of their own, and made no fences, and set out no trees, and established no landmarks, to lay the foundation of any future claim. The mounds which you here and there see, look, indeed, as if a portion of them had died and had been buried there; but those mounds and those boundless fields had been forsaken together. You ascend the Mississippi amid scenery unsurpassed in beauty probably in the world. You see the waters making their way along an interval of from two to four miles in width, between bluffs of from one to five hundred feet in height. Now the river makes its way along the eastern range of bluffs, and now the western, and now in the centre, and now it divides itself into numerous channels, forming thousands of beautiful islands, covered with long grass ready for the scythe of the mower. Those bluffs, rounded with taste and skill, such as could be imitated by no art of man, and set out with trees here and there, gracefully arranged like orchards, seem to have been sown with grain to the summit, and are clothed with beautiful green. You look out instinctively for the house and barn; for flocks and herds; for men, and women, and children; but they are not there. A race that is gone seems to have cultivated those fields, and then to have silently disappeared—leaving them for the first man that should come from the older parts of our own country, or from foreign lands, to take possession of them. It is only by a process of reflection that you are convinced that it is not so. But it is not the work of man. It is God who has done it, when there was no man there save the wandering savage, alike ignorant and unconcerned as to the design of the great processes in the land where he roamed—God who did all this, that he might prepare it for the abode of a civilized and Christian people."

The direction of the Mississippi at this place, and for several miles above, is nearly south. Opposite the village three islands, lying nearly in a straight line, one above the other, divide the river into two parts—the largest body of water flowing on the right hand of the islands. The upper island is small, containing less than ten acres of land, and is still uncultivated, though the trees with which it was but a short time since densely covered, are fast disappearing, and it will soon be brought under tribute to the husbandman.

The second island is some eight or ten rods below, and contains about forty acres. It is a beautiful spot of ground, covered thickly with a great variety of thrifty timber, among which the sugar-maple is conspicuous. The banks are high, bold and rocky on the upper end, gradually descending at the lower almost to the water's edge. Near the middle of the island a small bluff rises some ten or fifteen feet high, with a slope as nicely and beautifully turned as if it had been the work of art. It forms a semicircular curve at the lower end, gradually widening toward the upper, making one of the most charming building-sites that can be imagined. Near the lower end of this island commence the rapids in the main stream, the water foaming, bounding, and dashing over the rocks, which lie scattered across the bed of the stream as far as the falls.

Franklin Steele, Esq., owns this island, having entered it in 1848, as soon as it was surveyed. It is considered valuable property, the proprietor having been offered four thousand dollars for one half of it.

The third island lies immediately below, so near the last-mentioned that they were formerly connected by a slight bridge. It contains, on a rough estimate, some fifteen acres, and is not yet surveyed. A small house has been erected upon it by the mill company, as a pre-emption claim. On each side of this island are the falls of St. Anthony. Below the falls are two small islands, near the right shore. The falls of the main channel are several rods above those on this side, the greater volume of water having worn away the soft crumbling rock much faster. The recedence of the falls on both sides is so rapid as to be almost yearly perceptible; making the suppositions of some geologists highly plausible, that originally they were as low as Fort Snelling. During the high water of 1850, huge masses of rocks were torn from the islands washed by the falls, and carried a considerable distance down the river; large blocks of sand and limestone detached from the ledge of rock over which the water is precipitated; and altogether, the falls underwent a greater change than had been observed for many years.

Franklin Steele, Norman W. Kittson, and Mr. Stumbough, made a claim on lands in this vicinity, as early as 1836 or 1837, soon after the Indian title was obtained by government. The land, however, was not surveyed and entered till 1848. Charles Wilson seems to have been the first American who ever made a permanent residence here, having arrived in the spring of 1847. There was then but one house in the place, standing on the bluff some thirty rods below the mills, and built of logs. Roving Frenchmen and trappers may have temporarily resided here previously, but not as permanent settlers. Mrs. Ard Godfrey may claim the honor of having given birth to the first of the fair daughters of St. Anthony; and her husband, A. Godfrey, Esq., that of having commenced the first improvement of the water power at the falls. Under his superintendence, in the fall of 1847, the dam and saw-mills owned by the St. Anthony mill company, were begun, and the first saw put in operation in August, 1848. Others were completed soon after, making eight saws now running, of an average capacity of six thousand feet each per day. R. P. Russell, Esq., erected the first frame dwelling in the town, in 1847, and opened the first store. There are at present four organized churches—presbyterian, episcopalian, methodist, and baptist. Two school districts, known as Nos. 5 and 6, were organized in the village in 1850. In addition to the public schools taught in these districts, several flourishing select schools have been maintained since 1850. The whole population of the place may be safely estimated at two thousand souls.

The legislature, in 1851, passed "An act to incorporate the University of Minnesota at the Falls of St. Anthony." The law provides that "the proceeds of all lands that may hereafter be granted by the United States to the territory, for the support of a university, shall be and remain a perpetual fund to be called the 'University fund,' the interest of which shall be appropriated to the support of a university." The law further provides that the object of the university shall be "to provide the inhabitants of this territory with the means of acquiring a thorough knowledge of the various branches of literature, science, and the arts;" and that "the government of the university shall be vested in a board of twelve regents, who shall be elected by the legislature," and whose duties are prescribed in said law. "The university shall consist of five departments, to wit: science, literature, and the arts, a department of law and medicine, the theory and practice of elementary instruction, and the department of agriculture."

The university shall be located at the "Falls of St. Anthony." "The regents shall make a report annually to the legislature, exhibiting the state and progress of the university in its several departments, the course of study, the number of professors and students, the amount of expenditures and such other information as they may deem proper," etc. On the fourth of March, 1851, the legislature met in joint convention and elected the following gentlemen as regents for said university, to wit:—

Alexander Ramsey, Henry H. Sibley, C. K. Smith, Henry M. Rice, W. R. Marshall, Franklin Steele, Isaac Atwater, B. B. Meeker, A. Van Vorhees, Socrates Nelson, N. C. D. Taylor, and J. W. Furber.

The board of regents met at St. Anthony, October, 1851, for the transaction of business. The subject of the removal of the present site of the university engaged the attention of the board. It has been thought by some of the friends of the university that its present location is in closer proximity to the business, and especially the manufacturing carried on in town, than would be desirable for a seat of learning. The subject has been referred to a committee for examination, and to report whether any more eligible site can be obtained in the vicinity of St. Anthony.

The two townships of land donated by Congress to the university, have not yet been located. It was thought advisable to defer the location till after the ratification of the Indian treaties, in order that wider range might be afforded to make a selection most favorable to the interests of the institution. The matter is one of great consequence to the interests of the university, and will receive the attention of the regents as early as practicable.

One of the first steps taken by the board of regents, in behalf of the university, was the establishment of a preparatory department. This is now in a flourishing condition. It is under the direction of Prof. E. W. Merrill, a gentleman of much experience and success in teaching. It was opened for the reception of students November 26th, 1851. Since that time about one hundred and fifty students have been connected with the institution. The number has been steadily increasing each term, the present numbering eighty-five pupils. It is gratifying to observe that an interest is felt in the institution in different parts of the territory. Several students from abroad, have recently availed themselves of the advantages it affords.

There have been six students pursuing the study of the languages, seventeen algebra and geometry, sixteen physiology, the same number book-keeping, twenty-nine philosophy, and six astronomy. The books used are the same as recommended by the superintendent of public instruction.

No provision has yet been made for procuring apparatus suitable for the illustration of the natural sciences, and experiments therein. Great inconvenience is experienced from this cause. By a resolution of the board of regents, all the expenses connected with the preparatory department, are defrayed by private subscription. Many of the friends of education have already contributed generously toward this object. But it is believed there are others, who would only need to be informed that the want above alluded to is felt, to cheerfully contribute the means for furnishing the necessary apparatus.

The town of St. Anthony now contains over two thousand inhabitants, and is most beautifully picturesque in its position. It contains beautiful building sites, and now boasts several elegantly-built cottages, which would do honor to any city of the Union. Its rapidly increasing business, and population, together with its magnificent water power for manufacturing purposes, betoken another "Lowell," to rival old New England Massachusetts.

STILLWATER was first settled, October 10, 1843, by John M'Kusick, formerly from Maine; Elam Greely, from Maine; Calvin F. Leach from Vermont, and Elias M'Kean, from Pennsylvania, proprietors of the Stillwater Lumber Company; having selected this site on account of its valuable water-power, for the erection of a saw-mill, which was put in operation early in the spring of 1844. The simple board shanties of the first settlers, together with the mill, remained the only buildings in the place until the fall of 1844, when the first frame house was built by A. Northrup for a tavern stand.

From this time, the place steadily grew in importance. In 1846, a postoffice was established, and Elam Greely appointed postmaster. In 1848, the town was laid out by John M'Kusick, one of the proprietors thereof. About this time the county commissioners authorized the building of a courthouse at this place, which was completed in 1850. A schoolhouse was also built in 1848, schools having been established as early as 1846, and held in private houses. A presbyterian church, being the first in the town, was erected in 1850.

The settlement of the Arcola mill, which ranks next in age, was commenced in 1846, by Martin Mower, W. H. C. Folsom, formerly from Maine; and Joseph Brewster, from New York, who erected a saw-mill at this point. Since which many other buildings have been built, which, together with the mill, gives this place the appearance of a thriving little village.

The first settlement of Washington county was commenced in 1837, at what is called Taylor's falls—by Baker, Taylor, and others of the Northwest Lumber Company. About which time, the government treaty, with the Sioux and Chippewa Indians was concluded for the land, the Sioux owning the southern, and the Chippewas the northern portion of the land in this county. July 17th, 1838, the treaty being ratified by Congress, consequently several settlements were commenced about that time. Several by the French, along the shores of Lake St. Croix, as well as the more important settlements of the Marine and Falls of St. Croix.

The first steamboat that navigated the river St. Croix was

the Palmyra, July 17th, 1838, having on board the original proprietors of the Marine and Falls of St. Croix saw-mills, together with their necessary supplies and machinery, for the erection of the mills at those places.

The settlement of the Marine mills was commenced in 1838, by Samuel Burkleo, formerly of the state of Delaware, Orange Walker, from Vermont, and others of the Marine Lumber Company, who succeeded in erecting a good saw-mill, for the manufacture of pine lumber. Other buildings of different kinds have since been built, together with one large and commodious tavern stand. This place is a business point of considerable importance.

At this time, the jurisdiction of Crawford county, Wisconsin territory, extended over all this territory northwest from Prairie du Chien. Joseph R. Brown was chosen representative to the legislative assembly of Wisconsin, to represent the wants of the population; and, among the many representations of the wants of the people, was the organization of a new county, which was granted by the legislature in 1841, as will be seen by their act, November 20, entitled "An act to organize the county of St. Croix." At the time prescribed by law for holding the court, up came the judge to hold the court at the seat of justice; and on arriving at Dakota, the seat of justice, to his great astonishment, the only building in the town was a rough log-cabin, occupied by a lone Frenchman, who it appears was employed by the proprietor of the town to take care of the county-seat in his absence. This kind of reception not meeting the expectations of the judge, he very naturally took back tracks, and thus ended the judicial proceedings for St. Croix county. It was soon after attached to Crawford county, where it remained until 1847, when it was again organized for judicial purposes, and the county-seat established at Stillwater, where the first United States district court was holden in what is now Minnesota territory, being the June term of 1848. There being no courthouse, the court was held at the store of John M'Kusick, by the Hon. Charles Dunn, judge of said court.

POINT DOUGLAS is situated at the junction of the Mississippi and Lake St. Croix. In 1839, ten acres of the present town-site were claimed by Mr. Joseph Mozoe, who erected and occupied the first house (a log-cabin, now standing on the bank of the river) in the present town; and, in 1840, Mr. Calvin Tuttle became the purchaser of this land, who extended his claim to one hundred and sixty acres, which was subsequently, in the year 1844, sold to Messrs. Burris & Hertzell, merchants of this place. In 1839, Mr. Joseph Langtoe claimed about ten acres of land adjoining the above, which was subsequently sold to Captain Frazier, who increased the amount to eighty acres, which was, in 1843, sold to Burris & Hertzell, and in 1844 purchased by Mr. David Hone—this latter gentleman having at this time, adjoining the village, about one hundred and ninety acres of land, which he has by industry and good management succeeded in putting under fence and in a good state of cultivation; which has produced, for several successive years, crops that will average to the acre, of wheat, forty bushels; corn, forty bushels; barley, forty-five bushels; potatoes, two to three hundred bushels—all of which, owing to the great home demand, has realized a profitable return for the labor expended. Other gentlemen in the neighborhood have been equally successful in raising crops, although on a smaller scale. The lands lying between the river and Lake St. Croix are of fine quality, and filling up with an industrious and intelligent class of citizens, who appear determined to test fully the character of the soil, and provide for themselves and families at least a comfortable home.

In the year 1849, the town was surveyed and laid out in lots of fifty feet front by one hundred and fifty feet deep, the streets running at right angles, and generally fifty feet wide. The land rises gradually from the Mississippi river, which is its southern and principal front, until it reaches the base of a gradually-rising hill, the summit of which is about one hundred feet above the summit or level of the lake and river. From this elevation a very extensive and interesting prospect may be had of the lake, the lands on the west bank of the Mississippi, and the fine lands of Wisconsin. The eastern front, or lake side of this town, from its elevated position, will be the most agreeable and pleasant for family residence; the surface being gently rolling, and affording easy grades for draining the town, and having sufficient timber, which can be turned to good account in ornamenting and shading the streets and residences.

To those in search of health and pleasure, Point Douglas and surrounding country present many attractions; the fine air, the beautiful lake where fish of various kind abound, and where those in quest of aquatic excursions can nowhere find a more suitable field for such enjoyments.

A visit to Vermillion river and falls is no less attractive: the river winding its way unseen through an extensive and beautiful prairie until within a short distance of the precipice, then rushing with all the wild confusion of a Niagara or St. Anthony over craggy and disjointed rocks of about one hundred feet in depth until it reaches the river below, and finally finds a rest in the bosom of the Father of Waters one mile above this town; the river above and below the falls affording fish of fine quality, such as trout, bass, pickerel, chub, &c. A ride of a few miles to Rush river, in Wisconsin, through a fertile country of woodland and prairie, is no less inviting to those in search of piscatorial enployment, abounding, as do other rivers and lakes of the country, with fish of excellent quality.

The late appropriations of Congress for improvements within the territory, makes Point Douglas the starting-point of two principal roads: one to Fond du Lac, on Lake Superior; the other to Fort Ripley, one hundred and sixty miles above, on the Mississippi river.

Fort Snelling is situated at the confluence of the Minnesota and Mississippi rivers, on the west side of the Mississippi. The buildings of the garrison are upon a high bluff, probably two hundred feet above the level of the water in the rivers, and which stretches to the north and west in a gently-undulating and very fertile prairie, interspersed here and there with groves of heavy timber. The steamboat-landing of Fort Snelling is directly opposite the mouth of the Minnesota, from which a low island extends about two and a half miles down the Mississippi.

MENDOTA, which lies about half a mile below the mouth of the Minnesota, has been for many years a trading-post of the American Fur Company, and is still a depôt of goods and provisions for the supply of the traders, who, at this time, have penetrated much farther into the Indian country. But it has, till lately, been included in the military reserve of Fort Snelling. It has not attained that degree of prosperity so remarkable in the villages of St. Paul and St. Anthony, and which its far more favorable position might justly have secured for it.

From the summit of Pilot Knob, which lies back of Mendota, a view may be obtained of the surrounding country as far as the eye can grasp, affording to the spectator a sight of one of the most charming natural pictures to be found in this territory, so justly celebrated for scenic beauty. The view describes a circle of eight or nine miles—a grand spectacle of rolling prairie, extended plain and groves, the valley of the Minnesota with its meandering stream, a bird's-eye view of Fort Snelling, Lake Harriet in the distance—the town of St. Anthony just visible through the nooks of the intervening groves,—and St. Paul, looking like a city set upon a hill, its buildings and spires distinctly visible, and presenting in appearance the distant view of a city containing a population of one hundred thousand human beings.

Besides the older and larger towns, there are many *germinal cells*, along the navigable streams, hastening into existence. We have on the Mississippi, Wabashaw, Minnesota city, Red Wing, Hastings, Mendota, and perhaps others unintentionally omitted. Then on the Minnesota river are Shakopee, Le Sueur, and Traverse des Sioux. And yet above these, at the confluence of the Blue-Earth and Minnesota, in the foreground of a most charming picture of varied and picturesque scenery, stands the fair beginning of the future city of Mankato.

CHAPTER IX.

THE AGRICULTURAL RESOURCES OF THE TERRITORY, MANUFACTURES, ETC.

THOSE who are desirous of removing to a new country ought to prefer Minnesota for the business of farming. To begin with, if you are of that incorrigible class of persons who have taken it into their brains that no part of this great globe is habitable, by reason of the cold, to a higher degree of latitude than about forty degrees north, we have no use for you. Stay in your doorless cabins, and go shivering about in your thin, slazy garments of jeans, through the mingled frost and mud, and the icy sleet and chilling fogs of that most execrable of all climates—an hermaphrodite region, half-tropical and half-frigid—a cross of the north pole upon the equator. Stay where you are. We want here a race of men of higher physical and mental powers, of more meat and muscle, of more force and energy. The whole of the British islands—the nursery of that vigorous stock of the human family, which, first taking root in the rocky shore of the Atlantic, has, in two hundred years, uprooted the forests filled with barbarous Indians, and, like the prolific locust-tree, spread wider and wider its annual shoots, until its shadows are reflected from the Pacific—those British islands lie more than five degrees north of St. Paul. The whole of England, Ireland, Scotland, Belgium, Holland, and a part of France, lie north of the extreme northern boundary of Minnesota. We are now addressing those over the whole globe who have been invigorated by the cold. I do not know where to look on the face of the earth, as far south even as latitude thirty-nine degrees, for a race of people who would be worth having in Minnesota. We can dispense with the rusty Spaniard, the idle Italian, the stupid Turk; but we want all the middle, northwestern, and eastern states, and all the people of the islands and the continent of the north of Europe to know what advantages Minnesota offers to them.

We take it as an axiom, that individuals and states must be supplied with mainsprings. A man will last longer upon a treadwheel than rusting out in a dungeon. The hard-fisted Yankee, who wars through his lifetime with Nature, to win a little field among the ledges of New Hampshire, outlives two or three generations of "suckers," who settle down on the fertile bottoms of the Illinois, amid vast savannas of Indian corn. The Yankee is *never* satisfied while anybody in the world has a better house or better-educated children than his own. Whenever Nature pours profusion into the lap of man—when results come without exertion—man ceases effort, and his powers are no longer developed. This is the inevitable result, to individuals and to states. Nature spoils her children by enriching them. This result is the surest in a rich, southern soil, as the climate itself, as well as the profusion of Nature's supplies, invite to indolence and ease. The honey-bee, taken to the tropics, it is said, will provide stores for one winter; but, after that, is as improvident as a house-fly.

This is a condition of things not to be found in Minnesota. The length of the winter and the invigorating climate invite man to exercise. He seeks for it—has an appetite for it, as much as an Englishman has for roast-beef, or for a tramp with his gun. His powers are all right; he has a good boiler in him, and steam to work off.

The human family never has accomplished anything worthy of note, besides the erection of the pyramids, those milestones of ancient centuries, south of latitude forty north. The history of THE WORLD is written chiefly above that parallel. South of it existed slavery, in one or another form, always, to a great extent, in both ancient and modern times; and wherever Consumption contrives to place a saddle upon the back of Production, and ride, there will be want and wretchedness; for Nature has ordained it, for the true welfare of man, that every human being shall labor, in some honest and useful vocation.

But there are prejudices against our climate. Some insist upon it that we can not raise Indian corn. Show them prolific fields of it, as we now can hundreds, the naked ears glittering like gold in the mellow sunshine of autumn, and the ground beneath almost paved with yellow pumpkins, and yet they look incredulous, and shake their heads, and say: "It won't do. I was here last June, and your springs are too late. You can't make *cawn-crap y'here*, no how you can fix it, stranger!" These wise people have a theory that maize is adapted solely to the latitude they came from; and they are as stubborn in maintaining it as the geologists are in their theory that there can be no mineral coal north of the Illinois coal-beds; although it is actually found here, in various localities, ranging south from the Crow-Wing river as far as the mouth of the Blue-Earth, of the most admirable quality. If we could not raise Indian corn, we should remember that, with the exception of a part of Italy and Spain, all populous Europe subsists very well without it. But maize, I admit, is the cereal crop of America. I subscribe to all Mr. Clay's beautiful eulogium upon it; and perhaps the most valuable quality of this grain is its adaptation to *longitudes* rather than *latitudes*. There is not an Esquimaux Indian basking by his lakeside in the sunshine of his brief, hot summer, who can not raise and ripen one variety or another of maize. From the delta of the Mississippi to the remotest spring-branch that supplies Lake Itasca, the head of the river, this crop can be raised, and is raised and ripened every year. What folly, then, to contradict these palpable facts! The same reasoning applies to wheat; yet, in fact, we live too far south for sure crops of winter wheat. Those choice wheat-lands of Europe, on the shores of the Baltic, are far north of us. At Red river, many hundred miles north of St. Paul, they raise better wheat than ever goes into the markets of Milwaukee or Chicago. There is not a plant of any description, raised in Wisconsin, that does not ripen here. We have tomatoes here, abundant and ripe, in a garden which was not fenced until June. Last season we gathered cucumbers in November, which were planted very late, for pickles.

Our soil is generally productive; though much of it is sandy, it is a very productive soil—not as compared with the middle or eastern states, but as compared with Wisconsin and Illinois. There are fields here which the French have cultivated without manuring for twenty years, which produce good crops, barren as the soil may look to a "sucker" from the bottoms of Eel river or the Big Muddy. The farmers here, on the average, get larger crops per acre than we have ever seen raised in any other part of the west. We do not say that all Minnesota is fertile; but that it will compare favorably, in fertility, with any portion of the world.

Consider, then, our advantages in regard to health. No bilious fevers, no shaking with ague in the harvest-fields, no loss of crops by sickness. Is this nothing?

Of the extent and value of our home market for produce, it is needless to speak. In no other part of the West is there anything like an equal demand for agricultural products; to supply the Indian tribes on the Minnesota and Mississippi rivers; to supply the forts, and to supply the great and increasing business of the pineries, and the manufacture of lumber. Every farmer has a natural tariff to protect him, equal to the cost of shipping the same kinds of produce which he offers in market, from several hundred miles below, by steamboat; added to the insurance and the profits of the produce dealer, all which is more than fifty per cent. premium in his favor, over the farmer who lives down the river, and who has no such home market as ours at his door. Add to this the cheapness of choice lands in Minnesota, our freedom from the burden of a state government, and the moral, intelligent, and industrious character of our people, and the immigrant, if he is a man, and expects to live by exertion, will find more inducements to make his home in Minnesota, than in any of the bilious regions south of it.

There is a demand here for all kinds of farming, and especially for dairying and stock-farming. But in speaking of farmers particularly, I would not be understood to intimate that there is not abundant encouragement for other branches of industry. Where farmers can thrive, all other interests are safe.

Our market for all that can be raised in Minnesota, for years to come, will be ample, and *prices as high as can be obtained in any city of the West.* I can demonstrate this in few words. The non-producing classes among us comprise upward of forty thousand Indians, and some five thousand whites, the latter divided into traders, merchants, lumbermen, soldiers, mechanics, and manufacturers. If it be argued that the former will diminish with the advance of the settler, it can also be shown that the latter, from the very nature of our country—its inexhaustible water-power, and its interminable forests of pine—will increase in a corresponding ratio. The Indians and the soldiers must be fed by the general government. The supplies for this purpose are now drawn from the agricultural states below us. The trader, also, and the hardy forester that fells the tall pines, procure their flour and pork, and the grain that subsist their cattle, from Illinois, Iowa, and Wisconsin. This will not, it can not be the case when our own fertile acres are subdued by the plough. Look at our prices-current at this time, viz., April 10, 1853—before the arrival of the first boat from below with *our supplies*—flour, six dollars per barrel; oats, fifty-five and sixty cents per bushel; and potatoes, seventy cents. Butter twenty-five cents per pound, and eggs and poultry not to be had for love or money.

I want it distinctly understood, that our land is capable of producing all the crops that are raised in the central and western states. Fifty and even sixty bushels of oats are frequently produced from an acre of ground. Potatoes will yield, in a favorable season, three hundred bushels to the acre. No one competent to judge doubts the efficacy of Minnesota as a wheat-growing region, although this crop has not been thoroughly tested as yet. Our prairies are not large, as in Illinois and other states. Groves of timber are thickly interspersed over them, and refreshing springs of water, crystal lakes, and clear running streams, everywhere abound. If sheep husbandry or cattle rearing be the business you wish to engage in, this country is the place for you. The whole territory, prairie and woodland, is one immense natural pasture.

In view of all the facts we have stated, we can not place our finger upon the map of this great country at any point—California not excepted, with all its shining dust—that presents greater inducements to immigrants than Minnesota. Single men, as well as those with families, of industrious habits, will find employment. Farmers and mechanics that have energy and perseverance can not fail to succeed. A small amount of means will do to commence upon. A quarter section of land and a small outfit, with industry, will afford a competency. Mechanics of all kinds are in demand; their labor and wares will command a high price. All the products of the soil find a ready cash market, at prices that richly reward the farmer.

The projected line of railroad from New Orleans to the falls of St. Anthony will, when completed, bring us within one day's (twenty-four hours) travel of St. Louis, and within two days of New Orleans. A twelve hours' journey in the other direction, by railroad, will bring us to the richest mines on the shores of Lake Superior, and all this, without equalling the speed at present attained on some of the eastern roads. What, then, is to prevent this place becoming one of extensive manufactures? Our water-power is unlimited, and easy of improvement. The materials to be manufactured are near us; and the Mississippi is a great highway for the transportation. Even now, the cotton and wool of the south and west could be brought here and returned to the producers at much less expense than it could be brought to and from New England; but with such a line of railroad as is contemplated, we are brought into the immediate neighborhood of the mines of Lake Superior and the plantations of the south. And who shall say that the mineral of one, and the cotton of the other, will not soon be wrought in all the forms of art, at the falls of St. Anthony?

The proposed route from St. Louis lies through the valley of the Des Moines and Blue-Earth rivers, crossing the Minnesota river about sixty miles from its mouth. There is a natural grade through these valleys the whole distance, and there is no portion of the west more fertile than the lands along the whole line. There is probably no railroad in the world which passes through so rich an agricultural country for so long a distance. In addition to that, there are vast mines of fossil coal in the valley of the Des Moines, which such a road would render invaluable.

The greater part of the lands along this route is now owned by the United States. What a field of enterprise is here opened for the immigrant, and one, too, that multitudes are even now commencing to improve. A line of settlements is established along the valley of the Minnesota river, as far as the mouth of the Blue-Earth; and several towns and villages of considerable magnitude are already rising into importance. All this is done before the Indians are removed from the soil.

I have received from Alexis Bailly, who resides at Wabashaw, foot of Lake Pepin, on the Sioux or Minnesota side, a sample of the winter wheat raised on his farm last season; also specimens of the soil in which it grew, and of the subsoil. Mr. Bailly says in his note, which accompanies the package: "I will only say relative to the wheat, that it was seeded late in October last, and was in consequence of my absence this summer, a good deal neglected, and notwithstanding that, it yields above forty bushels per acre."

Mr. Bailly is one of the best-informed citizens of Minnesota, and having been largely engaged in the Indian trade, has resided many years in the territory. I place a very high estimate upon his opinion of the capacities of our soil and climate for agricultural pursuits. He does not doubt that Minnesota contains a large quantity of wheat-growing soil, which can not be surpassed for the profitable cultivation of that very valuable crop.

Every experiment made last year in the cultivation of winter wheat, has resulted in the most gratifying success. I have not been able to learn a single case of failure. This invaluable crop finds a genial soil and climate at the foot of Lake Pepin, on the St. Croix; in the immediate vicinity of St. Paul; and at Long prairie, north forty-six degrees. Minnesota, on both sides of the Mississippi, must therefore be noted on the agricultural map as a wheat-growing region, unsurpassed, in all probability unequalled, in the hitherto cultivated regions of the west. I say, unequalled, and firmly believe that experience will abundantly verify this opinion.

During the winter our soil is torpid, and a stranger to alternate thawing and freezing. During most winters it is covered with a thick mantle of snow, but there have been winters when there was little or no snow; but during such seasons there were no winter thaws, and, as a general fact, the soil was not subject to heaving on the breaking up of winter. The reason why most of our soil does not heave, is that it contains a due admixture of sand — the kind of soil that neither bakes nor heaves: there is no better.

The surface-soil in Mr. Bailly's wheat-field, as shown by the specimens, is a rich black loam, containing a large proportion of humus. The sub-soil is argillaceous — a friable yellow clay.

I should like to see some of our farmers attempt the experiment of raising sheep. It appears that sheep might be raised in this country with profit to the owner. Of course the farmer would want sheds to keep them in during the winter, for the warmer an animal is kept the less food it requires to sustain life. The fact that the ground is so long covered with snow during the winter, would of course make it more expensive to keep them during that period of the year, but I believe it could be done with profit to the farmer. At any rate, I want to see the experiment thoroughly tried before believing to the contrary. Every spring our butchers bring up a large number of sheep. Having just been sheared, they are generally the poorest-looking animals ever beheld; and it is almost enough to make one sick of mutton to look at them. But after they have run around town for a few weeks, picking off the short grass to be found in our streets, they become as fat as sheep generally get to be in any country. They could not be recognised as the same flock, unless one saw them every day, although they might have forty ear-marks.

Now is the time for the "sheep business" to be gone into in Minnesota with a certainty of success and profit. All the wool in the United States is being bought up in advance of the clip, at enormous prices. The rise is mainly effected by the gold discoveries in Australia, where the shepherds have deserted their flocks by hundreds and thousands, and gone to mining. The supply of the coarser wools used in English manufactures is thus cut off to a great extent; and the consequence must be a rise in the price of the staple throughout the commercial world.

In again referring to the subject of wheat-growing, I would say that the doubt that has heretofore existed relative to the adaptation of Minnesota soil and climate to the growth of winter wheat, can no longer exist, as the experience of the two last years has fully demonstrated that winter wheat is as certain and as profitable a crop in Minnesota as in New York or Pennsylvania. Corn is more certain and fully as profitable as in either of those states. The cultivation is no more expensive, the markets as convenient, the yield as abundant, the prices as good, and owing to the healthy climate, the life of the farmer is longer in Minnesota, than in any portion of the Union.

In concluding this interesting topic, and most valuable of all the interests of Minnesota, let me refer to the agricultural societies already formed, and in successful operation. These societies were chartered by act of legislature in Ramsey and Benton counties, in 1851 and 1852. The Benton county society met for the first time on the 16th December, 1852, at which session Capt. J. B. S. Todd, U. S. A., delivered an interesting address. Captain Todd, though occupied in the service of the United States, commanding the frontier post of Fort Ripley, deserves much credit for the personal attention he has paid to agriculture—proving himself a practical farmer indeed, by cultivating a large tract of land in Benton county, with the most gratifying success.

Captain Todd, referring, in his address, to the agricultural statistics of Benton county, gave the society the following facts:—

"Mr. J. Russell, residing at Sauk Rapids, has under cultivation one hundred and twenty acres. This is the second year of cultivation; forty-five acres were this season sown in spring wheat, and yielded one thousand bushels — being an average of twenty-two bushels per acre; forty-five acres were sown in oats, producing fifteen hundred bushels, averaging thirty-five bushels per acre; the remainder was planted with corn, winter-wheat, potatoes, turnips, and other articles necessary to a farmer for his own use. A part of the corn planted was the eight-rowed flint variety, and was successful. His main crop was the small Red Lake variety, planted the last of June. This was a failure, owing to the quality of seed, and the lateness of planting. Most of the corn that came ripened well; little attention was paid to it after planting. Last year the experiment of raising winter-wheat was not satisfactory, as was generally the case; and is to be attributed to the want of snow, so unusual with us. This year four or five acres have been sown, and thus far with every prospect of success — rutabagas yielding as high as twelve hundred bushels to the acre."

Twelve hundred bushels of turnips to the acre is a good crop, and worth talking about; but the other productions are worthy also of particular notice, as showing that the farm spoken of, although in its infancy, is capable of yielding a handsome income to the proprietor.

The following is given as a proof of what can be done in beef and pork, and other productions: —

"The farm of Mr. Gilman lies six miles north, and is an example of our timbered bottom lands, lying directly on the river, and for fertility of soil is not exceeded by any; it contains one hundred acres under cultivation. In 1850, there were fifty acres sown in oats, yielding two thousand five hundred bushels, averaging fifty bushels to the acre, and thirty-eight pounds to the bushel. Four hundred bushels were sold at fifty cents, and the remainder at an average of eighty-seven cents; twenty acres were grown in corn, yielding one thousand bushels, or fifty bushels per acre, and sold at one dollar per bushel. This year it has been mostly planted in corn. The seed was taken from last year's growth, cribbed in the usual manner, but from severe freezing, was so much injured as to require three plantings; that which ripened is considered as good as can be grown. The samples before the society speak for themselves; the remainder was fed to stock. Mr. Gilman has killed six thousand pounds of beef, and two thousand pounds of pork this fall, of his own raising and fattening. But a small quantity of oats were sown. Wheat has not been tried. The yield of buckwheat is as thirty to one. This farm was opened in 1850.

"The farm of Mr. John Depue lies eleven miles north of this, and is an admirable specimen of the prairie lands in the northern part of the county. It lies on the north bank of the Platt river, about two miles above its junction with the Mississippi, upon the second bench in the edge of a beautiful growth of oak, and extending into a prairie destined soon to become one of the most thickly-settled parts of the country. It now embraces one hundred and forty acres of cultivated land, was begun two years ago, and planted in corn, oats, potatoes, turnips, &c. It produced twelve hundred bushels of oats, sold at one dollar per bushel; two hundred bushels of corn which matured well, without special attention, for which two dollars per bushel was offered and refused; five hundred bushels of potatoes, and one thousand bushels of rutabagas—the surplus potatoes, over the demand for the farm, were sold at seventy-five cents—the rutabagas were fed to stock.

This year it produced eighteen hundred bushels of oats, now selling at the door for seventy-five cents, and two hundred and fifty bushels of spring-wheat of superior quality. The proprietor has fattened and killed his own pork and beef, and with commendable resolution, determines to do so in future, or go without. Winter-wheat was tried last year, but failed as a crop, under similar circumstances with that of Mr. Russell."

This society is a valuable institution, not only to Benton county but to the whole territory; for by the publication of its proceedings, rivalry is created among the farmers of other counties, and attention attracted in the states, and in foreign countries, to the ease and rapidity with which a husbandman can get rich in this inviting country; and renewed efforts will in consequence be made by those now engaged in agriculture, each county endeavoring to outstrip the other, and immigration will increase to such an extent as to exceed the anticipation of the most enthusiastic well-wisher of the territory."

These statistics of Capt. Todd referred to the year 1852, and the increase upon these facts within the past year, will be readily conceived by all.

I can not close this agricultural chapter without stating, that in another year, settlements can be made in our valleys without having Indians for neighbors. Thousands have been waiting for these very lands to be purchased and brought into market, who will be on the ground early to make settlements.

This territory has not so many small streams as New England, but immensely more beautiful lakes and level country. In many portions, too, there is not so much, nor so great a variety of timber; but we have fine prairies and natural meadows, and sufficient woodland for all necessary purposes. And we have one kind of wood here, which, though small, promises to be of much value; it is the *basket-willow.*

There is much said of late in agricultural and other papers about the immense profit of cultivating the *osier;* and it is also stated that five millions of dollars' worth of it is imported from France and Germany every year. Yet there is considerable of the best variety of this article growing wild in our immediate vicinity. This might be much improved by cultivation, and readily supply the place of the imported willow. We have a German here who has been familiar with the cultivation of it in his own country, and who has been busily engaged the past season in making most beautiful baskets from our native growth. He informs me that this is the best article of the kind he has ever seen; that it is tougher and stronger than the imported willow. It is not, of course, so straight and uniform in size as though it was cultivated, but this is easily remedied, and the cultivation of it will be commenced early the coming spring. It will not be at all strange if within five years the basket-willow should become an important article of export from this territory.

CHAPTER X.

FACILITIES FOR TRAVEL — RAILROADS THROUGH AND TOWARD MINNESOTA.

To those who think of coming to this territory, it is a matter of interest to know what are the facilities for travel, where are our markets, whence we obtain our merchandise, and where we are to send our products when we are so prosperous as to have a surplus. To these questions we will endeavor to give as concise an answer as possible. Our present line of communication with the east is by the way of Galena and Chicago. Those coming from the east can reach Chicago, either by a trip around the lakes, by the Michigan Central railroad, or Southern Michigan railroad; and a complete chain of railroad, around the south side of Lake Erie, from Chicago to New York, Boston, and almost any other place you please. From Chicago west, the railroad is already completed to Rockford, between eighty and ninety miles, and within another year will be completed to Dubuque or Galena — thus connecting the upper Mississippi with all the cities of the east. Another railroad is in progress from Milwaukee to Prairie La Crosse, a small but rapidly-growing town on the Mississippi river, nearly two hundred miles above Galena. This is being pushed forward with such enterprise, that it is expected to be completed in about one year. The eastern portion of it is already in operation, penetrating far into the interior of the state. Minnesota has already become attractive to the health and pleasure seekers of our eastern cities. But when these facilities for travel shall be fully realized, the falls of St. Anthony will rank with Saratoga, Newport, and the White mountains, as a place of summer resort. Much of our merchandise already comes from Boston and New York, notwithstanding it has to be carried near a hundred miles by wagons across Illinois. The amount will of course be increased with the ease and cheapness of transportation.

But there is another enterprise commenced, which promises even more for our territory than those I have mentioned. *It is a continuous line of railroad from New Orleans to the falls of St. Anthony!* running on the west side of the Mississippi river, through the best portions of Arkansas, Missouri, Iowa and Minnesota. The following extracts from the St. Louis News, of October 9, and from the Minnesota Democrat, of October 20, 1852, will give a more complete idea of the enterprise:—

"One of the greatest and grandest railroad improvements of the age is now engrossing the attention of a large number of the most enterprising capitalists in the west. A work of vast magnitude, which we supposed would not be contemplated for many years to come, is already in progress, and before six years expire we may be able to exchange, by railroad transportation, the staple products of the northwest for the fresh and ripe fruits of the tropics, and, measuring distance by time, St. Paul will be as near New Orleans as it now is to Galena. The enterprise is truly magnificent. That it is practicable no one acquainted with the subject can doubt. That it will be accomplished, is already assured by the intelligence we this day present to our readers. The wealthiest and most sagacious capitalists of St. Louis have embarked in the enterprise, with a far-seeing and patriotic determination to achieve success. Thousands of capitalists along the line of the proposed chain of roads will coöperate with zeal and liberality. New Orleans will embark in the work with enthusiastic energy, and before six months pass away the New Orleans and Minnesota Railroad will be hailed, throughout the west and south, as one of the greatest improvements of the age. As the St. Louis News remarks, in a strain of enthusiasm, which the subject naturally inspires: 'No grander scheme was ever projected for the promotion of man's empire over the very climates of the earth, and no enterprise has ever been unfolded that will take stronger hold upon the hearts and imaginations of men.

"A railroad from Minnesota to New Orleans, competing with the great Father of Waters throughout its course, and joining in close fellowship the six months' snows of Lake Superior with the perpetual summer of the gulf of Mexico! That is the latest project to which the extraordinary enterprise of the republic has given birth, and one which, in its gigantic proportions, is little likely to be paralleled. Mr. Whitney's scheme for uniting with iron bonds the waters of the two great oceans, exceeds it in immensity, but will bear no comparison with it in regard to feasibility. His route for the most part runs through arid wastes, now, and for generations to come, devoid both of necessities and facilities for an undertaking of the kind. The plan of which we speak is dissimilar to it in all respects save one. In proportion, the line from the extreme north to the far south yields the palm to the indomitable advocate of the Pacific line, but in every other particular it is immeasurably superior. It starts from a point just opening to civilization, it is true, but one that is manifestly destined to achieve an unexampled growth; and thence, running southward, it opens to market the broad prairies of Iowa, exacts tribute from the fertile soil of Missouri, and, having stopped for breath at the commercial emporium of the west, proceeds to traverse the gorgeous savannahs of Arkansas and the rich plantations of Louisiana, finally pouring its accumulated treasures into the lap of New Orleans. A route, in round figures, of some two thousand miles, already possessed of an enormous river traffic, and more or less settled at every important point.

"We are not dreaming dreams, or indulging in fancies at variance with facts. We record a project now occupying attention along both banks of the Mississippi, which has received the cordial approval of cool business men, and which will shortly be presented to the country in a plain business aspect. The merchants of St. Louis have taken the lead in its behalf, with a spirit that betokens early and good results. Their efforts must command the assistance of New Orleans, which is at length awakened to the necessity of land as well as water communication. Arkansas and Iowa are pledged by their action in other matters to a cordial coöperation, while the infant giant, Minnesota, enters into it with a spirit at once characteristic and hopeful.

"The project is pregnant with great considerations, political and commercial. It will unite climates unlike in their nature and products, and will give a common aim and interest to people differing widely in their circumstances and pursuits. It will form a new guaranty for the perpetuity of the Union, and will contribute more than legislation to smother sectional strife. It will secure to the extreme northwest its legitimate markets, and will more rapidly attract to it the capital and labor needed to develop its magnificent resources.

"In this grand work the people of St. Paul and St. Anthony have a common and united interest. When it shall have been completed, 'the sister cities' will be viewed as upper and lower towns of the same great metropolis, which will be to the northwest what New Orleans is to the south, and St. Louis to the centre—a railroad and commercial terminus, a grand centre of trade, and also, what neither of these points can ever become, the manufactory and workshop of the west.

"No portion of our flourishing country promises to enjoy a more brilliant destiny than Minnesota; and St. Paul and St. Anthony conjoined must become the commercial and manufacturing heart, not only of Minnesota, but of the vast domain surrounding it, stretching from Lake Superior to the Rocky mountains, and embracing the intervening area as far north as human enterprise can extend."

To some this may seem visionary; but on a careful examination of the facts in the case, I am confident that every intelligent man will agree with the editor of the St. Louis News, that "no grander scheme was ever projected," and that it is not only "possible," but "practicable," and "inevitable."

A railroad of one hundred miles, of easy and cheap construction, would connect the navigable waters of the Mississippi with the navigable waters of the Red river of the north. Another road of one hundred miles would wed the Mississippi to Lake

Superior. Already roads are in contemplation, which will unite Minnesota to the tide waters of the Atlantic and the gulf, bringing the best market to the door of the producer, and giving to our agriculturists, at all seasons of the year, the choice of an eastern or southern market.

A road is also projected from St. Paul to Green Bay. This will bring us within ten hours of Lake Michigan, and, as soon as the road from Toronto to Georgian bay is completed, within fifty-six hours of Toronto. In addition to the arguments usually urged in favor of grants of public land to railroad and other improvements, two particular reasons apply in this case, which should induce the federal government to aid the enterprise. The road would run through an unsettled and unsurveyed tract of country, and will open it to settlement. Few other roads are so situated. It will terminate in a territory of the United States, and will so expedite its settlement, as to shorten the period of its territorial existence, and relieve the federal treasury of the burden of its support. Hitherto railroads have been constructed, because the settlement and business of their respective localities were supposed to demand them. The experiment of building a road in order to settle a country and make a business, is yet to be tried. Mr. Whitney proposed such an experiment in his Pacific scheme; and if we reflect what the Erie canal and the railroad upon its banks have done for the settlement of the northwest, we have a significant hint of the efficacy of such means.

The editor of the *Minnesota Pioneer*, in speaking of this subject, says: "Among the important acts of the last legislature, may very properly be classed the various railroad charters passed during the session. We are aware that they are looked upon by many as chimerical, but we can not recognise *anything* as chimerical in the settlement of the great valley of the Mississippi. Our long residence in the West has enabled us to observe the rapid progress of civilization. The anticipations of the most sanguine have been so far surpassed, that we can not at this time concede the power of imagination to get beyond reality in western improvement, and western progress.

"We can look back a few short years, when the commerce of the Mississippi and Missouri was carried on by keel-boats, and we once made a quick trip from St. Louis to Minnesota in forty-one days. At that time the idea of navigating the Upper Mississippi with steamboats, above the foot of the lower rapids, would have been considered much more chimerical than would a project for throwing a suspension bridge across Behring's straits at the present day. We made a trip on horseback from the Mississippi to Chicago, and could get neither eggs nor pork to eat at any of the squatters' huts we stopped at. Now there is produce enough raised between the Mississippi and Illinois rivers to feed half of the starving population of Europe. We travelled in a stage (an open wagon) from Galena to Chicago when the trip was made in eight days, and when the *possibility* of staging on that route was by no means clear to the proprietors, and each passenger was obliged to walk and carry a rail to assist the team through the sloughs. Now a railroad is near completion which will travel over the same space in eight hours. We were at one time one of the only three white men residing within the limits of the present state of Iowa, which now has a population of over four hundred thousand. In our own beautiful territory we have made many trips between Prairie du Chien and Mendota, and from Mendota to Traverse des Sioux, when the hotels we lodged at were in the open air, and our table furnished from the supply we carried, or from the game killed on the route. Yet, with the blessing of God, we hope yet to travel in a railroad car, on a continuous route from the Minnesota river to New Orleans, and very *probably* to San Francisco.

"Each railroad charter granted at the late session, with one exception, is a connecting link in some great chain of road which is not only contemplated, but progressing south or east of us. Does any one doubt the completion, at an early day, of the Louisiana and Minnesota railroad? Does any one for a moment believe that the Illinois central railroad will rush up to the shore of the Mississippi opposite Dubuque, survey for a moment the vast expanse of country west of the Father of Waters, and then, affrighted, turn and seek again the shores of the Atlantic? No such thing; there is nothing in those beautiful prairies, fertile fields, or busy manufacturing towns, west of the Mississippi calculated to deter the 'iron horse.' Thousands are now living who will see him bound across the bridge which will be thrown over and high above the surface of the stream, and rush forward to the valley of the Minnesota, through the most lovely, healthy, and wealthy agricultural portions of the globe. After a momentary pause, to select the route, his progress is again onward, with caloric speed to the shore of that copper-bottomed inland sea, Superior, where he will neigh in concert with his brothers from the Atlantic in the east, and from Puget's sound in the great northwest.

"Does any one doubt the early completion of a railroad from the Mississippi to San Francisco? In a few years his doubts will be dispelled, and stern reality will show a revolution in the commerce of the world. Our teas, and all our Asiatic stuffs which we now receive by a tardy, dangerous, and expensive route through Europe and our Atlantic cities, will be brought direct from the Pacific, and supplies will reach the Atlantic by way of Minnesota.

"Those who may have doubts on the progress and early completion of these improvements, we ask to look back on the past. Examine the railroads now in operation in the eastern states, where the expense of constructing one mile of road will construct five miles over our flat prairies. If any one doubts the business being sufficient to support these roads, we would refer him to the debates in the New York legislature during the consideration of the charters for the road between Buffalo and Albany. The opponents of those charters based their arguments on the supposition that a railroad would destroy the business of the canal. But time has shown that the canal has not the capacity to do the business necessary, in addition to that done by the railroad. And while further privileges for transportation have been granted the railroads, the enlargement of the canal has been found necessary.

"Of the St. Paul and St. Anthony railroad we need say but little. Although isolated and alone, its early completion is just as certain as that the sun will rise to-morrow morning;

and the foolish rivalry between St. Paul and St. Anthony will then cease."

Eastern capitalists are now investing in this last enterprise, and the contractors are expected on to build the road the ensuing spring. It is more than probable that before this volume meets the reader's eye, the work will be surveyed and under full headway.

I desire to call the attention of capitalists abroad, and our neighbors at home, to the value, importance, and practicability of constructing, at an early day, a railroad from St. Paul to Fond du Lac or Lake Superior. We are informed by those acquainted with the topography of the country between the two points, that the route is a good one for the construction of a railroad.

The Lake Superior country is the greatest mining district in the world, and will support and soon contain a vast population engaged in that branch of industry. Its mineral wealth is inexhaustible, and its copper and iron ore the best that have yet been discovered. The copper ore of the famous mines of Cornwall, England, yield but about eight per cent. of pure metal—that of Lake Superior twenty per cent.

The iron of Lake Superior is preferred among the iron-workers at Pittsburgh to that of Sweden, and commands a higher price. Its remarkable malleability peculiarly adapts it for boiler iron and machinery. Messrs. Foster and Whitney, in their late geological report to the United States government, speaking of the iron of this district, say: "It is to this source that the great West will ultimately look for its supplies of the finer varieties of bar-iron and steel. The 'iron mountain' of Missouri becomes insignificant compared with these immense deposites. This region also contains extensive beds of marble, which will prove of much economical value for fluxing the ores and in yielding lime, while, with care, blocks for architectural and ornamental purposes can be obtained. Flesh-red is the prevailing tint with veins of a deeper hue. The novaculite slates are valuable, affording hones equal to the Turkey or Scotch stones."

A railroad from St. Paul a little more than one hundred

miles in length, will unite the lake and the Mississippi, and make the most important business point on the Mississippi above St. Louis. It would be the direct and travelled route from the Mississippi valley to Lake Superior, and open up to the farmers of Minnesota a valuable market for their surplus products. They have nothing to export now, but will, in a few years, have an abundance.

It can not be long before the canal around the falls of Ste. Marie will be constructed, and then with the proposed road, we will have a complete lake and railroad communication with all the commercial cities of the east. I hope to be able to present facts that will tend to convince all that have the prosperity of Minnesota at heart, as well as those who are seeking safe railroad investments for their capital, that we have not too soon called their attention to the proposed enterprise.

Argument is unnecessary to convince any person of common information, that the construction of this road is of immense importance to the prosperity of Minnesota in general, and St. Paul in particular. It is true that the road will not pay if immediately constructed, but now is the opportune moment—the very time to obtain the necessary grant of land from Congress. The sooner the better; and then all doubt about the construction of this vast improvement will be removed, and St. Paul will loom up on the map as a prospective city of the first magnitude.

Construct this road and the mineral of Lake Superior destined for the Mississippi valley, and gulf commerce, will pass through St. Paul, as well as a large proportion of the agricultural supplies, and southern products consumed on the lake. On the other side of the river, we have a country destined ere many years, to become the most flourishing agricultural region of the west, and this road will make St. Paul the dépôt of its products to supply the lakes, and for shipment east and to the North Atlantic. This road will bring St. Paul as near in cost of transportation to the eastern cities, as Galena will be with her railroad finished, which will insure the continuance at St. Paul of the great mercantile centre for the trade of the northwest. A large city will also grow up at the head of Lake Superior, which will be a benefit to St. Paul, because it will be the dépôt of the lake trade. The two cities will be partners and mutual aids in prosperity; and, making, at the same time, a monopoly and a division of the northwestern trade, they will sustain each other in its accumulation and possession. Their relative position and mutual interests will be the same as exists between Cincinnati and Cleveland, both of which cities have been vastly benefited by the iron road which unites their prosperity and destiny.

This improvement, as well as all others that will secure cheap and expeditious means of travel and transportation to and from the states, will increase the productive wealth of the territory and the happiness of its citizens generally, and very soon obviate the objection to Minnesota that it is too far away from the populous portions of the Union. Railroads will annihilate the formidable distance which separates us from our old homes and friends in the states; railroads will bring thousands and tens of thousands of people and millions of money to our territory, that would not otherwise come; railroads will save our people millions of dollars in the value of time and expenses of travel and transportation; railroads will increase our steamboat business, and secure to Minnesota the numerous advantages of an old country combined with those of a new.

If Congress could be induced to grant sufficient land for the construction of a railroad from St. Paul to Lake Superior, the following results would *immediately* follow: It would be universally conceded that St. Paul *must* become the great commercial city of the northwest for all time to come. The country on the east side of the Mississippi would be very soon taken up and occupied. Property on the east side of the river would enhance in value far beyond the most sanguine expectations of its present owners. No attempts would then be made to establish, on the Sioux side of the river, at Mendota or any other point, a commercial centre as a rival of St. Paul.

Now take up the map, and look at future results. There is Lake Superior, the shores of which are more valuable in copper and iron than any other portion of the globe; and will soon contain a dense population of persons engaged in mines and incidental pursuits, all of whom will be consumers of the products of agriculture and manufactures. Here, then, is another California, with California customers. The soil near the lake is inferior, but farther to the south and west are the fertile lands of Minnesota, destined to become the most valuable grain-growing region of the United States. The experiments made already in the cultivation of wheat in Minnesota fully justify this opinion.

Look at the map, and you will see that the mineral of Lake Superior may be transported to the gulf of Mexico, via the proposed road and the Mississippi river, cheaper than by any other route. The removal of the obstructions at the rapids will obviate every difficulty. The proposed road will therefore greatly increase the demand for steamboat transportation, not only in carrying down the mineral of the lake, but also in bringing back the products of the south which constitute a part of northern consumption.

The proposed road will open a new route to the east, via Lakes Superior and Huron, and by railroad thence to Toronto; thence across Lake Ontario, and by railroad to Boston, New York, and Philadelphia, where our future merchants will be sure to purchase nearly all their goods, except perhaps groceries. The same route will provide our future farmers with easy access to the eastern Atlantic markets.

One of the future resources of Lake Superior will be its immense and inexhaustible fisheries, the most valuable, all things considered, in the world. This branch of industry will employ, at some future day, a large amount of capital, and a numerous population, dependent upon some other region for most of their agricultural supplies. It will also furnish a large amount of business for the proposed road and steamboats on the river. Construct this road, and all the fish, copper, and iron, of Lake Superior, consumed in the Mississippi valley, and transported beyond the gulf via the southern ports, will naturally and of business necessity be reshipped at St. Paul.

Construct the proposed road, and St. Paul will be an important point, and, with St. Anthony's falls, a favorite resting-place for the thousands who in pursuit of pleasure or business will hereafter make the grand tour of North America.

The magnificent enterprise of the NORTH PACIFIC RAILROAD has been already commenced. Under the able and vigorous management of Governor Stevens, we may look for the successful completion of the survey for this route within a few months.

The general plan is to operate from St. Paul, the starting-point, toward the great bend of the Missouri river, and thence on the table-land between the tributaries of the Missouri and Saskatchawan, to some eligible pass in the Rocky mountains. The route will connect favorably with the waters of the Mississippi, Red river of the North, Missouri, and Columbia, the most important navigable streams of the United States.

The expedition started upon the great work, provided with everything essential to its success. The result will be of incalculable value to this country, and will open up a new and brilliant era for Minnesota.

One of the first objects to be accomplished is the opening of an immigrant route from St. Paul to the north Pacific, which will be done by next season.

The information gathered on the expedition will be presented to the country at the earliest possible time. The government has issued instructions that, after the completion of the field examinations, the expedition will rendezvous at some point in the territory of Washington, to prepare the usual reports, and send to Washington at the earliest practicable moment a summary of the principal events of the expedition, and a railroad report to be laid before Congress on or before the first of February, 1854.

The tide of immigration on the Pacific is flowing northward to the neighborhood of Puget's sound, a fine country, abounding in great natural resources. The capital of the new territory of Washington, Octavia, will no doubt be located in that vicinity, on a site which will become a commercial city of the first rank.

The distance from St. Paul to Puget's sound is only about fourteen hundred miles, and a direct route would pass over a rich country, affording an abundance of pasture for stock, and good water for man and beast. No deserts intervene, and there is no doubt but that the best passes through the Rocky mountains are to be found on this route. This is the opinion of scientific men engaged in the work of survey; and, relying upon other sources of information, there is sufficient reason to believe that such is the fact.

It is now the opinion of some of the best-informed men of the country, and which is entertained by several of the most able and influential United States senators, that the CENTRAL PACIFIC ROUTE, by way of the South pass, is impracticable. The country through which that route passes is generally unfit for cultivation; the altitude of the summit is greater, the snows deeper: that route, in brief, is out of the question. It is believed, however, that there is a route farther south, through Texas or New Mexico, and along the Gila to San Diego, or through Walker's pass to some point farther north.

The other route, upon which the public mind is becoming settled as the best road, is that now being explored by Major Stevens. It passes through a better country than any other named, and its eastern termination will strike the most populous and productive zone of the continent. That its completion will be witnessed in a few years we have no doubt. As the work progresses, population will keep in its advance, opening farms, building towns and villages, thus uniting the Atlantic and Pacific by one continuous chain of civilization. St. Paul being at the junction of the road and the navigable head-waters of the Mississippi, must become a great central entrepôt of trade and travel, and soon grow up into a commercial city of the first class.

If the route is found as favorable as is now believed, measures should be taken at the next session of Congress to provide protection by next season for emigrants who may desire to take that road to the Pacific. A cordon of military posts will be necessary to keep the Blackfeet Indians in check. This road (marked out by the exploring party, and protection extended to emigrants) will at once become the great route to the Pacific. In the spring and early summer, our levee, from the lower to the upper landing, would be lined with steamboats, and the town filled with voyageurs and their effects.

The progress of St. Paul, thus far, is without parallel in the infant growth of western towns; but, in view of the reasonable prospects, its growth for the next few years will be far more remarkable, and with this progress the whole territory will advance with equally rapid strides.

I regard this Pacific railroad project as the great enterprise of the age, in comparison with which all others, however important in a local point of view, sink into absolute insignificance. The day which will witness the junction of the Atlantic and Pacific coasts, by means of a perfect railroad communication, will be remembered as one on which the bonds of union between the extremes of our country were riveted for all time to come, and the commerce of the world secured to our own citizens.

From the knowledge we have, imperfect as it is, of the topography of the region to be traversed, we are justified in the conclusion that the northern route is far more favorable for railroad purposes than those hitherto proposed. The celebrated Kit Carson, in a lately-published letter, denies the practicability of any other of the southern routes than that through Walker's pass; and we know that even that is liable to objection, because of its winding and circuitous character, which will necessarily increase the length and the expense of railroad construction to an indefinite extent.

It is stated that Major Ogden, a chief factor of the Hudson's Bay Company, long resident on the Pacific slope, and whose occupation required him to become acquainted with the nature of the country between Puget's sound and the Cascade mountains, asserts that it is eminently favorable for the construction of a railroad. Old trappers, who have many times traversed it, corroborate his impressions. The passage of the Cascade and Rocky ranges will constitute the great obstacles to be overcome; but as the depression of these mountains is much greater in the high latitudes of forty-six and forty-seven degrees, it is reasonable to conclude that the passes are correspondingly more practicable than those farther south. Little is known of the country between these ranges; but the valley of the north fork of the Columbia extends through it, and will probably afford a line for a railway should all others present insurmountable difficulties. I know that from the base of the Rocky mountains, on this side, to the Mississippi, few obstructions will be met with, as a continuous and for the most part level prairie is to be found between those points.

The railroad across our territory to Puget's sound, and that from our northern boundary to the gulf of Mexico, once completed—and the latter may be regarded as a mere question of time—what bounds can be conceived to the prosperity of Minnesota? The very fact that such measures are proposed, and will sooner or later be perfected, must have a direct tendency to increase immigration to our territory. We have a fine climate, a soil rich in mineral and agricultural resources, and a profusion of good wood and pure water. The MEN only are needed to profit by a proper use of these advantages, and to add by their industry and enterprise to the general wealth. We are daily receiving additions to our numbers; and when it is known that Minnesota is to be made the great thoroughfare in the communication between the eastern and western confines of the Union, we may set it down as a fixed fact that immigration will flow in like a flood, and our fertile prairies and woodlands teem with the life and energy of a numerous but not redundant population.

At a railroad meeting held at St. Paul, on the 24th day of August, 1853, Dr. Otis Hoyt, of Hudson, Wisconsin, the enterprising president of the Northwestern railroad, addressed the meeting, giving a brief history of railroads and railroad projects in the United States. The railroad spirit had commenced in Massachusetts and rapidly spread in every direction, carrying with it wealth and prosperity. New York, looking with a jealous eye to the increasing wealth of Massachusetts, had, in the face of all the derision and contempt heaped upon the Erie canal, which was called "Clinton's Folly," "Clinton's Ditch," &c., caught the spirit, and thereby had herself become immensely wealthy.

The cost of the various railroads in New England and New

York, ranged from forty-three to sixty-three thousand dollars per mile, but are all paying large dividends, and the immense profits of many of the roads in New York was truly wonderful. In the old states, experience shows that if the business along the route of a proposed railroad will pay three fifths of the expense of constructing and operating it, the increase of business before the road could be completed, would be equal to the remaining two fifths.

The speaker had become well acquainted with the route of the proposed railroad from Madison to St. Paul, and from its feasibility believed the cost of construction could not be more than fifteen, or at most eighteen thousand dollars per mile. He had statistics (which he read) showing the business now done on the route, would pay more than fifteen per cent. on the cost of building and completing the road.

The estimates below are compiled from data as accurate as could be obtained, and are certainly less than the business actually done, and will bear no comparison with the amount which the road would do when constructed.

"WISCONSIN RIVER, LAST YEAR.

700 tons freight at $7.50 per ton	$5,250
1,000 passengers at $12	12,000
Total	$17,250

BLACK RIVER.

300 tons freight at $10 per ton, which is boated up from the Mississippi in flat boats	$3,000
500 passengers at $3	1,500
Total	$4,500

CHIPPEWA, MENOMINEE, AND EAU GALA, EAU CLAIRE.

800 tons freight, $13 per ton	$10,400
1,200 passengers at $3	3,600
Total	$14.000

ST. CROIX VALLEY.

Freight estimates taken from merchants and lumbermen	$28,400
Passengers at $4.40	19,050
Total	$47,450

ST. PAUL.

153 arrivals from Galena and below and as many departures, averaging 75 passengers each way at $4 per passage	$81,800
15,300 tons freight at $7.50 per ton	164,750
Total	$196,550
Grand total	$279,660

Allowing an increase of business of three fifths made by the existence of the railroad, which is a safe calculation in a new country with rich farming lands yet unoccupied, it would make $447,500.

Allowing also an increase of business of thirty per cent. per annum—which is far below the actual increase for the last four years without railroads—at the end of the next four years it would amount to the round sum of nine hundred and eighty-four thousand dollars per annum, or the interest of seven per cent. on fourteen millions of dollars.

Allowing that the cost of the road is four and a half millions, which is the gross estimated cost from Madison to St. Croix, and that only one half of the business is done by railroad, the stock will yield an income of eighteen and a quarter per cent. on the investment.

Furthermore, the increase in the value of lands on the line and about the large towns, will amount to more than enough to build five such railroads.

It is a well-known fact that the construction of railroads, even in the eastern states, has caused an increase of business on the line of the road between the commencement and completion of the road of about thirty per cent. The increase in the West has been much greater, and we believe that, owing to the peculiar and various resources of the district of country through which the road between Madison and St. Paul would pass, would justify an estimate of an increase of one hundred and fifty per cent. in the business that will naturally flow to that road, between the present and the period when the road will be completed, allowing the work to be hastened by the most energetic exertions for its completion.

The charter of the Northwestern railroad was granted by the legislature of Wisconsin, April 17, 1852, and the Western Minnesota charter was granted by the legislature of Minnesota, March 3, 1853. These roads are designed to connect on the St. Croix, and extend from Madison, in Wisconsin, by St. Paul and St. Anthony, to the western boundary of the territory, and ultimately to the Pacific.

It will be recollected that the line of this road will pass through and connect with the most valuable and extensive pine region in the northwest. It will also be borne in mind that the lumbering business is at this time being extensively increased in all the lumbering districts, preparatory to meeting the increased demand for lumber which must follow the construction of railroads to intersect the Mississippi.

The road contemplated, and which will doubtless be completed at an early day, from Galena through Iowa, to the Minnesota valley, with a branch to St. Paul, will, in connection with the Wisconsin Northwestern road, open our territory, to the markets, either in the south or east, in a manner to give Minnesota a decided business advantage.

CHAPTER XI.

STEAMBOAT AND RIVER TRADE, ETC.

PERHAPS the arrival of the first steamboat at Minnesota, was as important an epoch as any event since the discovery of that river by Jonathan Carver, or the wonderful advent of Hennepin, sixty years earlier at the falls of St. Anthony. It is difficult for us to imagine how civilization could have breasted the strong current of the Mississippi, in birch canoes; and it is very certain, that without the aid of steam, there would have been here no territorial government of Minnesota, no St. Paul, and but few to take an interest in the history of those early times in Minnesota.

The first steamboat that ever came up the Mississippi river to the mouth of the Minnesota river, was a stern-wheel boat named the Virginia, in May, 1823. It was a day long to be remembered. The Dakotas were then in full possession of both sides of the river. The Indians say they had dreamed the night before, of seeing some monster of the deep, which frightened them very much. As the boat approched the mouth of the river, they stood, in multitudes upon the shore, men, squaws, and papooses, gaping with astonishment to see the huge monster advancing against the current. They really thought it some enormous water-god, coughing and spouting water in every direction, and puffing out his hot breath. The peasants of Europe would not be worse frightened, if Mount Etna should get upon legs, and travel across the continent, belching forth fire and lava. The women and children fled for the woods, their hair streaming in the wind, while some of the warriors, retreating to a more respectful distance, stood their ground until the boat passed and landed. The boat being one of those awful high-pressure boats, which blow off steam with a noise like unbottling an earthquake, when she "blew out" shook with terror the knees of the stoutest braves; and in a twinkling, every red skin had vanished in the woods, screaming and shouting with all their might.

On the 17th of September, 1819, Col. Leavenworth, with some troops, first came up, and established a cantonment near Gamelle's, at the ferry on the west side of the Minnesota river. He next removed his quarters to camp Coldwater, a little way up the Mississippi, at the place where the two-story stone hotel now stands upon the prairie. In the winter of 1820 and 1821, soldiers were sent up to Rum river to get out pine lumber to build Fort Snelling. In the meantime, square timber was hewn, of hard wood, along up the shore and on the islands of the Mississippi, to make two block-houses, for immediate use, at the present site of the fort, which were so far completed as to be occupied by the troops in the winter of 1822 and 1823; after which the work of building the garrison was crowded on with much vigor. The labor of the building was done, nearly or quite all, by the soldiers. The fort, however, when completed, cost about ninety thousand dollars.

The following summary shows the least height of the thermometer, with the coldest days during the past seven years, together with the closing of the navigation, the first arrival in the spring, and the total number of arrivals yearly:—

In 1844, there were forty-one arrivals. Navigation closed November 24th. In 1845, forty-eight arrivals. The Minnesota and Mississippi closed November 24th and 26th. The coldest day of 1845–'6, was February 26th. Thermometer eighteen degrees below zero. In 1846, there were but twenty-four arrivals. The decrease was caused by low water. The rivers closed November 26th. The Minnesota opened again December 1st, and closed finally December 3d. Coldest day of the winter, January 27th; thermometer twenty-seven degrees below zero. In 1847, there were forty-seven arrivals. The Minnesota closed November 24th, and the Mississippi the 29th. Coldest day of the winter, January 9th; twenty-eight degrees below zero. In 1848, sixty-three arrivals. Rivers closed November 8th. The Minnesota opened again, but closed in a few days. Coldest day of the winter, February 18th; thirty-seven degrees below zero. In 1849, eighty-five arrivals. Rivers closed December 6th and 8th. Coldest day, December 30th; thirty-one degrees below zero. In 1850, one hundred and four arrivals. Rivers closed December 3d. Coldest day, January 30th, 1851; thermometer thirty-two and a half degrees below zero. In 1851, one hundred and nineteen arrivals. The Mississippi closed November 28th. In 1852, one hundred and seventy-one arrivals. The Mississippi closed November 18th.

The last boat arrival of 1851 was the Nominee; she left on the 20th of November. The last boat arrival of 1852 was the Black Hawk, Captain Lodwick; she left on the eve of 10th November.

The periods of the first arrivals in the spring are as follows, viz.: —

1844, April 6th, Otter, Captain Harris; 1845, April 1st, Otter, Captain Harris; 1846, March 31st, Lynx, Atchison; 1847, April 17th, Cora, Throckmorton; 1848, April 7th, Senator, Harris; 1849, April 10th, Dr. Franklin No. 2, Harris; Highland Mary No. 2, Atchison, and Senator, Smith, arrived same day. 1850, April 19th, Highland Mary No. 2, Atchison, and Nominee, Smith, arrived same day, crowded with passengers. 1851, April 4th, steamboat Nominee, Captain Smith, arrived at six A. M., with one hundred passengers. She left Galena March 31st, and arrived at Stillwater April 3d; was much retarded by high winds, &c. 1852, April 16th, Nominee, Captain Smith, and Excelsior, arrived the same day. 1853, April 11th, West Newton, Captain D. S. Harris. The Mississippi was clear of ice this year, at St. Paul, on the 1st of April. The steamboat Greek Slave, which wintered here for the first time, started upon the 4th of April for the Minnesota river. She returned upon the 9th, with one wheel-house carried off from contact with the trees. She went up as far as Mankato city, at the mouth of the Blue-Earth river. On the 10th, she started down to force a passage through Lake

Pepin, met the West Newton coming through, and returned in company with her on the 11th.

Average closing of the navigation, November 26th. The average spring arrivals of the above is the 8th of April. On an average, the boats cease running two weeks before the close of navigation here, and are detained below Lake Pepin the same time in the spring after the river opens at St. Paul; the navigation being interrupted from the 15th of November to the 8th of April—less than five months in all.

Above and below the lake, the river is only closed on an average of less than four months in the year, viz., from 26th November to 25th March.

The Mississippi closes unlike most streams. Its current being swift, the ice does not stay fixed for many days after the river is nearly covered with it. But the ice keeps pressing along, and, if the weather does not relax, the ice becomes more thickly set over the stream in patches; then the patches huddle and crowd, and climb and dive, till the hour of sealing their destiny fixes them for four and a half months *in statu*. So the river is left rough with the protruding edges of the flakes which were suddenly arrested in their rampant career.

The number of steamboat arrivals at St. Paul, in 1852, was one hundred and seventy-one. Of these, one hundred and thirty-one were from Galena, twenty-two from St. Louis, thirteen from the Minnesota river, three from the St. Croix, and one from Lake Pepin. There were seventeen different steamboats here that year; about double the number that has ever been here in any former year.

The Nominee made twenty-seven trips from Galena, including once that she only came to the Pig's Eye bar, and not including the trip in the spring that she only came up to the foot of Lake Pepin.

The Dr. Franklin made twenty-nine trips. This does not include the last trip she made, when she left her St. Paul freight at Point Douglas, and carried the mail back with her.

The Excelsior made nine trips from St. Louis.

The Tiger made nine trips—three from Galena, three from Mankato, two from the St. Croix, one from Lake Pepin.

The Franklin No. 2 made seven trips from St. Louis.

The Caleb Cope made five trips from Galena.

The St. Paul made eleven trips — seven from Galena, and four from St. Louis.

The West Newton made fifteen trips from Galena.

The Ben Campbell made eight trips from Galena.

The Black-Hawk made twenty-one trips — fourteen from Galena, three from Mankato, two from Babcock's, one from Traverse des Sioux, and one from the St. Croix.

The Jenny Lind made five trips — two from Galena, one from Babcock's, one from Traverse des Sioux, and one from Holmes'. She also made one trip to Point Douglas, which is not included in the above reckoning.

The Martha No. 2 made seven trips from Galena.

The Greek Slave made nine trips from Galena.

The Luella made four trips from Galena.

The Enterprise made two trips — one from Galena, one from Little Rapids on the Minnesota.

The Regulator and Geneva each made one trip from St. Louis.

From this it will be seen, that in 1852 there were fifty-two arrivals more than the year previous, notwithstanding the season was three weeks shorter, and an extreme low water for more than half the time. This is an increase of about forty-five per cent., and had the water been favorable for navigation, the season of 1852 would doubtless have showed an increase of over seventy per cent.

Another fact worthy of note is observable from an inspection of these statistics. It is this: while the number of arrivals from Galena has been increasing yearly, and has almost doubled since last year, the number from St. Louis has been rapidly diminishing. The account stands thus: In 1850 there were forty arrivals from St. Louis; in 1851, thirty-five; and in 1852 there were but twenty-two. The rapid decrease the latter year may in a measure be accounted for by the low water; but this does not explain it all. The fact is, Galena, with her fifteen or twenty steamboats, nearly monopolizes the carrying-trade between St. Louis and that city, and all points above; and although our trade with St. Louis has largely increased, yet the number of boats making trips from that city to St. Paul has diminished in as great a proportion; and we consider it very doubtful, supposing next season to be favorable to navigation, whether it will show much of an increase in the number of arrivals from St. Louis.

It seems impossible that Congress can overlook the immense national importance of making the navigation of the Mississippi unobstructed from St. Paul down to the gulf of Mexico. Why is it? Can it be because the states down the river are so ravenous for grants of public land, that the government is unwilling to give us an appropriation of money for the rapids, in addition to grants of land to the states, for fear of doing too much for the West? The West wants cheap communication more than lands; and the main artery more than little rivers. If we had a railroad from St. Paul to New Orleans, we should not rest quiet if it were obstructed at Rock island and Keokuk; but having a river, which is better, with only two obstructions in it, which might be removed for less money than the cost of a week's idle debate in Congress, we sleep over it, and let Congress sleep over it, for a quarter of a century, and continue to let our little steamboats crawl, and scratch, and scrabble over the rocky bottom of the river every year, carrying but a little goods at a time, and that in lighters. Make the navigation of this river what it ought to be, and our boats would double in size and capacity; insurances and freights, and the cost of pilotage, would soon fall one half. In every foot of lumber we raft, in every bushel of grain we ship, in every cup of coffee we drink, we are taxed, in consequence of the want of cheap navigation on this river. *The whole west, from Pembina to the gulf of Mexico, ought to light down upon Congress, and sting that stupid body, besiege it, harass it, beleaguer it, into immediate compliance with the demand of half a continent.*

The number of steamboat arrivals the present year will be upwards of three hundred—of course including those from the Minnesota river. The increase from forty-one to over three hundred, from 1844 to the present time, certainly speaks volumes of the future navigation, besides the prospective railroads yet to radiate to and from St. Paul. Six or seven steamboats have navigated the Minnesota river this season, each loaded with freight on every trip. One boat, the "Clarion," has paid for herself several times from her freight and passenger proceeds. It is no uncommon thing to see from six to ten boats lying at the St. Paul levee, all freighted.

CHAPTER XII.

THE INDIAN TRIBES — SIOUX, CHIPPEWAS, AND WINNEBAGOES.

* * * "Arts shall every wild explore,
Trace every wave, and culture every shore."

In Mr. Campbell's poem, "The Pleasures of Hope," we find this striking and very true prophecy; and, in Minnesota, before ten years shall have passed away, it will be well verified.

A treaty with the Sioux Indians has been consummated, and that their stay on the ceded land will be short, no one can doubt. A new home will then present scenes which will penetrate the heart of every family; while the pale faces, who occupy their new territory, will experience alike the usual pleasure and privation of frontier life.

The change which is soon to take place, reminds one of the sad reality and fatality which have befallen all the tribes of Indians in North America which have come in contact with the whites, and were of necessity compelled to sell their lands. Indeed there is no uncivilized shore on the face of the globe where the white man has trodden, but his controlling influence has been felt by the people who inhabited it. What, then, does the history of the past present of the Sioux? What, then, will the annals of the future reveal, of their wandering from region to region, of their poverty, of their vices and their degradation — outcasts and exiles from the home of their childhood?

About thirty years ago the Sacs and Foxes resided east of the Mississippi river, and their number was probably twice or thrice as great as at present. Their villages, their fields, and the unbroken forests, presented primitive life and primeval grandeur; but soon came the pale-faces among them, and the woodman's axe was heard to break the solitude of ages, and warn them of an impending fate. Their struggle against improvement was in vain. And where are they now? and what is their condition? They were removed west of the Mississippi, and

> "Where prowled the wolf, and where the hunter roved,
> Faith raised her altars to the God she loved."

Their homes, where old men had sung to youth the achievements which they had gained in strife, and where they had repelled the attacks of deadly foes, were changed into fields for harvest, and their songs and their chivalry thought of only as dreams of things that were. Again, after a few brief years, the white man claimed the home that had given birth to the youth of their nation; and since then they have been removed, until they have finally found a home — if such it can be called in this day of emigration — on the Missouri river, where they may linger out a few years of wretchedness.

The fate of the Sacs and Foxes is but what has followed other Indian tribes, and the Sioux must alike share a miserable destiny, and dwindle away, and, like many nations, once powerful, become extinct; and then a few centuries shall sweep by, and, as mouldered empires of the earth, the glory of their chivalry and power will be known but in history and song.

The Sioux number more than twenty-five thousand souls, and their territory extends from the ceded lands in Iowa and Missouri, to the territory belonging to the Assiniboins and other tribes, which divides their northern boundary from British America. Their limits extend southwestward across the Missouri, as near to the Rocky mountains as their roving bands, known as the Tetons, can follow their buffalo ranges. The Sioux of the plains, by far more populous bands than those who live nearer the Mississippi, are roving bands, and subsist by hunting the buffalo. As many as nine hundred lodges of them were encamped together on the plains last summer. These bands, although they are for the most part classed in several divisions, are really independent of each other. In fact, the individuals composing each band are nearly independent of each other. There is really no government, no delegated power or constitutional trust among them. If they have any government, it may be called democratic. A chief, except so far as he secures influence in the tribe by personal qualities independent of his office, can do nothing. As matter of form, rather than of fact, the bands constituting each division recognise the chief of some one of the bands as their head-chief in council. With slight difference of dialect, the Sioux all speak the same language. Their habits, customs, superstitions, are substantially the same. Some difference in the fashion of combing the hair, and in the style of dress, is observed in different bands. Our information of the western bands is comparatively little. For convenience, I will commence with a notice of the Sioux who inhabit the southeastern extremity of their territory, and follow with a notice, in order, of the bands that are found in our progress up the west bank of the Mississippi, the valley of the Minnesota, and thence westward, until we reach the wild Tetons, who occupy the western or annexation end, and extending indefinitely toward the Pacific ocean.

The first division is that of the Medawakantwan, or Spirit Lake Sioux, in the southeast. This division comprises seven bands or villages, which contain an aggregate of about twenty-two hundred souls. They sold their lands east of the Mississippi, in 1837, by treaty at Washington. They receive ten thousand dollars annually, and five thousand dollars more to be paid them by the direction of the president of the United States (who has never yet directed). Also for a period of twenty years after the date of the treaty, they receive twenty thousand dollars annually in goods, and five thousand dollars more in provisions.

The bands constituting this division are :—

1. Wabashaw band—chief, Wabashaw, who is also nominally head-chief of the division. Population three hundred.

2. Red-Wing band—chief, Waukoota. Population, three hundred.

3. Kaposia band (just below St. Paul)—chief, Little-Crow. Population, four hundred.

4. Black-Dog band—chief, Gray-Iron. Population, two hundred and fifty (five miles up the Minnesota river).

5. Lake Calhoun band—chief, Cloud-Man. Population, two hundred and fifty.

6. Good-Road's band—chief, Good-Road. Population, three hundred.

7. Six's band—chief, Shakopee. Population, four hundred and fifty.

The next division is that of the Wahpetonwans; composed of three bands, living on the waters of the Minnesota river, to wit:—

1. The Wahpetonwan band, numbering one hundred and fifty, at Little Rapids—chief, Plumstone, who is nominally head-chief also of this division.

2. The Lac-qui-Parle band, one hundred and twenty-five miles above Traverse des Sioux, on the Minnesota river, numbering four hundred—chief Big-Gun.

3. Big-Stone Lake band, fifty miles northwest of Lac-qui-Parle, numbering one hundred and fifty. These have no chief, being a branch of the Lac-qui-Parle band. Their head man is called The End. They are very shiftless.

The next division is that of the Sissetons, composed of three bands. No head-chief is acknowledged by this division.

1. The Traverse des Sioux band, numbering three hundred and fifty—chief, Red-Iron. (He is an industrious man, who is every day at work.)

2. Little-Rock band, numbering two hundred and fifty—chief, Sleepy Eyes.

3. Lac Traverse band, numbering three hundred and fifty. (This lake is the source of Red river of the North.) Chief, The Orphan.

There are other fractional bands of the Sissetons, also; among which are the Five Lodges, numbering about five hundred. They are about forty miles west of Lac-qui-Parle; chief, Red-Thunder. The germ of the Five Lodges was a

9*

family of murderers, it is said, who wandered away from the Sissetons many years ago, with the band of Cain, and constituted a little Nauvoo of their own, where rogues from other bands found refuge. They now number one hundred lodges; and have more vigor and more energy, if less docility and morality, than most other bands.

The next division is that of the Wahpekootays, numbering about three hundred; chief, Red-Legs. These people inhabit the fine region between the head-waters of the Blue Earth and Des Moines rivers. They constitute but one band.

The next division is that of the Yanktons of the Minnesota valley.

1. The Cut-Head band, numbering two hundred and fifty—chief, Waunahtaw, also head-chief of this division.

2. People-of-the-poles band—chief, uncertain. Number, one hundred.

3. The band-who-do-not-eat-buffalo-cows. Number, one hundred.

The next division is the Tetons; chief and population unknown. Their bands are—

1. The Ogolawla.

2. The Sioune; and probably some others.

The next division is that of the Yanktons of the Missouri, of whose chiefs and numbers I have no reliable information. These are the Sioux, who are called by Lewis and Clark, "The Big Devils."

The Rev. S. R. Riggs, a missionary long resident among the Dakotas, advocates strongly the "community system" among these Indians, and bases his ideas upon many important facts; and it is conceded the reverend gentleman is in the main correct. Indians have no regard for the laws of *meum* and *tuum*, and the only way to teach them this requisite is by a "community system," making the head of each family independent of the chiefs. The reverend gentleman, in an article published in the *Pioneer*, illustrates as follows:—

"Among people pursuing the hunter's life it is not strange that the principle of common property, to a certain extent, should be developed. In hunting the deer and buffalo it is generally found most advantageous on the whole to go in companies. This is especially true of the latter. The *tatanka* of the prairies go in large herds and are soon driven off, if chased constantly and without system. Hence the necessity, in the buffalo hunt, of the '*soldiers' lodge*,' which is an organization for regulating the time and manner of surrounding them. Several years ago, when buffalo were plenty in this region, the writer spent many sabbaths at the *Wahpetonwan* encampment on the *Pomme de terre*, and several times preached in the soldiers' lodge. A few extracts from memoranda made at that time, will convey some idea of the department of the interior in a Dakota camp.

"In their language, the soldiers' lodge is called *tiyotipi*. This *tiyotipi* is their legislative and judicial hall. No one goes to kill buffalo except when a chase is determined on by the soldiers in this lodge. If any one should dare to do so and thus drive away the buffalo, the soldiers would break his gun, cut up his blanket, &c.—that is, according to their language, 'soldiers kill' him.

"The tent is one of the largest and best in the encampment. Dry grass is spread around in the inside. The fire is the middle. Beyond the fire are two bunches of grass wrapped around and fastened to the ground by means of pins. On these two bunches of grass lie two pipe-stems, one blue, the common prairie color, and the other red, which is used only on special occasions. By the side of them is a pipe with an ordinary stem, which is commonly used. A little tobacco-board, and two or three sticks to clean the pipe with, form the complement of the smoking apparatus. Still beyond the pipe-stems lie two bundles of sticks, one of which is black, the other red. There are the soldiers, the evidences of their membership and the emblems of their authority. When the *tiyotipi* was organized *red sticks* were given to all such as had participated in killing enemies, and *black* ones to the younger men and boys. At the first meeting each one brought his stick; and these were collected and bound up in the two bundles. When the *tiyotipi* is dissolved, these sticks, they say, will be tied to a tree-top.

"Four of the real soldiers, or those represented by the red

sticks, are chosen as principal men in the lodge, whose place is immediately opposite the door. The side, to the right of the judges, is appropriated to chief soldiers, while the left is occupied by young men. A *cyanpaha*, or crier, and cook, are appointed, whose duty it is to be ever present in the lodge. All orders issue from the *tiyotipi.* The proclamations were made at this encampment by a man nearly blind, who has since been killed by the Chippewas. In the morning he stood out and publicly announced the name of a young man who was sent out to ascertain where the buffalo were. On his return he spoke to no man by the way, but proceeded to the soldiers' lodge, and after smoking with the red pipe-stem, whispered his message in the ear of the *cyanpaha,* who made proclamation of the same.

"When meat is plenty in the camp, there is no lack of it at the soldiers' lodge, although it is entirely dependent for its supplies on the free-will offerings of the women. But, then, every woman who brings a piece of meat has her name and the fact proclaimed throughout the camp. When they are out of wood at the *tiyotipi,* the crier stands out and makes known the fact, and every boy takes up an armful from his mother's wood-pile and hies away with it to the soldiers' lodge.

"When animals are hunted in this way, all engaged have of right some claim on what is killed. The laws regulating the distribution in these cases are set forth in the following extracts from a letter written some time since by *Waumdiokiya*:—

"In the buffalo-hunt, whoever kills one takes home the skin, half the breast, a hind-quarter, the ribs of one side, the tongue, the paunch and the fat thereof. These are his portion. He who comes up second takes half the breast, the ribs of one side, one hind-quarter, and the large entrails. These are his portion. The third who comes takes the head, the back-bone, the rump, both arms, and the small entrails. These are his portion.

"When one kills a deer, he takes home the skin, the rump, and both the hind-quarters. These are his portion. He who comes up next takes one side, one arm, the neck, head, and paunch. These are his portion. The third takes one arm, one side, the back-bone, the lights, and entrails. These are his portion.

"When one shoots a bear, he takes the skin, the heart, and the entrails. These are his portion. The man who comes up next after him takes the rump and both the hind-legs. These are his portion. The next one that comes takes one arm, one side, and the fat of one kidney. These are his portion. Whoever comes next takes one arm, and one kidney with the fat thereof. If there are many people, the remainder is divided into many portions."

These are the laws of division in the chase among the Dakotas. So well understood are they, that we seldom hear of difficulties occurring among the claimants. But the common-property system does not stop here. When a man has brought home his portion of meat, it immediately passes into the hands of his wife, or other principal female of the family. Sometimes it is all consecrated to making a feast. But if this is not the case, and all the families in the encampment are not so fortunate as to be supplied, the neighbor-women gather in, "beseeching and besieging" for a portion. And so it often happens that the skilful and industrious hunter and his family eat less of what he brings home than his more indolent neighbors. The skin, however, is his, to use or sell. But, on the whole, it must be acknowledged that the community system, so far as we have regarded it, solely in connection with hunting, although less productive of injurious results here than elsewhere, does still encourage idleness rather than industry. In the hunter's life it may be pleaded as a necessity, but this plea can not be made for it in other circumstances.

A Dakota boy is taught to shoot birds and squirrels, and whatever living animal crosses his pathway. They are common stock; they have no owners, and each one kills what he can. In this way he grows up with very loose ideas of the rights of property. If his uncle or his brother has two horses, and does not yield to his wishes in giving him one, it is no more difficult to shoot or stab the horse than to kill any other animal. The feeling that a man has a right to whatever he sees, and can lay his hands on, grows, in too many instances, with an Indian's growth. And this feeling is one of the outlines of the common-property system.

All Indians are excessively fond of their own amusements, and I append a description of a "round dance," at Traverse des Sioux, during the treaty of 1851:—

"The commission, and in fact our whole camp, was present, and perhaps one thousand Indians of the various bands. The theatre of this religious dance was a circular enclosure made up of the limbs of the aspen stuck in the ground, interwoven with four arched gateways, one toward each point of the compass, making an area about the size of a large circus.

"A pole was planted in the middle of the area, with an image cut out of bark, designed to represent the 'thunder-bird,' suspended by a string from its top. At each of the four arched gateways stood another pole and image of the same description, but smaller than the one in the centre. Near the foot of the central pole was a little arbor of aspen-bushes, in which sat an ugly-looking Indian, with his face blackened, and a wig of green grass on his head, who acted as sorcerer, and uttered incantations and prophecies with fervent unction, and beat the drum, and played on the Indian flute, and sang, by turns, to regulate the various evolutions of the dance.

"Before this arbor, at the foot of the central pole, were various mystical emblems: the image of a running buffalo, cut out of bark, with his legs stuck in the ground; also a pipe and a red stone shaped something like a head, with some colored shavings, moss, or other material, on the cranium, to represent hair. This red stone is said to represent the spirit of evil, to be appeased. At a signal given by the sorcerer, the young men sprang in through the gateways, and commenced a circular dance, in procession, around the sorcerer, who continued to sing and to beat his drum; and occasionally changed the order of dancing, or afforded the dancers a respite by blowing upon his flute. The dancing is the same sort of double-hop, or shaker-step, which we see in their medicine and scalp dances. After fifteen or twenty minutes of violent exercise, the dancers ran out of the ring, returning after a short respite.

"In the third set, a few horsemen, in very gay, fantastic

costume, accompanied the procession of dancers within the area, by riding around outside of the enclosure. In the fourth and last set, a multitude of boys and girls joined the band of dancers in the area, and many more horsemen joined the cavalcade that rode swift and more swiftly around the area, some dressed in blue-embroidered blankets, others in white; and every horseman, as he skilfully and swiftly rode, a subject for the painter, the music quickening and the excited performers flying like a whirlpool of fantastic men and horses—an exhibition so rare and strange, that in New York a "Welch" would make a fortune out of it in a month, as an equestrian show. Suddenly, at the end of the fourth act, several rifles were discharged at the poles upon which the thunder-birds were suspended, cutting them all instantly down; when the curtain fell, and all dispersed. So ended the round dance—the most imposing exhibition, probably, that is ever seen among the Sioux."

It would be useless to try to convey to the reader unaccustomed to savage life, an intelligible idea of the infernal noises and uncouth gestures of these red devils, when engaged in any of their dances. For a *scalp-dance*, at nightfall, they light their camp-fire, and with naked bodies painted, some jet black, others bright red, or buff, or striped in the most fantastic manner, form a circle round the fire, holding the scalp aloft, suspended in a hoop; and when they commence to leap and bound, set up the most unearthly yelping, whooping, and howling, twisting their bodies into every conceivable contortion! The squaws, too, becoming excited even to frenzy, howl worse than a pack of famished wolves, creating a pandemonium, as seen from a distance through the gloomy forest by the lurid glare of the camp-light, more shocking and spectre-like than the worst scene described by Danté in his "Inferno."

The *Medawakantwan* bands of Sioux or Dakotas receive annuities under the treaty of September, 1837, amounting to ten thousand dollars in money; and besides this annuity money they receive every year ten thousand dollars in goods, five thousand five hundred expended in the purchase of provisions for them; and eight thousand two hundred and fifty "in the purchase of medicines, agricultural implements, and stock, and for the support of a physician, farmers, and blacksmiths, and for other beneficial objects;" and all these sums to be expended annually for twenty years from the date of the treaty. A stipulation in the first article of this treaty provides that a "portion of the interest" on the whole sum invested, "not exceeding one third," being five thousand dollars annually, is "to be applied in such manner as the president may direct," has been the occasion of much evil. Thus far, no use has been made of the money, and it has accumulated from year to year until it amounts to more than fifty thousand dollars.

The seven bands of the Medawakantwan Sioux—the only branch of the Dakota family with whom we have heretofore had formal treaty stipulations—are scattered over a broad tract of country, extending from the village of Shakopee, twenty-five miles up the Minnesota river, to the village of Wabashaw, one hundred miles below its mouth, on the Mississippi. The Dakota or Sioux nation (*Dakota* is the name they prefer, and the original one, *Sioux* being given them by the French traders long since) is the most numerous perhaps of any Indians on the continent—numbering, the different tribes and bands, between twenty and thirty thousand. They are divided into numerous bands, and have separate interests in the lands they claim, but are united in a common language, intercourse, marriage, &c., and unite for common defence. At what time they came into the possession of the country can not, I think, be correctly ascertained. I have conversed with some of the most aged among them, say eighty years old, who were born in the vicinity of St. Paul, and have heard of no other place as the residence of their fathers. They have been and still are a warlike people, and their wars with the surrounding tribes have been numerous in former years, but now confined principally to the Chippewas, which can be dated back from time immemorial. Taking their country as a whole, it is a good country, and a portion of it not exceeded for farming purposes in any part of the Mississippi valley. The land is said not to be so good as you approach near the Missouri—prairies are large, with scarcity of timber, and too much sand.

With regard to minerals, I can not say much. The red pipestone is found in abundance on a stream that discharges itself into the Missouri. Many have seen this beautiful rock, and some blocks of it adorn our national monument.

That part of the nation that inhabit the plains, and over toward the Missouri, live mostly by the chase, raising only a small quantity of corn. Buffalo and furs are becoming scarce, and they will be compelled before long to adopt some other method of subsistence, or become extinct. That part of the nation who live in the vicinity of the Mississippi and lower Minnesota rivers have Indian farmers and annuities, which enable them to subsist without depending entirely upon the game.

With regard to civilization and Christianity, the Dakotas are behind many other tribes of our northwestern Indians, although they have had considerable advantages of missionaries and schools. It can not be said, I think, that they are inferior to other nations, or even the white race, in mental capacity. I have seen many children, and adults also, that, it appears to me, would be susceptible of the highest culture, and that Nature has been profuse in her gifts. There appears to be a want of effort, or motive, to stimulate them to action. The time must come when they will be incorporated with us as a people, living under our laws, adopting our habits, or disappear before the overwhelming wave of the Anglo-Saxon race.

The Chippewas, or as some write, the "Ojibways" are generally reported to be the most chivalric of their race, and are a nation of whose dialects, mythology, legends, and customs, we have the fullest accounts.

The sub-agency of this tribe was removed in July, 1850, from Lapointe, in Wisconsin, to Sandy Lake, in Minnesota territory.

The Chippewa or Ojibway nation of Indians, constitute about eight thousand, of which near four thousand five hundred reside in this territory; the balance in Wisconsin and Michigan.

They occupy both shores of Lake Superior; and the Ojibways, who live beyond the Assiniboins to the far northwest, and the Knisteneaux, or Krees, who dwell beyond them again, are all branches of the same great people.

A recent writer correctly describes them: "The Chippewas are small in person"—(This remark in regard to their size does not apply exactly to the woods Chippewas, west of the Mississippi)—" and of a quiet and meek aspect; they have an indomitable spirit, and a prowess that shrinks from no encounter; they are the Poles of the North, whose wont is to stand, without regard to odds, and fall every man on his track, rather than fly."

Migrating from the east late in the sixteenth or early in the seventeenth century, they first settled at the falls of St. Mary, from which point they gradually pressed westward; and eventually compelled the Dakota nation to abandon its ancient seat around the head waters of Mississippi, whose rice lakes and hunting-grounds the Chippewas at this day possess, and beyond to the Red river of the north.

In consideration of the cession by the two treaties of 1837 and 1842, the United States stipulated to pay them for twenty and twenty-five years, twenty-two thousand dollars in money; twenty-nine thousand five hundred dollars in goods; five thousand dollars in blacksmithing; one thousand two hundred dollars for carpenters; six thousand dollars for farmers, and an agricultural fund; four thousand five hundred dollars for provisions and tobacco; two thousand dollars for schools; and agreed to pay forty-five thousand dollars to the Chippewa half-breeds, and one hundred and forty-five thousand dollars in liquidation of their just debts. For those made by the treaty of 1847, they were paid down forty-five thousand dollars; and the Mississippi portion of them were allowed one thousand dollars annually, for forty-six years, to be paid in money, or to be applied toward the support of schools, or the employment of blacksmiths and laborers; and the Pillager band certain stipulated articles of goods, of the value of about three thousand six hundred dollars for five years.

The entire Chippewa tribe are divided into fifteen families, upon the totemic principle, to each of which are four subdivisions. Each family has a crest or symbol of some bird, fish, or animal, called, in their nomenclature, the totem; to the origin of each of which some legend attaches. The system is ancient, and dates as far back as their most unnatural and absurd traditions extend. Though divided by thousands of miles, and unconnected for generations, members of the same totem can not intermarry or cohabit with one another. The totem descends in the male line.

A work upon the Chippewas was prepared by the late W. W. Warren, himself a quarter-breed of this nation, and is now being published. Upon the Chippewas, I have thus necessarily been brief, and refer the curious to Mr. Warren's book for further information. The Chippewa country lies between the head of Lake Superior and the Red river of the north—from latitude forty-six to forty-nine degrees.

The Winnebago Agency is located about forty miles back from the Mississippi river, on Long Prairie river, about one hundred and forty miles north from St. Paul. Long Prairie is about sixteen miles long, and on an average one and a half miles wide, stretching from the northeast to the southeast; and from the high and central location of the agency buildings lying around it, presents a highly picturesque and agreeable view. This tribe numbers about two thousand five hundred souls. The first recorded treaty by the United States with this tribe was made in 1816. They were again included in a treaty made at Prairie du Chien in 1825, and at the same place, in the year 1829, another treaty was made with them, by which they received thirty thousand dollars in goods, and eighteen thousand dollars annuity for thirty years, and three thousand pounds of tobacco, and fifty barrels of salt annually for the same period. And again they treated in 1832, with an annuity of ten thousand dollars for twenty-seven years, with a stipulation to establish a boarding-school for them at Prairie du Chien, for the same period, at an annual cost of three thousand dollars, and three thousand seven hundred dollars more annually, for farmers, blacksmiths, physicians, &c. They also made a treaty at Washington in the year 1837, by which they sold all their lands east of the Mississippi. Under this latter treaty the government paid two hundred thousand dollars in liquidation of their debts; one hundred thousand dollars to their relations of mixed blood; expended seven thousand dollars for their removal west; gave them fifty thousand dollars in horses and goods, and paid for provisions, erecting a grist-mill, breaking and fencing ground, and incidental expenses, the sum of forty-three thousand dollars. It was also agreed to pay to them annually, for twenty-two years, ten thousand dollars in provisions, twenty thousand dollars in goods, twenty thousand dollars in money, and five thousand dollars to be devoted to education, agriculture, &c. They made a treaty at Washington city in 1846, by which they agreed to remove to the Upper Mississippi, and which they did in the year 1848. In this last treaty they disposed of all their interest or claim in any lands whatever, on condition that the United States should give to them "a tract of country north of the Minnesota, and west of the Mississippi river, of not less than eight hundred thousand acres, and pay them one hundred and ninety thousand dollars for the following purposes, to wit:—To liquidate their debts, for their removal and subsistence, for breaking up and fencing lands at their new home; and including ten thousand dollars of it for manual labor schools, and five thousand dollars for grist and saw mills. The balance, being eighty-five thousand dollars, is to remain in trust with the United States, at five per cent., for thirty years; and the interest thereon is to be paid to the tribe yearly.

The Winnebago schools are now under the direction of catholic missionaries.

It is a lamentable fact that the educated of this tribe are the most worthless, which clearly shows that they should first be taught to labor and acquire property; after which, they will see not only the use but the necessity of becoming educated.

It is to be hoped that they may yet become a civilized people. They raised last year on Long Prairie, the following quantities of produce:—

Corn	300 acres	12,000 bushels.
Potatoes	50 "	10,000 "
Wheat	10 "	300 "
Turnips	50 "	10,000 "
Oats	40 "	4,000 "
Garden vegetables	10 "	

On the Mississippi:—

Corn....	100 acres	2,000 bushels.
Potatoes......................	10 "	1,000 "
Turnips.......................	80 "	8,000 "

The crops at this agency are unusually good, and the Indians can not want for food. They have assisted in ploughing, planting, and harvesting. Those that have horses put up hay enough to keep them through the winter. I find that they are not only disposed but anxious to work; and many of them will do as much work in a day as a laboring man among the whites.

This year nothing of any consequence will be raised. The Indians have all left Long Prairie, through fear of the Chippewas—two of whom they lately murdered—and everything at the agency is going to destruction.

In August of the present year, a council was held between the Winnebagoes and Governor Gorman, by which the Winnebagoes exchanged their old lands at Long Prairie for a tract on Crow river, with the reservation of the right of way for the Pacific railroad, and to which tract they wish to remove forthwith. Much confliction of opinion exists among the people of Minnesota, relative to the exchange, and many of the white settlers are loud in expressing their dissatisfaction. However, it may turn out best for all parties, though it is doubtful whether the general government will ratify the exchange. The title of this Crow River tract was extinguished by the Sioux treaty of 1851, and this grant to the Winnebagoes completely vests these lands in another Indian title, to the exclusion of the original owners, the Dakotas. The treaty of 1851 was made at a large expense to the United States, at the urgent solicitations of white settlers, who were eager for the possession of good farming lands; but under the present Winnebago exchange, they are forbidden the Crow River country, said to be among the best for farming purposes. This matter is much mooted in St. Paul, and without expressing an opinion, I present the facts alone.

CHAPTER XIII.

THE SIOUX TREATY OF 1851—COUNTIES, COURTS, ROADS, ETC.

The following is the treaty of Traverse des Sioux, between the United States and the *See-see-toan* and *Wah-pay-toan* band of Sioux or Dakota Indians:—

"Articles of a treaty, made and concluded at Traverse des Sioux, upon the Minnesota river, in the territory of Minnesota, on the twenty-third day of July, eighteen hundred and fifty-one, between the United States of America, by Luke Lea, commissioner of Indian affairs, and Alexander Ramsey, governor and *ex-officio* superintendent of Indian affairs in said territory, *commissioners*, duly appointed for that purpose, and the See-see-toan and Wah-pay-toan bands of Dakota or Sioux Indians.

"Article 1. It is stipulated and solemnly agreed that the peace and friendship now so happily existing between the United States and the aforesaid bands of Indians shall be perpetual.

"Art. 2. The said See-see-toan and Wah-pay-toan bands of Dakota or Sioux Indians agree to cede, and do hereby cede, sell, and relinquish, to the United States, all their lands in the state of Iowa; and also all their lands in the territory of Minnesota, lying east of the following lines, to wit: Beginning at the junction of the Buffalo river with the Red river of the North; thence along the western bank of said Red river of the North to the mouth of the Sioux-Wood river; thence along the western bank of said Sioux-Wood river to Lake Traverse; thence along the western shore of said lake to the southern extremity thereof; thence in a direct line to the junction of Kampes-ka lake with the Tchan-kas-an-da-ta or Sioux river; thence along the western bank of said river to its point of intersection with the northern line of the state of Iowa, including all the islands in said rivers and lakes.

"ART. 3. In part consideration of the foregoing cession the United States do hereby set apart for the future occupancy and home of the Dakota Indians, parties to this treaty, to be held by them as Indian lands are held, all that tract of country on either side of the Minnesota river, from the western boundary of the lands herein ceded, east of the Tchay-tam-bay river on the north and to the Yellow Medicine river on the south side—to extend on each side a distance of not less than ten miles from the general course of said river: the boundaries of said tract to be marked out by as straight lines as practicable, whenever deemed expedient by the president, and in such a manner as he shall direct.

"ART. 4. In further and full consideration of said cession, the United States agree to pay to said Indians the sum of one million, six hundred and sixty-five thousand dollars ($1,665,000) at the several times, in the manner, and for the purposes, following, to wit:—

"1. To the chiefs of the said bands, to enable them to settle their affairs, and comply with their present just engagements; and in consideration of their removing themselves to the country set apart for them as above, which they agree to do within two years, or sooner if requested by the president, without further cost or expense to the United States; and in consideration of their subsisting themselves the first year after their removal, which they agree to do without further cost or expense on the part of the United States, the sum of two hundred and seventy-five thousand dollars ($275,000). *Provided*, That said sum shall be paid to the chiefs in such manner as they hereafter in open council shall request, and as soon after the removal of said Indians to the home set apart for them as the necessary appropriation therefor shall be made by Congress.

"2. To be laid out under the direction of the president for the establishment of manual-labor schools, the erection of mills, blacksmith-shops, opening farms, fencing and breaking land, and for such other beneficial objects as may be deemed most conducive to the prosperity and happiness of said Indians, thirty thousand dollars ($30,000).

"The balance of said sum of one million, six hundred and sixty-five thousand dollars ($1,665,000), to wit, one million, three hundred and sixty thousand dollars ($1,360,000), to remain in trust with the United States, and five per cent. interest thereon to be paid annually to said Indians for the period of fifty years, commencing the first day of July, eighteen hundred and fifty-two (1852), which shall be in full payment of said balance, principal and interest; the said payments to be applied under the direction of the president, as follows, to wit:

"3. For a general agricultural, improvement, and civilization fund, the sum of twelve thousand dollars ($12,000).

"4. For educational purposes, the sum of six thousand dollars ($6,000).

"5. For the purchase of goods and provisions, the sum of ten thousand dollars ($10,000).

"6. For money annuity, the sum of forty thousand dollars ($40,000).

"Art. 5. The laws of the United States prohibiting the introduction and sale of spirituous liquors in the Indian country, shall be in full force and effect throughout the territory hereby added, and lying in Minnesota, until otherwise directed by Congress, or the president of the United States.

"Art. 6. Rules and regulations to protect the rights of persons and property among the Indians, parties to this treaty, and adapted to their condition and wants, may be prescribed and enforced in such manner as the president or Congress of the United States from time to time shall direct.

"In testimony whereof, the said commissioners, Luke Lea and Alexander Ramsey, and the undersigned chiefs and headmen of the aforesaid See-see-toan and Wah-pay-toan bands of Dakota or Sioux Indians, have hereunto subscribed their names, and affixed their seals in duplicate, at Traverse des Sioux, territory of Minnesota, this twenty-third day of July, one thousand eight hundred and fifty-one.

"Signed by "L. Lea, [seal.]
"Alex. Ramsey, [seal.]"

Also by the principal chiefs and headmen of the See-see-toan and Wah-pay-toan bands.

"Signed in the presence of Thomas Foster, secretary; Nathaniel M'Lean, Indian agent."

The treaty with the lower bands of Sioux was signed at Mendota. Little Crow, who writes his own name, led off. These Indians receive for their lands an amount somewhat less than was paid for the lands of the upper bands. They will receive, after removal, two hundred and twenty thousand dollars to settle their obligations, remove and subsist them; and after that, cash annuities of thirty thousand dollars per annum, or three fourths as much as was stipulated in the treaty with the upper bands; and the same ratio, three fourths, as much of annuities that are not cash annuities, for fifty years.

There will have been paid out in all, at the expiration of the fifty years, a little less than three millions of dollars for the entire purchase. The Indians were paid in cash thirty thousand dollars, being part of the funds unpaid to them, and remaining due, as arrearages, by the terms of their treaty of 1837.

All the annuities guarantied in both treaties that have been made will be added together and paid out per capita to all of them together. These are the figures (nearly):—

The lower bands receive in all	$1,044,010
Of which there is to be paid down at their removal (within one year after the ratification)	220,000
The remaining $824,010 will be put at 5 per cent. interest for fifty years—the principal then to revert to the United States; this interest will yield to them annuities as follows, for fifty years:	
Cash	30,000
Civilization fund	12,000
Goods and clothing	10,000
Schools	6,000
Whole payment to lower bands	$1,044,010
" " upper bands	1,665.000
Total purchase-money	$2,709,010

To the people of Minnesota the most interesting political event that has occurred since the organization of the territory is the extinction, by the treaties of Traverse des Sioux and Mendota, of the Sioux title to immense tracts of land upon the western side of the Mississippi. These treaties bridge over the wide chasm which could alone obstruct the advance of Minnesota to the lofty destiny evidently reserved for her.

By the two former treaties, the Dakota Indians relinquish to the government their right of usufruct to all the country previously claimed by them east of the Sioux-Wood and Big-Sioux rivers, extending over four degrees of latitude and five of longitude, and covering a superficial extent of forty-five thousand square miles. This vast district Nature has marked out for exalted destinies.

Prior to the ratification of the Sioux treaties of 1851 there were but ten counties in the territory, viz.: Ramsey, Washington, Benton, Chisago, Wabashaw, Itasca, Hennepin, Dakota, Pembina, and Cass. Of this number, but five, viz., Ramsey, Washington, Benton, Chisago, and Pembina, were organized for judicial purposes. And in Pembina no court has yet been held. The judge assigned that district by the legislature of 1852 refused attendance. Of the above counties, five are situated on the west side of the Mississippi, in what was then Sioux country, and were attached to Ramsey, Washington, and Benton counties, for judicial purposes.

The most important local measure of the session of 1853 is the organization of counties west of the Mississippi. There are now eleven counties organized in the territory recently purchased from the Sioux Indians. Their names are—Pierce, Scott, Fillmore, Nicollet, Goodhue, Wabashaw, Le Sueur, Blue-Earth, Sibley, Dakota, and Hennepin. Pembina and Cass counties are also on the west side.

Since the consummation of the magnificent Sioux treaties, a new era has not only dawned, but come forth in full, refulgent light upon our territory. Eleven counties have been called into existence west of the Mississippi, where but a very few years ago there was not a regularly-established settlement, and where the savage was sole "monarch of all he surveyed."

When I consider that all those counties, now but sparsely settled, will, in a very few years, be filled with a population from the states east and south of us, and that without the organization of these counties no means would have been afforded for the establishment of common schools, the location and improvement of the highways, the establishment of ferries, or the enjoyment of judicial privileges, I am led to believe that the act organizing counties was one of the most important of the session.

It is a well-known fact that an American, with a small family of children, will forego many pecuniary advantages, rather than locate where he can not have access to a school; and I firmly believe that the character as well as the numerical strength of the population west of the Mississippi within the next year, will be very much affected by the passage of the law.

Immigrants may now locate in any portion of the territory with a knowledge that any settlement containing *five* families may be set off as a separate school district, and be entitled to receive from the county treasury a *pro rata* of all the school-tax collected in the county. County commissioners and other county officers are to be appointed by the executive immediately, that all the machinery of county governments may be put in operation during the summer, preparatory to the election of county officers next fall.

The following table shows the amount of taxable property in the old counties for 1851–'52 :—

Counties.	Taxable Prop. 1851.	Taxable Prop. 1852.	Terr'l. Tax, 1851.	Terr'l Tax, 1852.
Ramsey	$782,113	$1,060,820	$782 11	$1,060 82
Benton	64,775	103,170	64 78	103 17
Washington	335,172	343,760	335 17	343 76
Chisago	new co.	46,890		46 89
Hennepin	new co.	43,525		43 53
Totals	$1,182,060	$1,598,165	$1,182 06	$1,598 17

It is estimated that the amount of warrants issued in 1852 will not exceed in sum $885, leaving in the treasury a considerable surplus, if we consider the uncollected taxes as assets.

THE COURTS.

On the 19th of March, 1849, President Taylor appointed the following-named persons judges of the supreme court of the United States for this territory, to wit:—

Aaron Goodrich, of Tennessee, chief-justice;

David Cooper, of Pennsylvania, } Associate justices.
Bradley B. Meeker, of Kentucky, }

On Sunday, 27th May, 1849, Governor Alexander Ramsey reached St. Paul, and on the 1st day of June, he proclaimed the organization of this territory, recognised its officers, and required obedience to its laws.

On the 11th June, 1849, the governor issued his second proclamation, dividing the territory into three judical districts, as follows:—

The county of St. Croix constituted the first district, the seat of justice at Stillwater; the first court to be held on the second Monday in August, 1849. The seat of justice for the second district was at the Falls of St. Anthony; the first court to be held on the third Monday in August. The seat of justice for the third district was at Mendota; the first court to be held on the fourth Monday in August.

The chief-justice was assigned to hold the courts in the first district, which duty he performed in accordance with the governor's proclamation. This was the first court held in this territory; it remained in session six days. Judge Meeker was assigned to hold the courts in the second district, which duty he performed; there was no cause pending in this court. Judge Cooper was assigned to hold the courts in the third district, which duty was performed by him. No cause pending in this court.

There was at this period fifteen lawyers in the territory.

Up to this time we have had three trials for murder. The accused was in one case acquitted by the jury, and in another found guilty of manslaughter, and imprisoned in Fort Snelling for a period of one year.

A Sioux Indian was tried in the November term, 1852, before the chief-justice of the territory, for shooting and killing a white woman, and notwithstanding able efforts made to clear him by his legal advisers (J. J. Noah, and D. A. Seccombe, Esqs.), he was convicted and sentenced to be executed. His counsellors, however, filed a bill of exceptions, upon which the final issue now hangs. Meanwhile the Indian has been confined in jail.

The first term of the supreme court for this territory was held at the American house, in the town of St. Paul, on Monday, the 14th January, 1850, Judges Goodrich and Cooper being present. There are at this time two courthouses in the territory — one at St. Paul, the other at Stillwater. Two terms of the supreme court are held at the capital each year, commencing on the last Monday of February, and the first Monday of September. Such other special terms are held as the judges may deem necessary, and shall from time to time order.

In accordance with a law passed at the last session of the legislative assembly, the terms of the district court of the territory are held at the times and places following :—

In the county of Ramsey, on the third Monday of April, and the third Monday of October; in the county of Washington, on the first Monday of April, and on the first Monday of October; in the county of Chisago, on the first Monday of June; in the county of Benton, on the second Monday of June, and second Monday of December; in the county of Hennepin, on the first Monday of April, and the first Monday of September; in the county of Dakota, on the second Monday of September; in the county of Scott, on the third Monday of September; in the county of Le Sueur, on the fourth Monday of September; in the county of Blue-Earth, on the first Monday of October; in the county of Nicollet, on the second Monday of October; in the county of Wabashaw, on the second Monday in June; in the county of Fillmore, on the fourth Monday of June.

The counties of Ramsey, Washington and Chisago, constitute the first judicial district, and the Hon. Wm. H. Welch is district judge thereof.

The counties west of the Mississippi river, except the counties of Pembina and Cass, constitute the second judicial district, and the Hon. A. G. Chatfield is district judge thereof.

And the counties of Benton, Cass, and Pembina, constitute the third judicial district, and the Hon. Moses Sherburne is district judge thereof.

Either of the district judges are authorized and empowered to hold any of the district courts assigned to any of the other district judges, or any of the special terms appointed to be held, not within his own district, or any of the chamber duties within each district, at the request of the district judge to whom such district is assigned.

For judicial and other purposes, to enforce civil rights and criminal justice, the county of Itasca is attached to and made a part of Chisago; the counties of Cass and Pembina are attached to Benton; the county of Sibley is attached to Hennepin; the county of Pierce is attached to Nicollet; the county of Rice is attached to Dakota; and the county of Goodhue is attached to the county of Wabashaw.

GOVERNMENT ROADS.

The policy which has been pursued in the application of the several appropriations made for the construction of roads in Minnesota, by act of Congress, of July 18, 1850, has been—firstly, to make the surveys, and prepare maps and estimates, for the use of the department at Washington having control of the appropriation; secondly, to apply the unexpended balances to the construction, as far as possible, of the roads.

The surveys of the several roads have been completed, with the exception of the contemplated one from Mendota to the mouth of the Big Sioux river.

An appropriation of ten thousand dollars has been made for the purpose, and the road is now being surveyed, from the mouth of the Big Sioux, on the upper Missouri, to a point at the mouth of the Minnesota river, opposite Fort Snelling. They are ordered to report upon its adaptability for railway purposes, it being contemplated to make this the northerly branch of the Pacific railway.

This country is unexplored, the surveys of government lands being four hundred miles east of the Sioux river. It will pass through the country lately acquired from the Sioux Indians, who still roam the "Traverse des Sioux" unmolested, but this progressive age will not permit those fertile tracts to remain in undisputed possession of either Indians or buffalo. The party consists of Captain Reno, of the United States army, chief; Captain Tilton, late chief-engineer of railroads in Indiana, chief-engineer; Mr. Cross, formerly of the army, assistant-engineer; and twenty men, principally of the fur companies of St. Louis, to be furnished with Colt's pistols and the patent rifle. Captain Tilton, chief-engineer, is intrusted with the duty of making a report upon the practicability of this country for railway purposes. The result of the labors of the party will be placed before the department, in accordance with a resolution of Congress last winter, making an appropriation of one hundred and fifty thousand dollars, for surveys and explorations connected with the Pacific railroad and its branches.

The road from Wabashaw to Mendota has been surveyed, and a portion of the road, with a number of bridges along Lake Pepin, are now under contract, and are to be completed as soon as practicable.

The road from Point Douglas to Fort Ripley has been rendered available at all seasons of the year; and bridges, with suitable approaches, have been built over Coon creek, Elk river, and Rock creek. This road is a military and commercial thoroughfare, by which the Chippewa and Winnebago Indians, the troops at Fort Ripley, and the traders at Pembina and Selkirk receive their supplies. Thirty miles of this road are also under contract.

The road from the Mississippi river to Long Prairie, heretofore almost impassable in seasons of high water, has been much improved; and bridges have been built at the two crossings of Swan river. Nine miles of this road are now completed.

Twenty-four miles of the Point Douglas and St. Louis river road have been constructed, opening, from Stillwater northward for that distance, a good highway. The extension of this road is required to bring into market the extensive and richly-wooded, but inaccessible region, lying north of the Marine mills, and open to settlement and the enterprise of our lumbermen, tracts of valuable land, now lying waste for want of means of communication with them. Nineteen miles of this road are under contract, and will be finished this season. This will complete it from Stillwater to the vicinity of Sunrise river. Forty thousand dollars have been appropriated on this road alone.

CHAPTER XIV.

MISCELLANEOUS MATTERS.

Every good thing has its alloy. The perpetual summer of the tropics produces inactivity in man, as well as a superabundance of spontaneous fruits to supply his wants. The herdsman upon the pampas of South America, with his innumerable cattle that are reared without the expense of feeding or shelter, with all his apparent resources of wealth, is poor—but little better than a savage. The farmer upon the American bottoms, who turns over his hundred acres of black furrows in one field, which presently becomes as it were a young forest of green maize, waving and rustling in the sultry breezes of August, as he sits in the open space between his two log cabins, at noonday, feeble and enervated, and his little pale children, shaking with ague, gather around him, and he listens to the shrill cry of the locust—and sees far off upon the Mississippi river, the steamboat—even the steamboat—hot, panting, exhausted, smiting the sluggish waters with feeble strokes; his very heart sinks within him—and he sighs for the cool, bracing mountain air, or the stimulating sea-breeze and the sparkling spring water; and would exchange all his corn-fields and his acres for a garden among the sterile rocks of the north, with its rigors, its snow-banks, and its little painted schoolhouses. So California has its alloy! ah, much more alloy than gold. It may be considered an axiom, that the richest lands are not found in the most healthful climates. Nature delights in making an equitable average in the distribution of her favors; although her equivalents at first thought may not all seem quite fair.

What shall it profit a man to choose lands, watered by creeks full of fever and ague, and horn-pouts and lily-pads, producing one hundred bushels of corn to the acre, and worth twenty cents per bushel, rather than lands watered by trout brooks and mossy springs, producing only fifty bushels of corn per acre, worth seventy-five cents per bushel?

Settlers, what do you want? Will it satisfy you to get land, as good as there is in New York or New England, where the climate is even better, and the market all you please to ask? Such lands you can find. We have warm, sandy loams, rich argillaceous soils, clay lands, precisely like the barrens of Michigan, all—all productive lands, far better than they look—and, in fact, such as will soon make an industrious farmer rich. Or will you be satisfied with nothing but the flat, unctuous prairies of Illinois, extending in unbroken plains, and watered by stagnant creeks? If so, in God's name go there and settle, and when the great blazing sun sets, and leaves you there upon the chill naked prairie, your children sick and uneducated, and without one hope or aspiration rising above the dead level that surrounds you there, remember—remember that these things have been told you.

This immense region is bountifully watered by the Mississippi, Minnesota, and Missouri rivers, and the Red river of the north, and their numerous tributary streams, which traverse it in every part. At a point about seventy or eighty miles above the falls of St. Anthony, west of the Mississippi, commences a large and remarkable forest, which extends to the southward, nearly at a right angle, across the Minnesota river, to the branches of the Mankato or Blue-Earth river. This vast body of woodland is more than one hundred and twenty miles in length, and from fifteen to forty in breadth. Many beautiful lakes of limpid water are found within its limits, which are the resort of myriads of wild fowl, including swans, geese, and ducks. These dense thickets along its border afford places of concealment for the deer, which are killed in great numbers by the Indians. The numerous groves of hard maple afford to the latter, at the proper season, the means of making sugar, while the large cotton-woods and butternuts are converted by them into canoes, for the transportation of themselves and their families along the water-courses and lakes. At the approach of winter, the bands of Dakotas or Sioux, save those who rely exclusively upon buffalo for subsistence, seek the deepest recesses of the forest to hunt the bear, the deer, and smaller fur-bearing animals, among which may be enumerated the raccoon, the fisher, and the marten. In this beautiful country are to be found all the requisites to sustain a dense population. The soil is of great fertility and unknown depth, covered as it is with the mould of a thousand years. The Indian is here in his forest home, hitherto secure from the intrusion of the pale faces; but the advancing tide of civilization warns him, that the time has arrived when he must yield up the title to this fair domain, and seek another and a strange dwelling-place.

Minnesota now occupies no unenviable position. The government granted us, secures us all in the full possession of privileges almost if not fully equal to those enjoyed by the people of the states. With a legislative council elected from among our own citizens, our own judicial tribunals, with ample provision for defraying the expenses of the territorial government, and with the right of representation in the halls of Congress, surely we can have no cause of complaint so far as our political situation is concerned. It is for ourselves, by a wise, careful, and practical legislation, and by the improving the advantages we possess, to keep inviolate the public faith, and to hasten the time when the star of Minnesota, which now but twinkles in the political firmament, shall shine brilliantly in the constellation of our confederated states.

As a territory, but yesterday without a name, or political existence, our growth has been of the most satisfactory character. Health has prevailed within our borders. Our new soil has not failed to respond gratefully to the labors of the husbandman; and already in places, our prairies, scarcely abandoned by the disappearing buffalo, are assuming a robe of cultivated verdure. The enterprise of our hardy lumbermen has met with a liberal return; and there has been a rapid augmentation of this important element of wealth, and rich source of revenue, so invaluable to ourselves, as well as to the country on the great river to the south of us.

In the eyes of the world, Minnesota is a peculiar country It is to their view elevated morally as well as physically above the horizon of other new countries, as it were in an illusion of *mirage.* The world regards it not as the Eldorado of gold, but of a happy home for cultivated man.

Emigration to the West has heretofore been nauseously associated with the idea of low latitudes, the miasms of flat lands, and consequent disease and heart-sickening disappointments. It has, too, been associated with back-woods institutions—lynch law, the bowie-knife, uncertain means of education, and a gospel ministry on horseback. Minnesota presents another picture, and is truly a phenomenon in the eyes of the migrating world. It occupies a high latitude, has a quickly-drained surface, and is the inviting home of intelligence, enterprise, good laws, schools, and churches.

In a moral view especially, the world anticipates much for Minnesota. For a people, like trees, are exponents of the soil on which they subsist and the atmosphere they breathe. The observation of the world has made this an axiom—like country, like people. Considering then our location upon the earth, is it not evident that our territory is not only a peculiar land, but that it is to be the home of a peculiar people? We who are here, migrated with that idea before us, and we are still guided by it. That portion of the emigrating class who entertain the same idea, will of course come here too.

California is a phenomenon too, but she addresses her claims to another and a different class of people from those who appreciate Minnesota; besides, she is not materially unlike the other Spanish provinces which have in earlier times been famed for gold alone. But our territory addresses itself to a wiser and a better class than the mere seekers of gold. It addresses itself to that class who value a good home for a man, a land of moderate affluence, law and order, intelligence and virtue. If its destiny is to be the best home for that large class of people toward the rising sun, who seek a new home, does it not behoove us to see that this destiny is well carried out. The pilgrims at Plymouth did their duty to their posterity, and that people have been prospered. William Penn and his followers did their duty, and their posterity have been prospered.

The present population of Minnesota are responsible for her future prosperity. It is for us to lay the foundations of good institutions or of those planted in error which in time will fall.

Let generous and good men be sustained in their philanthropic purposes, but let individuals who seek personal aggrandizement at the expense of law and order be rebuked.

Minnesota is destined to assume a high rank among the states the Union. The high-toned character of the population, so different from that usually found upon the frontier—their obedience to law—the zeal manifested in the cause of education, the disposition universally shown to make every sacrifice to place the prosperity of the territory upon a sure basis—the aversion felt to all schemes which may in any wise entail embarrassment or debt upon the future state, and the general anxiety to maintain the character of the territory unblemished, afford a sure guaranty of the moral principles by which the people will always be guided, and upon which their government will be conducted. The munificent grants of land made by Congress for the university and for the maintenance of common schools, will be husbanded with great care, so that the benefits of education may be extended to every one who is desirous to avail himself of such privileges. The population of the territory has more than quadrupled since the census of 1850, and it is morally certain that there will be an addition to it of thirty thousand souls in the lapse of another year. The immigration to Minnesota is composed of men who come with the well-founded assurance that, in a land where Nature has lavished her choicest gifts—where sickness has no dwelling-place—where the dreaded cholera has claimed no victims—their toil will be amply rewarded, while their persons and property are fully protected by the broad shield of law. The sun shines not upon a fairer region—one more desirable as a home for the mechanic, the farmer and the laborer, or where their industry will be more surely requited—than Minnesota territory.

We shall raise cattle for those states where they can not do it so well. Our beef and horses will be as much more valuable than the same products of the states below us, as are the agricultural products of New England superior in quality to those of the general west. Our meats will have a higher flavor, and our horses more activity. We shall grow wool to great advantage, all the way to Pembina, five thousand miles north. We shall grow flax, and prepare it for the eastern market at our numerous places for water power. We shall export potatoes, a source of income which of itself would sustain us, as it now nearly sustains Nova Scotia. But I believe that our chiefest reliance as an article of export, will be our manufactured lumber. We have facilities for this branch of business that can scarcely be found elsewhere. All the states on the Mississippi, two thousand miles to its mouth, and the West Indies and Mexico, would be our natural markets for this production. No section of the world could compete with us. The pine may here be converted, and principally by machinery, into a thousand forms—from a meetinghouse to a noggin. St. Anthony will delight to fill orders.

In the order of things it can not be but the mines on our lake shore will be the foundation for wealthy towns, the lake itself the field of the most important fisheries, and as a consequence, there will be avenues of trade opened between the head of southern and northern navigation. The capital of distant cities emulous for this trade will be invested in these works. Labor will flow in at the call of capital, and population will increase in ratio with the profits of such investments. There are a hundred topics of intellectual speculation like these, that I might take up, but our chickens are so many that I will not attempt to count them, but ask the world to come and see them hatch.

We have the attractive country, and with these sources of population at our command, who can even approximate to a correct estimate of our future increase? I will certainly be safe to anticipate the proportional increase for the next five years, as equal to at least double that of any other portion of the west during the *past* five years.

I hope that thousands of immigration companies will be formed during the present year, and that those engaged in organizing them will not overlook the superior advantages of Minnesota. I sincerely believe that no other portion of the west presents so many attractions to the enterprising immigrant as our own territory. A large portion of it is situated upon the navigable head-waters and tributaries of the Mississippi, thus being in intimate communication with the richest and most thriving portion of the Union.

Most of the lands so situated are in the Sioux country, and may be taken possession of by actual settlers before they come into market, and fall into the hands of speculators. Those who enrich the soil by their labor ought to be its owners. Although we entertain this opinion, we condemn no man for speculating in land. While the system of land speculation continues, every one is justified in striving to share in its advantages.

No fact is more evident, than that both the settlers and the territory would be in a far more prosperous condition, if our lands were owned by none but those who occupy or improve them by their own labor and capital.

The Sioux treaties having been ratified by the senate of the United States, more than twenty millions of acres of land are open for settlement, *before it can be surveyed*—BEFORE IT CAN BE MONOPOLISED BY SPECULATORS. The sun never shone upon a more beautiful or fertile land. A more salubrious country, old or new, exists not in the broad domain of the east or west.

Go to work, men, in the states—men of industry, enterprise, and intelligence. Organize your emigration companies, shake the dust from your feet, and hasten on to the wild lands of Minnesota, which bid you take them, without money and without price.

You will have nothing more to do than come and take possession of the lands. Your "claims" thus made will be a sufficient title till these lands shall have been surveyed and brought into market.

From the Iowa line to the Minnesota river—from the Mississippi reaching beyond the head-waters of the Blue-Earth, lays a broad scope of territory, unsurpassed in all the necessary qualities of a richly-favored agricultural country—rolling prairies, heavy timber, well watered, and quite exempt from malarious influences. So easy of access, that navigable rivers wash two sides for hundreds of miles in length. Those who settle upon the Minnesota will have steamboats at their doors, while those who fill up the more central portions will not wait long for the iron road.

No kind of evil conduct on the part of the press or individual writers, is more reprehensible, or should be condemned with more severity, than that of deliberately planning the inveigling and misleading of immigrants by false representations and exaggerated coloring to valueless property.

The majority of home-seekers from foreign parts have a nice little sum of gold carefully stowed away, the fruit of years of toil and saving, which, upon landing in a new and strange country, is their present dependence, and upon the wise disposal of which their future happiness and prosperity mainly depend.

While our newspapers and writers have said very much in favor of settling in Minnesota—have insisted strongly upon her agricultural, mercantile, and lumbering interests, they have dealt very little in exaggerated statements, or inflated inducements.

Much excitement prevails about this time on the subject of towns in the valley of the Minnesota river. Now, honestly speaking, there is not a city from its mouth to its source. That bustle, activity, and enterprise, are busy at many charming eligible points is true, and it is not less true, that towns will grow up in the valley, which most of the older writers call a second Nile. But the towns are yet *in futuro.*

The offering of lots in these sites for sale at reasonable prices, can not be considered an illegitimate speculation. We all know that the Minnesota valley is unsurpassed in beauty and fertility, and as a charming place of residence, where industry will be rewarded by an overflowing abundance, which has but few places to equal it.

That a dense population will soon crowd the banks of the

river, and that, at the favorable points, these people will congregate together, forming towns and cities, there can be no doubt; then, should the rise in property hold in any proportion to that in St. Paul, it is hard to say what lots really are worth in the best located town-plots at this moment.

It can not be expected that we shall feel as much interest in the creation of these towns as the settling of the agricultural portion of the country. It pains me to think that tens of thousands are toiling in the far East, upon a stingy, beggarly, wornout soil, yielding scarcely sufficient to keep soul and body together, while in that delicious valley the most luxuriant growths fall uncropped to the ground. With the voice of a Stentor, Minnesota might proclaim to all nations, "Come unto me all ye who are hungry and naked, and I will feed and clothe ye." But she should add, "Bring a good stock of industry, ambition, patience, and perseverance, and don't expect to find large cities, with marble palaces, but a rich, open soil, with plenty of wood and stone for building." Armed with fortitude and a small capital, we say come, and when you come, go to work, and blessings will rapidly multiply around you.

But there is a class of immigrants who are deserving of reproof, for their desire to cavil and find fault with everything not suited to *their* ideas of accumulating wealth without trouble or difficulty. The following article from the pen of Major J. J. Noah, from the *Minnesota Pioneer*, gives a correct idea of the "grumbler" and his reproof:—

"Minnesota must create some noise in the world, and some anxiety on the part of adventurers to visit and examine its resources. Every boat comes thronged with new faces, all eager in inquiring what and how chance may favor them in their whims, caprices, and predilections. Mr. Simpkins, an old citizen, meets a friend from the east, a schoolmate and boy-companion, just arrived from home to take a peep at this region of bears' meat and buffalo. Simpkins is naturally glad to see his old friend, Mr. Codger, and after the natural inquiries of bygone days, they walk up Third street, arm-in-arm.

"Meeting Mr. Enterprise, another old citizen, Simpkins introduces Codger, and dialogues as follow:—

"'Mr. Enterprise, this is my old friend Codger, from old New York; boys together; come up here, wishes to see the country, locate a land-warrant, build a farm, get married, &c.'

"After Messrs. Codger and Enterprise shake hands, and the compliments of a new acquaintance have passed, Codger puts Enterprise upon his cross-examination without mercy or justice.

"'Fine country this!' quoth Codger; 'how long have you been here—three years, eh? town built up in too great a hurry. Any back country to support all this? Potatoes raised here? Corn won't grow—too cold! Wheat thrive here? Plenty of buffaloes and deer, I suppose; no trouble to kill them? Afraid of Injuns—won't they tomahawk a fellow?' And so on through a multitude of inquiries, until Mr. Enterprise is seriously troubled which to answer first, or to inform Simpkins that his friend is either aberrated or foolish; and as soon as he can get a word in edgewise, he quietly remarks:—

"'Mr. Codger, I came here some three years since from the state of Pennsylvania, with my family and a little money. I bought a town lot in St. Paul, which was then in embryo, containing a few scattered houses, a government just formed, and laws scarcely fledged. I found a scant population, mostly men of intelligence and energy, who assisted and welcomed my advent among them. I became possessed of the presentiment of a bright future for Minnesota, and building a shelter for my family—rolled up my sleeves, and worked at anything I could get to do. As my character was known, so my credit and standing increased. A slight acquisition of capital gave me opportunities to speculate in town property; but I worked all the while, drove a team, chopped wood, and not finding society as exacting as in the east, I progressed in means as the country progressed in importance, and as other men of different occupations followed the same course, you see that St. Paul has become a metropolis, and the country filled with enterprising farmers, breaking prairie, raising crops, and making themselves useful citizens. All this has not been done without labor, nor has there been few obstacles to this sequel. Poverty has waged her bitter war against us—jealous countries have belied and attempted to injure our growth, but it is some satisfaction to know that we have succeeded, built up a country and a name in the far northwest, and made it of such importance, that the whole Mississippi valley feels our slightest pulsation, and gazes with eager eyes upon our minutest transactions.

"'Do not fancy for a moment, sir, that the progress of these events has been a matter of course. We all have fought for them, and battled for their success. The farmers, the pine forests, the Indian trade, the lumber interests, the magnificent water power, the manufacturer, the tradesman, the physician, the lawyer, the editor—all have combined jointly and singly to bring about these results, and to each belong their share of praise and their quota of remuneration. If you wish to settle here, locate your warrant, build your shanty, plough up a few acres, fence them, sow some potatoes, live economically, and work your way quietly into affluence, possessed of a fine farm, a good name, and bright prospects. But if you have come here with a desire to cavil and find fault, doing nothing to advance yourself, you will discover your error too late to retrieve. Be enterprising, and do not foresee difficulties, but rather prepare to surmount pyramids of disadvantages!'

"A word to new-comers. It is wholesome advice, and will prove true. If a man comes to Minnesota to settle, his way to fortune will not be smooth. Let that be clearly understood. Do not cavil or find fault, but come prepared for work and labor. Be enterprising—and persevere. If you go back to your home in the East, underrating our country merely upon a cursory glance, you do us great injustice as well as yourself. Let your motto be 'onward;' time will accomplish all; and when by population our internal resources develop themselves, you will be proud of your remote home, the 'New England of the West.'

"As for minute details, they are now unnecessary; let every man come and see us for himself—then *judge*. If, when here, he will only put himself at anything he findeth for his hand to do, and then DO IT, *with all his might*, he can not fail of ultimate success."

THE HEALTH OF MINNESOTA.

As health is THE peculiarity of the territory, and its enjoyment being the greatest blessing bestowed by Providence, we have cause to be thankful to him for casting here our lot.

It is the constant remark of visiters among us, old and young, that there is something in our atmosphere or climate — they know not what — which exhilarates the mind, and sharpens the appetite. I have seen many persons arrive here in feeble health, languid and depressed in spirits, and, after a short stay, depart renewed and refreshed in body and mind.

It will no longer be unknown, or doubted, that Minnesota possesses, in a degree unsurpassed, the two great elements of health : — a climate in harmony with the most perfect condition of the human body, responsive to the demands of every physical necessity ; the picturesque scenery, the topographical grandeur, and the charming variety of natural beauty, combined with allurements to active enjoyments — the ride, the walk, excursions by land or water, fishing in silvery lakes, the hunt, and the innumerable rational sports suggested by our climate and natural advantages. These unite to gratify and exhilarate the mind of the invalid, and are of all physic the most pleasant, soothing, and curative, for the body.

In addition to natural advantages, Art will contribute by her handiwork, the appliances, elegant and useful, essential to the comfort and gratification of visiting invalids. The accommodations of the hotels in St. Paul, St. Anthony, and Stillwater, are not surpassed, if equalled, in any towns of like extent in the West. But these establishments do not satisfy the luxurious wants of the wealthy classes who fly from the heat of the South, and the dust of thronged cities, to more healthy, pleasant, or sequestered summer retreats. The increasing demand will soon supply hotels of the first class, furnished in the most sumptuous style.

As a resort for invalids our climate is peculiarly inviting. When the summer comes, many citizens will be fleeing away for a few weeks from the sultry beams of a city solstice, and seeking refreshment and repose in more congenial climes.

The limpid lakes of Minnesota, and the cool and sparkling spray of St. Anthony's falls, should no doubt attract a large number. I hope the day is not far distant when our friends living in the cities toward the southern end of the great Mississippi will build country-seats in our vicinity. There is no place on the globe more healthy or more beautiful than Minnesota. Her prairies are studded with silvery lakes and traversed by pearly streams; flowers of almost every variety meet the eye. We have mineral springs equal to any in the world; our lakes abound with fish, and our forests and prairies furnish ample amusement for the sportsman. Gentlemen residing in New Orleans can come here by a quick and delightful conveyance, and bring all that is necessary to make them comfortable during the summer months, and at a trifling expense. For a small sum of money they can purchase a few acres of land on the river, and build summer-cottages. I am satisfied they will find it the cheapest, most convenient, and pleasant mode of spending their summer months. Here every facility will soon be offered for educating their children. A university that will vie with the best in the Union has been liberally endowed by the government. But a short time will elapse before many of the children of the southern valley of the Mississippi will be sent to this healthy region to be educated. Let them come—they will be cheerfully welcomed as kindred who drink with us out of the greatest river in the world!

Pleasure-seekers will find Minnesota a joyous Eden during the summer months, and from present indications myriads of them will turn their steps hitherward the approaching season. The etiquette, expensive dress, and formality, of eastern and southern "watering-places," &c., can here be thrown aside, and men and women both look and act just as God intended they should, without let or hinderance from anybody.

There is now living at Prairieville, on the Minnesota river, an old voyageur by the name of Joseph Montrieul, who is ninety-four years of age. Seventy-four years ago he came from Montreal, and has lived ever since within the bounds of what is now known as the Minnesota territory.

He has never resided but among the Dakotas, except when

he made a journey to the Pawnees with a trader by the name of Campbell, the year after his arrival from Canada—that is, seventy-three years ago. A very strong proof of his honesty and faithfulness is, that during upward of seventy years he has lived with but three or four employers, in the humble capacity of voyageur and laborer about the trading-posts.

Thirty years ago he lived with Mr. J. B. Farribault, of Mendota, who resided on the island opposite Fort Snelling. The island was then well and beautifully wooded. On it they planted corn and vegetables, and sowed wheat, all of which was very productive; but in the year of "the high water," as it is remembered by the old inhabitants, all the buildings were swept away.

With the exception of that year—after which it appears to have been abandoned—the island was seldom overflowed to such an extent as has been the case of late years.

The old man says "he never saw the falls of St. Anthony," and boasts of it with something of the same feeling which the man did whose only claim to notoriety was that he had never read the "Waverley novels." Although still vigorous, he is quite deaf, and one of his eyes is much dimmed; but he managed to shoot a duck last fall, and said that "he hoped to kill a number in the spring." In his young days he is said to have been an excellent shot.

The accounts he relates of the state of the country on the Minnesota river seventy years ago are very interesting. The traders on that river then were Colonel Dixon, at Mendota; Campbell, near Little Rapids; Fraser (father of Jack Fraser), at Traverse des Sioux; two brothers of the name of Hart, and Mr. Patterson, at a place now known as Patterson's Rapids, forty miles below Lac-qui-Parle. He seemed to think that there was no trading-post higher up, but further inquiries will, we think, prove that there were trading-posts near the sources of the "St. Peter's," as the Minnesota was then called, at least one hundred years ago.

Long subsequent to Montrieul's first arrival at Traverse des Sioux, there were thousands of buffalo in that neighborhood. They were even sometimes seen on the prairies in the vicinity of where Fort Snelling now stands. The land was then extremely rich in animals and game of all kinds, but yet both the traders and Indians sometimes suffered great privations for want of food.

The fur-trade engendered a peculiar class of men known by the appropriate name of bush-rangers, *coureurs des bois*, half-civilized vagrants, whose chief vocation was conducting the canoe of the traders along the lakes and rivers of the interior; many of them, however, shaking loose from every tie of blood and kindred, identified themselves with the Indians, and sank into utter barbarism. In many a squalid camp among the plains and forests of the west the traveller would have encountered men owning the blood and speaking the language of France, yet in their wild and swarthy visages and barbarous costume seeming more akin to those with whom they had cast their lot. The renegade of civilization caught the habits and imbibed the prejudices of his chosen associates. He loved to decorate his long hair with eagle-feathers, to make his face hideous with vermilion, ochre, and soot; and to adorn his greasy hunting-frock with horse-hair fringes. His dwelling, if he had one, was a wigwam. He lounged on a bear-skin, while his squaw boiled his venison and lighted his pipe. In hunting, in dancing, in singing, in taking a scalp, he rivalled the genuine Indian. His mind was tinctured with the superstitions of the forest. He had faith in the magic drum of the conjurer; he was not sure that a thunder-cloud could not be frightened away by whistling at it through the wing-bone of an eagle; he carried the tail of a rattlesnake in his bullet-pouch by way of amulet, and he placed implicit trust in the prophetic truth of his dreams. This class of men is not yet extinct. In the cheerless wilds beyond the northern lakes, or among the mountain solitudes of the distant west, they may still be found, unchanged in life and character since the day when Louis the Great claimed sovereignty over the desert empire.

Probably the world has never produced a race of more hardy, athletic pedestrians than the voyageurs and trappers who range through the wild regions of North America, between the great lakes and the Pacific ocean. The unwritten legends of their experience of border and savage life, and of their perilous adventures, would, if written, make volumes of stirring romance. One of the duties performed by voyageurs is the transportation of baggage, supplies, and canoes, across portages. For this purpose they use the "portage-collar," which is a strap passing around the forehead, attached at each end to the burden or pack to be carried, which is also partly supported upon the back. In this manner a voyageur often carries (in packs) a barrel of flour a distance of five or six miles. Squaws carry burdens in the same manner. In this way we have often seen them in St. Paul, carrying heavy loads of cranberries, or of corn, in a sack. The voyageur often finds "a repose," that is, something to place his burden upon while he rests, every three miles in crossing a portage. This mode of transporting was not only common among trappers and voyageurs, but until lately it was universal among the Indians, especially the Chippewas, who, until recently, had few if any horses. We saw in St. Paul, not long ago, Jack Fraser, of whom Captain Marryat makes mention in his travels in the northwest. Jack is a wiry-looking man, aged about fifty-two years, the son of a highland Scotchman by an Indian mother, and one of the most intrepid of the Sioux braves. At the war-dance, Jack wears thirty-two eagle-plumes, each plume representing a scalp taken. He never engages in the medicine-dance, or any of the Indian orgies except the war-dance, and he dresses invariably in the fashion of the whites, although he has a strongly-marked Indian face. He is a nephew of Wakouta, chief of the Red-Wing band of Sioux.

The prospects for builders and mechanics are certainly inviting.

All building and other town improvements have heretofore been confined principally to St. Paul, St. Anthony, and Stillwater. This season, however, there will be a very great demand for mechanics and laborers in other portions of the territory, and there is no doubt but the steamboats will be perfectly crowded after the opening of navigation. The towns of Red-Wing, Hastings, Mendota, Minneapolis, Shakopee, Henderson,

Le Sueur, Traverse des Sioux and Mankato city, are preparing for a vigorous improvement, and will give employment during the summer to a great number of mechanics and laborers. In addition to the above, Capt. Dana will probably employ, about fifty mechanics, and as many laborers, in the construction of the new fort on the Minnesota river. The Indian department will also give employment to many persons in the erection of the agency buildings, mills, &c. Connected with the improvements in the valley of the Minnesota, may be noticed the transportation of supplies which will give employment to from fifty to one hundred persons during a great portion of the summer and fall. It is a well-known fact, that until the Minnesota river is improved at the rapids, and the snags taken out in many of the bends in the river, steamboats, in ordinary seasons, can not navigate the Minnesota above the rapids, *more* than three months during the summer. During the remainder of the season keel and flat boats will be used which will give employment to a great number of boatmen.

At the Mississippi Boom from eighty to one hundred persons are employed, exclusive of those necessary for running rafts of logs and lumber down the Mississippi. The booms on the St. Croix, Rum river, and at the falls of St. Anthony, and the lumbering business of the St. Croix, require some three hundred men. As many more will be wanted on the government roads.

In addition to all enumerated above, ten thousand persons are required to raise flour, pork, beans, and potatoes, to feed the lumbermen, mechanics, laborers, merchants, troops, Indians, and loafers of the territory.

The Indians' days of residence about St. Paul are numbered. Their lands are all purchased, so that in a very short time they will take up their line of march in the direction of the Rocky mountains; and the forests over which they roamed, the waters by which they dwelt, will know of them no more. Their mausoleums of the dead will be trampled under foot and forgotten, and not a monument will remain to record the history of a great nation that is passing away for ever. A feeling of commiseration steals over me while contemplating their actual condition. Needy, improvident, ignorant, superstitious. With sorrowful hearts they hear the exulting cry of the foreigner, that "Westward the star of empire takes its way," and as the hungry crowd of mixed nations press forward, with gladdened hearts at the prospect before them, with this triumphant motto emblazoned on their banners, dispossessing and shoving onward the moody savage — what tears, what suffering, what gloomy forebodings of the future — what home attachments broken up for ever, load the soul of the helpless child of nature, is with the white not esteemed a matter worthy of instant thought. The good missionary who labors for their spiritual good, and who asks no home out of this sterile portion of Christ's vineyard, takes up his bible, his prayer-book and cross, to follow these homeless creatures to the still more cheerless regions of the remote north.

CHAPTER XV.

CONCLUSION — A VISION — SCENE IN ST. PAUL TWENTY YEARS HENCE, ALL OF WHICH I SAW, AND PART OF WHICH WE ALL EXPECT TO BE.

"*Coming events cast their shadows before.*"

"I would recall a vision, which I dreamed
Perchance in sleep — for in itself a thought —
A slumbering thought, is capable of years,
And curdles a long life into one hour." — BYRON.

I WAS seated within my study during a late cold and stormy afternoon, in that melancholy portion of the year — November. The blazing fire leaped and crackled joyously upon my hearth in pleasing contrast with the raging storm without. Sitting in my old arm-chair I watched the descending snow-flakes; and the rapid hurrying to and fro of the many dashing sleighs and other equipages; musing the while upon the many scenes of life thus constantly presented to my eyes, and moralizing upon the hopes, the fears, and the future of the busy throng that floated by so rapidly. From musing, I soon fell, "as is my custom of an afternoon," into a pleasing slumber, silent and undisturbed for hours. And now, while sleeping in that comfortable old arm-chair, all of a sudden my fancy portrayed the following "*vision.*"

Methought that time had shot his arrow suddenly forward some twenty years and odd, and in manhood's prime, and life and health, I stood upon the lofty bluffs, overlooking the great and populous city of St. Paul. Beneath and around me, on every side, a hundred lofty spires glittered in the morning sunlight, while still farther in the distance countless habitations of humble pretensions, suburban cottages and lovely gardens seemed vying in a common race to cover all the plain, and from the grassy vale and shady nook looked cheeringly up, or from gentle hill slope, or clinging to the steeper sides of the semi-circular bluffs, looked down and smiled. The summits of the bluffs were crowned with the residences of the merchant-princes of St. Paul—the homes of luxury, taste, refinement, ease, and elegance. Just below, and almost at the doors of these merchant-princes, a hundred richly-laden boats, from all parts of the upper and lower Mississippi, the St. Croix, and Minnesota, lay proudly at the levée, loading and unloading freights, while the song of the laborer reached even to the bluff whereon I stood. Other steamers and sailing craft of every size were constantly arriving and departing, or passing to and fro, while ferry-boats were crossing and moving about in all directions. From opposite to Fort Snelling away down to Carver's Cave, the city stretched her snowy front; and then across the river to the south, and away off over the bluffs to the north, as far over the plain as the eye could reach, villages of lesser note, the rural palace and the princely mansion, with here and there a single cottage, with lavish and benignant hand were strewn along the vale. City, town, and hamlet, the hill, the valley, the bluffs, almost like mountains, and the far-off plain, with the mighty Mississippi and the deep blue of the far off Minnetonka, were before me. The sky above me was unobscured by a vapor—

> "So cloudless, clear, and purely beautiful,
> That God, alone, was to be seen in Heaven."

And from the crest of Minnetonka's wave, on zepherous footsteps wandered to my lips a breeze refreshing and sweet.

It was morning. The sun had scarcely cleared the horizon, and already every street and avenue of the city was crowded with a joyous and excited population. Men, women, and children, in gaudy apparel—the aged and the youthful—all classes, castes, conditions, and complexions—were mingling in the utmost confusion. And there was the passing to and fro of squads of military in full uniform; firemen in gay shirts and caps; members of benevolent and civic societies, in rich regalia and insignia of their several orders; officers of the army and navy, soldiers, policemen with badges and maces; marshals on horseback, in gaudy sashes and rosettes; while squads of mounted cavalry and lancers were charging hither and thither. A thousand flags and banners floated over the city, and from the boats along the levée; and the flashing of tinseled uniforms, of bayonets, of sword and lance, of fire-engines and gay equipage of every kind, threw back the sunlight. The ceaseless roll of drums, and the clangor of martial music, were mingled with the roar of artillery, which from early dawn had continued to peel from one end of the city to the other; and on the river, and from St. Anthony and Mendota, and from where Fort Snelling *used to stand*— the lofty site now covered with a growing town — cannon answered cannon, and in tones of thunder reverberated from bluff to bluff — from plain to plain, and from shore to shore — dying off at length toward Lake Pepin to the south.

It was the Fourth of July, eighteen hundred and seventy-six; and on that day, representatives from the several old Mississippi valley states, from Nebraska, and the other new states and territories extending westward to the Rocky mountains; the people from the North, too, from Pembina, and the old Selkirk settlement, formerly so called — now the state of Assiniboin (pronounced Assin-i-bwaw), and even from old Fort York, on Hudson bay, together with the people of Minnesota, generally, had congregated in St. Paul, for the twofold purpose of celebrating the centennial anniversary of American Independence, and to witness as well the opening of the great Atlantic and Pacific railway, from Boston, New York, and Philadelphia, *via* St. Paul, to Oregon and California, its terminus being San Francisco.

In connection with all this was the first despatch, to be sent in words of living fire, upon that day, along the wires of the Great Britain submarine, and North American telegraph line, from London, *via* the states, to San Francisco.

The full time for the consummation of a mighty and glorious event had finally arrived, which for twenty years had been anxiously looked for, hoped for, sighed for, ay died for! The hour was near at hand, in which the most sanguine expectations and long-cherished desires of the civilized world were about to be completely realized ; and a great "national highway," for travel and commerce, as well as for thought and intelligence, opened and established from the rising to the setting sun. More especially was it a consummation which Minnesota, since the hour when her first constitution had been given her, the third of March, 1849, had long devoutly wished. The ratification of the Sioux treaties in 1852, and the formation of other treaties in 1860, which extinguished the Sioux and Chippewa titles to all the land within her limits, from the Missouri on the west to the old boundary of forty-nine degrees to the north, had also been events of considerable magnitude in their day, and afforded great joy to youthful Minnesota. But the great enterprise was now completed, and never in all her history, save at the incorporation of the "Republic of Mexico" into the American Union, some ten years previous, or the annexation of "Canada and Cuba," which happened some five years before, St. Paul had never seen such a day of rejoicing.

The sun had scarcely reached the zenith, when the roar of the cannon, the sounds of martial music, and the approach of an immense procession, with banners floating to the breeze, attracted my attention far up the river to the southwest. I turned, and beheld a scene which for a moment rendered me almost delirious with excitement. When I recovered myself, the pageant had approached so near, passing immediately in full view of the eminence on which I lay, as to enable me particularly to survey what I shall now attempt to describe.

Spanning the mighty Mississippi, just above Wabashaw street, was a splendid suspension bridge, with a pier upon the sandy island in the stream, and a magnificent arch on either side. From Mendota (now a town stretching its summit up around Pilot Knob), down along the bluffs on the south side of the river, was the great railway ; extending across the river by a double track some twenty feet apart, and thence, throughout our own St. Paul, away off to the southeast toward the Atlantic seaboard.

Supported on each hand by an immense escort, composed of *our entire population*, came the "first train of cars from San Francisco," the departure of which had been announced here by telegraph a short time previous.

First came an open car, or platform, extending across from one track to the other, richly draped and ornamented with banners, and containing a band of fifty musicians, who played "*Hail Columbia*." Next came two splendid locomotives, one on either track, moving abreast. On the one upon the right, I read "*Atlantic;*" on that upon the left, "*Pacific*." Over these, extending across from track to track, and for three hundred feet in the rear, was a continuous platform, supported on wheels, covered with rich and gorgeous tapestry, forming upon the most magnificent scale "a grand triumphal car." Immediately in front, on the right and left of this platform, arose two columns of beautiful proportions, about thirty feet in height, and of alabaster whiteness. On the one I read "*The Union*;" on the other, "*The Constitution*." From the tops of these columns, the intervening space was spanned by an arch, composed of the "coat of arms" of the several states of the Union, carved in bas-relief on separate blocks of marble; and upon the keystone of the arch, I read the familiar motto, "*E Pluribus Unum*." On this point perched an immense spread eagle, glittering with gold, and holding in his beak a likeness of "The Father of his Country," in a plain gold setting, enwreathed with laurel; while high above, and over all, floated the "star-spangled banner." Immediately under the arch was an altar of pure white, upon which I read "Freedom," and from the top of the altar arose a square shaft of white, some four or five feet in height, and on the several sides of which I read, "Peace, Prosperity, Happiness," "Truth, Justice, Equality," "Education, Arts, Commerce," "Agriculture, Manufactures, Mines." On the top of this shaft rested a vase of pure gold, bearing the inscription, "California and Minnesota, the twin sisters, are this day indissolubly bound together by an iron band." In this was contained water from the Pacific ocean. On either side of this stood a beautiful young woman, in the bloom of health, dressed in muslin robes of snowy whiteness, trimmed with gold and evergreens, and bearing appropriate emblems, typical of the genius of "Peace" and "Commerce." Immediately in the rear of these a figure, representing Neptune with his trident, was standing in a rich and gorgeous chariot drawn by dolphins; and falling from the rear of the chariot, and strewn over the entire length of the great platform, were shells and precious stones, and gold and silver ores.

This was to typify that our advancement in the arts and sciences had induced even the "god of the ocean" to forsake his native element, and, availing himself of human skill, to take the overland route from one part of his dominions to another; and, further, that the commerce of the seas would henceforward take this route; while the shells and precious stones falling from his chariot seemed to remind us that this great undertaking was destined to be literally paved with the riches of the deep.

Immediately in the rear of this group, arranged on either side of the platform, were separate pedestals, four feet six inches in height by three feet square, placed at a distance of nearly six feet apart, and extending in parallel rows over two hundred feet in the rear. These pedestals were fifty in number, twenty-five on either hand, and were emblematical of the "fifty free and independent states of the American Union," which included the Canadas on the north to the isthmus of Darien on the south, and from Cuba in the southeast to the Russian settlements in the northwest, from the equator to the frozen regions. Upon each of these pedestals I read the name of a state; and on the tops, standing erect, were fifty beautiful young women, between the ages of eighteen and twenty years, in the full bloom of health and womanhood. These were dressed in flowing drapery of white, adorned with roses, and on the head each wore a crimson-velvet cap, ornamented with a single star of gold. Each bore an emblem (vegetable, mineral, or artificial) of her particular state, while an endless chain of roses and orange-flowers, in graceful festoons, extended from hand to hand, and was emblematical of the common interests which unite us as a people. The blue eyes and fair complexions of the north in union, though in contrast, with the dark eyes and olive complexions of the south. Immediately in the rear of these, and occupying the remaining portion of the "car triumphal," was the president of the United States, himself a citizen of Minnesota, members of the cabinet and heads of departments, deputations of members from both houses of Congress, foreign ministers resident at Washington, executive officers of several of the Pacific states (all returning from an excursion trip from Washington to San Francisco); and lastly came a delegation of aborigines, consisting of the chiefs and headmen of the nations of the plains. Then came another detached car, similar to that described in the first instance, containing a band of fifty musicians, playing the "Star-spangled Banner."

Thus appointed and arranged, the train arrived opposite to the business centre of the city, advanced upon the bridge, and halted. Then a Christian minister (the Rev. E. D. Neill, I think), accompanied by the president and secretary of state, with heads uncovered, proceeded from the extreme rear through the long avenue of young women representing the several states; and as they passed along, each successive state stood with head uncovered, in token at once of their respect for religion and their fidelity to the general government. This movement served also as a signal for the multitude to follow suit, and who accordingly acquiesced during the following ceremonies:—

Arrived in front of the triumphal arch, the minister briefly invoked the blessings of Jehovah upon the great enterprise before them, and for the welfare of the country at large. He then stepped aside, and the chief magistrate of the nation having closed the discoursive part of the ceremonies with a few appropriate remarks, a signal was given, whereupon the sisters "Peace" and "Commerce" gracefully inverted the "golden vase," and the waters of the Pacific ocean were mingled with the waters of the mighty Mississippi. The bay of San Francisco was wedded with the Atlantic and gulf of Mexico, and the bright drops of the Sacramento were mingled with and flowed with those of the "Father of Running Waters."

At that instant another immense train arrived in fifty hours from New Orleans, sixty from the Rio Grande, and *four days from the city of Mexico.* It contained a pleasure-party, numbering by thousands. Among them were the wealthy planters, their wives, and little ones—the dark-skinned creole gentlemen and ladies—together with the dark-eyed senoritas and gayly-dressed caballeros from the old halls of the Montezumas. They were coming to spend a few weeks amidst the noise and spray of the "Little falls," or *Minne-ha-ha,* and of our great St. Anthony. The eastern train from Philadelphia, New York, and Boston, and another from Lake Superior, and still another from Pembina and Assiniboin, near Lake Winnipeg, also came rattling in, alive with human freight from the east, the north, and northeast.

Then the mighty throng of assembled thousands raised a loud hosannah, and methought the chorus of their mighty voices resounded adown the flowing stream, and over the gulf and broad Atlantic, and then re-echoed across Europe's peopled surface with redoubled force, till in the wilds of Russia it reached the last and only home of the despot—the descendant of the Nicholas of 1853—who had long since laid mouldering in a tyrant's grave. Then did the heart of the last of the line of kings and emperors which this fair earth shall ever witness, grow faint within him, as he saw his inevitable doom portrayed as plain as the "handwriting upon the wall," and heard his death-knell proclaimed in tones of might and wrath, which told him that an avenging GOD was nigh! Ay, he listened, while the pallor of death stole over his guilty features, and the craven-hearted usurper of the rights of man, and violator of all his Maker's laws, did tremble for very fear—ay, trembled like an aspen-leaf, as he heard the voices of the mighty host exultingly jubilate on that "centennial anniversary" of a nation's birth-day—the greatest nation, too, which old Time and events have yet given to the world, its population now being sixty millions.

Then rose the serf, the Cossack, and all the republicans of Europe, led on by the aged heroes Kossuth and Mazzini, and a host of others, and struck a tremendous and final blow for freedom — the goddess of Liberty flitting and hovering over the scene — until at length a loud, triumphant shout came ringing back across the ocean and gulf, and up the noble river to the spot where the multitudinous host were still pouring forth their anthems of praise to the God of hosts — proclaiming to them that the final victory between Liberty and Despotism had been fairly won, and that Tyranny had sunk his frightful head amidst a perfect cataract of blood. The prediction of Napoleon had been verified in one sense — and, in 1876, all Europe was at last REPUBLICAN. . . . . Louis Napoleon had long since sunk into insignificance, oblivion, and contempt; and poor, unhappy France, now so no more, had become a true republic.

At that instant, the ceremonies being over, amid the roll of drums, and the clangor of martial music, the discharge of muskets, the roar of artillery, and the deafening huzzas of an excited and countless multitude on the land, upon the bridge, and upon the water beneath — the train moved on toward the eastern seaboard, and *I awoke from my dream.*

CAMP-FIRE SKETCHES,

OR

NOTES OF A TRIP FROM ST. PAUL TO PEMBINA AND SELKIRK SETTLEMENT ON THE RED RIVER OF THE NORTH;

TO WHICH ARE APPENDED

A DESCRIPTION OF PRINCE RUPERT'S LAND, ETC.

NOTE.

THE object of the expedition narrated in the following pages was to form a treaty with the Red Lake and Pembina bands of Chippewa Indians for their country lying in the valley of the Red river of the North, and south of the British line. Governor Ramsey was appointed commissioner to treat with them, and Dr. Thomas Foster appointed secretary. The treaty was formed, but was afterward rejected by the United States senate.

SKETCHES BY A CAMP-FIRE.

CHAPTER I.

THE OUTWARD MARCH.

Our party consisted of the following persons, viz.: Governor Ramsey, Hugh Tyler, Dr. Foster, Rev. John Black, of Montreal, J. M. Lord, F. Brown, Pierre Bottineau, Joseph Courserole, and myself. Our escort consisted of twenty-five dragoons from Fort Snelling, commanded by Lieutenant Corley, and accompanied by six two-horse baggage-wagons; our own baggage and provisions being carried on light Red-river carts, with eight French-Canadian and half-breed drivers. In number we comprised about fifty souls in all.

A portion of the civil party took the steamboat "Governor Ramsey," at St. Anthony, on Monday, August 18, 1851, and proceeded to the Thousand isles, below Sauk rapids, where the balance of the party, with the horses, carts, and a light riding-wagon, awaited their arrival. After uniting, we all proceeded on to Russell's, above Sauk rapids, and on Wednesday crossed the Mississippi, and camped the first night about two miles west, in the Sauk river valley.

Thursday, 21st.—Fine, clear, cool day. We struck tents and were away early; rode fifteen miles over prairie, and along the valley of Sauk river, bordered on either side with thick woods, and interspersed here and there with strips of woodland and a thick undergrowth of bushes. Then passed over the worst piece of road between Sauk rapids and Pembina. The dragoons were busy for several hours in repairing it for the passage of the teams. It was a piece of swamp-land, about fifty yards in width, and covered by a bad "corduroy" road.

Three, P. M.—Proceeded on three miles, and found the dragoons encamped for the night at another bad crossing of swamp-land, near a creek. It took them several hours to repair it with bushes, grass, &c. Encamped near by also, to await our turn to-morrow. Our march to-day was eighteen miles.

Friday, August 22.—Clear, cool, and pleasant. The weather is now delightful—the sun quite hot at noonday, and the nights cool and bracing. Up at daylight, and away on our march at seven, A. M. The dragoons off before us.

After proceeding two miles, we crossed Sauk river, passing over to the southwest side. We found a good ford, about four feet deep, the bottom being gravelly with a few boulders. The hills are very high, and skirted with heavy timber, on the right bank. We then emerged on to a beautiful rolling prairie, extending as far as the eye could reach; bordered by timber, stretching in belts on either side; that to the right bordering on Sauk river, and bearing away off to the northwest. We soon came to a swampy place, where the dragoons mired their horses. Grass was then mowed, a causeway made, the horses crossed on it, and the heavy teams drawn over by ropes. We soon after discovered a he-bear, "loping" off over the prairie at full speed. Several of us gave chase at once, and after pursuing him through swamps and marshes for half an hour, and wounding him severely, the dragoons came up, surrounded him, and finished the job by killing him with pistol-balls. Tyler, in a two-horse wagon, joined us in the chase, and came in just at the death.

We halted at noon, and took a cold bite and a cup of tea. In the afternoon we rode on some twelve miles farther, and encamped in some brush and timber, where the water was bad and mosquitoes worse. The country passed over to-day was rolling prairie, thickly interspersed with marshes and small, sluggish streams, the ground ascending for fifteen miles, then descending to the camp five miles. We found it a very hard march, with the bear-chase, the bad roads, and much detention in passing over the swamps and marshes.

SATURDAY, 23d.—Fine, clear morning. Up, as usual, at daylight; breakfasted on tea and herring, and supped last night on herring and tea—rather hard living. Dr. Foster, on being asked at noon yesterday if he would have a piece of the neck of a cold goose, replied, "Yes, sir-ee, it is *neck or nothing*—of course I will!" We to-day rode over the rolling prairie, full of strips of marsh, when, after a march of ten miles, we came to an almost impassable swamp. We crossed with some difficulty, by pulling the carts and horses across by ropes, during which the Rev. Mr. Black and I completely mired our ponies, and came near going with them to the bottom, if there was any. After this, we took a cup of tea to refresh ourselves; proceeded on twelve miles farther, then encamped on the banks of a lake, where we had fine spring-water, and altogether the best camping-place we have yet had, the situation and scenery around being very beautiful. The carts arrived at sunset; we then erected tents, cooked and ate supper after night, amid hosts of mosquitoes, which were finally driven off by a strong southwest breeze.

SUNDAY, 24th.—Cloudy and cool, with rain in the morning, with thunder and lightning. All hands busy fixing tents more securely, digging trenches around to drain off the falling water, &c. Being Sunday, we remained in camp all day. Last night four of our horses broke their lariats and ran homeward at the top of their speed, but were caught, most fortunately for us, by the dragoons, at their camp twelve miles behind us, Had they not been there, we should have been obliged to have followed the beasts clear back to Sauk rapids, ere we could have overtaken them.

To-day, our French-Canadians and half-breeds, who have charge of the provision and baggage-carts, have been shooting pigeons, ducks, &c., also making new cart-axles; and the day has not seemed much like Sunday. Yesterday afternoon, while several of us were riding on ahead, we started up a skunk along the road, and immediately gave chase, when such shying and dodging, to keep to windward of the beast, was never seen before. We nearly rolled off our horses with laughter. Now came the doctor, sidling up very cautiously, and fired two shots with a revolver, then beat a precipitate retreat as the skunk fired at him. Lord then pranced up on Billy, and fired one shot at the spot where it smelt the loudest, then turned tail, too, and fled. Gabou finally despatched the varmint with a tomahawk.

Monday, 25th.—Up and away early; once more upon the road; had a very fine ride of about fourteen miles to White Bear lake, as it is called, from the fact of white bear being so plenty, perhaps. This is a beautiful lake, eight miles long and several wide; the banks of woodland and rolling prairie. We halted on the north shore, about one mile distant, for several hours. Dined on roast skunk (not the one killed on Saturday, though), ducks, and prairie-hens, ham, pork, &c. Some of the party are very fond of skunk, either roasted, fried, or stewed, and attribute the peculiar smell of the meat to the fact that the animal lives on garlic—a very garlicky explanation!

In the afternoon we rode to Pike lake, twelve miles farther; we reached it at sundown, and found a very beautiful spot, indeed, and heavily wooded around a portion of its banks. The lake is full of Pike fish, hence its name, which was given to it by Captain Pope. The dragoons are encamped quite near us, having been ahead all day. Mosquitoes are very bad, although the weather is quite cold and bracing. The country passed over to-day was a rolling prairie, with small streams of water running through the ravines; all of which are tributary to the Minnesota. To-night our carts failed to reach us, and remained about four miles behind. Fortunately, Brown came riding up at dark and informed us of the fact, and also brought two wild geese and some prairie-hens along. The latter and one goose were roasted, as we sat huddling round the fires (for the evening air was cold), and were devoured with great gusto; a little boiled ham, salt, and hard bread, were obtained from the dragoons, which added additional zest to the camp-fire meal. Some of us then betook ourselves to the dragoon camp, and slept in tents; the rest disposed themselves around the fire, and in the carriage, and so passed the night, Dr. Foster, for one, half frozen. And this is life upon the prairie; right ready and willing are we to make the best of everything, and suit ourselves to circumstances.

TUESDAY, 26th.—Up early and breakfasted with the dragoons, on a cup of coffee and piece of hard bread. The morning very cold for the season. Overcoats necessary, and all hands sitting around the fires. Wind east, and very fresh; a fine, bracing morning, the best for travelling we have yet had. The carts soon arrived and passed on ahead, and at eight, A. M., we followed, and after a fine ride of ten miles, we arrived at Elk lake, and stopped to feed and dine upon the prettiest spot we have yet seen. It was upon the western bank of the lake, upon a knoll, high above the water, the banks of the lake being high and covered with a skirt of woodland; the waters, agitated by a strong breeze, rolling wildly below. This lake is some two miles long, and full of headlands, and small isles all heavily timbered. A most charming spot for a residence when the country becomes once settled; at present the whole place is wild and beautiful. Since writing the above, the rest of our party have arrived, and I find it is not "Elk" lake, but one new to all the party, and to us nameless. Governor Ramsey, therefore, called it Lake Fillmore, in honor of the president; quite a compliment, too, by-the-by, considering that it is much the finest of the kind we have yet seen. We had a very good dinner to-day, consisting of bouillon, made of geese, ducks, &c., with ham, pork, coffee, bread and butter, &c. This afternoon we pursued a very circuitous road over a more rough and rolling country than we have yet passed, broken by deep ravines and full of lakes, ponds, &c. Some of the lakes were very beautiful; our road passed over the outlet of one of them at its mouth, where it poured over the rocky bottom and formed a creek thirty feet in width. At sundown we reached the banks of a large creek, or perhaps of the Chippewa river, and after crossing found the dragoons encamped on the open prairie, on the western bank. We also camped near them, and had wood and good water plenty. Our march to-day was about twenty miles, though so circuitous that I doubt if we made more than ten miles on our regular course. The stream upon which we are encamped is a very rapid one, and flows over a rocky bed of boulders.

WEDNESDAY, 27th.—Cool, cloudy, and quite cold early in the morning; fine weather for travelling. Up at daylight, and away upon our march at half-past five, one hour earlier than our earliest start heretofore. Rode about ten miles over an elevated prairie, full, as usual, of lakes and ponds; crossed a stream about sixty feet in width (Potato river), and stopped for our dinner on the banks of a fine lake, partly wooded on its shores, with a gravel bottom. After a rest of several hours we proceeded on five miles, and found the dragoons encamped on the bank of another fine lake, the shores well wooded. As it was but four, P. M., we pressed on some five miles farther, making twenty-five miles march to-day; then camped on the prairie; no wood in sight; carried enough on the carts for the getting of supper and breakfast. A pond full of dirty, dark grass was near by, out of which we got our water. Two of our party brought in a large quantity of geese, ducks, and prairie fowls, to the camp, to-night. Indeed, wild game of the feathered kind is getting to be a drug upon our hands, as we get more daily than we can use. The country we passed over to-day was an elevated plain for the most part, with less woodland and fewer lakes, and the growth more even and of a poorer quality than that below. We are now passing on to the dividing ridge between the head waters of the Red, Minnesota, and Mississippi rivers.

THURSDAY, 28th.—Cloudy and cold in the morning; very unpleasant, with slight rain; warmer in the afternoon, with thunder and lightning. Wind southeast to southwest. Up at daylight, and upon our march at six, A. M. Rode some ten miles over a flat, dry, and very uninteresting country, destitute of lakes, and the grass dry and in some places already burned off, with stagnant ponds and a sluggish creek, at which we stopped to dine. We could procure no wood, save what we carried with us, and the water was also very bad. At noon we started on again; the country continued bare and flat, with no timber in sight, till we approached the Sioux Wood river, where we arrived at four, P. M., after a march of twenty miles, and one hundred and forty from Sauk rapids.

The Bois des Sioux is a stream about thirty miles in length, and flows from Lac Traverse into Red river, by a course due north. We crossed about four miles above its mouth, where it was fifty yards in width, and four and a half feet deep, its course being very crooked. We camped on its bank, alongside the dragoons, all hurry and bustle in the midst of a gust; supped on soup made of two wild geese, with onions, potatoes, and condiments; called bouillon by the half-breeds. At ten, P. M., a very heavy storm of thunder and lightning came up suddenly from the southwest. The rain descended in torrents, the winds blew, thunders roared, lightning flashed, the tent flies snapped, flapped, and cracked; the water rolled in under our oil-cloth floor, while we remained all safe and dry and went to sleep amid the raging and roaring of the tempest.

Friday, 29th.—Cloudy and very damp early in the morning; cleared up about ten o'clock; fine, cool, and pleasant, with a good breeze from the north. The troops having made a raft yesterday afternoon, they began to cross early this morning, rafting over their goods, and drawing the wagons over with ropes; swimming and wading the horses over at two different fords, about one hundred and fifty yards apart. They were all over at half-past ten o'clock, and then came our turn; all our goods, provisions, baggage, &c., were turned out on the grass to dry, which opportunity I availed myself of to examine and take a list of all. The carts were drawn over by ropes, the goods taken over on the raft, and the horses swam across all at the lower and deeper ford. After all was again repacked we started at two, P. M., and after pursuing a northwest course about eight miles, over a flat, marshy prairie, we crossed over the Wild Rice river on a rustic bridge of logs, and camped on the other side, near the dragoons, whom we found already there and comfortably fixed. The

Wild Rice is a narrow and very crooked stream, with high banks, and resembles a deep ditch of dirty water. It is skirted with woodland at intervals. We are now three or four miles down Red river, below the mouth of the Sioux wood, above which it takes the name of Ottertail river. Our distance from Red river, to the west, is some three miles; the woods bordering its banks being visible during our ride this afternoon. Our whole journey to-day has not exceeded ten miles; to-morrow, we have a march of twenty-five miles to the Shayenne, which we cross thirty miles above its mouth; and I am told that we will not see Red river until our arrival at Pembina, as our road skirts along the high ground on the western slope of the valley, distant on an average some thirty to forty miles. This detour is necessary to avoid the marshes, swamps and bad places along the bed of the valley and nearer to the river.

Saturday, 30th.—A fine, clear, warm, day—the finest we have yet had. This morning a false alarm raised all the camp at half-past one o'clock; a fire was made, the kettle put on, water boiled and after putting the tea to draw, we all returned to bed again, determined that nothing should "draw" us out again till morning. Our road to-day lay over a flat and marshy prairie, with no lakes or streams, the woods along Red river alone being visible, away off to the right. At noon we halted at a stagnant pool of dirty water, cut down two small dead poplars (all the timber we could find), boiled our coffee and had a cold bite for dinner. The sun was very hot, huge bottle-flies and gnats very bad, and our horses most used up. At three this afternoon we started on again, and rode twelve miles, to the Shayenne, that is, the Rev. Mr. Black and I, who ride together. Here we found the dragoons encamped on the top of the steep wooded bank, on the south side of the Shayenne; the turbid, narrow, river rolling rapidly about two hundred feet below, and a vast expanse of rolling prairie away off to the north on the other side. The country passed over this afternoon was a level, marshy prairie for the most part, with sand-hill knolls like mounds, and excavations as though done by hand, at intervals. As we approached within six miles of the Shayenne, the timber in groves became more abundant, with rolling prairie, hills, mounds, and valleys leading us to suppose we were immediately on its banks. The dragoons were deceived in common with the rest of us and thus led some ten miles beyond their usual march; making a distance of thirty miles. At their camp we found Dr. Foster and a friend, who had rode on at noon in search of the Shayenne. After partaking of a good supper in Lieutenant Corley's tent, and waiting till nine o'clock for the arrival of our carts and balance of the party, the Rev. Mr. Black and I re-caught our horses, and rode back by the light of the new moon, in search of the stray wanderers; after a ride of some two miles we came in sight of their camp-fire, to our great joy, and soon came to the camp, at ten, P. M.; the tents were pitched on the open prairie, just on the side of a swamp, where the water was pretty good; also some wood handy, and but few mosquitoes, which at the dragoon camp were far worse than I ever saw before, or heard of, or imagined; in fact, no imagination could do them justice —they must be seen and felt to be appreciated. I rode a cream-colored horse, and was unable to distinguish the color of the animal so thickly was he covered on my arrival there. During supper they swarmed around like bees hiving, and entered the mouth, nose, ears, and eyes, and had it not been for a cool, fresh, evening breeze, they would have been unbearable. Dr. F. remained with the lieutenant at the camp all night, and I have since learned that they were almost literally devoured alive, albeit they had the protection of mosquito bars; which on this occasion did not amount to much. Dr. F. was phlebotomised to the extent of several pounds of blood; and finally took refuge on the open prairie, muffled up in a lot of blankets, and exposed to the keen night wind, which still proving ineffectual in resisting their attacks (as he says they even penetrated through his boots), he finally, at daylight, threw off all disguise, and almost distracted took refuge in a smudge among the tents. He to-day looks dry, and has very much of a smoked appearance, besides being weak. He feels that he has been victimized by hordes and legions of winged devils — a mosquitoed martyr. At our own camp I slept comfortably without a bar, and had no more bills presented than I could settle, without disturbing pleasant slumber.

SUNDAY, 31st.—The last day of summer and a cool and pleasant one—with a fine breeze, the very counterpart of yesterday, which was exceedingly warm. We rose late this morning and started about seven o'clock—soon came to the Shayenne again, and after passing the dragoon camp, and down the high, steep hill on the south side, we passed the river on a rough log bridge; the muddy stream flowing below deep and silently, like a large canal, the banks steep, muddy, and heavily wooded. The country through which the Shayenne flows is much broken and quite hilly, with knolls and sand-bands rising upward in much confusion. On the north side of the stream the country is quite low and flat, almost on a level with the river, and forming a strange contrast with the high bank opposite. It rises, however, in the course of a mile or more, and we ascended another level prairie when our hunters discovered two bull-buffalo about a mile ahead. They immediately equipped and started, and soon surrounded and killed both. The carts and balance of the party then proceeded to the spot; about half a mile from the road, and on discovering water, we encamped on the open prairie for the balance of the day. The buffalo were skinned, the choice parts cut out, and the liver and kidneys fried for dinner. It was not as good as that of beef, and I must taste the steaks before I decide as to the merits of bull-buffalo. As this was the first buffalo seen or taken, it afforded for a time much excitement. Guns, pistols, etc., were reloaded, handkerchiefs were tied around heads, waists belted, stirrups tightened and away they went, best fellow foremost, and Dr. Foster himself in the carriage this time (instead of Tyler), in hot pursuit.

MONDAY, September 1.—The mosquitoes this morning were almost as bad as on Saturday night, the air being warm and sultry, and weather cloudy, and our camp being on the flat, marshy prairie, near a swamp. There was no satisfaction in eating even buffalo meat, which, by-the-by, is not so good as a beef-steak, by any means, being dry, tough, and more tasteless. If broiled, and well-seasoned, it might answer better.

We passed over a flat, marshy prairie this morning for ten miles, and crossed over Maple river on a rough log-bridge, which being there, saved us much trouble, as the banks were high, and the stream deep, very crooked and ditch-like, with some timber on its banks. This afternoon we passed on six miles further, and camped near a ravine of water just on the road; the mosquitoes, as usual, very bad.

We to day left our escort of dragoons at Maple river, where they arrived just before we left, at three, P. M., having presented the poor fellows with a portion of our buffalo meat to feast on. Our horses now look lank and lean; between long marches, flies and mosquitoes, and no grain, they have fared badly; we hope to have cool weather, and perhaps a frost soon. As for the mosquitoes, they have been almost unendurable all day. The weather is warm; mercury was sixty-five degrees at sunrise, and our march only about fifteen miles. Soon after camping to-night, our hunters rode out and shot another buffalo, which had been discovered lying in the high grass about a mile off from camp. He proved to be a bull, and ran most furiously for a mile or two before he was surrounded and brought to bay. During the chase, Pierre Bottineau's horse stumbled, and threw his rider violently to the ground. He was picked up insensible, terribly stunned though not much hurt. He was bled, brought to camp in the carriage, and put to bed. The choice portions of the buffalo only were taken, and the carcass left to the tender mercies of a band of wolves, who howled, barked, and preyed over it all night.

Tuesday, 2d.—A very warm day; sun shines very hot, and the flies and mosquitoes are extremely bad. We made a march of twelve miles, and stopped to dine in some timber on the banks of Rush river, another small ditch-like stream. Rode on six miles farther in the afternoon, and camped with the dragoons, who had come up at noon, passed us, and gone ahead. They had just killed another buffalo, and were cooking large quantities of the meat for supper—buffalo now becoming quite plenty.

Our camp to-night is on the open, wide, and apparently boundless prairie—no wood in sight, and none to use save what we carry with us. The country is flat, and very uninteresting, the water stagnant, and prairie marshy. No signs of Red river, we being still away off some forty miles to the left. The mercury at sunrise to-day was down to forty-three degrees, not quite cold enough, however, to deaden our tormentors, yet, who are almost as active as ever.

WEDNESDAY, 3d.—Up at four o'clock, and away at five, A.M. Rode ten miles, and halted for our noonday rest; dined on a knoll above the prairie, near a small stream of water. The mercury this morning stood at sixty-six degrees, the air very warm from the south, and a thunder-storm away off to the north. The mosquitoes, as usual, very bad early in the morning. The wind, however, was strong this afternoon, and blew the most of them away, and we were not troubled so much till night again; very glad for that respite any how—our tormentors are continuous and excessive generally, Made a march of ten miles this afternoon, and camped on the prairie near a pond of water, though we had no wood, save what we carried with us.

Most of the party started on a buffalo hunt this afternoon, and did not return till after dark, when they came in shouting and yelling like wild Indians. They killed two bulls, and the dragoons killed three. The country passed over to-day was more interesting, being high-rolling prairie. Our road led over a ridge of rolling land, running east and west, though no timber has been visible since at noon yesterday.

THURSDAY, 4th.—Up at daylight; the mosquitoes being too bad to allow of much sleeping. They kept us awake, in fact, most of the night; the inside of the bars containing quite enough to worry a man, and keep him slapping and fighting instead of sleeping, while the tent was black with them, and their humming noise sounded like bees hiving. Six buffalo were discovered this morning within a few hundred yards of the camp, but as our horses had run off we could not follow them. Some of the hunters went out on foot, but could not approach near enough to get a shot. After riding some eight miles this forenoon, we came to a branch of Goose river, and found the dragoons there, and busy drying their buffalo meat over smoke. Here we found the first timber seen in two days; it bordered the high bluff on the south side of the pretty valley through which this branch of Goose river meanders in a very tortuous manner, in common with all these prairie streams. We crossed the valley, and ascended the high hill on the north side, where we dined and took a bath in the clear cool stream besides. The wood on this side being scarce, we cooked no dinner. Our meals to-day consisted of cold boiled pork and buffalo. The streams and crossings in this valley, unlike those between the Red and Mississippi, flow deep through the prairie, and have for the most part hard sandy or gravel bottoms. The soil is lighter, and contains more sand; there is also far less woodland, and a less luxurious growth of vegetation. We came up to no more *bad places*, where horses swamp and teams get mired; but pass over all obstructions in the way of streams and swamps without any difficulty. This afternoon we rode some twelve miles, and camped on a knoll above a small stream of clear good water (though very warm). Having no wood, we were obliged to boil our kettle, and the French boys their pork and buffalo, over a fire made of dried buffalo chips.

Only a few mosquitoes on hand, and those driven to leeward by the strong smoke and smell of the buffalo chips. We kept them all out of the tents too, and had the most comfortable sleep we have had since starting; which makes amends for last night's torments, and is like a change from purgatory to the third heaven. A splendid aurora borealis was witnessed from the camp last night; a glorious display which is very seldom equalled.

Our escort, which is always far ahead or out of timely reach in case of need behind, passed us at our camp at noon, and are out of sight ahead to-night. After supper we were serenaded by a large band of wolves, which prowled round our camp, and howled most fearfully all night long.

We utterly disregard all wolves, Indians, and other *varmints.* This afternoon, I chased a large drove of greyish brown wolves for a mile or two, and shot a number of them. In the distance when first seen, they looked large like elk or deer, and one black one moved like a buffalo. Our march to-day was from sixteen to eighteen miles.

FRIDAY, 5th.—Clear, fine, and pleasant; sun very hot, with a good breeze from southwest. Rode ten miles in the morning, over a gently-rolling prairie, ascending one ridge and down another, with nothing but level prairies and ridges ahead, one after another in succession, with knolls, ponds, and a small lake or two by way of variety, and a strip of woodland away off to the right. Halted at ten, A. M., on a branch of Goose river, though not so large as the one passed yesterday; in fact it is now a mere rivulet of three or four feet wide. The water good and rather cool. Having but little wood to cook, we dined on herring, tea, and crackers.

This afternoon we made about ten miles, and camped at dark on the brow of a hill near a small stream; the dragoons were encamped in the edge of some timber, about two miles ahead. A very pleasant, clear evening, and the mosquitoes scarce; supped on buffalo-meat and tea, and slept comfortably and soundly.

SATURDAY, 6th.—Cloudy and cold, quite a change since yesterday; mercury forty-eight degrees at dawn. At eleven, A. M., rain commenced falling, and a heavy thunder-storm passed around the horizon, a portion visiting us. Wind fresh from the north, requiring gloves and overcoats. Up at daylight, and away on our march as usual very early

Rode some twelve miles, and overtook the dragoons at ten, A. M.; made a temporary halt till eleven, then proceeded some three miles farther and awaited the arrival of the carts, which came up at three, P. M. We then camped on the south side of a small stream, a branch of *Salt river*, and prepared for a comfortable night's rest, and a quiet spending of the sabbath.

* * * * *

The dragoons had previously encamped on the north side of the same stream, and had just killed another buffalo in the midst of the thunder-storm. Our route still lies over prairie, interspersed with belts of timber, and stretching north. The banks of the brook upon which we have encamped are also slightly wooded, and I believe we will now have plenty the rest of our journey. We have now been four days without any, save what we carried with us, and all the old empty barrels, boxes, &c., have been brought into requisition.

We were amused this morning by Joseph Courserole, a young half-breed Sioux, who is our chief cook, &c. He was making a speech to the camp in the presence of the French boys around the fire. He spoke and gesticulated with all the earnestness of the real Indian, and was encored by loud "hohs" from the awakened sleepers in our tent. He spoke in Sioux, and I suppose from his manner, he told wonderful things. He was born away out to the northwest of our present camp at Devil's lake, and was raised at Mendota by the Hon. H. H. Sibley. He is now an excellent hunter, the best shot in the party, and promises to become a celebrated voyageur, and unrivalled in the chase. One of the party was taken sick to-day. We camped together *this time*, and medical attendance was at once on hand.

Among the fifty people who compose our party, are an old Canadian Frenchman, and a companion younger than himself. The old man passed nearly all the earlier portions of his life on Red river, and till some twenty years ago, when he moved to Missouri territory, and has been living ever since away out among the Blackfeet Indians. He is now returning to live and die at the Selkirk settlements. He and his companion ride in a two-horse wagon, drawn by two grays, and, although they camp with us, they cook and eat at their own camp-fire, and sleep without a tent, either under their wagon or alongside on a bed of robes and blankets on the ground. The old gentleman is active and yet vigorous, though his head shakes with age.

Pierre Bottineau, who contracted to take our goods and provisions from Sauk Rapids through to Pembina, is a half-breed Chippewa; of a highly-nervous temperament, with Indian features strongly marked, very swarthy, dark hair, tall, muscular, and active, and is about thirty-seven years of age. He is an excellent hunter and voyageur; was born in, and has spent his whole life in wandering in and exploring, this territory and adjacent country. He has along eight carts, each loaded with about five hundred pounds of freight, and six Canadian French boys as drivers; also two half-breed men of the Chippewa tribe — one his own brother.

The finest exhibition of the aurora borealis I ever witnessed occurred to-night, beginning at nine o'clock.

To attempt a description, however, is the height of vanity. The Rev. Mr. Black and I gazed long upon it as a most remarkable manifestation in the heavens, before we could tear ourselves away and retire to rest. How long it continued after midnight I can not say.

Mr. Black, who has spent his life in Canada and Scotland, says it is much the finest exhibition he has ever seen; and Pierre has never seen its equal this side of Hudson's bay, where they are extremely common and very beautiful. We are now in latitude forty-eight degrees north, and I suppose will have frequent exhibitions of them.

SUNDAY, 7th. — A most beautiful, cool, clear, calm, and quiet day — the pleasantest we have yet had. The camp is quiet; the people are all reading or sleeping; no mosquitoes to annoy us — the cold, fresh air from the north, having rid us for a while of their hateful presence. Our camp is a most beautiful one, and is situated on the south side of Saline river, a small stream only a few yards wide. On the opposite side near by is the dragoon camp, with the horses grazing in the little valley between; the whole forming a pretty and very interesting sight.

It is three weeks to-day since we left St. Paul. Three weeks of daily travel across prairies, swamps, and streams, up early and down late. Three weeks of a bold, wild, free sort of life — which I enjoy the more the further we advance, and could travel on to Oregon without tiring. We have no long and tedious marches, made amid "the winter of discontent," and in rude, rough, and boisterous weather, but all is Indian summer, amid joyous ease, comforts, and many pleasures. Another aurora to-night — soon over; a brilliant moonlight evening; air cold, mercury down to forty-five degrees.

Some of our party of French boys have been out gunning to-day, and returned with lots of geese and ducks; others have been busy putting on new cart-axles, their usual Sunday employments. With these exceptions, things in and around both camps have been religiously quiet.

Monday, 8th.—A most beautiful, clear day, with a cool and pleasant breeze from the north. The morning the coldest we have yet had, the mercury being down to thirty-six degrees at sunrise—almost a frost. We were up early; struck tents, caught the horses, which were quite refreshed and strengthened by the rest and good pasture, and at seven, A. M., once more took up our line of march to the north. The dragoons sounded bugle, and were off ahead of us. After a march of four miles, we came to a stream supposed by us to be the Big Salt river. It flowed over a hard, and in places a stony, bed, through a deep and narrow valley; the hill-sides in some parts being heavily wooded with good-sized oaks. A range of cone-like hills, extending from the left of the road, resembling a line of mounds. The road then lay over a gently-ascending rolling prairie; a small stream of water, and a stony granitic ridge occurring occasionally. Some of the boulders in the beds of the streams, and especially on the ridges, were quite large. Some of the latter were painted in red stripes, and on one I noticed a blood-red hand, and four horse-shoes of a yellow color.

We then passed into the pretty valley of the Little Salt, and halted for dinner on its banks, after a very pleasant ride of about twelve miles, according to our usual mode of computing distances, viz., three miles an hour, on a slow walk. The banks of this small river are also heavily wooded with oak, and we have found amidst them some few more of those curses to a voyageur, warmed into life and energy by the noonday sun—I mean mosquitoes.

We started on again at three, P. M., and proceeded about five miles; and encamped for the night on the north side of quite a stream, called Cart river—the water clear and cold, and flowing over a bed of sand and gravel, and through thick woods, at times emerging and breaking through the open prairie in large, deep ravines, one fourth of a mile in width and over one hundred feet in depth, the stream in some places being very deep and broad, and thickly bordered with an undergrowth of bushes. The scenery around to-night is wild, romantic, and quite beautiful. A furious thunderstorm is coming up: the low mutterings are heard, while the forked lightnings are played all around the horizon in the distance, and the night is as black as the "dark, unfathomed caves of ocean." And now comes down the deluge, a perfect avalanche of falling waters, though the heaviest of the storm has passed around us to the south.

Tuesday, 9th.—Another fine, clear, cool day; mercury forty-eight at sunrise. We made a march this morning of about fifteen miles, and halted for dinner near a beautiful stream of cold, clear water, flowing over a sandy bottom, intermixed with slate and gravel, in common with all the streams we have crossed to-day. The country travelled over has been very beautiful—a rolling prairie, interspersed with heavy belts of timber on all the numerous streams, with a thick undergrowth in many places. The country is much better adapted to farming purposes than that passed over on the ridge between the Red and Shayenne rivers which we crossed on our last week's march. We are now descending the slope into the low lands bordering on Red river, and the country since Saturday morning's march has much improved in appearance and the land in quality. Fine farms could be located in the country we are now passing over, and for grazing purposes it can scarcely be equalled. Small lakes are abundant, and vegetation good.

This afternoon we proceeded about five miles, and halted early on an elevated ridge of timbered land, above a wide prairie before us, bounded on the far side to the northeast by the Poplar isles, just dimly visible in the distance. These islands are groves of young poplars thickly collected together for miles over the low, flat prairie, like the wooded isles of ocean.

Wednesday, 10th.—Cloudy, cool, yet very pleasant. Up at half-past three o'clock; breakfasted about daylight, and off on our march at sunrise. Rode ten miles, and reached Tongue river, as it is called—a stream of cold, clear water, and a branch of the Pembina. Here we overtook the dragoons, encamped, they having been ahead for several days. Here we also found the governor and Tyler, they having gone on and left us yesterday, to overtake and stop our escort—and compel them to accompany us into Pembina, from which we are now distant only some thirty miles.

This afternoon we travelled eight miles, when the horses giving out, we camped on the open prairie, without wood, and no good water, and the mosquitoes nearly as bad as at the Shayenne. To-night we have had a heavy thunderstorm, to avoid which and our unremitting persecutors we betook ourselves to the tents, and thence inside our mosquito-bars, and lay secure from both. We passed through the "Poplar isles" to-day, and found it to be a flat, swampy, and uninteresting portion of country. The dragoons are out of sight ahead again to-night.

THURSDAY, 11th.—Cold and cloudy, with rain and mist nearly all day; wind northeast, and by far the most unpleasant day we have yet had. Up late, and breakfasted in the rain for the first time on the march. Rode about twelve miles, and at noon reached Bottineau point, a prominent point of woods on Tongue river. Here we halted and dined in the high, wet grass—our last meal out. It consisted of ducks (of which we shot about fifty on the banks of Duck lake, near by), also pork and boiled buffalo-tongues, potatoes, tea, &c., with wild plums for dessert which we found on some scrubby trees on the river-bank, and, though not fully ripe, were quite a luxury.

At two, P. M., we started on, and soon found the dragoons again. They were encamped in the edge of the woods on Tongue river, where they remain till to-morrow. We now had eight miles of swampy prairie to cross, and at four, P. M., came in sight of the first houses at the Red river settlement, much to our great joy; as a house was as much of a novelty to us after a tramp of five hundred miles across the unpeopled prairies, as the first sight of land is to the weary and tempest-tossed mariner.

The houses were full of half-breeds, who saluted us with the discharge of guns, &c. Dr. Foster and Mr. Lord rode on ahead, and were treated to milk and potatoes—a treat equal to that of the milk and honey received by the wandering children of Israel of old. A mile beyond we came to the junction of the Red and Pembina rivers, and found the trading-post of N. W. Kittson, Esq., and the settlement called Pembina in the angle at the junction. Here we found half a dozen log-dwellings, and a quantity of half-breed and Chippewa lodges; the American flag flying from the top of a tall flag-staff; with barns, stables, haystacks, horses, cattle, &c., and things generally looking very comfortable. On the muddy banks in front stood an admiring group of several hundred whites, half-breeds, and Indians, of all sizes; with any quantity of dogs, very large and wolfish: and amid this Babel of cries, yelps, barks, and shouts, from the said big dogs and little papoose Indians, we came to a halt and reconnoitred, on the south side of the Pembina and west of the Red river, standing almost glued fast in the sticky, tenacious mud, caused by the rains and annual overflow of these two rivers for three years past. The timber upon their banks is dead (drowned out), the ground destitute of grass, with tall, rank weeds three and four feet in height abounding.

The rivers are very muddy and deep, with but little current. Red river is about one hundred yards in width, and the Pembina twenty-five yards. The country is very flat all around, and the streams heavily wooded, while a thick growth of young, dead willows line the water's edge from Pembina to Selkirk settlement. Mr. Kittson and Messrs. Rolette and Cavileer soon visited us and took us over to the town, giving us the freedom of the place, besides sending some Selkirk butter and eggs across to us at camp. Our carts arriving at dark, we built a rousing fire, pitched tents, covered the banks with grass and weeds, spread our oil-cloths and mattresses, and were once more comfortable.

This is our last night "out of sight of land"—slept our last sleep on the tented prairie for the present, which I regret, as it is far preferable to a bed of down within a palace. Slept well, too, considering the multitude of discordant and almost unearthly sounds which struck upon our drowsy ears, accustomed to quietness and calm. Now are heard the Indians shrieking and beating upon drums at their camp across the Pembina; and those big dogs keep howling dismally, like a host of wild, voracious wolves. The dark and cloudy night is made hideous with hell-like wailings; and the mournful, sighing wind bears to our ears the sharp and piercing cries from a hundred deep-toned throats, sounding in their awfulness like the despairing howlings of the damned. So much for our first night at Pembina.

We have thus made the march from Sauk rapids to this place in twenty travelling days, being twenty-two in all, and from St. Paul just twenty-five days. Messrs. Kittson and Cavileer came through a short time since in twelve days, or about nine and a half days of marching time, the quickest trip on record.

Friday, 12th.—Weather cool and pleasant; the mercury forty-eight degrees at sunrise. This morning we rode a few miles out of town, and met the dragoons advancing, and then *escorted them* to the junction of the Pembina and Red rivers where we all crossed the former stream, to the settlements beyond. We found a busy scene on going over. The houses are built around an open space, and the square courtyard (so to speak) is filled with a miscellaneous crowd of half-breeds, Indians, of all sizes, with their lodges of bark and skins, together with horses, cattle, carts, dogs, &c., in great variety and numbers.

The houses are built of logs, filled with mud and straw; the roofs thatched with the latter, and some covered over with bark. Around the angles of the yard are various warehouses, an icehouse, blacksmith-shop, and the trading-house, or store, which is covered completely over with large squares of bark, and looked like an entire barkhouse. In front, toward the river, are barns and stables, haystacks, &c., with numerous horses and cattle feeding, and a general appearance of thrift, comfort, and industry, pervades the scene—so new and interesting to us all, after a three-weeks' jaunt across the prairies, in which we did not meet a single human creature, not even a roaming Chippewa or Sioux.

We took possession of Mr. Kittson's house, which he had

kindly placed at our disposal, and celebrated our arrival by a sumptuous dinner, in which *hot corn* and potatoes, onions, &c., as big as pint tin-cups, formed the principal item in the vegetable line. These were grown in the gardens here, and are the only productions of the soil now cultivated at this place; no farming whatever being done, on account of the annual floods in the valley of the Red river, for three years past—the waters having risen to the height of thirty-one and thirty-three feet above low-water mark, flooding all the country, and inundating the houses at this place to the depth of two and three feet. Mr. Kittson was obliged to leave the post at this place last spring, and take up his residence for a month upon the surrounding highlands. These floods, should they continue, will prove a serious drawback to the settlement of this valley, the half-breeds being loath to put in crops when they are liable to be swept off annually.

Mr. Kittson had some six thousand rails swept off from his place last year. To obviate this difficulty, a new town and an agricultural settlement has been laid out by Mr. Kittson, and the Rev. Mr. Belcourt (the catholic priest stationed at this place), on what is called the Pembina mountain, thirty miles to the west of this place, and bordering on the river Pembina. The situation is a very eligible one, in a fine farming region; the land is excellent, and the timber abundant. The town is called "St. Joseph's," and is situated upon the eastern slope of the longitudinal ridge of land, called Mount Pembina, which is in places heavily wooded, and presents an Alleganian appearance as it is approached or skirted along toward the east.

Since our arrival, the name of "Waucheona," the Chippewa term for *mountain*, has been selected by Dr. Foster, and adopted by Mr. Kittson, as the name of the embryō town; he being opposed to exhausting the whole calendar of saints, and making every one of them stand as godfather to every town, lake, mountain, or stream, in the territory.

In consequence of there being no farming operations carried on here now, we found no grain on hand to feed our horses, excepting barley, and that is brought up from the Selkirk settlements, one hundred miles down Red river. Barley is a stronger feeder than oats, yet not so good as corn. It produces more than oats, say about forty bushels to the acre; and the price below ranges from fifty cents to a dollar per bushel, the former being the standard price when no extra demand takes place.

This afternoon I took a walk across "the line," two miles below, in company with the Rev. Messrs. Black and Tanner, the latter a half-breed Chippewa. About half way down, we passed the residence of the Rev. M. Belcourt, a large, two-story frame-house, situated alongside of a rude log-church, surmounted by a wooden cross.

The site is a very pleasant and commanding one, upon the high ground about half a mile back from the river, and safe from floods. Gardens, out-houses, and vehicles, were scattered around, and an air of comfort, and the rude enjoyments of a far-off *home*, were visible. I am told that all the half-breeds here are catholics, with perhaps a few exceptions, and that Mr. Belcourt has resided among them, at the settlements below, and here, the long term of twenty-three years and upward. He is at present at the Mountain. At the *line* (forty-nine degrees) we found an elm-post, which was planted in the ground, upon the river bank, by Major Woods and Capt. Pope, bearing date, August 14, 1849. Just beyond is the first trading post and buildings of the Hudson's Bay Company, in this direction, a rival post of Kittson's. The buildings are built of logs and mud, one story high, and thatched with straw, are very warm and comfortable, and built around an open square. Here we found an old Scotch gentleman, named Sittare, an employee of the Bay Company, and who has charge of this place. He is a native of the Orkney Isles, and has resided in British America the still longer term of forty-eight years. A lifetime spent amid such solitudes *is enough* to make a man a misanthrope, and no one need wonder at it if I were to say that the old gentleman was not the most agreeable personage that I have met in this direction.

His only companions were a few half-breeds; the trading-house was closed, no trade, or business of any kind on hand, and the whole place was dull and desolate. Slept in our tent to-night, as of old; it is pitched in the court-yard, in front of the main buildings, with large fires burning around, and at each, is assembled a motley group of whites, half-breeds, and Indians; while in the distance, the dogs are howling, the braves and younger squaws are dancing promiscuously around their lodges, singing and beating drums for their amusement, and perhaps as a lullaby to us. They succeed most admirably, in making the black night as hideous as possible. Our escort of dragoons, are encamped about one fourth of a mile back upon the prairie, and their camp of snow-white tents, with the American flag flying gayly in the breeze, presents qnite a pretty appearance, in contrast with the half-breed and Indian lodges, which are dotted here and there, separately, and in little hamlets of a dozen, all around as far as the eye can reach.

Saturday, 13th.—Cloudy, cold, raw, and windy, most of the day. The wind is keen from the northeast, and feels like that of a winter's day in milder latitudes. The mercury was down to fifty degrees at sunrise, and only rose to sixty-five degrees. Early this morning, a large Mackinaw boat started for the settlements below, in quest of barley; ourselves and escort requiring three hundred bushels. The boat was manned by eight half-breeds, six of whom were oarsmen. They will occupy two days in going down; two more in collecting the barley, and getting it thrashed, as it now stands out in the fields in shocks; five days to ascend the crooked, sluggish stream, and will bring about one hundred and sixty bushels; after which they will return for another load, and immediately on their second arrival, say about the 1st of October, we will start homeward. To-day the half-breeds and Indians were served out rations; the Indians received flour and pemmican for three days' subsistence; and the half-breeds the same; with an additional allowance to each family of four pounds of sugar, and one pound of tea, they all being great lovers of that beverage. This occupied all the morning. The Indians number some five hundred, and the half-breeds, who drew rations, about fifty families. The latter are living here during their attendance on the treaty, in skin-lodges; though I am told they have comfortable log-houses, when settled perma nently at home; and when not out on their semi-annual hunt. I have observed a number of their houses along the banks of Pembina and Red rivers, and understand the rest to be at the Mountain, and away out at Devil's lake, about one hundred miles to the southwest. Their occupation at present is exclusively that of hunters; and their life is naturally a free and easy, and a careless one; hunting buffalo and making pemmican and ox-carts, occupy all their time. These carts are made entirely of wood, not even an iron nail is used, wooden pins, and thongs, and bands of hide, being substituted. The only tools used are an axe, a hand-saw, a three-quarter, and an inch auger, with chisels of the same size. The carts are sold for thirty shillings; which is the average price, except in the hunting seasons, when in demand, they sell as high as ten dollars. A pair of wheels alone, are then worth five dollars. They are very strong, and will carry twelve hundred pounds of buffalo and pemmican.

The fall hunt comes off soon after the conclusion of the treaty. The usual time for starting upon the summer and fall hunts, is the 10th of June and September. Nothing but pemmican and dried meat is secured on these two hunts; the robes being all taken in the winter, when the hair is long; the party returned from their summer hunt just before our arrival here. They were unsuccessful too, for once, and returned quite poor and empty-handed. The had a desperate fight, about the 20th of August, with the Yankton Sioux, who were one thousand strong, and all mounted upon horses; the affair took place away off upon the Missouri plains, upon the western slope of the Coteau des Prairies, and resulted in the victory of the half-breeds after they had been entrenched behind their carts and an earth embankment, for a day or two. I did not ascertain the number killed on either side.

Sunday, 14th.—Cloudy, cold, raw, and windy; quite unpleasant and unseasonable. An over-coat is necessary out of doors, this morning, and fires in the house, for comfort; the weather, as well as other matters, serves to remind us of our northern latitude. To-day we had preaching by the Rev.

John Black, in the dining-room of the governor's house; a novelty most certainly, in this far distant region. The congregation consisted of about a dozen whites, and three half-breeds. The Rev. Mr. Tanner also officiated, sang, and prayed, in English; and this afternoon, he preached in the open air, to the assembled Indians in the Chippewa language. Some of them paid close attention, sitting in a circle upon the ground; while others were listless and wandering, and others stood looking on from a distance, with the dragoons and half-breeds. The Chippewa is a beautifully sounding language, like the Italian. Mr. Tanner uses the Chippewa testament and hymns, which were translated by his father, who was for many years a prisoner among them, and wrote a book thereon. Mr. Tanner is about thirty-five years of age, and a very superior man for his class; he was born on the east side of Red river, opposite this place; was educated at Mackinaw, and has acted as a missionary among the Indians at Red lake, for the last five years. He removed to this place a week ago, and intends farming, teaching school, &c., for a livelihood after the conclusion of the treaty. His wife is a half-breed, and they reside at present, in a lodge in the yard at this place. He is a fluent and earnest speaker, and discourses with great fervor and much eloquence to his red brethren, and is calculated to do good, if any can be done among them; he has been with them on their buffalo-hunts to the Missouri plains, armed like the rest; and has hunted buffalo and made pemmican all the week, and preached the gospel to them on Sundays—this being one phase of missionary life upon the prairies. He also has a half-breed brother, a real heathen as he styles him, who ranks as a chief among the Indians, and who lives among them, and accompanies them upon their hunts. This afternoon, things are dull and quiet; the Indians are strolling around, or lying idly in their lodges; the squaws are lugging huge loads of wood upon their backs, which they cut upon the river's bank, and secure by a strap passing over their shoulders and around the forehead; their bodies bending beneath the heavy load. Dozens of dirty children, half-clad in a piece of still dirtier blanket, are also playing around. The half-breeds are sitting around the fires in the yard; some lying in their lodges, and others standing at a respectful distance, listening to Mr. Tanner. Their young priest, M. Lecombe, has come down from his residence at the mission-house since vespers, and is holding a consultation with the governor. He seems to be a very intelligent, fine, young fellow; and intends accompanying us homeward to St. Paul, on his way to Montreal; where the Rev. Mr. Black came from, on his way to Selkirk settlement; thus keeping up an equilibrium in religious matters, and effecting a change between these two distant regions, in the persons of two ministers of different faiths; which is pleasant to contemplate, and which will be of great advantage to all concerned.

THE TREATY.

MONDAY, 15th.—Still cold, raw, windy, and unpleasant; wind east-southeast; it looks, feels too, very much like snow, and has for several days past; the mercury was down to fifty at sunrise. At noon the Indians met, and the treaty commenced in front of the governor's house; his excellency, with Dr. Foster as secretary, and others, were sitting at a table at the front door; the principal chiefs, braves, and head men of the Red lake and Pembina bands of Chippewas, were sitting on low seats in front, while around behind them in a semi-circle stood a numerous crowd of half-breeds and Indians, men, boys, squaws, and papooses, accompanied by their dogs, who, for once during our stay here, were quiet. The governor opened the council by an address of some length, which was interpreted by the Rev. Mr. Tanner and James Nolen, to them; as also their replies made in return. An old Indian, named "Clear-Weather," replied twice to the governor's remarks, in which he was quite pert and facetious as he thought, and ended by wanting a plain statement of our business there, and what we were going to do for them—what we were going to offer them, told bluntly and without any circumlocution or ornament; he wanted no "sugared words or honeyed phrases." He was not at all satisfied with what had been said to them, and wanted something more definite, explicit, and to the point, and then they would go and make up their minds upon it, provided their great father would present them at least two bullocks in the meantime, as they were extremely hungry and could not deliberate on empty stomachs. The governor then told them they were women, and not the great Chippewa hunters he had thought them; that it was their duty as children to present their father with something to eat, after he had travelled such a long weary journey across the prairies purposely to meet them; but as he was now satisfied that they were squaws, and knew not how to hunt, he would go himself this afternoon and kill them some buffalo, and asked them "if they would have cows or bulls!" This little sally or bit of by-play put them all in good humor, and the council closed till ten, A. M., to-morrow. The dignitaries and potentates of this region of the earth then walked off majestically and proudly; and these stoics (?)—these men without a tear (?)—were seen no more. In plain terms they *vamoosed,* in double quick time, lugging off their tobacco on their shoulders, and driving off their cattle, with loud shouts, to camp, where the rest of the day was devoted to gormandizing, and to-night we have hell let loose again among them.

Tuesday, 16th.—Cloudy, cold, windy, and rainy. At daylight a rainstorm set in from the southeast, and continued nearly all day. A regular old fashioned equinoctial; mercury down to fifty-four and only rose to sixty-one degrees. No council was held that day in consequence of the storm. The Indians all invisible; all at home in their lodges, surfeiting themselves on ox meat and pemmican. Things very dull and gloomy; everywhere around the tent-fires are all extinguished, and the star-spangled banner droops and hangs straight down the tall flag-staff, reared high in air above. The mud in the court-yard is as tenacious as pitch, and glues a man to the ground as soon as he steps out. We were, therefore, compelled to be sedentary; spent the day, for my own part, in reading "Major Long's Second Expedition to the Source of the St. Peter's River, Red River Valley, and Across the British Line, in 1825–'26;" also prepared and packed up provisions for a canoe trip to-morrow down to Selkirk settlement, Fort Garry, &c.

WEDNESDAY, 17th.—The weather has cleared off finely, and is cool and pleasant; wind west-southwest, and the sun quite warm; the mercury sixty-one degrees at sunrise. Rose at daylight and prepared for a start down the river, in company with the Rev. John Black, in a bark canoe, with two *Bois Brulés** as voyageurs. Our canoe was fifteen feet long, and three feet wide, and was pretty well loaded down with ourselves, our bedding, baggage, and provisions. We started at seven, A. M., and paddled down the crooked, muddy river at the rate of some four miles an hour, stopping several hours to breakfast and dinner upon the river bank, and more frequently to haul out our leaky, frail canoe, and pitch the bottom with melted epinette, a vegetable gum used for that purpose. We saw large flocks of geese and ducks swimming among the dead willows along the banks, and could have shot large quantities, but we had not time to stop and pick them up. The ducks were all quite tame, and would approach within a few feet of our canoe, being so unused to the sight of human beings as to feel no fear. Other birds are numerous, among which I notice the eagle, hawk, crane, crow, plover, blackbird, and pigeon; also observed a fish-duck diving after fish; he was a fine large fellow, with a long bill, and a bright scarlet head; he swam toward us boldly, and thereby saved his life by his fearless confidence.

Red river is a very uninteresting stream; its waters are a liquid mud and have a very disagreeable taste, and affect the bowels of all persons unaccustomed to their use. The banks of the river are low, and extremely soft and muddy; you sink in knee-deep immediately on stepping foot on shore, where you stick and flounder about considerably before reaching the dry, hard prairie-ground above.

Along its whole course, both banks, within the margin of the stream, are covered with the thick growth of drowned-out willows before spoken of, while farther back on the prairie, fine large trees, majestic oaks and elms, are in the same con-

* Half-breeds; the name signifies burned wood.

dition; and now stand towering aloft like high, giant skeleton sentinels, throwing out their dry and leafless limbs across the water, as if to guard its passage. Each tree is marked at the height of some thirty feet above the water by the heavy drift-ice during the spring freshets; and the bark of all the timber to that height is of a dirty mud color, which, with the dead, drowned-out trees, presents a very disagreeable aspect. In some places the timber merely skirts the banks on both sides, and a broad expanse extends far on either hand; at others the timber extends farther than the eye can penetrate, and no prairie at all is visible for many miles, all being a desolate solitude of dead and dying skeleton trunks of leafless trees. There are some trunks in the river too forming snags; the water is very deep, current sluggish, say about one mile an hour generally, and in some places almost imperceptible, with not more than half a mile of straight channel at a time; for while its general course is due north it twists and turns in a very serpentine manner, to all points of the compass. The river contains no islands, and the only rapids are down below Selkirk settlement. A fine steamboat navigation will be found from there up to the junction of the Bois des Sioux, a distance of nearly four hundred miles; and one far better than that of the Mississippi above St. Anthony. We passed by the mouths of a number of small streams, viz., the Red Grass, Marias, Gratiaro, &c., which all resemble deep crooked ditches, and pour out additional quantities of thick, dark mud-colored water, the washings of the rich and fertile prairies, now blooming with numerous flowers, through which they flow.

This is a splendid evening, the finest we have had for a long time; the sun is setting beautifully into the bosom of the far-off prairie, as it were, while all Nature is calm, still, and composed; the silence only broken by the dipping of our paddles, the occasional chirping of a bird, and the rapid rising of the scared wild fowl from out the smooth, calm surface of the water as we approach. We halted at sunset, about forty miles distant from Pembina, and have a good camp in a thick woods, where the only drawback to our comfort is the mosquitoes, which are as usual extremely annoying to us. The warm sun to-day unfortunately revived them from the torpid state in which the late cold storm had thrown them. We have our bar put up, tent-fashion, the corners being fastened to four stakes, and the raised apex or centre is secured to a bent pole, which keeps it upright and tightly stretched. Our bed consists of a robe and three blankets, with our coats and overcoats, &c., for pillows. We are upon an old camping ground, where two hundred and fifty cords of wood has been cut and piled around for the use of the settlements below this winter. The night is very clear and fine, the face of heaven is smiling amid myriads of twinkling stars; the northern horizon is lit up with the rays and dancing beams of an aurora, while the woods and silent flowing river are illuminated by our camp-fire; our voyageurs are fast asleep upon the ground before us, and not a sound is heard, save that of the crackling, leaping flames and the low tone of our own voices as we chat merrily. And now as my companion reads a chapter in his French pocket-bible, and I pencil down these sketches of fact and fancy by the light of the burning fagots—but hark! we have company it seems, and are not so lonely as I thought—that was the hoot-owl's cry; and sounds like the wailings of a friend in misery—*that* was the cry, long drawn out and dismal, of a distant wolf; and now they are heard yelping and barking furiously, like a pack of hungry curs. And what was THAT—more unearthly than the fierce war-whoop, which almost freezes the young, warm blood, and turns the stout, athletic frame to stone? Was it a " demon-spirit or goblin damned," or the mere howling of the rising wind, the precursor of another storm, I see arising in the distant horizon! Ha! I see two gleaming, fiery eye-balls in the thicket of the underbrush: " *Take that,* to light you to better quarters;" I hurl a blazing fire-brand toward the varmint, who, with another dismal cry, leaves us to quietness, and to repose and sleep.

THURSDAY, 18th.—A fine, clear, beautiful day; cold early in the morning, and warm through the day, with a pleasant breeze; the storm has blown over for the present. We were up and away at daylight, stopping several hours to dine and breakfast. While cooking our morning meal, some half dozen horsemen came galloping down the road along the western bank, and passed on down without calling on us; they were half-breeds returning from the treaty. There is less woodland along the banks to-day, and we have a fine open view of the immense prairies on either side. Occasionally we pass hay-stacks, enclosed by a rude fence, to which the settlers drive their cattle in the winter season, from the settlement below.

The banks are still very low and muddy, and covered with a line of the same young dead willow. We camped to-night, again, on the top of a high bank we found after a long search till dark for a choice spot. It was covered over with bushes and heavy timber, and alive with ravenous mosquitoes. The evening is damp and cloudy, heavy masses of dark clouds are rising in the west, and a storm is coming, sure. We retired early, very much dissatisfied at not reaching the settlements to-night, which we ought by all means to have done. Our voyageurs, however, being paid so much per day, have not hurried themselves; and, besides, our canoe is so leaky and out of order, that we have frequently to land, empty all our goods upon the muddy bank, and gum the bottom with melted epinette. We are, consequently, about twenty miles above Fort Garry, and some ten miles above the nearest house, at the upper end of the Half-Breed settlement, which extends along both sides of the crooked river, in the shape of a long serpentine village, down as far as Fort Garry, at the mouth of the Assiniboin.

Friday, September 19.—This morning we arose at daylight, in the midst of a dense fog and mist, wind northeast; cold and raw, and has the appearance of another regularly built north-easter. At five, A. M., we started, anxious to get down to more comfortable quarters; and at half-past seven we came in sight of the first houses; stopped, had breakfast, and while eating the barge came up with a large sail hoisted, moving slowly against the current, without the assistance of the oars. She contained a hundred and sixty bushels of barley, and will be ten days upon the trip; some of the men being sick, detained them longer than they should have been. We then proceeded on down the river, in the face of a heavy gale of wind, and huge rolling waves, nearly all the balance of the day, although the distance by land was but nine miles to Fort Garry. As we were much retarded, we at length deserted our voyageurs and canoe, and taking to the shore, we walked on down the settlements on the right bank of the river, at times following a good road along the river, and then taking a near cut through the woods from point to point, and cutting off the bends. After losing ourselves several times, and only finding our way with considerable search and difficulty, we finally arrived opposite the fort at three, P. M., heartily fatigued and glad to rest at the house of M. Narcisse Marion, a French-Canadian, and the father-in-law of N. W. Kittson, Esq. We found him very kind, hospitable, and communicative, and anxious to hear the news from above; i. e. from Pembina, St. Paul, and elsewhere. In an hour our boat arrived, and we then proceeded on down to the residence of Mr. Alexander Ross, on the west side of Red river, and about a mile below. The old gentlemen met us on the bank, welcomed us to Selkirk, and escorted us up to his house; a white, rough-cast, two story stone, which stands upon a large bend of the river, and commands a view both ways; and that view is certainly the finest I have seen for a long, long time.

FIRST GLANCE AT SELKIRK SETTLEMENT.

A village of farmhouses, with barns, stables, hay, wheat, and barley-stacks, with small cultivated fields or lots, well fenced, are stretched along the meandering river, while the prairies far off to the horizon are covered over with herds of cattle, horses, &c., the fields filled with a busy throng of whites, half-breeds and Indians—men, squaws, and children—all reaping, binding, and stacking the golden grain; while hundreds of carts, with a single horse or ox, harnessed in their shafts, are brought in requisition to carry it to the well-stored barn, and are seen moving, with their immense loads rolling along like huge stacks, in all directions, Add to this the numerous wind-mills, some in motion whirling around their giant arms, while others motionless are waiting for "a grist." Just above, Fort Garry sits in the angle at the junction of the Assiniboin and Red rivers, with a blood-red flag inscribed with the letters H. B. Co., floating gayly in the breeze. Opposite is the catholic cathedral, built of stone in 1832, and still unfinished. The bare, rough, unplastered wall, in front, is cracked and shattered, and is surmounted by two steeples; one finished, and containing a chime of bells; the bare timbers of the other tower aloft, dark with age and nakedness. I visited the interior this afternoon, and found a very spacious nave, which was being remodeled, as also the galleries; and men were at work on scaffolding, painting the arched ceiling of a deep mazarene blue, and ornamenting it with wreaths and festoons of flowers; the work, so far as completed, is done in a very artist-like manner. A number of priests reside upon the spot; a large frame convent painted red adjoins it on the south, and the congregation is composed principally of half-breeds from up Red river.

For a distance of two miles up the Assiniboin river, to the west, are seen the farms and dwellings of the pensioners; the former well fenced and cultivated, the latter of frame and logs, one story high, mostly rough-cast, or white-washed over, with gardens, &c., attached, and comfort and plenty attending and smiling around them. Many other objects of interest worthy of notice strike the eye, but the above suffices for a first glance at Selkirk. The scene that has met my eyes this afternoon, has become daguerreotyped upon my optics, never to be effaced. As I saw thee to-day, Selkirk, so shall I always see thee; and to the latest hour of my existence, thy beauties, as faintly portrayed above, will, to my mind's eye, at least, remain indelibly imprinted. We spent the night with Mr. Ross and family, and found him to be a very intelligent and interesting old gentleman, full of information as regards this northwest region, and of Selkirk colony in particular. He has published a book descriptive of the country west of the Rocky mountains, Vancouver's, and the Pacific coast, where he spent some fifteen years of his life, prior to 1825, since when he has been residing in this colony, and has been for a long time one of its leading citizens.

SATURDAY, 20th.—Cloudy, raw, and cold, most of the day; very unpleasant out of doors; but as my time here is precious, I paid no attention to it. What is wind or weather to a man who never expects to get to Selkirk in his life again, and has but three short days to stay, now that he is here, and that, too, in the very centre of the continent, and a whole month's march of twenty miles per day to the west of sundown? Spent the day in visiting around the settlement; called at Fort Garry, and made the acquaintance of Major Caldwell, a Highland Scotchman, the governor of the colony, and of the seventy families of pensioners sent out by the British government. Also met Mr. John Black, a very polished gentleman, who has charge of the Bay Company's post here at the fort, Dr. Cowan, and Messrs. Pelley, Lane, and Logan, junior. Close by the fort is the fine large mansion-house of Mr. M'Dermott, a very wealthy Irish gentleman, who came out to the colony in 1812. As he was one of the pioneers, a free, good, hearty, sociable gentleman, an every man's man, who has an open house for friend or stranger, I paid my compliments to him, and to his son-in-law, Mr. Ballantine, a very polite and friendly personage, as are all I met. Here I met a number of the fair ladies of the settlement; ladies of much beauty, educated and accomplished, and of some fortune, I am told. Wine was passed around, and much pleasant conversation indulged in; and I, a stranger, found myself almost at home. Who could leave such company? I could not, and the consequence of it was, that I found myself up, and in a very lively mood, till after the witching time of night, in close confab with—*the old gentleman*, all about the colony, in which we discussed its affairs, past, present, and prospective, at great length. Mr. M'Dermott can talk more and faster than any half dozen men I ever met before, and would have regaled me till the early dawn to-morrow, without tiring. I had also the honor to meet and make the acquaintance of Recorder Thom, formerly editor of the *Montreal Herald*, the most ultra, radical sheet in Canada. Mr. Thom is a leading man here, and is very active, energetic, and possessed of considerable talent. He is at present the clerk of the court, at a salary of £750 per annum, though he is not allowed to act as such, or enter the court, so objectionable is he to the half-breed population; and an editorial published in the *Herald*, during the Canadian troubles in 1837, it seems has arrayed the French-Canadians, too, in deadly hostility against his person. Numerous threats have been made against him; and his life heretofore, at times, has not been safe. Away with politics, however; I did not intend to touch on this; and so, kind reader, a good night to you. "The iron tongue of midnight has tolled twelve," and I'll see Selkirk shovelled off down Red river, an island made of it in the very centre of Lake Winnepeg, before I will write another word to-night.

SUNDAY, 21st.—The weather this morning is cloudy, with a Scotch mist at times; afternoon warm, clear, and pleasant. I started this morning on horseback, in company with Mr. Ballintine, to see a portion of the lower settlement, down Red river. We rode over a good road, about one hundred yards in width, which extends to the rear of the line of houses, a row of five-acre fields lying in between; while on the river-bank, in front, there is nothing but a footpath. The English and Scotch portions of the settlements extend in a continuous village along both banks, following all the turns of the crooked river, from the upper to the lower Fort Garry, a distance of twenty miles. The latter is called the stone fort, is much the largest and best, and is the residence of Governor Colville of Prince Rupert's Land. Below this fort an Indian village extends for miles; while up the Assiniboin, scattered settlements of pensioners and half-breeds stretch along to White-Horse plain, a distance of some twenty-five miles; making in all an extended settlement of whites, half-breeds, and Indians, of nearly seventy miles, and comprising a population of whites and half-breeds of some six thousand souls. We rode down about ten miles, to the middle or log church; the other two, one of which is of stone, are situated at each end of the English settlement, near the forts, so that no one has to travel over a distance of five miles to some one of the three: quite a desideratum in the winter, when the thermometer is down to forty-five and fifty degrees below zero! These churches are episcopalian, are large and commodious, and are surmounted with high steeples, each containing a sweet-toned bell. The officiating ministers are Bishop Anderson, Rev. John Chapman, and others, all of whom I have had the pleasure of becoming acquainted with. The congregations are large and respectable, and would prove creditable to any western settlement in the states. I met the people on their way to church to-day — some on foot, some in carts, and others in more stylish vehicles, all well dressed and happy looking.

They appear to have all the creature-comforts, and to revel in abundance. Each farmer has a frontage of six chains upon the river, which extends back two miles, though little of it to the west of the main road is cultivated; the fertile prairies, carpeted over with wild-flowers, lying a beautiful and unprofitable waste, save for grazing purposes, and a portion of its annual crop of wild hay.

We returned at two, P. M., and dined at the upper fort, with Dr. Cowan, and Messrs. Pelley, Landee, and Logan. This evening we took a stroll up the Assiniboin, along the north bank, among the pensioners. Thirteen families reside within the fort; the balance are stationed for two miles up the river: those nearest having twenty acres of land under cultivation, the others forty acres. All the duties incumbent upon them toward the government are, to appear on parade each Sunday, and to drill twelve times a year. I therefore saw them at home with their families, and out strolling along the river, all in their uniform. Although much better off than they ever could be at home, yet I am told they are great grumblers, and are very much dissatisfied with their condition, and very unreliable as a police force in case of an emergency.

I had the pleasure of meeting the ladies of the fort this evening; and although they are from the Orkney isles, a rude region amid the inhospitable northern seas, yet they will compare favorably with any I have ever met amid the fashionable life of an eastern city.

MONDAY, 22d. — Cloudy and very damp early in the morning. It cleared off soon, however, and remained bright, clear, and warm, and now at last seems like a delightful Indian summer. After buying up all the half-breed and Indian curiosities, and everything else of interest I could find, I bade adieu to everybody; wrote a hasty letter to the people of St. Paul, by an express which starts immediately; dined once more with the very clever fellows at the fort, and then with much reluctance started homeward. And now, in leaving this hospitable colony, I desire to pay this tribute to its people. Amid all my wanderings over this earth of ours, I have never been more kindly treated, nor made the friendship of a more whole-souled people; I have never in so short a time become so much attached to any place, nor left it with one half the keen regret, I now do this. As I pass slowly along the lonely road that leads me from thee, Selkirk, mine eyes do turn continually to gaze upon thy smiling, golden fields, and thy lofty towers now burnished with the rays of the departing sun; while the sweet vesper-bell reverberates afar, and strikes so mournfully pleasant upon mine ear. I feel satisfied that, though absent thousands of weary miles, my thoughts will always dwell on thee with rapturous emotion.

Pembina, Thursday, 25th.—Cloudy, with rain, thunder, and lightning, in the afternoon. I reached here yesterday evening, stiff and sore from the long march of seventy miles; and found that most of our party had started down Red river, on Monday morning last, in two canoes, with eight *Bois Brulés* in each. As I came by land, I missed them all. The treaty was concluded on Saturday evening last, having occupied all the week. The Indians and half-breeds have all left.

Friday, 26th.—Cloudy, cold, and windy from the north; very unpleasant. Mr. Kittson's ten carts started for the fall hunt of buffalo, and will wait for the balance of the party at the mountain till our arrival next week—at which place the governor promised to meet and speak to the assembled half-breeds. The brother of the Rev. Mr. Tanner arrived from the plains yesterday, with his cart surmounted with an immense pair of elk-horns, which we intend to take with us to St. Paul. They are the largest I have ever seen, have some ten prongs, and measure about five feet from point to point. Although

Tanner is a half-breed, and dresses like them, he ranks as a chief among the Chippewas, and should have been present at the treaty. He says he kept away on purpose, apprehending difficulty: a wily sort of politician in Indian tactics, it seems, like some of our own *vote-dodgers*. He is a very tall, muscular, and active fellow, with a very dark complexion, long, dark hair, and black eyes, and is from forty-five to fifty years of age.

He is one of Mr. Kittson's most successful and reliable hunters, and brings in annually about five hundred dollars' worth of furs. Unlike the rest, he is very careful and prudent of his money, rather close in his dealings, strictly honest, with an aversion to getting in debt.

He has a family, consisting of an Indian wife and half a dozen children, who accompany him upon his hunts, and spend the winters out on the Missouri plains, and along the Assiniboin, inside of the British line. He left to-day for the Mountain and Selkirk settlement, to get such of his supplies as were not to be obtained at this place; his brother, the Rev. James Tanner, accompanying him.

I feel much interested in them, on account of their father, John Tanner, whose own published narrative I expect to have the pleasure of reading, and of whose history I have read an interesting sketch in Major Long's second expedition to these regions, besides gleaning considerable verbal information from different persons here concerning him.

SATURDAY, 27th.—A fair, clear, and very pleasant day; the sun warm, atmosphere hazy, and a pleasant breeze prevailing—regular Indian summer, superlatively fine in the forty-ninth degree. Things are very dull here at present, and all hands long to be off.

The dragoons are busy cleaning up carbines, pistols, knives, &c., and getting ready for the homeward march, and lots of buffalo-cows and bear. Some twenty-five lodges of Indians are still present, "loafing" around by day, and singing and dancing all night long, beating drums, and making the darkness generally as hideous as night was ever made.

The Red-lake Indians have all left for home. They are a

better and more provident class, it seems, and raise large quantities of corn, potatoes, pumpkins, &c., while their missionaries grow winter and spring wheat in perfection. The Rev. J. P. Bardwell, the agent for the Oberlin board of missions, and Rev. S. G. Wright, who is stationed at Red Lake, left here for that place on Monday last, they having been down to Selkirk for some stock-cattle. Red lake is about one hundred miles to the southeast of Pembina, and is in latitude forty-eight degrees — being far to the north and west of Lake Itasca, the source of the Mississippi.

SUNDAY, 28th. — Another fine, clear, beautiful day; the mercury rose to seventy-two degrees. I am told there was ice this morning, though I did not see it. The first frost in this valley, north of the line, occurred on the morning of the 24th, and it was a very heavy one. I gathered wild-flowers in the gardens at Selkirk, two days previously, in latitude fifty degrees.

I took a ride to-day into her majesty's possessions, and called at the Hudson Bay Company's post just across the line. Spent some hours very pleasantly with the employers, who are in the "service," as they term it. The party of *Bois Brulés*, sixteen in number, who accompanied the governor's party down the river, returned by land this morning, with their canoes on carts. They left on Thursday, and reported that his excellency and suite would be here to-night. They did not come, and to prevent our disappointment we were treated to another brilliant display of aurora borealis, almost equal to the one described on the 6th instant.

MONDAY, 29th. — Cloudy, foggy, and misty, till ten, A. M.; the rest of the day warm and fine. The mercury rose to seventy-seven degrees.

Hugh Tyler and Lieutenant Corley arrived on panting and foaming steeds, at ten, A. M., having rode from the *Rivière Gratiaro,* thirty miles, since six, A. M. The governor, Dr. Foster, and guide, arrived an hour after. They left Fort Garry on Saturday afternoon; camped out two nights by the way; had a tent and cart, plenty of provisions, and got along right pleasantly. They were much pleased with the place and people, and were feasted to perfection—were almost killed with kindness, and are still suffering from the effects of it. I find they were nearly as much pleased with everything they saw as I was myself, and were made perfect lions of, comparing their reception to that of old Kentucky and Virginia hospitalities of fifty years ago.

CHAPTER II.

THE HOMEWARD MARCH.

Tuesday, Sept. 30.—We are busy to-day preparing for a start homeward. The dragoons crossed the mouth of the Pembina this morning, and proceeded a short distance on the other side, and camped, to await the arrival of the barley from Selkirk, which is all that detains us now.

An Indian talk and council came off this morning in our house between the governor and an old Indian named "Clear Weather," one of the dissatisfied party who refused to sign the treaty. He came in *sans ceremonie,* followed by about thirty others, all smoking, and affecting great dignity. Mr. Tanner was sent for, to act as interpreter; and, after an impressive silence, the great orator deigned to speak. He was short of breath, he said, and could not speak as he wanted to, but such as it was he gave freely and without restraint. He had many faults to find, and many questions to ask, stating that he had been sick, and, if well at the time of the treaty, it would not have been formed, &c.

Much other talk to the same purpose followed this, and the governor then replied in a long explanatory speech, to which the Indian rejoined by wanting at least *two swallows of meat apiece*—thus falling at once from the sublime to the ridiculous, and showing the object of the visit to be a begging expedition and no more! We having no beef left, gave them a lot of tobacco, and so broke up the conference—the dignitaries departing, after shaking hands all round, and apparently well satisfied with their success. This scene occupied an hour, and its principal effect was to retard our dinner just that much, the council being in our dining-room.

Wednesday, Oct. 1.—Cool weather, with a rainstorm; wind west. Busy weighing and preparing our freight and baggage, and getting ready for a start homeward. The carts are all loaded and sent over the Pembina, together with the horses, all ready for a start to-morrow. This evening is wild and tempestuous, with rain; the howling winds sound dismally, and are prognostics of the approach of rude, rough winter. It is time we were off for the city of St. Paul. We expect fine weather yet, as the Indian summer is to come. We are well prepared at all points to make our journey pleasant; have a good stock of provisions, which, with plenty of buffalo-cow and bear, will feast us most luxuriously. Well, "a good digestion waits on appetite, and health on both." We are all improving finely, and hope for a still pleasanter journey homeward than we had when outward bound.

Thursday, 2d.—Weather cloudy, cold, and windy; very raw and boisterous from the north. A very good hint for us to be upon our southern march. We took it, and left *instanter*, after a three-weeks' residence at Pembina and Selkirk settlement.

Governor Ramsey, Mr. Tyler, Dr. Foster, Pierre Bottineau, accompanied by Mr. N. W. Kittson and Charles Cavileer, Esq., left for the Pembina mountain, or new town of St. Joseph, thirty miles to the west, on Pembina river. They expect to meet there the assembled half-breed hunters, who are about starting on their buffalo-hunts, and afterward rejoin us at our second night's camp, on Tongue river. The dragoons and the balance of our party, with the carts, are also off, and are dimly seen far away upon the prairie. I am alone in the deserted camp; a solitary half-breed hunter holds my horse, as, lying by the blazing fire, I write these random sketches, and ruminate for a long, long time. But I must put up book and pencil, and away. Good-by, my lonely half-breed—good-by, Pembina: I shall never, perhaps, set foot within your bounds again; and although I have almost left my heart at Selkirk, far beyond thee, I still turn gladly with my back to the rude north blasts, and look forward to a meeting with older, warmer, and truer southern friends, to whom I hasten. Adios!

Our party is increased by the addition of M. Lecombe, a young catholic priest, who has been living at St. Joseph with M. Belcourt, and is now on his way to Montreal via St. Paul and the states. He messes with us, and is a very agreeable and accomplished young fellow. George Morrison, a Pembina half-breed, also accompanies us to Crow-Wing. As we return over the same route we came, I will not describe the every-day affairs of our camp-life as minutely as when on our outward march, nor say anything further of the country. I have doubted the propriety of describing our homeward route at all; I will therefore be brief.

Sunday, 5th.—Nothing worthy of note thus far. I rode in the carriage to-day by way of change, my horse being lame, and read "Simpson's Arctic Discoveries." We are now near the spot where the tragic scene occurred which ended in his death and the murder of two of his companions, June 14, 1840. I have felt much interest in the narrative of the unfortunate man, and his untimely death. It appears that while on his return to the states, with the news of his arctic discoveries, he became deranged from over-excitement on the subject of his explorations, and in a fit of madness shot two of his voyageurs and then committed suicide. He was on his way to London, at the time, to communicate with the admiralty department; but his remains now sleep amid these quiet scenes—his lowly grave is roamed over by the fierce, wild buffalo—and his requiem is nightly sung by howling wolves. Peace to his ashes!

Monday, 6th.—Most beautiful weather. To-day we have set fire to the prairies by accident in getting dinner. The dragoons ahead have done the same, and the strong wind bears it back on us with astonishing rapidity; we are enveloped in immense clouds of smoke, through which we travelled all the afternoon—the fire roaring all around and under our feet. Decidedly hot and uncomfortable. On taking out my thermometer to-night I found it *broken*. We will now have to depend on our own feelings for the state of the temperature hereafter—or else on the small *spirit* thermometers which are carried in the pockets of some of the party.

TUESDAY, 7th.—The sun rose red and fiery through the morning's misty haze, and appeared to be of the shape of a perfect dome, like that of the capitol at Washington—it was extremely beautiful.

This morning, when near Goose river, we discovered our first two buffalo, about a mile to the left of the road. The dragoons gave chase to one, and killed him after a long run. At noon *our* hunters, who had been on a scout ahead, returned with the tongues and a portion of the flesh of five buffalo they had just killed, and reported large droves ahead. We of course had the meat for dinner, broiled and fried, besides pork and ham, potatoes, coffee, etc.; in fact, a first-rate dinner. We are certainly living on the fat of the land, though as far as the buffalo are concerned, it is decidedly the lean kind of the prairie—the flesh being both lean and tough—as we find nothing but bulls—the cows at this season of the year being all to themselves, and undisturbed by their brutish lords.

After dinner we soon came among the buffalo, and found large numbers along both sides of the road. We immediately darted in among them, pell-mell, each fellow for himself, and then such yelling, shouting, firing, shying of horses, as their riders, with belted-waists, and handkerchiefs round their heads, swayed to and fro in their saddles, loading and firing while at full-speed, and in a manner that would have done credit to Ringgold's flying artillery at Palo Alto.

We soon had a number down, and then I reined up on the brow of a hill to reconnoitre. Horsemen were scouring hither and thither over the prairie, in all directions, the smoke of their rifles curling up above their heads, as, riding at full speed, side and side, and neck and neck, with the savage, shaggy, beasts, pouring in their broadsides into them, till one by one, the huge animals went down and bit the dust, while a hurrah, and wild, triumphant, shout came ringing across the prairie-surface, proclaiming the success of the elated hunters. Single buffalo, small droves, and large herds, were tearing around full-speed, occasionally halting to paw the dust, and bid defiance to the pursuers. I helped run down and kill my share at least. The last I ran a mile or two, and finally, he took back toward the carts, upon which he charged across the road, and dashed right through them—their horses rearing and plunging with affright. On he sped, and on I followed, amid the cries and shouts of the French boys. Two horsemen in advance headed him off soon after, when he turned furiously at bay, threw the earth in the air in clouds, and dashed at us continually. The rest of the party coming up, we surrounded him at a distance of fifty yards, and commenced a murderous attack upon him. The balls whizzed through the air, and as each entered his shaggy side, he quivered for a moment and then dashed at his assailant, who turned, of course, and fled. After a dozen shots he reeled and fell staggering down the hill, and headlong pitched into a creek, his blood pouring in streams from mouth and nose, and spouting in jets from out his side, mingling with, and discoloring the water, so that it ran, apparently, a stream of blood—hence we named it Bloody creek. It was very amusing to see Jim Lord's horse "Billy Button," as Lord would ride him up toward the wounded beast, till attracting his attention, the buffalo would dash at him, giving a number of successive leaps, and moving stiffly like a hobbled horse, when Billy Lord would turn tail to, and flee. Thus repeatedly would they take a *bee-line* for a hundred yards or more, leaving nothing but a yellow streak behind, at which the spectators laughed immoderately. We killed, in all, about twenty, and took out their tongues, leaving their carcasses to the wolves. We saw, in all, from five to ten thousand, the plains, as far as the eye could reach, being dotted with them. At our camp to-night they are all around us, some within half a mile.

WEDNESDAY, 8th.—A beautiful warm, clear, day. We were up at daylight, but did not get off for an hour after sunrise, which is a very late start for us, and is caused by the French boys all being up last night on guard against the *Indians*. One of them, who was sitting by the fire cooking and eating about midnight, was certain he saw two Indians in the road, and within thirty or forty feet of the camp. One lay down, and appeared to be sneaking and watching, preparatory to seizing one of the horses. The alarm was given, guns loaded, pistols primed afresh, and, after much talking, gesticulation, and preparation being made for an hour, Pierre and all his men moved down the road a hundred yards or more, and then, like the king of France, valiantly marched back again—bringing in all the horses, and tying them to the carts. It was clear and moonlight at the time, yet my own opinion, and that of *our* party is, that not an Indian could be found with a hundred miles, and that it was all the resulted of a lively imagination, heightened by fear. Pierre was once chased through this very section of country by a gang of hostile Sioux, and all his companions killed and scalped. He has never got over the fright, and with the French boys, and other half-breed Chippewas, is always talking of, and expecting to see the Yankton Sioux popping on to them. We have had lots of buffalo all along the road to-day, and have had some fine and very exciting chases. We killed several just in the road, in fact, they were so plenty that we chased none except those directly in our path. We reached Goose river at noon—dragoons once more overtook us. We all dined together on the high plateau, on the south side of Goose river, and had once more a reunion of our large family. This afternoon we travelled ten miles and camped upon the prairie.

THURSDAY, 9th.—Cloudy and cold, with a southeast rain-storm almost all day. A regular old-fashioned equinoctial. We rose this morning about one o'clock, being roused very foolishly at that hour—no one knowing the right time. We then had breakfast, and Dr. F. and I started on ahead, at least an hour before daylight, and still too dark to see the road—had to trust to our horses altogether. At daylight it began raining, and continued falling rapidly all the morning. We rode some four miles, and then awaited on the top of a long, high, rolling, prairie, for the arrival of the carts and balance of the party.

To amuse the doctor, and keep our spirits up, having none along to take down inwardly, I gave a gratuitous exhibition on horseback of the most pathetic scenes from "Hamlet," "Romeo and Juliet," "Richard III." "Macbeth," "the Lady of the Lyon," and "the Men of the Buffaloes"—varying the performance with a specimen of "Bombastes Furioso," and a farce or two, including the "*Dead Shot.*" The doctor approved in the proper places, like a most excellent critic, according to the merits of the various parts.

About ten o'clock, A. M., a large herd of buffalo cows were discovered to the left of the road ahead, several miles distant. Preparations being hastily made for an attack, our hunters, after a spirited chase, captured five. The herd contained from one hundred to one hundred and fifty, among which were a number of calves. After dinner we rode on four miles, and came up with the advance party, assembled round the carcass of one of the cows, the meat of which had been cut up, preparatory to being jerked at leisure, and eaten fresh. The cow was very fat, more tender, and much smaller than the bulls killed previously; also resembled more closely the domestic animal. The portions we were unable to carry with us were left to the tender mercies of the wolves, which were already in sight, attracted by the scent of blood, and only awaiting our departure to fall to work.

The afternoon was cold and rainy, chilling us to the very marrow; our road being over flat, swampy ground. We camped just before night at Rush river, in a grove of majestic trees immediately on the river's bank; the dragoons had already camped, and some one of our party had previously built a large fire, by which we stood in the drenching rain, drying ourselves in front, while taking a soaking in the rear. Our tents were pitched, horses staked, supper cooked of buffalo cow-steaks, etc., and we passed the night amid the terrors of the elements, and they made a time of it. We marched a distance this day of twenty-five miles, equally hard upon the horses as ourselves.

Friday, 10th.—Cloudy and cold all day, and from eight o'clock, A. M., a rain-storm. We should have remained camped all day, instead of marching; the dragoons, too, were far ahead of us. I walked as usual several hours, but finally took refuge in the carriage from the pitiless storm. Wind strong, and cold enough for snow. After proceeding ten miles, we mired our horses and carriage in endeavoring to cross a muddy stream, and had to draw them out with ropes. We were all miserable, and pushed ahead, without halting for dinner, a distance of six miles, to the banks of Maple river, wet, hungry, and cold. Pierre Bottineau and two others were there before us, endeavoring to kindle a fire, one holding an umbrella, while the others blew the dry material preparatory to piling on the wet twigs and limbs. To those who are unacquainted with the mode of lighting fire upon the prairie in a drenching rain, a description will be found interesting. Some dry Kinne-kin-nick bark is generally carried along, cut very fine for the purpose of smoking; this being the Indian and half-breed substitute for tobacco. A small portion of this, together with a little tow, or paper (if to be had), is placed in as dry a place as possible, and shielded from the rain by holding over it a hat, or cap, or blanket; some wet powder is then thrown on, together with a little of the dry explosive, and the whole ignited with flint and steel. Fine chips, and shavings of the dry inside of a stick of wood, are then thrown on to the little pile; and in a few minutes a cheerful fire is blazing amid the torrent, and a blaze large enough to roast an ox is leaping upward — on which each voyageur, as he comes up with his gathered arm-load, throws his contribution, swelling the flames still higher, then gathers closely around, while the steam and smoke from his scorching garments ascend in perfect clouds.

SATURDAY, 11th. — Again cloudy and cold, with rain and a slight snow-storm in the morning; north wind, and very disagreeable. We determined not to travel to-day, and lay abed late to keep ourselves warm. Our breakfast consisted of roast buffalo-ribs, boiled meat, potatoes, coffee, &c., and we spent the rest of the day drying our wet bedding, coats, boots, saddles, and blankets; the half-breeds busily occupied cutting up the buffalo-meat, and jerking it, by spreading it over a frame of poles, about four feet from the ground, and building fires underneath, which were kept burning day and night.

We have had a storm of much severity, and being upon the prairies, unprotected by any timber, we have felt it in its full force. To-night the sun set clear, and the western sky was most brilliantly illuminated. Fine weather will undoubtedly follow, the equinoctial being over now for certain. Indian summer will now return and resume its sway, after this temporary disruption of the elements.

Herds of buffaloes are around us to-night, and have even wandered in among our horses, close to camp. We are obliged to chase them out occasionally, for fear of accidents. Yesterday afternoon I could have shot them from the carriage, as they crossed the road continually, often being within fifty yards; indeed I often feared a herd would run us down in their mad, headlong career.

Sunday, 12th.—Fine, clear, and most beautiful day, and more to be appreciated after the disappearance of the sun for three days. Our carts were hauled over Maple river bridge, and up the steep bank on the south side, by ropes, all hands laying hold, albeit it was the sabbath. But all days are alike to us; the powers that rule our expedition having left their religious scruples and proprieties behind them.

We then set out, over the smooth, level prairie, for the Shayenne, distant from twelve to fifteen miles; the buffalo—bulls, cows, and calves—all around us, and running across the road in herds. A number were killed, and the tongues and a portion of the flesh secured. We reached the Shayenne, the southern boundary-line of the buffalo in the Red river valley, at noon. The dragoons had just crossed over, and their teams were winding up the steep bluff on the opposite side.

We dined, rested two hours, and made a march of eight miles in the afternoon. We stopped at the only clump of timber on the whole prairie, between the Shayenne and Wild-rice river, and here we found the dragoons encamped. Being out of the buffalo country, a portion of the excitements of the trip are over.

And now, if I can throw enough interest into our monotonous journey back to Sauk Rapids, to interest the reader, I shall be happy. Be it remembered, however, that these unpretending, rough notes, are written with pencil, with my knee upon the grass for a writing-desk, amid the smoke of evening, noon, and morning camp-fires, sometimes upon my horse, while leisurely pursuing my lonely way apart from the rest of the company; and as first written, they appear to you.

In consequence of our resting yesterday and travelling to-day, amid all the bustle and confusion of the camp, besides buffalo-hunting, etc., it is extremely hard to realize it is the holy institution of the sabbath that has again dawned upon us so beautifully. I think of the quiet Sunday far away at home, and in the crowded cities of the East, where the bells are gayly chiming in the ears of their thousands of hearers, who should be worshippers, and answer to their call.

MONDAY, 13th.—Cloudy, cold, and windy, all the morning, with rain-showers at noon. Overcoats and exercise on foot necessary to comfort. We started early, and reached the "Wild Rice" at one o'clock, P. M., having made a march of sixteen miles. Drew the wagons, carriage, and carts, over by ropes; then camped in double quick time, and all hands fell to cooking. Dinner and supper combined, was ready at four, P. M. It consisted of boiled buffalo cow and potatoes, fried cow and hearts, coffee, stewed peaches, and a hash made of cold meats, potatoes, onions, lard, pepper, and salt; all well mixed, prepared, and cooked by Dr. F., assisted by the young priest, Mons. Lecombe, Gabou, and Pierre. All hands then fell to with an avidity unexampled in all the hungry, voracious feats on record, and devoured the meal ravenously. I have been thinking that we will scarce know how to live in houses, or eat at table, when we get into civilized life again. There is a romance and strange wild pleasure in the life we lead at present, so that the ordinary every-day routine of business life among the busy haunts of men away down to the southeast (St. Paul), will seem irksome and monotonous; and we will all have to be broken into the traces of quiet, sedentary, domestic life again,—which will perhaps prove all the pleasanter and more to be appreciated, after undergoing a temporary interruption to its enjoyments.

TUESDAY, 14th.—Election day in Minnesota, for members of the house and council. Well, they have a delightful day for it; sun warm, air cool and pleasant. Go it—organizers, disorganizers, and coalitionists—to the mark, ye whig whigs and democratic democrats—give one day to your beloved Minnesota. We talked, too, of holding an election of our own, and were only deterred by the fact that no one would be a candidate. It was voted unanimously to take a "horn." The governor's whiskey was tapped, prairie mint gathered, and juleps made; the standing toast being that of Falstaff—"If sack and sugar be a fault, God help the wicked!"

We crossed the Bois des Sioux four miles south of where we crossed going out, and swam the horses, rafted the goods, carts, wagons, &c., over as before. We then camped for the night on the banks of the Sioux wood.

Wednesday, 15th.—A beautiful, cool, clear day. Marched twenty-five miles. We killed a large elk, and fared sumptuously on venison. Roast elk-ribs, with boiled steaks, with a nice mess of stewed heart and kidneys, formed our evening meal.

Thursday, 16th.—Two weeks on our homeward march. Weather very clear and pleasant, with ice in the morning. We reached Rabbit river by dinner, but had to carry our wood half a mile to camp. The governor prepared dinner for the first time. It consisted of a dish of stewed kidney, first parboiled, then fried in a pan, with lard, flour, and other condiments. In the meantime, a great talk was kept up by his excellency, about the *excellency* of the dish, and the superiority of kidney fat over all other fats; Doctor F. dissenting, and urging that the admixture of so much fat would render down the whole into good tallow candles, and moved that the mess be cast into moulds, and each man allowed to eat or burn his candle, as he pleased. Tyler interfered, and was told that it was none of his business—"too many cooks spoil the broth." "Don't let it burn, Gabou. Now, gentlemen, if it don't burn, it will be first-rate!" Dispute now arose as to how the gravy ought to be made; all hands differed in opinion. Lord's plan was sustained by the quasi cook, and adopted. Just then a big black bear was discovered close to camp, and all hands started in hot pursuit. The governor forgot his kidney fat, Doctor F., his candles, and, in his haste, almost extinguished himself in a neighboring lake. Lord even forgot his gravy, the stew was burnt, and in a minute the devil was to pay; but Bruin *got fits!* Pierre and Gabou took the lead on horseback, while the rest of us ran down and along the banks of Lake Constantia, till we were fairly out of breath.

Bruin ran like a race-horse, but could not save his bacon that time. Pierre shot first, and his ball only tore off a toe from the beast's fore foot. Gabou then fired, and his two balls passed through poor Bruin, who leaped, and fell headlong down the hill-side, and was dead before we reached him. He was skinned, and the meat placed on the carts; when, after the kidney dinner, we once more moved on.

FRIDAY, 17th.—Cloudy, with rain all day. We made a short march, and camped early, to avoid the storm, on the borders of a lake near Potato river. All hands then fell to at cooking. Doctor F. could be seen, with great slices of ham on a forked stick. Tyler was parboiling and frying the ham and eggs. The French boys put up elk-ribs to roast, and Pierre a skunk; he having killed two yesterday for the governor, who had taken a great fancy to them, and was very desirous to have another taste. The regular dinner consisted of broiled bear-ribs, eggs, coffee, &c.

The whole was eaten except the skunk, and his *excellency* refused to partake of it, on the ground that it was *very* good when he was *very* hungry, but that an ordinary appetite could not relish it. It would be a very *ordinary* one that could. He also says, there are too many kinds of meat *about*, and too much of it, for any one to fancy skunk.

Dr. F. and Tyler were appointed a committee of two, to see that he eats one at least before he goes to bed to-night, and not to let him off without. It is but *meet* that every one should have plenty of that which is most to his taste, and also skin and eat his own skunks, and not leave them for his friends. We then spent the rest of the day within our tents, and had a good time of it. The governor *ate his skunk* for supper, though he thought we were coming it rather *strong* over him. Our salt gave out to-day, and there is great grumbling in the camp. We have plenty of whiskey left, however, uncle being very liberal in his supply of *spirits*, which is a very useful and necessary article; as all our party are *mediums*, and go *rapping* at the spirit-kegs, filling up their flasks and bottles as regularly as clock-work.

The governor has now, however, locked up all the spirits in wooden boxes, so that the spirit world is closed to all the mediums save himself. He still *taps* three or four times a day, and always gets very satisfactory answers. He is, therefore, a firm believer in *the spirits*. Lord, however, if he can not tap himself, refuses to have any communion with them, and *has sworn off*.

SATURDAY, 18th.—We marched twenty miles to-day, passing by Lakes Pike and Fillmore, and camped on a small muddy stream. The dragoons left us two days ago, and are out of sight. They have been of no use to us whatever during our march. But Uncle Sam pays for it. Go on, fiery dragoons—joy be with you!

SUNDAY, 19th.—Cold and windy, but good travelling weather. We camped at Lightning lake, so called because the lightning here struck the camp of Major Woods and Captain Pope, while on their expedition to Pembina, in the summer of 1849. We also camped here over Sunday on our outward march. Our supper to-night was cold bear-ribs, crackers and coffee, eaten while sitting on a log around the fire.

This is our last sabbath west of the Mississippi, and we begin already to feel near home.

MONDAY, 20th.—An extraordinary day. Weather variable; mostly cloudy, and quite cold, with a rainy mist and snow-squalls at intervals. One minute it is snowing most furiously, then hailing till the ground is covered; the next the sun is shining warm and pleasantly. There appears to be a general disruption of all the elements. We rode eight miles, to Crow river, and found the crossing very bad. Dr. Foster's mare, poor Bessie, was completely mired, and was pulled out with a rope. The governor and Dr. F. were carried over on the backs of Pierre and Jarva, and I forded, with the big long india-rubbers belted around the waist, and occasionally sticking fast; while Lord took off coat, boots, pantaloons, and drawers, and waded *á la model artiste*—in the midst of our immoderate laughter.

We then proceeded two miles, and camped upon the prairie; helped the doctor along with the old mare, thrashing her along at every step with a long strap, and had hard work to get her along at that. Poor Bessie! with tail between her legs, and head hung down, she seemed shrunken by her bath to about one-half her former size, and, as the cold winds swept around her, she trembled, and looked most piteously. But cheer up, brave beast! Uncle paid a hundred dollars for you, and if you should now keel over, it would be truly a *dead* loss to him; besides, the doctor would have to walk the balance of the road, and he would be perfectly inconsolable — his grief would be greater than he could bear; so bear up, brave Bess!

We dined and supped together at three, P. M.; fare was fried ham and buffalo, coffee, etc. Spent the rest of the day around the fire, drying our moccasins and stockings, and fixing up generally. Retired early. The grass being all killed by the frosts for some time past, our horses have nearly given out. We are obliged to stop a dozen times a day, on the banks of streams, and in the little sheltered valleys where the grass is green, and there refresh our exhausted animals.

TUESDAY, 21st. — Cloudy and windy, and very cold; snow-squalls occasionally. We started early, to keep warm; and Doctor F. came near drowning his mare in attempting to cross a stream. She swamped, but after being lightened of her burden, to wit, the doctor in a saddle, with a knapsack and two overcoats behind, and a coil of rope of thirty feet and a stake, for a lariat at night. On the removal of all this, she rose to the surface, and, a rope being fastened around her neck, she was drawn out choked, with a "Yo, heave O!" and a "Pull now, boys, altogether, out she comes!" by all our force. In doing this poor Bess struggled and floundered considerably, and the mud and water flew as though a dozen porpoises just harpooned were there; the doctor meanwhile standing alongside of her, at a safe distance, over his boots in water, crying, "Pull, pull, you devils, pull — a long pull, a strong pull, and a pull altogether! out she goes!" We then took turns in driving her along, the doctor riding my horse, and I wading the swamps and streams in the big boots. Each one in his turn abandoned the poor beast, and the doctor in despair finally left her to her fate, and the tender mercies of the governor and Tyler, who were still behind, covering our rear, feeding their horses, and occasionally consulting the *spirits* of the place—that spirit which Shakspere calls "the invisible spirit of wine." It is but just to say, however, that before leaving them I took a draught myself, to shield me from the effects of the keen winds and snow-squalls.

We stopped an hour to warm ourselves by a fire which had been kindled at David lake, in a piece of woodland. We lay down in the tall grass, while the wind shrieked through the trees, the fire roared, and the snow commenced falling furiously. Just as we rose to start, we heard an awful yelling and shouting close at hand, to the right. Looking around we saw a blanket waving in the wind, at a distance of about two hundred yards, and occasionally a creature that appeared to be an Indian would spring up, and waving his blanket at us, again fell quickly down into the grass. Dr. F. thinking it might be some one in distress, started over afoot, but soon halted, turned back and refused to go any farther, unless accompanied by the rest of us. Not knowing the meaning of such an unusual performance—especially as we had been upon the ground for an hour previous without hearing anything—and believing it to be some *fool-caper* of one of the advance party, I rode ahead, till Gabou finally rode over to the spot, and after a sort of parley with the creature—during which it leaped about and waved the blanket, and then squatting suddenly down, it covered up completely; then, finally, lay down in as small a compass as possible, forming a living ball enveloped in a blanket, and so remained quiet and motionless. After this pantomime, Gabou pointed to a strip of woods about a mile off, and motioned us to go there. We found the supposed Indian to be "Amab," one of the French boys, who had been stationed there to direct all back travellers to the evening's camp in the timber, where we found all the carts had gone. We, therefore, followed their trail, leaving the silent blanket-enveloped sentinel as a sort of living finger-post to direct the others still behind. On arriving at the woods we found the carts and carriage—the horses picketed in the woods for shelter, and a huge fire blazing. The governor, Tyler, and the old mare, soon after arrived, and dinner being ready, all hands ate with their accustomed avidity, some in their tents, and some around the fire amid the falling snow. In the midst of our enjoyments, we could not but regret the loss of one of our party, who had come along the road, walking and leading *his* sick mare, before the fantastic sentinel was posted, and not observing that the carts had left the road, he kept on, although two guns were fired, and blankets waved, and shouts sent after him from camp.

Much pity was bestowed on him, and a great deal of wondering and speculation indulged in as to his whereabouts on such a night as this, without fire, food, or shelter. He is supposed to be at the crossing of Sauk river, fifteen miles ahead. Gabou set off, however, on his Indian pony in search of him, the snow falling in wild, fitful, gusts. We are yet some forty miles from the Mississippi, and are uneasy at the rapid giving out of our horses. Two of our half-breeds started on ahead this morning in hopes of reaching the river by night.

However, as we lie warm and comfortable in our tents to-night, upon our beds of mattress, robes, and blankets, with overcoats, boots, and saddles, for our pillows, we can listen undismayed to the keen howlings of old Boreas, and the patterings and rattlings of the gliding snows overhead—the first rude, rough harbingers of the precocious winter, disturbs us not.

Blow, winds, blow, snows may fall, and the winds may howl, for ourselves we care not, only for our poor beasts, and our absent voyageur.

Wednesday, 22d.—A beautiful, fine, clear, day, after the storm, cool and bracing. The old mare, Bess, was found standing in the same spot and position that she was left last night. She had apparently not laid down, or moved a muscle. She stood, in fact, a statue of a mare—perfectly rigid throughout the night, and exposed to the fury of the storm, we being unable to get her under shelter. The Dr., getting desperate, started on ahead on foot, while the governor, Lord, and Tyler, drove poor Bessie along with blows and shouts; but finally failing in this, they hitched Billy Button (Lord's horse), to her with a rope, using Lord's vest for a collar, putting it around Billy's neck, and attaching the rope around it, they thus pulled the mare by force; Bill drawing as if his life depended on it, and Bess holding back till fairly choked and obliged to go ahead. Thus they jogged along at the rate of a mile an hour, and till within a few miles of the river, when Bess suddenly fell over from sheer exhaustion, and never after stirred. They then sat down and smoked their pipes over her fallen body—shed a tear or two "over the left" eye-lash, and left her to her fate—"death and the wolves."

We all reached Sauk river, crossed and camped a few miles beyond. Gabou had found our lost companion there about ten o'clock last night. He had built a fire, picketed his mare, and was *just going to bed.* So they piled on the logs, took supper, and made a night of it in the woods which skirt the river bank. A dragoon horse which we picked up exhausted yesterday, gave up the ghost to-night—another *dead loss* to uncle; we have several more belonging to the dragoons, not yet quite dead but soon will be. The great bulk of the conversation to-night was on the death of the poor unfortunate mare of the doctor's; much merriment and wit was indulged in at the expense of both—the latter having been obliged to walk, and ride upon a cart *as a dernier resort* to get to port.

Thursday, 23d.—A fine clear, cool day. We got to within four miles of the river at Sauk rapids, and camped for the last time. The governor rode on ahead, and sent us oats from Russell's, without which we could scarce have got in. We had evening prayers, our custom of a night, by Monsieur Lecombe, for the last time, as to-morrow our camp breaks up.

Friday, October 24th.—We reached the Mississippi at ten, A. M., having made the march from Pembina in twenty-three days, and very glad to get back to the settlements again.

Saturday, 25th.—We started for St. Paul, taking some of the carts along, and sending our baggage on ahead in a two-horse team. Stopped at Big lake all night.

Sunday, 26th.—We reached St. Paul to-night, after an absence of just ten weeks.

The *Minnesotian*, of St. Paul, thus alludes to our arrival home, and sums up our journey in this wise: "The dragoons who accompanied the governor to Pembina, returned to Fort Snelling on Friday last, and on Monday, about eleven o'clock, the numerous friends of our worthy executive were delighted to take himself, and those who accompanied him, by the hand. The party was absent only ten weeks, and in that time travelled upward of twelve hundred miles, going and returning, besides consummating the important business of the expedition, in the highly satisfactory manner already made public.

"Their route lay to the west of the Red river of the North, until they struck the Pembina river, which they followed to its mouth. This is the site of Mr. Kittson's old trading post, the place where the treaty was made. They returned by the same route.

"The party, soldiers and citizens, all return in the most robust health, though somewhat bronzed by exposure to the weather. Their horses stood the journey home remarkably well, considering the grass was very much cut down by the frost. Dr. Foster lost his horse a day or two out from Sauk rapids, which was the only one lost by the governor's party. The soldiers lost two, we believe.

"Game in abundance was found on the route, both going and coming. Buffalo, elk, bear, geese, ducks, and brant, were killed in much greater quantities than could be used. Buffalo were more plenty on the return than in going out. Thousands lined the prairies during several days' travel. From sixty to a hundred were killed by the party, and any number could have been taken.

"Dr. Bond, who, from his close observation of meteorological subjects, has earned the title of clerk of the weather, informs us that the first frost which nipped vegetation in the valley of Red river, occurred on the 28th of September. Four days previous, he gathered flowers, fresh and blooming, in the gardens at Pembina. On Tuesday week, about one hundred miles west of Sauk rapids, they encountered a snow-squall.

"All the party speak in the highest terms of the country over which they passed, and of the hospitable entertainment they received at the hands of the people on both sides the line. The attentions of the Hudson's Bay factors and clerks, and the people of Selkirk settlement generally, are warmly alluded to. The former accounts are confirmed, that they are a frugal, hardy, and industrious people, surrounded by all the comforts of life that can be attained in that remote region."

NOTE.—These sketches up to the 29th September, 1851, descriptive of our "Outward March," and residence at Pembina and Selkirk settlement, were first published in the *Minnesota Pioneer*, at St. Paul, during the months of February, March, and April, 1852. The notes of the "Homeward March" have not hitherto been published.

CHAPTER III.

LETTERS FROM PEMBINA AND SELKIRK SETTLEMENT—DESCRIPTION OF THE SETTLEMENT.

The following letters, descriptive of the Selkirk settlement, were written during the short stay I made in that hospitable region, and were addressed to Col. D. A. Robertson, late editor of the "Minnesota Democrat," in which paper they were subsequently published. They form the connection between the "outward" and "homeward" march:—

Fort Garry, Selkirk Settlement, *September* 22, 1851.

Dear Sir: I avail myself of an express which is just leaving for St. Paul, bearing despatches from Dr. Ray, who has been exploring the coast from Victoria to Wollasten Land, from the one hundred and tenth to the one hundred and seventeenth degree of west longitude, in hopes of finding some trace of Sir John Franklin, and the straits which were supposed to extend through to the northwest in that locality.

He has failed in both, and intends next summer to turn his attention in another direction, satisfied that there is no longer any hopes in that quarter. His package has just arrived by Mr. Ross from the Norway house, on the northern extremity of Lake Winnipeg. It is to be forwarded immediately to the admiralty department, via St. Paul and the states. Mr. Adam Klyn is the bearer, and will reach you in fifteen days—a glorious opportunity for communicating a few lines to you—as good as it was unexpected; my time, however, is very precious, and will not admit of details.

Our party reached Pembina on the 11th instant, in twenty travelling days from the Mississippi at Sauk rapids. We had buffalo-hunts, bear-chases, plenty of smaller game, good roads, delightful weather, and every other pleasure, with some of the excitements and accidents attending a prairie trip, with nothing, however, of a serious nature; scarcely any sickness, and no annoyance except from the legions of winged devils in the shape of mosquitoes, gnats, and huge, tormenting flies, which all existed in swarms of countless millions throughout the trip. The treaty began on the 15th, with the Red-lake and Pembina bands of Chippewas, numbering in all about two hundred and fifty. Several hundred half-breeds were also present, and expected to participate in the making of the treaty, and were exceedingly disappointed when informed that their claims would not be respected, and that the government only recognised the Indians as the rightful owners of the soil, and intended to deal with them accordingly. The half-breeds had counted on the reception of a portion at least of the annuities as almost certain, and had hoped for the consummation of a treaty, in case their claims were recognised, with that view only; not with the more manly intention of coming into the full possession of the lands at an early period, and bettering their present miserable condition by their cultivation, and, as independent tillers of the soil, subsist without the poor, miserable pittance which it would be, at least in the shape of an annuity doled out to them from year to year, the very receipt of which would degrade and lower them as men and citizens of our territory. Their dependence upon annuities in prospective, and their keen expectancy of receiving them in common with their red relations, with their unwillingness to become honest tillers of the soil, shows them at least to be very deficient in self-respect, and to possess a very low and I think erroneous estimate of their own character. I hope, however, better things of this free, hardy, and very energetic class; and that they will take advantage of what will be done for them by government to improve their present wandering condition and mode of life, and elevate them among the ranks of "Nature's noblemen," for which position they are well qualified.

The land proposed to be purchased includes each side of Red river thirty miles to the east and west, and as far south as Goose river. This includes a portion of Pembina mountain and the new town of St. Joseph, thirty miles west of Pembina. An offer was made them of eight thousand dollars down on the ratification of the treaty, and yearly annuities of several thousands for twenty years.

I left Pembina, in company with the Rev. John Black, on the 17th, before the consummation of the treaty, and have since heard nothing definite. As the express passes Pembina, you will have later news. We were three days descending the Red river (ninety miles); and, although we have been suffering with an equinoctial since our first arrival at Pembina, yet I have been highly pleased with everything pertaining to this settlement, and I assure you I have seldom left a place with more reluctant feelings than those I experience at present.

I am about starting up the river in a bark-canoe, with two half-breed voyageurs, and will reach Pembina on the evening of the 26th, camping out three nights by the way. The weather is now delightful, it having cleared off this morning, and is as fine and warm as an Indian summer. The cathedral-bells across the river are ringing a merry chime, and I almost fancy myself away "down east" in a large Atlantic city—not in the Selkirk settlement, amid the very centre of the continent, and a whole month's march of twenty miles per day to the west of sundown—that is, St. Paul.

I find it very hard to be brief amid scenes like these, but my time and the circumstances in which I find myself situated compel me in what I have yet to say—not because it is "the soul of wit" to be so, but you are aware that necessity knows no law.

I have been treated in the most hospitable and kind manner by the people throughout the settlement, and by none more so than the people of the fort, whom I shall long remember. To Mr. John Black, who has command of "the company's" post at this place, Dr. Cowan, Mr. Pelley, and Mr. Logan, jr., and also to Mr. M'Dermott and Mr. Alexander Ross and son, I am under many obligations. I have this moment been introduced to Bishop Anderson of the episcopal church, a very affable and worthy gentleman. He has resided here two years, and in common with the other members of the several churches, of which there are three, is very highly esteemed. The churches would do credit to any western settlement in the states. The congregatious of each are large, and the character of the people for industry and morality is most excellent. I have found more of the noble traits, which dignify and exalt our race, existing among the people here, than any one unacquainted with them would imagine. Not to be too eulogistic, however, I will close; if I am deceived in them, it is an error of the head, not of the heart. More of this anon.

We expect to leave Pembina on the 1st of October, and to reach St. Paul on the 25th, perhaps not until the 1st of November. Our route will be out to the westward of the one we came, to Devil's lake, among the buffalo-cows and probably the bears. We anticipate a pleasant time returning, as the Indian summer soon sets in, and the mosquitoes will all be killed by early frosts, or else too much benumbed to "present their bills" with vigor: we expect to "settle" all that are presented without drawing upon Uncle Sam's treasury for an additional amount of funds.

Governor Ramsey comes down by canoe to-day or to-morrow, accompanied by Mr. Hugh Tyler, Dr. Foster, and Lieutenant Corley. The people here will give them a warm reception—one of the old-fashioned sort, such as you might have expected from men before human nature became corrupt. They are most heartily welcome, and their arrival looked forward to with interest and pleasure.

A letter from Governor Colville at the lower fort has just arrived, offering our governor and party the hospitalities of Prince Rupert's Land; and Major Caldwell, governor of the colony, is here upon the spot, to extend the same. But I must close, hoping to find you and all the good people of St. Paul "all correct" on my return.

PEMBINA, *Wednesday, September* 24, 1851.—11, P. M.

DEAR SIR: I have just arrived here from Fort Garry, after one of the heaviest marches I have ever before experienced. It happened in this wise: I was detained at the fort on Monday till four o'clock, P. M., as I was obliged to stay and once more dine with the very clever folks there stationed. I then left, and after crossing Red river on the ferry-boat, at the mouth of the Assiniboin, I proceeded on up, through the half-breed settlements, on the east side of the river, for about ten miles, over a good road; and when night fell, secured a guide, who piloted me for several miles to the camp of my two voyageurs, whom I had already sent up to the head of the settlement that morning with the canoe, and orders to await my arrival there. I also camped immediately, heartily tired of the tramp; and yesterday morning was off again at daylight, assisting the men to paddle, and going up against the current at about three miles per hour. At seven o'clock we stopped for breakfast, being just out of sight of the houses, which extend some fifteen miles by water above the fort. As our canoe leaked badly, the men informed me that it would take five days to reach this place, and proposed deserting her and taking to the prairie-road on foot—stating, too, that we could easily come up in about two days.

I was strongly inclined to let them come, and go back, or else in the canoe to Selkirk; or either proceed on up by water until I met the governor's party, or await his arrival where I was. But not liking the uncertainty attending the time of his arrival, and being loath to beat a "retreat backward," even if it were within the hospitable walls of a friendly fort, I decided very unwisely to go on.

I therefore employed two Chippewas, whom I found camped upon the bank; and the party of four then tied the baggage, bedding, and provisions, into four large bundles, and each taking one upon his back, secured by a strap passing in front over the forehead, and sometimes across the chest, we began our march; the men going along with their bodies inclined at an angle of about forty-five degrees, moving with a long, loping trot, which I at first found rather difficult to keep pace with; at times passing through a swamp or across a prairie-stream, when one of the party would drop his pack, and, returning, take me upon his back and carry me safely over.

At noon we stopped to prepare our dinner of tea, old ham, dried buffalo-meat, and hard bread, with a few condiments and extra fixings for a relish; and here we met a half-breed going down with a cart and two spare horses; he was also dining upon the road, where it passed a large bend in the river, and informed me that the governor had just gone down in two canoes, eight men paddling in each, and went very quick. I was by this time very sore and tired, as we had made a forced march of fifteen miles since eight, A. M., and I therefore negotiated with the man (who said, in answer to my first question, that "he spoke English a little piece") for the use of one of his horses to carry me back to the settlements. Feeling refreshed, however, after dinner, I determined to go on; we made the same distance in the afternoon, passing through a swamp at sundown, which was about half a mile in length, knee-deep at that—a mass of tenacious mud and water. We camped soon afterward upon the open prairie, with no wood to make a fire except a few rushes to boil our tea, and I retired wet and too fatigued to sleep or keep one moment in the same position. I fortunately had a bed consisting of a buffalo robe, three blankets, and a canvas-covered mosquito bar, which served to keep off the heavy dew, already falling. If you were ever too tired to be still, you can appreciate my situation. Well, I worried through the night, and on rising at daylight this morning, I found my pantaloons and things all frozen as stiff as horn, and having no fire, I was obliged *to put them on to thaw.* Walked on through the tall wet grass six miles, to breakfast on the Prairie Gratiaro, forty miles from Selkirk. I there overtook my men, and Mr. Adam Klyn and his companion, with a spare horse loaded with their baggage and provisions, the mail, &c., all *en route* for the good city of St. Paul. They had previously passed me two miles beyond, having left the fort yesterday at nine, A. M., and camped four miles behind me; but as they could not help me any, it was at least some satisfaction to know they bore one letter from me to you, if no more.

I also met there Mr. James M'Coy going down with three horses, one of which he very kindly offered me, saying, "It was better to ride back forty or fifty miles, than to go ahead to the 'Prairie au Maurais,' about twenty-five miles on foot." I proposed going that far at least, and wrote to Mr. N. W. Kittson, by the express, to send my horse immediately. I therefore thanked him very kindly and pushed ahead with a staff, and a firm determination to get through; forded streams and swamps with a perfect contempt for all obstacles, and at noon came to the lodges of two half-breed families, situated on each side of a deep stream, with any quantity of dogs and children, cows and calves; and I afterward, when too late, saw some horses in the distance. A pretty-looking, half-breed woman came paddling up the stream, in a log canoe, and soon put us all, bag and baggage, safely over, when, not accepting pay from us, she threw her arms around the neck of one of my voyageurs, named Laundry, and kissed him thrice — very *touching* and pathetic, truly! I walked on *solus* much refreshed, thinking of love and romance in the wilderness and prairie, and of Jacob and Rachel at the well.

At two, P. M., we stopped to dine on the banks of the only lake along the road; after which I distanced the men out of sight, and at five, P. M., reached the River Maurais, the hour and place I had fixed by letter as my resting-point. The men soon came up, and at sundown we started on, when I soon fell lame and was obliged to take off moccasins and stockings. The men were now out of sight ahead, on a full run, and night fast closing in. At length, at dark, after proceeding about three miles, I was overjoyed at meeting a half-breed mounted on my good old horse coming at full gallop. I quickly mounted into his place, and leaving him to camp upon the prairie, with the others, I returned in haste at least ten miles of the weary road through her majesty's dominions, and crossed the line two miles to the north of this as quickly as I would have done if one of her best regiments had been upon my heels. I reached here eventually at eight, P. M., as near a used-up man as well can be, without becoming entirely defunct.

When you consider that I was entirely unaccustomed to such tramps, and was but about twenty marching hours upon the road, and much impeded by the long prairie-grass at that, you will conclude I made considerable of a *march*.

I was especially desirous of reaching here to-night, in order to write a number of letters home by this express, and those who receive any of this date will value them accordingly, for they have cost me dear, I assure you. I have written a detail of my journey, for the reason that my lower extremities are aching as though compressed within a two-horse-power vice, and serve to remind me of the one thing continually, having bathed them in spirits and hot water, and anointed them with precious ointment, I will branch off at something else, merely remarking that the whole road up lies over a wide flat prairie of rich soil, bordered on the left with a belt of timber extending along the river; none of the other rivers, except the Maurais, are timbered. I met large numbers of carts going down to Selkirk to join the lower half-breeds in their fall hunt up the Assiniboin, keeping this time north of the British line, in consequence of a fight they had with the Sioux, over one thousand in number, in July. The summer hunt was unsuccessful. Very little pemmican was made, and but few robes secured, and the sooner the buffalo becomes entirely extinct, the better it will be for them. They will then give up their wandering, Arab mode of life, and go at farming or some other useful occupation for a living. At present they are as restless as regular Bedouins, and if they wore long beards, and had flocks of sheep and goats, one might think he was among the patriarchs of old—"the fathers of all such as dwell in tents."

The treaty was concluded on Saturday evening, after the usual amount of talk, and the following are its provisions. The Chippewas cede all their land from the line north, to the Goose and Buffalo rivers, and thirty miles each side of the Red river—say a strip sixty miles in width by about one hundred long—and they are to receive thirty thousand dollars cash on the ratification of it by the senate; eight thousand dollars thereafter cash, and two thousand dollars for schools annually for twenty years; the whole amounting to two hundred and thirty thousand dollars. I have not had time to examine the treaty yet, but suppose they remain upon the lands and have all the advantages as before, excepting where they may be settled upon and cultivated. They may consider it a present of the above amount, as during their own lifetime they will be but little intruded upon. It is midnight and my space is full.

PEMBINA, *Thursday, September* 25, 1851.

WE leave for St. Paul on Wednesday next, 1st October; our first day's march will be to the new town of St. Joseph on the Pembina mountain, as it is called, thirty miles to the west of this place, the governor having agreed to meet the half-breeds there, a number being about to assemble for the fall hunt. I have just learned that those from the settlements across the line are also coming up, and that there will be some three hundred lodges there. They will hunt, however, along the line, and on the British side, the buffalo being found on that side as well as ours, Captain Pope to the contrary notwithstanding. St. Joseph contains half a dozen houses and two stores. Rev. Mr. Bellecourt resides there, and is erecting a log church; and I have heard of Mr. Kittson's determination to break up the post at this place, and remove there too, the ground here having overflowed for the last three years successively, Red river rising thirty-one and thirty-three feet above low-water mark, and houses on the point between the junction of Red river and Pembina, being flooded to the depth of one and three feet this year and last. Mr. Kittson was obliged to leave and live upon hills near by for more than a month, last spring.

The heaviest floods known in the country occurred in 1824, '25, and '26; the latter year the waters rose sixty-six feet in height, and the whole country was completely drowned out; a large party left Selkirk in consequence and made an overland journey across the plains to St. Peter's and Galena, near which last place they settled.

These floods are a serious objection to this valley, and to Pembina in particular, the site of which is comparatively low; though I think that having occurred only at intervals heretofore, it will be many years before the like occurs again. Partly in consequence of this state of things, there is not a particle of farming done here now, and on our arrival we were obliged to send immediately to Selkirk, for barley for our horses. A dozen voyageurs, in a large barge, brought up one hundred and sixty bushels, and occupied nine days to make the trip, having to wait till this year's crop, which was cut and still standing in the fields, in shocks, was thrashed. They started back, on Tuesday, for one hundred and sixty bushels more, and upon their arrival we will march. Barley is worth in this settlement seventy-five cents a bushel, and costs us here about one dollar and fifty cents. Its usual price when no extra demand takes place, is fifty cents; and for wheat, seventy-five cents, the price paid by the Hudson's Bay Company, the year round; butter and eggs, sixpence; meat, fourpence; flour, three to five dollars per hundred pounds, according to kind, three of which are made. The people revel in abundance. The worst of it is, they have no proper outlet for their surplus produce, to stimulate them to increased exertions, but this is owing to their situation merely, and is an evil time alone can remedy, as they are brought nearer to us by the iron chain, and a market opened to rouse them into more activity and life. At present they pay seven shillings and sixpence, for their lands, per acre. Each settler has a frontage of six chains upon the river, and extends back two miles in depth. Only a small part, however, of this is cultivated. The houses are of logs, thatched and shingled; are warm and very comfortable; some of the larger are of frame, two-story, and a few of stone; all have a plenty of barns and stables, with a number of large stacks of wheat, hay, and barley, and as we happened there in their grain harvest, the people were all busy in the fields. The Indians and half-breeds, men, women, and children, reaping and binding grain; others, with horse and ox-carts, hauling in the same and stacking it. It afforded an interesting and novel sight in contrast with our early harvest of July. It usually takes place here about the 20th August, and is a full month later this year than common, the season having been very cold and wet up to the 17th August, up to which time fears were entertained for the loss of the whole crops. The weather fortunately changed, and for a month was very warm and fine. The grain all ripened, and the yield is large. Of wheat twenty to twenty-five bushels, and barley thirty-five to forty bushels, per acre ; spring wheat is sown from the 20th to 25th of May, and barley from the 1st to 5th of June ; potatoes, the largest and finest I have ever seen, produce largely, more to the acre, than in Minnesota. Indian corn matures, but is not raised to much extent; a small variety is grown. but the situation is too near Lake Winnipeg, which influences their climate, and the late spring frosts are apt to injure it. I am told that corn matures here better, and that the season is about one week later in the fall, than down below. We had hot corn on our table on the 12th instant, the day after our arrival here, which was grown in Mr. Kittson's garden, but it will never be much cultivated in these settlements, the other crops proving more valuable.

The English and Scotch settlers extend along both sides of Red river, from the Assiniboin to lower Fort Garry, or "the stone post," as it is called, about twenty miles below. This is far the best post of the settlement; eighteen windmills are scattered along the west bank, upon which this lengthy serpentine village of six thousand people, is principally situated, and along the line is a solitary water-mill, and another at Sturgeon creek, about eight miles up the Assiniboin, built by Mr. M'Dermott, a very wealthy and enterprising Irish citizen, who came out to the colony in 1812. He is, therefore, one of the pioneers, a free, good, hearty, and sociable gentleman. He is in fact an every man's man, and has an open house and a ready hand to offer to friend or stranger. To his son-in-law, Mr. Ballantine, I am much indebted also, for various kind attentions shown, and I can assure you, I never was among a kinder people.

The Rev. John Black, from Montreal, who accompanied our party out from St. Paul, was also very warmly welcomed; his arrival had been long expected and generally known among all classes.

As we passed down the settlement on our first arrival, people came out and took us by the hand, told us we were strangers, and asked if the new minister was not soon coming also. His Scotch parishioners have just built him a house, thirty by forty feet, of hewn logs, with shingle roof, which he will use as a church this winter, and afterward as a residence. They intend to build him one of stone next year. They made many inquiries concerning him of me, and were all much disappointed at finding he did not speak the Gaelic. That he was a gentleman and a Christian, a good French scholar, and spoke the English fluently, did not make amends altogether for his deficiency in not understanding Gaelic, which is the tongue they use.

The episcopalians have three fine churches surmounted by high steeples, two large ones built of stone, at each end of the English part, and near the forts, and one of logs near the cen tre. Bishop Anderson, who resides at the upper church, had also a fine academy, and a neat white two-story building, with grounds attached.

The catholics have a large cathedral opposite the upper fort, and the mouth of the Assiniboin, built of stone, in 1832, and still unfinished; the huge, massive, prison-like wall in front being cracked and shattered, and is surmounted by two steeples—one finished, the bare timbers of the other towering aloft, dark with age. The interior was being remodelled—carpenters were at work; the high, arched ceiling just painted of a deep mazarene blue, and men at work on scaffolding decorating it with wreaths and festoons of flowers painted in a very artist-like manner. I was told that the nuns at the convent just by were to have done that part of the work, though they were not present when I was there.

Some five or six priests are connected with the church, and the congregation are mostly half-breeds from the settlements up the Red river.

At the fort there are thirteen resident families of pensioners, and the remainder, to the number of seventy, reside within two miles' distance, up the Assiniboin, on the north bank. They have each twenty acres of ground, and those most distant up the river have forty acres, well fenced and cultivated, with neat one-story log and frame houses, painted white, and everything around them betokens plenty. None are incapacitated for manual labor, and many are quite young; and while some have lost nothing but a finger or thumb, others perhaps have lost less useful members, and are sound, active, and hardy fellows. Still they have done the state same service, and they know it too, and growl continually that they are not better off.

I can say no more concerning Selkirk or its people, for the express is ready to start.

The following is some additional information concerning Pembina and Selkirk:—

The attention of traders and merchants is at this time turned with a good deal of interest toward the northwest, more particularly the Red river or Selkirk settlement, and to Pembina, which is now merely a small trading-post within the American line. Before the running of the line of division between the American and British territory, on the forty-ninth parallel of latitude, Pembina was the headquarters of the Selkirk settlement. Since that time it has steadily declined, till within a year or two. The government has contracted to run a regular monthly mail, twelve times in the year, between St. Paul and Pembina, and hereafter communication may be considered as regularly established. The journey is made in the summer on horseback, and in the winter with dog-teams and show-shoes. The more difficult season for performing the service will be during the high-water months of May and June; for between Pembina and St. Paul there are fifteen or sixteen rivers which have to be crossed otherwise than by fording—usually by rafts and buffalo-canoes. Many of the streams are annually bridged over by the caravans of traders, and as often swept away.

The Red river settlement was originally projected by Lord Selkirk, a Scottish nobleman, largely interested in the Hudson's Bay Company. They held a vast extent of lands by charter from the British crown. Of the company he made an extensive purchase, and brought over his first colonists in 1813, and remained with them twelve months. Another accession was made in 1817, and another in 1823; and they now number, in Europeans, French Canadians, and half-breeds, about seven thousand souls.

One half the population are hunters, and the other half farmers. The main settlement, known as "Red River," is about sixty miles north of Pembina, or down the river, and is on an extensive plain, which extends, somewhat broken and interspersed with timber, east to Lake Winnipeg—to the west, a vast, unbroken plain to the Rocky mountains. The hunters, mostly half-breeds, do nothing but hunt buffalo. They make two grand excursions each year: one commencing on the 20th of June, and lasting two months; and the other on the 10th of September, and lasting till the 10th of November. They live wholly on buffalo-meat, and are engaged only in preparing pemmican meat and fat—the one used only for food, and the other for light. The regular price of it is four cents a pound, both fat and lean. The tongues and hides only of the buffalo are saved. The regular retail price of a tongue, dried, is twenty-five cents, and a good robe is two dollars. The hunters lead a free, happy, wild, romantic life, and are, when in the settlement, temperate and well-behaved.

The farmers raise wheat, oats, potatoes, barley, cattle, and sheep. Oxen are worth from fifty to sixty dollars a yoke; cows, from twelve to fifteen dollars; a good cart-horse, forty or fifty dollars; and a horse trained to hunt buffalo will bring one hundred and twenty-five dollars, and sometimes more.

Their wheat is equal to any in the world, weighing from sixty-five to seventy pounds to the bushel. Barley and oats are also heavy; and potatoes and all kinds of garden vegetables grow luxuriantly. *The land is never manured.* From three and a half to four feet of snow falls in winter, and rain is unknown from November to April. Corn is raised, but it is not relied on as a sure crop. The Hudson's Bay Company pay regularly only, however, for what they wish to consume, except in seasons of scarcity, eighty-seven cents a bushel for wheat, fifty for oats and barley, and twenty-five for potatoes. There is no export trade. They receive their supplies of dry goods, woollen cloths, and liquors, from York factory, a store of the Hudson's Bay Company, situated on Hudson's bay, seven hundred miles from Red River. It requires two months to make the journey, and there are thirty-six portages to be made in going that distance. The title of the settlement is "The Red River Colony," and it is ruled by a governor appointed by the queen. The magistrates, counsellors, and officers, receive their commissions from the committee of the Hudson's Bay Company. The jurisdiction of the governor extends a hundred miles in all directions from Fort Garry, except over the American line. Seventy pensioners at Fort Garry is all the military force, and they are under the command of Major Caldwell, the governor, who is also a pensioner.

The wheat and other grain is ground by windmills, of which there are eighteen, and two water-mills. There are no saw-mills, all the deals used being cut up by whip-saws. There are no fulling-mills, or manufactures of any kind.

Above and below the settlement on Red river there are extensive tracts of timber — of pine, oak, whitewood, poplar, and cedar. The ice gets out of Red river about the 20th of April, and it is closed about the 1st or 10th of November. The cold is sometimes excessive in the settlement. Mercury freezes once or twice every year, and sometimes the spirit thermometer indicates a temperature as low as fifty-two degrees below zero! When such a low temperature occurs, there is a pervading haze or smoky appearance in the atmosphere, resembling a generally-diffused yellow smoke, and the sun looks red as in a sultry evening. As the sun rises, so does the thermometer; and when the mercury thaws out and stands at ten or fifteen below zero, a breeze sets in, and pleasant weather follows — that is, as pleasant as can be while the mercury keeps below zero as continually as a fish in his own element, and coming up above the surface just about as often.

For weeks, sometimes, the wind will blow from the north — temperature say from five to ten degrees below zero. Suddenly it shifts into the south, and for six hours the thermometer will continue to fall. When, in summer, the wind blows a length of time from the north, it drives the water back, and Red river will have its banks full in the dryest seasons. The same thing occurs when the wind blows from the same direction in winter, although the sea and river are frozen unbrokenly ten feet thick to the north pole.

In the year 1670, Charles II. granted all the territory in North America, subject to the British crown, that was drained by waters flowing into Hudson's bay, to the Hudson's Bay Company — and, among other privileges, the exclusive right to deal and traffic with the natives. Besides this territory, they have extended their jurisdiction over the lands watered by the rivers that flow into the Arctic ocean, and also that vast country west of the Rocky mountains. Their territory, in fine, embraces all North America (with the exception of the Russian possessions in the extreme northwest, and Greenland in the northeast) that lies north of the Canadas, and the United States and its possessions. The southern boundary of the company commences on the Pacific coast, opposite to and including Vancouver's island, at latitude forty-nine, and extends on this parallel to the southeastern point of the lake of the Woods, thence on the highlands that divide the waters which flow into Lake Superior and the St. Lawrence from those flowing into Hudson's bay east to the Atlantic ocean. So much for the Hudson's Bay Company and its possessions, both of which may become objects of interest in a few years to us and our neighborhood.

Lord Selkirk, having obtained a grant from the company of a territory extending from Fort Garry a hundred miles in a circle, on certain conditions, came out with his colony, as before remarked, in 1813. They flourished and increased for some time. In 1825, 1826, and 1827, the Red river overflowed its banks, and produced universal distress — so much, that many of the most wealthy and influential citizens left the place; a party of whom, consisting of Messrs. Francis Langet, Philip F.

Schirmer, Louis Chetlain, Peter Reindsbacker, Antoine Bricker, Paul Gyrber, John Baptiste Verain, John Tyrey, and others, with their wives and families (German Swiss from Geneva and that vicinity, speaking the French language), came down and settled at Gratiot's Grove, near Galena, Illinois. At that time there were large smelting operations carried on by Colonel Henry Gratiot.

The party named came out to Selkirk in 1817—the first band being nearly all Scotchmen, but the second from the continent. Those emigrating to Illinois, the most of whom are now living, have been among the first citizens and worthy members of society, handing down their virtues to their children.

The origin of the floods which did such immense damage on Red river, in the years before named, has never been satisfactorily accounted for; but it is surmised that they came from the superabundant water of the branches of the Missouri, bursting over the low ridge which divides the waters flowing into the gulf of Mexico from those flowing into Hudson's bay.

The only tax which the colonists of Red River pay is four per cent. on all the goods they import, whether from England or elsewhere; and the Hudson's Bay Company pay the same on all the imports they sell or consume within the limits of the Red-River Colony. The company import goods and merchandise from England, and charge the consumer in the colony seventy-five per cent. advance on the London invoice prices, for freight, insurance, duty, land-carriage, and profit. They sell bar and sheet iron for twelve cents a pound; sugar, London crushed, twenty-four cents; tea, from fifty cents to two dollars; and other articles in proportion. The imports for the last five years have averaged one hundred thousand dollars, from all sources; and the one thousand dollars revenue is devoted to schools, roads, bridges, and internal improvements, all salaries being paid by the company. The colonists export comparatively nothing—the only article that will pay being furs (not including buffalo-robes), on which the Hudson's Bay Company have a monopoly, over which they watch with a jealous eye.

Since the route has been opened and travelled from Pembina to St. Paul, they have commenced to bring forward merchandise. Twenty per cent. duty is demanded of the Selkirkers on buffalo-robes, and thirty per cent. on their moccasins. Red River gentlemen express the assurance that they never can pay that tax, and that hereafter they will be obliged to avail themselves of the boats and ships of the "company." We presume Congress will look into this matter, and discriminate in their favor, unless there exist good reasons for a contrary course.

TRIBUTE TO THE PEOPLE OF SELKIRK SETTLEMENT.

How sweetly in this blest retreat
  The cool, calm evenings fall,
While scenes and sounds familiar once
  A far-off land recall!

Or morning, when the hill-side green
  Is bright with golden beams,
And flowers as large and fair as those
  Of childhood's wildest dreams.

How deep the solitude which reigns
  In yon thick forest-glades,
Where under tangled leaves and flowers
  Bright morn to twilight fades! —

While o'er thy fertile prairie wide
  The silvery streamlet flows,
Its music heard, but not to break,
  The spell of deep repose.

Selkirk! thy sweet vale contains
  All good this world can give —
Peace, health, and comfort — what remains
  To wish for, but to live?

I feel thy beauty and thy charms
  Demand from me no feeble praise:
I have no power, yet fain I would
  A better, warmer tribute raise.

For, could I leave this cheerful vale,
  And quit thy hospitable roofs,
Without one sigh, one keen regret,
  And of thy merits leave no proofs —

I should unworthily repay
  The kindness of those friends
Whose worth deserves as warm a lay
  As love or friendship ever pens.

My footsteps Fate, perchance, may lead
  To other lands and climes,
And treacherous Memory may forget
  The joys of bygone times:

But thou, sweet Selkirk, from my heart,
  Though weary then and worn,
Though care and sorrow cloud my path,
  Thy name shall not be torn!

I love thee — for thy woodland scenes
  Recall my childhood's hours;
And as my native state is dear,
  So are thy woods and flowers!

TABLE OF DISTANCES, BY THE LAND ROUTE, FROM THE MOUTH OF THE MINNESOTA TO THE PEMBINA SETTLEMENT.

From Fort Snelling.	Miles.	Total.
To falls of St. Anthony	7⅓	
To Banfill's, at mouth of Rice creek	9⅓	16⅔
To mouth of Rum river	9	25⅔
To mouth of Elk river	13	38⅔
To Big lake	8⅓	47
To Big meadows	18½	65½
To Sauk rapids	11	76½
To David lake	29	105½
To White-Bear lake	39	144½
To Pike lake	8	152½
To main branch of Chippewa river	11	163½
To Pomme de Terre or Potato river	10	173½
To Rabbit river	12	185½
To first crossing of Red river of the North	18	203½
To second crossing of Red river of the North	20	223½
To Wild-Rice river	13½	237
To Shayenne river	11	248
To Maple river	17	265
To Rush river	18½	283½
To second point of Rush river	9½	293
To point of ridge	16	309
To main branch of Elm river	7½	316½
To south branch of Goose river	8½	325
To Salt lake	8½	333½
To main branch of Goose river	10½	344
To crossing of Goose river	2½	346½
To Turtle river	18	364½
To Big Salt river	19½	384
To Little Salt river	9	393
To Little Hill river	12½	405½
To Steep Hill river	4½	410
To Hartshorn river	3	413
To Mud river and Poplar island	7	420
To branch of Tongue river	16	436
To mouth of Pembina river	10½	446½

TABLE OF SOUNDINGS OF RED RIVER OF THE NORTH, ETC.

	Feet.
From mouth of Pembina river to the mouth of Red-Lake river	15
From Red-Lake river above mouth	14
From Red-Lake river to mouth of Goose river	13
Over rapids near mouth of Sand-Hill river	6
Goose river above mouth	6½
From mouth of Goose river to mouth of Shayenne	11
Shayenne river above mouth	6½
From Shayenne river to mouth of Wild-Rice river	9
From Wild-Rice river to Sioux-Wood river	8½
Sioux-Wood river above mouth	4
Ottertail lake	19

APPENDIX.

PRINCE RUPERT'S LAND—THE HUDSON BAY AND NORTHWEST COMPANY—THE ESQUIMAUX, MONTAGNES, CREES, SAUTEUX, SIOUX, ASSINIBOINS, ETC.

THE following interesting matter, descriptive of Prince Rupert's land, etc., is from the pen of the Rev. G. A. Bellecourt, of Pembina, and was addressed to the Hon. Alexander Ramsey, president of the "Minnesota Historical Society." It was written in French, and its able translation was made by Mrs. Letitia May, of St. Paul.

The discovery of America, by Christopher Columbus, in 1492, gave a new impulse to the spirit of enterprise. From that period, bold navigators launched fearlessly out into the broad bosom of the ocean, and continued to make, from time to time, new discoveries in the field which had been laid open to them by the noble and devoted perseverance of their great predecessor.

It was about the year 1607, that the celebrated navigator, Henry Hudson, then in the employ of the English, discovered the magnificent bay to which he gave his name; and in 1611, pursuing his researches, he penetrated five hundred leagues farther north than any traveller had done before him. It was this same year that two missionaries, Fathers Masse and Biart, arrived in Canada.

Some time after this period, the English, in order to profit by the discoveries which had been made in their name by Hudson, commenced some settlements in the vicinity of Hudson's bay, and entered into a kind of traffic for furs with the

Indians, who descended, during the summer season, the various streams which pour their waters into this bay, bringing with them these trophies of their success in the chase.

These settlers built at first only a few houses in which to pass the winter. Here they suffered greatly from the scurvy, which broke out among them. But the strong desire of gain which actuated them, rendered them regardless alike of the ravages of disease and the rigor of the climate.

The French of Canada also wished to establish themselves in this region, pretending that, as that country formed a part of the same continent as New France, they had the right to trade with the natives that high up and even higher. Several of their adventurers had penetrated as far north as the bay of Hudson, as early as the year 1656, and in the intermediate time between that and the year 1680, when Groseillers and Radisson left Quebec for the above-named bay with two vessels, which were but poorly equipped for such an expedition. The persons engaged in this enterprise only succeeded in erecting a few forts, whence they sallied forth and attacked the English settlements in the neighborhood, and were in their turn attacked by them; thus exhibiting, in the horrors of civilization, more cruelty than the savages with whom they had come to trade. Such have been, at every period, among the sad effects of an inordinate love of gain. These dissensions between the English and the French did not cease till the ratification of the treaty of Utrecht.

The result of these wars between the two contending people was, that the English obtained the sole occupancy of the neighborhood of Hudson's bay, and both shores of Nelson river. But many French companies, established partly at Montreal, continued the commerce in furs; which they practised almost exclusively in all the rest of the northwestern part of North America, extending their expeditions even so far as the Rocky mountains. Many places in these regions still retain the names of celebrated personages and houses which existed at the time of their discovery; as, for instance, Lake Bourbon, Dauphin river, Fort la Reine; and a missionary, of whom I have not been able to learn the name, made several days' march up the river Saskadjiwan (*Kisiskadjiwan, current which turns round*).

We have no evidence that the French ascended higher up than three days' march above Lake Bourbon, along the river Pas, or Saskadjiwan. The first who left Canada with views of commerce in this country, was Thomas Ourry, who ascended the river Saskadjiwan, in 1766. Up to this time the Canadian traders did not venture any higher up than Grand Portage, at the northern extremity of Lake Superior. His voyage, which proved to be very profitable, encouraged others to follow his example. James Finley made a voyage also, which was equally happy. But as these adventurers, in travelling thus far into the interior, intercepted the furs which had before this time been brought by the Indians to Hudson's bay, the English traders became jealous of them, and advanced farther into the interior. From this we date the commencement of a long series of disorders and excesses, of which the details were the more revolting as the certainty of impunity gave free course to all the passions.

Joseph Frobisher undertook to penetrate farther than any of his predecessors had done, and went as far as Churchill, which is beyond the fifty-ninth degree of latitude. The following year his brother went as far as *L'Ile à la Crosse*. In 1778, Peter Pond entered English river, thus called by Frobisher, and pursued his course to the river L'Orignal, where he passed the winter. One day, after he had made some of the Indians drunk, he was so annoyed by them that, to rid himself of their importunity, he gave one of them so large a dose of laudanum that he was plunged into an eternal sleep. This murder cost the life of a trader and all his assistants. And any trader, or any white man, who would have dared to show his face in this place, or on the Assiniboin river, would have fallen a victim to the sanguinary vengeance of these exasperated savages, had not the smallpox broken out among them, and produced a diversion in favor of the whites. This dreadful scourge spread terror and desolation among all these people. Whoever was not attacked by it fled into the most profound depths of the forest, far from the presence of the whites.

About two thirds of their population perished. Their corpses lay on the ground; the masters became the food of their own dogs, or of the wolves. From this period is dated also the army of the great picotte (quarrel). This was about 1780.

This same year Peter Pond formed a partnership with Mr. Wadin. These two men were of a character too opposite to be united, as it soon appeared. At a festival given by Pond to Wadin, the latter was killed by the former, who shot him in the thigh with a pistol. The ball broke the artery, the hemorrhage from which could not be stopped; so he died. Pond was tried and acquitted at Montreal, but he was not acquitted in the eyes of the people who heard of the transaction. And, in general, the judgment pronounced in his case was considered as unheard-of, or as containing too much of the mysterious to do honor to the judge who pronounced it.

In 1781, four canoes filled with traders went up as high as "*Portage de la Loche*," some high lands between the Saskadjiwan river and the Polar sea. At last, in 1783, was formed the company, which has since become so famous, under the name of the Northwestern Company. The first factors were Benjamin and Joseph Frobisher, and Simon M'Tavish. It was first composed of sixteen partners. P. Pond and P. Pangman refused to join it, though the former changed his mind the next year. P. Pangman joined with Gregory, M'Leod, and M'Kenzie, in 1785.

These opposing interests were the cause of disorders of every kind; so much so, that these companies rendered themselves despicable even in the eyes of the savages, who were astonished to find that their own manners were much better than those of men whom, in other respects, they regarded as being greatly superior to themselves. In one of these difficulties, Gregory saw one of his companions killed before his eyes, and several of their assistants wounded. It was easy to be conceived, that their common interest demanded a sincere and cordial union. This they comprehended somewhat later; and at last, in 1787, all these companies united together, and thus increased the number of partners to twenty-six. The forty thousand pounds sterling, which their commerce yielded them at that time, was trebled in less than eleven years. In 1798 the company increased the number to forty-six, which caused some dissatisfaction, and led a small number of them to form a separate company. Nevertheless, the Northwest Company had become too powerful to dread any such divisions. It continued to prosper, in spite even of the opposition of the Hudson Bay Company.

This last company took advantage, as it still does, of a charter granted by Charles II, to his cousin Rupert. This document, although illegal according to the British constitution, has been strongly sustained. It grants the most absolute powers, and concedes a sovereignty more despotic than Charles himself possessed. Though the governmental department has sufficiently expressed themselves upon the subject of the illegality of this contract, yet the friends of this company have always been so powerful as to prevent an official declaration to this effect, by contending that the subject should first undergo a discussion in court. Thus, those who are opposed to the pretensions of this company, not having enough of money to sustain the process, fearing that gold and favor would prove the stronger argument, find themselves obliged to submit to a usurpation which they can not prevent.

Though they complained of these abuses a few years ago by petition, which was ably sustained at London, and which occasioned a good deal of excitement in England, the only effect produced here, was to abate in a small degree the boldness of the pretensions of this company, which tended to a perfect tyranny. In proof of this, I will adduce a few instances of their impositions:—On one occasion they seized the effects of a hunter, upon suspicion that he might exchange some of them with the Indians for furs. On another occasion they caused a hunter to be imprisoned for having given one of his overcoats to a naked Indian, for about its value in rat-skins. They also refuse to allow the missionaries to receive furs to sustain the expenses of public worship; while the Indians can not obtain any money from the company for their furs; and forbid the missionaries to buy leather or skins to protect their feet from the cold. These, and a thousand other grievances call so loudly for redress, that I think a small increase of the burden will cause the evil to correct itself.

About the year 1812, the Northwest Company had more than sixty trading posts west of the longitude of Lake Bourbon, and as high up as Slave lake, where they sustained a prosperous commerce. This success only inflamed still more the jealousy of the Hudson Bay Company. Everything that could be imagined to discourage their adversaries or hinder their prosperity, was resorted to without scruple, or the least regard to human life. They went so far as to burn up their bark canoes, and destroy their traps which were in the water, the sole means of subsistence in many places.

The hostilities which existed between the two companies assumed a more formal aspect about the time of the establishment of the colony of Lord Selkirk, that is, from 1812 to 1816. In 1815, eatables being very scarce in the establishment, the governor of the colony issued an order, forbidding any one to take any provisions whatever of food out of the boundary of the colony. Now it was well known that the company of the Northwest, ought to try to send provisions through this colony, for the numerous travellers who were coming from Montreal, and who depended upon their succor, to enable them either to continue their route or return to Canada. The agents of this company having been informed in time, of the order of the governor of the colony through which they had to pass, when they were descending the river Assiniboin, halted before they entered the territory of the colony, and sent a detachment of cavalry, composed of half-breeds, under the control of Cuthbert Grant, at that time clerk of this company, with orders to go by land to the mouth of Red river, in order to escort the canoes of provisions which were expected down every day. Though they made a large circuit in compassing the angle formed by the Assiniboin and Red rivers, this company of half-breeds were recognised from the fort of the colony, when they reached the mouth of the river Assiniboin. Immediately upon seeing them, Governor Semple ordered out two pieces of cannon and sent in great haste to assemble the settlers in the neighborhood, and without waiting for them to come together, took the field with such persons as he could collect at the moment. The half-breeds, who saw from a distance these movements near the fort, stopped to make observations. At last seeing an armed force coming out against them, they prepared to make a vigorous resistance, with orders, nevertheless, not to make an attack. When the English came within gun-shot, Mr. Grant sent a cavalier in advance, to make some arrangement with the governor; but the messenger, far from being listened to, received a discharge from a gun, which he avoided only by precipitating himself from his horse. He then hastened back to his companions. A combat immediately commenced, which lasted only a few hours, and was so well-conducted on the part of the half-breeds, that it cost them only one man; while on the part of the English, the governor and nineteen of his men lay on the field of battle.

This took place in the spring of 1816, at the time that Lord Selkirk, who had come to reside in Canada, was on his way to visit his colony. He was encamped at the extremity of Lake Superior, on an isle called "*Ile de Traverse*" opposite, though at a distance from Fort William, the principal dépôt of the Northwestern Company, when he learned the news of what had taken place at Red river, and the death of his protégé, Governor Semple. As he was escorted by a company of veterans, he re-embarked with the intention of taking Fort William, which he effected without a blow; for as his approach was unsuspected, he found the gates open. He thus took possession of this post and passed the winter there.

The next spring, he visited his colony, where he left some soldiers, and returned to Canada by way of the United States. After his arrival at Montreal, he instituted a suit against the Northwestern Company, much to the satisfaction of the bar, both of Upper and Lower Canada, who were the only persons benefited by it; for the case was removed to England, where it was never judged, after having cost enormous sums.

During his sojourn at Red River, Lord Selkirk had remarked that this little community were altogether destitute of the principles of religion and morals; accordingly, he suggested to the catholics of the place that they should address a petition to the bishop of Quebec, to send them a missionary. His grace, Joseph Octave Plessie, then bishop of Quebec, granted their request most willingly, and sent them, the following spring, 1818, Mr. Joseph Norb't Provencher, then curate of Kamouraska, as his grand vicar, and Mr. S. J. N. Dumoulin, then vicar of Quebec. Having quitted Montreal the 19th of May, they reached the place of their destination July 16th.

At their arrival, the colony was the emblem of misery. They had not yet tried to plant, except with the hoe, and that only to procure seed for the following year. During two consecutive years, the grasshoppers made such devastation among the crops, that they did not even gather seed, and were obliged to send for them to Prairie du Chien, on the Mississippi river, about a thousand miles distant. They also brought chickens from that place, which multiplied very rapidly. The crop of 1822 was passable, but the rats caused great destruction. As they had not yet procured cats, the country was infested by these vermin.

As the few animals brought from Europe by the Scotch colonies, had been destroyed during the troubles of the preceding years, they were obliged to procure some from Prairie du Chien. Some individuals imported several pairs of oxen, and some cows. At that time, a cow sold for twenty-five pounds. In 1825, an American drove four or five hundred oxen and cows to that place. The cows sold at from four to ten pounds each. Their number has since considerably increased.

In 1825, the snow fell the 15th of October in great quantity, and remained on the ground. Still more fell during the winter, which was one of the coldest which had passed for twenty-five years. The snow melted suddenly about the last of April. The water had already risen in the streams as high as the banks, when the ice, which had scarcely diminished in thickness, was dragged away by the violence of the current, and taking a straight course, rooted up trees and demolished edifices and whatever found itself in its way. The water rose five feet in the church of St. Boniface, nearly opposite the mouth of the river Assiniboin, which is one of the most elevated spots in that vicinity.

The fish, the principal resource of the inhabitants at this season of the year, were dispersed in this immense extent of water, and the fishermen were not able to take them. To crown their misfortunes, the bison that were ordinarily found in abundance near the river Pembina, went away, and about fifteen persons who had calculated on this resource, perished from hunger. The waters did not retire entirely till the 20th of July; when some persons risked sowing barley, which came to maturity.

After so many scourges of different kinds, one would think that the survivors would have been ready to abandon for ever a country which offered only disasters and difficulties. Some of them did indeed leave, and go to the United States; others lived, like the savages, by hunting and fishing, for several years, after which they returned to the culture of the earth: at last, having had good crops during several years, the remembrance of their misfortunes was effaced. The same scourge has not visited the place in a general manner till last year, 1852. The water rose a foot higher than in 1826, and the losses occasioned by it are still greater, and more difficult to repair. A greater quantity of fencing, grain, and property of all kinds, has been carried away and destroyed by the water; then the lumber being all destroyed or carried away to some distance from the colony, the expenses of building are much more considerable. We, at St. Joseph of Pembina, are beyond the reach of these misfortunes.

We have seen that the visit of Lord Selkirk to Red River, occasioned missionaries to be sent to that colony. The process which he instituted against the Northwestern Company, though never judged, was also productive of some favorable results. The great expense of sustaining this process, joined to those occasioned by the constant opposition of a rival interest, and still more, weariness of a life of incessant contentions, induced these two companies to unite, under the name and privileges of the Hudson Bay Company. Some of the members of the Northwestern Company, not willing to be known under a title which they had despised, preferred to retire from the commerce.

The union of these two companies took place in 1822. Since that period, the profits of the company have been very great; but, on the other hand, the people of the country have suffered by it in inverse proportion. The price of furs, as well as that of merchandise given in exchange, was regulated entirely by the company. The seller came and deposited his furs, and took from the trader's store, in exchange, such things as he wished; beginning by the articles of first necessity, and stopping when he was told he had enough. This absolute power engendered, as can be readily conceived, many abuses. The traders, seeing the people so submissive, became arrogant, and gave themselves up, without any shame, to every excess of immorality. At last, missionaries being sent out in every direction, men who had been civilized were made to remember their first education; a reform of conduct was the result, and honesty recovered its rights.

There was a mission formed near the Rocky mountains, above the river Saskadjiwan, on the little lake of Manitou. It was established in 1843, by Mr. J. Baptiste Thibault, a priest of the diocese of Quebec, who lived there till 1851. He left in his place, Mr. Bourassa, a priest of the same diocese of Quebec. Another mission was since formed at the isle of La Crosse, by Mr. S. Lafleche, a priest of the district of Three Rivers, and Mr. Als Tache, a priest of the diocese of Montreal. They both received a mission for this post, where they rendered themselves in 1845. Since that time, several priests of the society of Oblats, of Marseilles, have been sent on a mission to these mountains. Father Faraud has penetrated farther north than any of the others. He went as far as Great Slave lake. Chapels for worship have been erected in each one of these missions. Among all these churches, only one (the cathedral of St. Boniface) is built of stone; all the others are wooden edifices.

The parish of St. Francis Xavier, of Prairie du Cheval Blanc, about eighteen miles from the mouth of the river Assiniboin, existed as early as 1830. This spot is the least exposed to inundation of all the surrounding country. This parish is composed of emigrants from Pembina, where there were several commercial houses, and quite a number of farmers. But when Major Long, of the United States, had verified the point of the forth-ninth degree of latitude, Pembina proving to be on the American territory, the Hudson Bay Company caused the whole population to remove to their side, by menacing them with a refusal to let them have any supplies from their stores if they remained. Their missionary, Mr. Dumoulin, being returned to Canada, the whole colony finished by emigrating, though very reluctantly, to Prairie du Cheval Blanc.

Twelve miles higher up on the Assiniboin, I built a chapel among the Sauteux, where I had a very flourishing mission from 1832 till 1848, when I quitted this diocese to go to Pembina. During this time, I built another chapel, and founded a farm, about three hundred miles from the colony toward the east, at a point called Wabassimong, on the river Winipik. This mission was committed to the Oblats of Marseilles the year before I left it. At last being arrived at Pembina, in 1849, I constructed a chapel on Red river, a mile below the mouth of Pembina river, on the most advantageous site we could select. The inundations having decided us to establish ourselves near to Mount Pembina, about forty miles from Red river, I built another chapel of wood, fifty feet by twenty-five, two stories high.

The total population of the colony of Selkirk is about seven thousand souls, of which little more than one half are catholics; the others are divided between the church of England, presbyterians, and methodists. There is on Red river but one society of nuns not cloistered. These came from Canada, and are of the order of the sisters of charity called "grey nuns" (*sœurs grises*). Though instruction was not the object of their institution, they have been invited to this calling, and have fulfilled its important functions with success since their arrival in 1844.

MANNERS OF THE INHABITANTS OF THE COUNTRY.

The population of the country divides itself into three classes, viz.: the colonists who come from Canada or Europe; the half-breeds, and their children; and the savages. The Canadians and the Europeans have brought with them that spirit of nationality, which leads them to esteem themselves above the other inhabitants—half-breeds, &c. For the first, nothing is so good as Montreal; for the others, nothing is like London. The half-breeds being more numerous, and endowed with uncommon health and strength, esteem themselves the lords of the land. Though they hold the middle place between civilized and savage life, one can say that, in respect to morality, they are as good as many civilized people. Their character is gentle and benevolent. Their greatest vice is prodigality; they have also an extreme tendency to the use of strong drinks; nevertheless, the vivacity of their faith has wrought wonders among them in this respect. A number of them have taken a pledge to abstain entirely from the use of all intoxicating liquors; and many others, without having done as much, still hold themselves within just bounds. Though the half-breeds lose much of their time in idleness, I do not think this owes its origin to the vice of indolence, but rather to the absence of all commercial interest; that is to say, to the want of enterprises passably lucrative, or of rewards sufficiently inviting, to make them sustain the fatigues of labor. For they are capable of enduring to an astonishing degree the most horrible fatigues, and they undertake them with the greatest cheerfulness when circumstances call for it. They love gaming, but have no great passion for it; and it is rare that any one of them delivers himself to any excess in this vice. They have a taste for music, and above all for the violin; and a great many of them know how to play. They have a tendency to superstition, which arises from their origin; particularly in respect to dreams. Though religion teaches them what they ought to think about these things, they feel invincibly impressed with a sentiment of hope or fear, according to the nature of the dream. The third class of the population of the country are the savages, who have a still stronger spirit of nationality than the other two, though they admit that they are not so skilful in other respects.

The immense valley that empties its waters into Hudson's bay is inhabited by a great number of savage tribes, who all spring from four mother nations, absolutely distinguished from each other by their language.

1. All the people who border on the northern sea, from Mackenzie's river to the Atlantic ocean, belong to the tribe of the Esquimaux. All speak nearly the same language, have the same usages, same superstitions, and the same manners. Small in stature, their physiogomy is entirely characteristic; and offers nothing which attaches itself to the other American nations. They never form any alliances with other nations; who regard them as being as far inferior to them, as they themselves are inferior to the whites. The name of the Esquimaux is a corruption of the word Weashkimek, *the eaters of raw fish;* this word is Sauteux. They have, like the other savage nations, the use of the drum. Their habitations are usually made of snow or ice, and are warmer than one would be tempted to believe; but they have a humidity which is insupportable to any person not born in them. As they drink whale oil with great delight, they expose themselves to great dangers to catch this animal; which proves that they are not destitute of bravery. Without occupying themselves with the reflection that the fisherman and his canoe would make only a mouthful for one of these marine monsters, over whom they often pass in the chase of the whale—nor that with one blow of his tail, the whale himself, could throw them to the third heaven, like to the feeble bird, which strikes with its bill the crow who comes to deprive it of its young—they throw their slight darts at the back of the enormous fish, till they have rendered themselves masters of it. As no missionary has ever lived among this people, it is impossible to form any just estimate of their mental capacities.

2. The nation of Montagnes, who are divided into several different tribes, are the neighbors of the Esquimaux, and in-

habit a strip of land parellel to theirs, from the Rocky mountains to the neighborhood of Hudson's bay, and extending southward to the river Saskadjiwan. They are, perhaps, of all the savages of America, the only ones who have no kind of superstition or worship of imaginary beings. Great admirers of the whites, they imitate them as much as they can. This natural disposition, joined to the absence of all religious prejudice, has given to the missionaries who are sent there, every advantage they could desire. They are now nearly all Christians, excepting a certain number of families whom the bonds of polygamy, which they find difficult to break, hold still at a distance.

The name of Montagne is not a translation of the savage word *Wetshipweyanah*—*having the dress pointed*—because the cap, which covers their heads, is pointed and sewed to a cloak or sack which they wear, which, under points of view, makes them appear pointed at the top. This word is also of the Sauteux language. They live by hunting the cariboo, and some by hunting the bison; and on the fish with which all their lakes abound. These people are not warlike, no more than the Esquimaux.

3. The Crees who inhabit the two sides of the river Saskadjiwan, and with whom we should join all the Mashkegons, who belong to the same family, and who extend in all the country which borders the bay of Hudson on the west, south, and east, in a word, all the marshy country. The mother nation of these two numerous tribes seems to be the nation of the Sauteux, which extends from Canada to the river Saskadjiwan, where they are mixed with the Crees, and are known under the name of *Nakkawinininiwak*—the men of divers races. The word Crees is also not a translation of the savage word *Kinishtinak*—being held by the winds. That is to say, the inhabitants of those places, where the slightest wind keeps them from travelling: from which it appears, that the Crees originally inhabited the shores of the great lakes, such as Lake Superior; perhaps, also, certain portions of the lake of the Woods, which one can not cross except when the weather is very calm, and which they certainly inhabited at one time.

The word Mashkegon is a corruption of Omashkekok—the inhabitants of the marshes. The only way of travelling in all the immense region which they inhabit, is in canoes. I have met old men, in travelling through their country, who had never seen a horse.

The word Sauteux, which seems to have been given to this nation from their having a long time inhabited the Sault Ste. Marie, is not a translation of the savage name Odjibwek. This word has been the object of a great many suppositions: some say it was given to this nation on account of the form of their plaited shoes—*teibwa*, plaited; but this interpretation is not admissible, for the word does not contain the least allusion to shoes. Others say that it comes from the form the mouth assumes in pronouncing certain words, wishing always to hold on to the adjective *teibwa;* this is not more satisfactory. It is not uncommon that a word is somewhat changed when applied to a man or a nation. I could give a number of examples of this. I would venture then to say that the word Odjibwek comes from Shibwe; in order to make a proper noun Oshibwek, in the plural the pronouncing slowly of *shib*—root, to draw out; that is to say, to lengthen out a word by the slow pronunciation of its syllables; the particle *we* signifying articulate, pronounce; the *k* is an animated plural, which here can only be applied to men. In truth, the pronunciation of the Sauteux characterizes them in an eminent manner. The Ottawas, the Nipising, the Algonquins, the *Tetes de Boule*, the Montagnes of Canada, are so many tribes which belong to the same family. We must not confound the Montagnes of Canada with those of the north, who have nothing in common except the name. The Sauteux and the Crees have always been intimately united; and they have the same usages and the same superstitions, to which they are extremely attached.

Their principal religious meeting takes place every spring, about the time when all the plants begin to awaken from their long winter sleep and renew their life, and commence to bud. The ticket of invitation is a piece of tobacco sent by the oldest person of the nation, indicating the place of rendezvous to the principal persons of the tribe. This is a national feast, in which each individual is interested, being the feast of medidines. Each head of a family is the physician of his children, but he can not become so without having a preliminary instruction and initiation into the secrets of medicine. It is at this feast that each one is received. All the ceremonies which they perform are emblematic, and signify the virtue of plants in the cure of the various maladies of man.

Another superstition, proper to cure the evils which have place more in the imagination than in the body, is the Nipikkiwan. It consists in drawing out the evil directly, in drawing the breath, and spitting in the eyes of the sick person. The pretended cause of the suffering is sometimes a stone, a fruit, the point of an arrow, or even a medicine, wrapped up in cotton. One can not conceive how much these poor people submit with blind faith to these absurdities.

Lastly, curiosity, and the desire of knowing the future, has invented the Teisakkiwin. It consists of certain formalities, songs, invocations of spirits, and bodily agitations, which are so energetic, that you are carried back to the time of the ancient sybils; they seem to say to you, *Deus ecce Deus*, and then submitting to the questions of the spectators, for whom they always have a reply, whether it be to tell what passes at a distance, or reveal the place where objects which have been lost may be found. As the skill of the prophet consists in replying in ambiguous terms upon all subjects of which he has not been able to procure information in advance, he is always sure of success, either more or less striking. Besides, as one is ordinarily predisposed to the marvellous, anything that aids an imposture is easily overlooked.

I knew a man who was in great trouble on account of his horses, which he could not find just at the moment when all the hunters were about to go upon an expedition. Seeing he could not accompany them without his horses, he used every effort to find them. At last an old Sauteux came to him and proposed if he would give him a net (a net used to catch fish) he would go immediately and invoke his manitous; and he was very sure they would give him the desired information. As one can readily suppose, the offer was accepted; and after the ordinary formalities, the juggler said he saw the number of the horses, and described them otherwise faithfully, naming also exactly the place where they could be found. They were in effect found in the place he had indicated. Now this old man had himself hid the horses, in order to obtain from the owner, the net which he knew he possessed; and which he himself needed. I could cite many other instances of the same kind.

Dreams are for the Sauteux revelations; and the bird, the animal, or even a stone, or whatever it may be which is the principal subject of the dream, becomes a tutelary spirit, for which the dreamer has a particular veneration. As dreams are more apt to visit a sick person, when the brain is more subject to these aberrations, many such have a number of dreams, and consequently many tutelary spirits. They preserve images, and statues in their medicine-bag, and never lose sight of them; but carry them about wherever they go. The faith of the Sauteux in their medicine is such, that they believe a disease can be thrown into an absent person, or that certain medicines can master the mental inclinations, such as love or hatred. Thus it is the interest of these old men to pander to the young. It can not be denied that the Sauteux have some knowledge of medicine. And I have myself witnessed several cures, which did honor to their physician. I have, above all, followed with great interest the progress of a cure which an English doctor had pronounced incurable, nevertheless the Sauteux doctor pronounced its cure very easy; which indeed he effected in a very short time. The disease was erysipelas, degenerated into ulcers.

The Sauteux language is much richer than is commonly thought. It bears a great resemblance to the ancient languages. It has, like the Greek, the dual and the two futures. And, like that language, it has but few radical words, but their manner of forming words for the occasion by the aid of these radicals, gives a great facility of expression, the same as in the Greek. The conjunction " and," either by hazard or otherwise, is the same as in the Greek. This language is formed of radical and compound words. The radical words are commonly employed in the familiar style; but in oratorical style, the compound words are used. As for example, *ishpa, wadjin*, in compound style is *ishpatna*, the mountain is high; *mangeteya sipa*, the river is large, in the compound style is *mangittigweya*, &c. This makes the learning of the language rather difficult at first, nearly equal to the acquiring of two languages; but in return for this, one acquires an extreme facility in expressing his thoughts with all the force he desires.

The Sauteux have also their poetic style, which consists more in suspension and enigmatical phrases than in words. Their songs contain only a few words, with a great many notes. Their music is very strange, and consists more in guttural sounds than in modulations. Their intervals are generally *de tierce en tierce*, accompanied by a great many unisons. They have songs of war, of love, and of worship.

Their writings are composed of arbitrary hieroglyphics, and the best writer is he, who is most skilful in using such signs as most fully represent his thoughts. Though this manner of writing is very defective, it is nevertheless ingenious and very useful, and has this advantage over all other languages, since it paint the thoughts, and not the words. For it remains for genius to discover the means of writing the thought, and not the word; just as figures represent numbers in all languages. Though the Sauteux have no idea of the state they shall find themselves in after death, they believe in the existence of a future life. They have very strange ideas on this subject; in consequence of some of these, they place near the deceased his arms and the articles most necessary to life. Some have even gone so far as to have their best horse killed at their death, in order, as they said, to use him in travelling to the country of the dead. It is the general belief that the spirit returns to visit the grave of the deceased very often, so long as the body is not reduced to dust. During this space of time it is held a sacred duty, on the part of the relatives of the deceased, to make sacrifices and offerings, and celebrate festivals before the door of the tomb. In the time of fruits, they carry them in great abundance to the tomb, aud he who nourishes himself with them after they have been deposited there, causes great joy to the parents and relations of the deceased. Although I have seen an old man who believed in metempsychosis, it is not a belief of the nation ; he probably received this thought elsewhere.

The Sauteux have also some knowledge of astronomy ; they have names for the most remarkable constellations ; they have names, also, for the lunar months ; but their calculations, as can be conceived, are very imperfect, and they often find themselves in great embarrassment, and have recourse to us to solve their difficulties. The electric fluid manifested in thunder, the rays of light of the aurora borealis, are in their imagination animated beings ; the thunders, according to them, are supernatural beings ; and the rays of the aurora borealis are the dead who dance.

Their idea of the creation of the world goes no farther back than the deluge, of which they have still a tradition, the narration of which would fill volumes. This account is extremely amusing, and filled with wearisome episodes. Without attempting to narrate the whole of it here, I will tell that part which relates to the creation : "An immortal genius, seeing the water which covered the earth, and finding nowhere a resting-place for his feet, ordered a castor, an otter, and other amphibious animals, to plunge by turns into the water, and bring up a little earth to the surface. They were all drowned. The rat, however, succeeded in reaching the bottom. and took some earth in his paws, but he died before he got back ; yet his body rose to the surface of the water. The genius, Nenabojou, seeing that he had found earth, brought him to life, and employed him to continue the work. When there was a sufficient quantity of earth, he made a man, whom he animated with his breath." This genius is not the Great Spirit, of whom they never speak except with respect ; while Nenabojou is considered a buffoon of no gravity.

This account contains one thing very important. It is that in speaking of the creation of plants, &c., it speaks of their nutritive properties ; and thus offers a resource for the sustenance of life in times of scarcity ; showing what roots, plants, and mosses, can to a certain extent preserve life. Improvident, not to say more of them, like all savage nations, the Sauteux pass rapidly from abundance to want.

There grows in the prairies a kind of turnip, which can appease hunger. When this root is chopped up, dried, and beaten, the Sauteux make a soup of it, which, when mixed with a little meat, becomes very nourishing; and thus, the food which would scarcely have sufficed a single day, is made to last several days. There is also a wild onion, of which they make much use. The ginger which grows in the woods, is employed as pepper in their repasts. In the spring, they find a kind of root, the shape of which resembles a ligne, vulgarly called a *rat's tail.* It is very abundant, of a good flavor, and very nutritive. Another root, named *ashkibwah*—that which is eaten raw—is very abundant, and contains much nutritive substance. The fibres of the trees, above all of the aspen, are used by them in time of scarcity; also a kind of bush or shrub which is found in the woods, called *pimattik.*

In the rocky countries, there exists a kind of moss very well known to travellers, of which the utility has been appreciated in more than one adventurous circumstance. It is the famous *tripe de roche.* This moss is of the nature of the mushroom. As there are some mushrooms which are real poisons, so there is a kind of *tripe de roche* which, far from nourishing, produces death. That which is green, and has small, round leaves, is the most nourishing, and most easily digested. With this, and a duck, a partridge, or a fish, one can make a succulent soup sufficient to nourish several men.

The Sauteux have a great passion for gaming. They pass whole days and nights in play; staking all they have, even their guns and traps, and sometimes their horses. It has happened that, having nothing more, they have staked even their wives upon the play.

Their love of intoxicating liquors is, as among all the other savage tribes, invincible. A Sauteux, who was convinced of religion, wished to become a Christian; but he could not be admitted without renouncing indulgence in drunkenness to excess. He complained bitterly, that the Hudson Bay Company had reduced his peoole to such a pitiable state, by bringing rum into the country, of which they would never have thought if they had not tasted it. The Sauteux are one of the most warlike of nations. From time immemorial, they have had the advantage over their numerous enemies, and pushed them to the north. They treat the vanquished with the most horrible barbarity. It is then that they are cannibals by virtue; for though we see sometimes among them cases of anthropophagy, they have such a horror of it, that he who has committed this act is no longer sure of his life. They hold it a sacred duty to put him to death on the first favorable occasion. But during war they make a glory of cannibalism. The feast of victory is very often composed of human flesh. One sees a trait of this barbarity in the names they give to their principal enemies; as, for instance, the Sioux, whom they call *Wanak*. As I have remarked before, it is not rare that they add to or retrench a little their proper names, which renders their interpretation rather difficult for strangers. In the word I have mentioned, *bwan* is put for *obwan*, which signifies a piece of flesh put on the spit; thus the word *abwanak*, which they have finished by calling *bwanak* or *pwanak*, signifying those whom one roasts on a spit. In their great war parties, after the victory, the Sauteux build a great fire, then plant all around spits laden with the thighs, heads, and hearts, &c., of their enemies, after which they return home.

4. The Sioux, to whom we must join the Assiniboins, inhabit a portion of the valley of the Hudson bay, viz.: the upper part of the Red river, and the river Chayenne, which is tributary to it. But many endeavors have been made to conclude a solid peace with the Sioux; and though each time has been with the appearance of success, their acts of treason have always destroyed these bright hopes. The Sauteux complain bitterly of their want of faith.

The nation of the Assiniboins, who separated themselves from the Sioux, according to tradition, on account of family disputes, took its name from the rocks of the lake of the Woods, where they first lived after their separation. Their name comes from *assin*, rock, and *bwan*, Sioux — *Sioux of the Rocks*. It is impossible to fix the date of this separation; for at the arrival of the first missionaries to Hudson's bay, Father Gabriel Marest, in 1694, wrote, speaking of the Assiniboins, whom he called *Assinipoils*, that this tradition was regarded as being already very old.

The Assiniboins are numerous, and from their habit of living in large encampments, are formidable to their enemies. This tribe, like the Sauteux and the Crees, their allies, are not hostile to the whites. A traveller can pass through this nation with more security for his life than in a civilized country, which can not be said of the Sioux. One can not travel upon the highlands of the Missouri and Red rivers, without often being seized with horror by the narrations occasioned by the view of places and scenes of a crowd of acts of barbarity and treason, that have been perpetrated by this people, of which one sees in history but an example from time to time. It is a horrible sight to see, as I have seen in different places, the skeletons of human beings, confounded in a heap with the bones of savage animals. Without these imminent dangers, which such sights recall to the mind of the traveller, these prairies would appear a paradise. Filled with game of all kinds, they offer at each moment a new point of view, and a variety of perspective most astonishing—lakes, where the herds of bison come to slake their thirst, and where the majestic swan and the wild goose repose themselves in passing—the limpid streams, where the beavers expose their ingenious work to the admiring gaze—petrifactions, mineral waters of various kinds, flowers, and strange plants, all unite to amuse and interest the intelligent traveller in search of the useful and the agreeable.

The nature of the territory separated from that of the United States by the 49th degree of latitude, is such, that it seems necessary that one should have first visited the country before determining the line and making a choice. With the exception of a straight strip of land, say a degree parallel to the 49th degree of latitude, all the rest of the country of the bay of Hudson is filled with lakes, marshes, savannas, and rocks. Except a small portion, on which is established the colony of Selkirk, there is not a spot of land that will produce corn. One can hardly imagine the sad eventualities to which the people of this country are subjected, who can never count on the resources of agriculture, being six hundred miles from any point where they can obtain supplies. It is thus that the people north of Saskadjiwan are exposed from time to time, to the terrible alternative of dying of hunger or of eating one another, when in the interval that the fisheries fail, it happens that the chase fails also.

It is for this reason that our neighbors of the colony of Selkirk view with envious eyes the beautiful territory which extends south of the forty-ninth degree, from Rainy lake to the Rocky mountains. The left bank of the river of Rainy lake, for the space of about eighty miles, is covered with all kinds of wood, of which the extreme height indicates the fertility of the soil. The country which belongs to the United States, is filled with advantages in respect to water-power. It is on account of the inferiority of the advantages of their territory, that our neighbors feel a strong opposition to our establishment.

At the foot of the beautiful mountain of Pembina, which is more than two hundred feet above the level of the river Pembina which divides it, and on its first table rises the little village of St. Joseph. It is divided by squares of twelve chains, and subdivided by lots of six chains. Its streets are one chain (sixty-six feet) wide, which adds to the beauty of the town, rendering the extinction of fire easier and favoring the free circulation of air and the health of the citizens. Everything wears an air of vigor in spite of the little protection they have thus far received from the general government. The least effective step, such as a garrison of soldiers, however feeble it might be, the construction of a public edifice, a court of justice, a prison, a house of correction, or anything that would prove the indubitable intention of government to protect us, would draw to this place a great portion of the population of Selkirk and elsewhere. The soil is very fertile, and the frosts never occasion any damage. Our gardens yield us an abundance of melons of all kinds; a fruit which is not known in the gardens of the Selkirkers. In 1851, the first frost felt at St. Paul was on the 6th or 7th of September; while at St. Joseph the first frost was not until the 2d or 3d of October. They raise potatoes which weigh about two pounds each, and carrots eighteen inches long and four in diameter. If the country were explored it would show, without doubt, great mineralogical advantages. At a short distance from our establishment, there are certain indications of iron and coal—these two articles are the most important for this country. The river Pembina furnishes water-power for any force required; there is also stone in abundance and very easily obtained.

THE MOUNDS OF THE MINNESOTA VALLEY.

The Rev. S. R. Riggs, of the Lac-qui-Parle mission, gives the following interesting account of the mounds of the Minnesota valley:—

In the Minnesota valley mounds are numerous. They may properly be divided into:—First, natural elevations, pahas, or pazhodans, as the Dakotas call them; second, such as are partly natural and partly artificial; and third, elevations which have been formed by certain processes. Pahas, or pazhodans, are found scattered over the prairies, some of the more prominent of which may be seen from a great distance. Such is Heyokatee, *the house of Heyoka*,* situated near the Mayawakan or Chippewa river, some ten miles or more above its junction with the Minnesota. This natural elevation appears at some distance to the right of the road, as one comes from Black-oak lake to Lac-qui-Parle. But even this is hardly

* Heyoka is the *anti-natural god* of the Dakotas—represented by an old man wearing a cocked hat, with a quiver on his back, and a bow in his hand. In the winter, it is said, he goes naked, and loves the northern blasts; while in summer he wraps his buffalo-robe around him, and is still suffering from cold.

to be compared with the "pahawakan," or *sacred hills*, in the valley of the James river, which are more than one hundred feet high, and can be distinctly seen from the farther border of the Coteau des Prairies, a distance of about forty miles. In passing from one point to another on the prairie, the *pahas* are very serviceable as guides to the traveller.

These natural elevations, where they are found near Indian villages, have been used as burial-places. Among the Dakotas, the native way of disposing of the dead is that of placing them on scaffolds. A *paha*, or conspicuous point, is preferred as the place of erecting such scaffold, that it may be seen from a distance. At the present time, burial soon after death is practised to a considerable extent by the Dakotas of the Minnesota valley, including those still on the Mississippi; and where they still prefer to place upon scaffolds at first, they not unfrequently bury in the course of a few months. But their graves are so shallow that, to cover the dead sufficiently, they are often obliged to carry up earth; and it is probable that formerly they carried up more than they do at present. To prevent the body from being dug up by wolves, they generally enclose the grave by setting up around, in a cone-like form, billets of wood. The decomposition of the bodies, and the rotting of the palisades and scaffolds, enrich the ground, and cause a more luxuriant growth of vegetation, which, of itself, directly tends to add to the size of the mound. Then this rank vegetation forms a nucleus for drift. Then the grass and dust which the wind blows over the prairie, lodge, and make the elevation still greater. On the hill, a short distance east of the ruins of Fort Renville, to the northwest and in sight of the mission-houses at Lac-qui-Parle, there is a *paha* of this kind, in which, in years gone by, many persons have been buried. It now presents on the top a very irregular surface, partly owing to the interments thus made, and partly to the burrowing of the gophers in it. On the southwest side of the Minnesota, a short distance back of the Wahpetonwan village, there is another mound, which has been long used as a burying-place. Similar ones may be found near all Dakota villages.

If the question be asked, Why do the Dakotas prefer these mounds as the places of deposite for their dead? I answer:—First, as before suggested, that the place may be seen from a distance all around. As they wail morning and evening, they can conveniently look to the abode, not only of the body of their departed friend, but, as many of them believe, of one of the spirits also. Secondly, all *pahas* are under the guardianship of their god Heyoka. And thirdly, a hill may be regarded as a more congenial place of rest for a spirit than a valley; and thence, too, the earthly spirit may the better hold communion with the one which has gone to the east along the "iron road," or is above, making progress on the "wanagi tachanku" (the via lactia), or *spirit's road.*

The third species of elevations which I shall notice, have the form of embankments rather than mounds. They are artificial, found usually in the river bottoms or low planting lands, and formed by carrying out, spring after spring, the corn-roots and other trash from off the field, and piling them along the outer edge, or on the row between two fields. In many instances of patches that had been planted for ten or twenty years previous to the introduction of the plough, I have seen these embankments from two to three feet high, and of all conceivable shapes; some rhomboidal, some hexagonal, some oval. I remember having noticed them first, many years ago, in the old plantings at Little Six's village, where I presume they may still be traced, as I am not aware that those old fields (which were on the opposite side of the river, and about two miles below the site of the present village), have ever been ploughed. The thought has occurred to me that, perhaps some of what have been regarded as Indian fortifications in other parts of the country, may have a similar origin.

In connection with these remarks on mounds, it is proper to give some description of a very interesting excavation and fortification, which is found a few miles above the mouth of the Pa-zhe-hu-ta-ze or Yellow Medicine river. It is on the south side of the Minnesota, and within sight of the mission-station lately commenced by Dr. Williamson. I visited this memorial of another race. The excavation extends around three sides of a somewhat irregular square, the fourth being protected by the slope of the hill, which is now covered with timber. After the filling-up of years, or perhaps centuries, the ditch is still about three feet deep. We found the east side, in the middle of the ditch, to measure thirty-eight paces; the south side, sixty-two; and the west side, fifty. The north side is considerably longer than the south. The area enclosed is not far from half an acre. On each of the three excavated sides there was left a gateway of about two paces. The earth was evidently thrown up on both sides; but the embankments have now almost entirely disappeared in the level of the prairie. Within the enclosure there are numerous very slight elevations, which seem to mark the places occupied by the dwellings of those who were once entrenched here. It would be interesting to know what were the form and character of these houses; but all we can learn from the present appearance of things is, that they were probably partly made of earth.

This is by far the largest and most interesting fortification that I have seen in the valley of the Minnesota. How long ago was this ditch dug, and by whom? It evidently bears the marks of some antiquity; and it was not probably made by the Dakotas, as it must date many years beyond their occupancy of this country. Some band of Indians, perhaps a little in advance of the Dakotas in civilization, here entrenched themselves against the attacks of their enemies. As we stood within the enclosure, and contemplated the work, we naturally asked the question, Who did this? And from the deep silence of antiquity the only answer we received was, WHO?

THE BROPHY SETTLEMENT.

THIS flourishing farming settlement is situated six miles northeast of St. Paul, and four and a half miles from St. Anthony. It was first settled by Michael Brophy, a soldier of the Mexican war, who went into this wild region, accompanied by a beautiful and accomplished wife, in the fall of 1850. He here entered a warrant for one hundred and sixty acres of land amid this beautiful region of woodland, prairie, and charming lakes, and, like Blannerhasset, dwelt alone away from the noise and bustle of the rising towns. No "Burr" was there to trouble him, save the *burr-oaks* in groves, which he soon cleared away, and putting up his cabin, commenced a permanent improvement. He soon attracted the attention of other adventurers seeking for homes and fortunes. Through his obliging manners, and his readiness in conducting strangers through the country, and giving them all the information in his power, as well as by the hospitalities extended at his home he drew many settlers to his neighborhood. The earliest pioneers succeeding him was a company of enterprising young men, known as the "Bachelors," who located there in the spring of 1851. Their names are, James R. Lawrence, Henry M'Kenty, Patrick Powers, C. E. Shaffer, and Andrew Jackson Morgan. The latter forsook "the art preservative of arts," and the setting of types for the setting of stakes, the following of the plough, and a residence with the other "Bachelors" in a house of tamarac logs.

Here they opened up their farms and flourished amid the beauties of Brophy. By industry, untiring perseverance, and a rapid meeting with and battling all opposing obstacles with resolute hearts, and with contented minds, they here dwelt peacefully, and laid the foundations for future wealth and independence. Other settlers followed, and the land is now being rapidly taken up. To those in search of a good farm, with all the necessary requisites of soil, wood, and water, combined, with an easy access to two good markets at very convenient distances, the Brophy settlement affords advantages that are seldom met with elsewhere. The soil consists of a rich clay and sandy loam—the two being often found on the same quarter section. It produces well—nay luxuriantly, as any one may see by a few hours' ride amid the fine farms now opened. Oak openings and rolling prairies are interspersed to suit the various tastes of all, and many fine locations on the various lakes are yet unoccupied. It is destined to become the most flourishing farming settlement in the neighborhood of St. Anthony or St. Paul, from the fact that a number of enterprising men are now located there, and all other things being equal, it has obtained a start which nothing can retard. The whole settlement for many miles is beautifully interspersed with lakes, of all shapes and sizes. The most beautiful of these is Lake Johanna, situated in the very midst of the settlement. It is three miles in circumference, and is surrounded by beautiful headlands, peninsulas, and high bluffs. The waters are of a crystal clearness, and abound in all kinds of fish common to the territory. The shores are sandy and full of pebbles, among which cornelians, agates, etc., are occasionally found. Lake Johanna is indeed a most romantic, lovely spot, and your eye loves to linger upon its quiet, peaceful, surface, while the setting orb of day throws on its surrounding scenery a flush of variegated light, which glows and kindles like the rose which tints the fair soft cheek of an eastern *houri*.

LIST OF OFFICIALS.

The organization of the territory of Minnesota having been made during the administration of President Taylor, the first official appointments were made (as is the precedent) from the ranks of the political party then in power, consequently the first executive officers of Minnesota were whigs. But the administration of General Pierce succeeding, the first incumbents were removed, and the important offices of the government of Minnesota were filled by appointment of the democratic president, and otherwise, as follows:—

Governor and Superintendent of Indian Affairs—Willis A. Gorman, of Indiana, *vice* Alexander Ramsey, formerly of Pennsylvania.

SECRETARY OF THE TERRITORY—J. T. Rosser, of Virginia, *vice* Alexander Wilkin, of Minnesota.

CHIEF-JUSTICE—William H. Welch, of Minnesota, *vice* H. Z. Hayner, formerly of New York.

ASSOCIATE-JUSTICES—A. G. Chatfield, of Wisconsin, *vice* David Cooper, formerly of Pennsylvania; and Moses Sherburne, of Maine, *vice* Bradley B. Meeker, formerly of Kentucky.

UNITED STATES MARSHAL—W. W. Irwin, of Missouri, *vice* J. W. Furber, of Minnesota.

UNITED STATES DISTRICT-ATTORNEY—Daniel H. Dustin, of New York, *vice* Henry L. Moss, of Minnesota.

LAND-RECEIVER AT STILLWATER—William H. Holcombe, of Minnesota, *vice* Jonathan M'Kusick, of Minnesota.

LAND-REGISTER AT STILLWATER—T. M. Fullerton, of Minnesota, *vice* Allen Pierse, of Minnesota.

LAND-RECEIVER AT SAUK RAPIDS—William H. Wood, of Minnesota, *vice* A. Christmas, of Minnesota.

LAND-REGISTER AT SAUK RAPIDS—George W. Sweet, of Minnesota, *vice* Reuben H. Richardson, of Minnesota.

AGENT FOR THE WINNEBAGOES—J. E. Fletcher, of Iowa, *vice* A. M. Fridley, formerly of New York.

AGENT FOR THE SIOUX—R. G. Murphy, of Illinois, *vice* N. M'Lean, of Minnesota.

AGENT FOR THE CHIPPEWAS—D. B. Herriman, of Indiana, *vice* J. S. Watrous, of Wisconsin.

POSTMASTER AT ST. PAUL—William H. Forbes, of Minnesota, *vice* J. W Bass, of Minnesota.

POSTMASTER AT ST. ANTHONY—Orrin W. Rice, of Minnesota, *vice* Ard God frey, of Minnesota.

COLLECTOR OF UNITED STATES CUSTOMS AT ST. PAUL—Robert Kennedy, of Minnesota, *vice* Charles J. Henniss, of Minnesota.

COLLECTOR OF UNITED STATES CUSTOMS AT PEMBINA—Philip Beaupré, of Minnesota, *vice* Charles Cavileer, of Minnesota.

CLERK OF THE SUPREME COURT—Andrew J. Whitney, of Minnesota, *vice* James K. Humphrey, of Minnesota.

LIBRARIAN AND PRIVATE SECRETARY—R. A. Smith, of Indiana, *vice* Wallace B. White, of Minnesota.

DELEGATE IN CONGRESS—Henry M. Rice, *vice* Henry H. Sibley (whose term of service has expired, the delegate being elected for two years).

ATTORNEY-GENERAL—Lafayette Emmett, *vice* L. A. Babcock, resigned.

ADJUTANT-GENERAL—Sylvanus B. Lowry, *vice* James M'Clelland Boal.

TERRITORIAL AUDITOR—Socrates Nelson, *vice* A. Van Voorhies.

TERRITORIAL TREASURER—Roswell B. Russell, *vice* Calvin Tuttle.

SUPERINTENDENT OF SCHOOLS—George W. Prescott, *vice* Rev. E. D. Neill, resigned.

MINNESOTA AND ITS RESOURCES.

The following letters, from distinguished and well-known sources, are offered for perusal to the readers of this work, as evidences of the appreciation which the subject of "Minnesota" commands within the territory. As complimentary to the author, they have given him much encouragement toward the success of the book; while they reflect in a great measure the tone which every true friend of western settlement should cheerfully respond to:—

(*From Hon. Alexander Ramsey.*)

St. Paul, *June* 21, 1853.

J. S. Redfield, Esq.—*Dear Sir:* Mr. J. Wesley Bond, a resident of this place for three years, and who in that time has enjoyed more than ordinary facilities for the acquisition of much valuable and interesting information of the current history and statistics of this territory, has prepared, and proposes to publish, a work illustrating the present condition of Minnesota. Such a work is a desideratum at this time; and Mr. Bond, from the large store of interesting facts that he has been industriously collecting, and his acknowledged abilities as a ready and fluent writer, I am convinced will satisfy the wants of the public in this regard.

The interest that has been excited all over the Union in reference to this region of the northwest will secure the book a ready sale, and I trust it may be convenient for you to aid Mr. Bond in bringing it before the public.

Very respectfully yours,

Alex. Ramsey.

(*From His Excellency Governor Gorman.*)

Executive Department, St. Paul, Minn. Ter.,
June 25, 1853.

J. S. Redfield, Esq.—*Dear Sir:* Mr. Bond has written a history of Minnesota, that is favorably spoken of here. He desires to make some arrangement for the publication. I have no doubt but that it will have a large circulation and ready sale. Any facility you can afford to the end desired will be regarded as a favor to the territory and to myself.

Most respectfully,

W. A. GORMAN.

(*From Isaac N. Goodhue, Esq., late Editor of the Minnesota Pioneer.*)

ST. PAUL, *June* 20, 1853.

J. S. REDFIELD, ESQ.—*Dear Sir:* In the states east of us there are probably more inquiries for information respecting Minnesota than for any other point of settlement in the new localities of our continent. As editor of the "Minnesota Pioneer" newspaper, I have had occasion to observe a remarkable degree of avidity with which information of our territory has been sought by eastern people who contemplate emigration to the west. I am confident that Mr. Bond's manuscript respecting our territory will meet with a ready sale whenever it is offered to the public—especially in the states east of us. As to the qualities of the work, I can assure you, that, if they are such as I have found in his frequent communications to the readers of the Pioneer, they are admirably suited to the purpose intended.

I wish Mr. Bond entire success in his enterprise, and doubt not he will attain it under the auspices of your establishment, if he shall be so happy as to receive your material encouragement.

Very respectfully, your obedient servant,

I. N. GOODHUE, editor "Minn. Pio."

(*From Rev. E. D. Neill, Secretary of the Historical Society of Minnesota.*)

ST. PAUL, M. T., *June* 18, 1853.

MR. J. W. BOND—*Dear Sir:* The work, entitled "Minnesota and its Resources," that you have prepared, and asked me to examine as secretary of the Minnesota Historical Society, has been perused with pleasure. The articles from your own pen, and those collated from the files of Minnesota papers, are such as will often be referred to by the Minnesotian. I have no doubt that, when the book is published, it will meet with a rapid sale, not only in Minnesota, but at the east, for it conveys just the sort of information the immigrant desires. The only book that has been published on Minnesota is Seymour's work. This gentleman (now no more) was a lawyer in Galena. Without practice, and very needy, he made a hasty trip to the territory, not being absent from Galena more than two weeks; and, after borrowing a book of travels, by Long, from one of my friends, returned and wrote the "Sketches of Minnesota," which have been the only sources of information at the command of the immigrant.

I hope that you will lose no time in forwarding your book to some eastern publisher, for such a manual is much needed.

Very truly your friend,

E. D. NEILL.

(*From J. Esaias Warren, Esq.*)

ST. PAUL, *June* 20, 1853.

J. S. REDFIELD, ESQ.—*Dear Sir:* I take pleasure in submitting to your careful perusal the MSS. of an exceedingly interesting work on Minnesota, which I think it would prove greatly to your interest to give to the world in a permanent form. The author is an excellent writer, and has been for years a resident of the territory. He has done ample justice to his subject, and this is saying as much as could be said. The immigration is now so great, and so rapidly on the increase, that a new work on the country is much in demand, and could not fail to command an extensive and ready sale. Hoping that you will be able to undertake the publication of the work, I have the pleasure to subscribe myself

Your friend and obedient servant,

J. Esaias Warren.

(*From J. J. Noah, Esq.*)

St. Paul, *June* 18, 1853.

J. S. Redfield, Esq.—*Dear Sir:* My personal friend, J. W. Bond, Esq., has handed me for perusal a "paper" on Minnesota, comprising researches and useful information rarely to be met with in the literature of the pres-ent day, which he tells me he is anxious to have published by your house. In recommending your acceptance of the same, I feel perfectly confident of its certain success, stored as it is with information more perfect and varied than the casual, speculative writer cares to fill his volume with. Mr. Bond has devoted a long residence here to literary pursuits, and his "Camp-Fire Sketches" were looked upon as ably written, as well as instructive and agreeable. As an editor, I have had abundant opportunity to note the cra-vings of popular taste; and the lapse of time since the publication of a "pla-giarism" on Minnesota, by Mr. Seymour, of Galena, has developed this focus of western civilization, until it has become an object of much attention throughout the United States. Consequently something really original and practical is in high demand; and, upon a careful examination of the effort of Mr. Bond, I do not hesitate to urge its speedy publication.

With respect I subscribe myself your ob't servant,

Jacob J. Noah.

(*From Hon. H. Z. Hayner, late Chief-Justice of the Territory of Minnesota.*)

St. Paul, *June* 22, 1853.

J. S. Redfield, Esq.—*Dear Sir:* With feelings of pleasure, permit me to add my testimonial to the able effort of J. Wesley Bond, Esq., who has be-stowed much care and labor upon "Minnesota and its Resources," and which he contemplates offering to you for publication. The production of such a work, with information known to be peculiarly correct, aside from any pub-lic character its statistics may assume, must, in my judgment, meet with suc-cess and unbounded public approbation. The eyes of the Atlantic popula-tion are continually gazing, in the dim obscurity of distance, toward the Great West, the immense resources of which remain yet to be developed by the hardy sons of New England and the down-trodden masses escaping from tyranny to find happy, peaceful homes within our vast domain. I know of no country better adapted to the confidence of western immigration than Min-nesota; and, in order that such confidence may be generally diffused, I can safely recommend the work of Mr. Bond to the inquiring public. The liter-ary reputation of the author is enviable, and I trust you may find it conve-nient and profitable to embark in his enterprise.

With respect, your ob't servant,

H. Z. Hayner.

PHILOSOPHERS AND ACTRESSES

By ARSENE HOUSSAYE. With beautifully-engraved Portraits of Voltaire and Mad. Parabère. Two vols., 12mo, price $2.50.

"We have here the most charming book we have read these many days,—so powerful in its fascination that we have been held for hours from our imperious labors, or needful slumbers, by the entrancing influence of its pages. One of the most desirable fruits of the prolific field of literature of the present season."—*Portland Eclectic.*

"Two brilliant and fascinating—we had almost said, bewitching—volumes, combining information and amusement, the lightest gossip, with solid and serviceable wisdom."—*Yankee Blade.*

"It is a most admirable book, full of originality, wit, information and philosophy Indeed, the vividness of the book is extraordinary. The scenes and descriptions are absolutely life-like."—*Southern Literary Gazette.*

"The works of the present writer are the only ones the spirit of whose rhetoric does justice to those times, and in fascination of description and style equal the fascinations they descant upon."—*New Orleans Commercial Bulletin.*

"The author is a brilliant writer, and serves up his sketches in a sparkling manner." *Christian Freeman.*

ANCIENT EGYPT UNDER THE PHARAOHS.

By JOHN KENDRICK, M. A. In 2 vols., 12mo, price $2.50.

"No work has heretofore appeared suited to the wants of the historical student, which combined the labors of artists, travellers, interpreters and critics, during the periods from the earliest records of the monarchy to its final absorption in the empire of Alexander. This work supplies this deficiency."—*Olive Branch.*

"Not only the geography and political history of Egypt under the Pharaohs are given, but we are furnished with a minute account of the domestic manners and customs of the inhabitants, their language, laws, science, religion, agriculture, navigation and commerce."—*Commercial Advertiser.*

"These volumes present a comprehensive view of the results of the combined labors of travellers, artists, and scientific explorers, which have effected so much during the present century toward the development of Egyptian archæology and history."—*Journal of Commerce.*

"The descriptions are very vivid and one wanders, delighted with the author, through the land of Egypt, gathering at every step, new phases of her wondrous history, and ends with a more intelligent knowledge than he ever before had, of the land of the Pharaohs."—*American Spectator.*

COMPARATIVE PHYSIOGNOMY;

Or Resemblances between Men and Animals. By J. W. REDFIELD, M. D. In one vol., 8vo, with several hundred illustrations. price, $2.00.

"Dr. Redfield has produced a very curious, amusing, and instructive book, curious in its originality and illustrations, amusing in the comparisons and analyses, and instructive because it contains very much useful information on a too much neglected subject. It will be eagerly read and quickly appreciated."—*National Ægis.*

"The whole work exhibits a good deal of scientific research, intelligent observation, and ingenuity."—*Daily Union.*

"Highly entertaining even to those who have little time to study the science."—*Detroit Daily Advertiser.*

"This is a remarkable volume and will be read by two classes, those who study for information, and those who read for amusement. For its originality and entertaining character, we commend it to our readers."—*Albany Express.*

"It is overflowing with wit, humor, and originality, and profusely illustrated. The whole work is distinguished by vast research and knowledge."—*Knickerbocker.*

"The plan is a novel one; the proofs striking, and must challenge the attention of the curious."—*Daily Advertiser*

NOTES AND EMENDATIONS OF SHAKESPEARE.

Notes and Emendations to the Text of Shakespeare's Plays, from the Early Manuscript Corrections in a copy of the folio of 1632, in the possession of JOHN PAYNE COLLIER, Esq., F.S.A. Third edition, with a fac-simile of the Manuscript Corrections. 1 vol. 12mo, cloth, $1 50.

"It is not for a moment to be doubted, we think, that in this volume a contribution has been made to the clearness and accuracy of Shakespeare's text, by far the most important of any offered or attempted since Shakespeare lived and wrote."—*Lond. Exam.*

"The corrections which Mr. Collier has here given to the world are, we venture to think, of more value than the labors of nearly all the critics on Shakespeare's text put together."—*London Literary Gazette.*

"It is a rare gem in the history of literature, and can not fail to command the attention of all the amateurs of the writings of the immortal dramatic poet."—*Ch'ston Cour.*

"It is a book absolutely indispensable to every admirer of Shakespeare who wishes to read him understandingly."—*Louisville Courier.*

"It is clear from internal evidence, that for the most part they are genuine restorations of the original plays. They carry conviction with them."—*Home Journal.*

"This volume is an almost indispensable companion to any of the editions of Shakespeare, so numerous and often important are many of the corrections."—*Register, Philadelphia.*

THE HISTORY OF THE CRUSADES.

By JOSEPH FRANÇOIS MICHAUD. Translated by W. Robson, 3 vols. 12mo., maps, $3 75.

"It is comprehensive and accurate in the detail of facts, methodical and lucid in arrangement, with a lively and flowing narrative."—*Journal of Commerce.*

"We need not say that the work of Michaud has superseded all other histories of the Crusades. This history has long been the standard work with all who could read it in its original language. Another work on the same subject is as improbable as a new history of the 'Decline and Fall of the Roman Empire.'"—*Salem Freeman.*

"The most faithful and masterly history ever written of the wild wars for the Holy Land."—*Philadelphia American Courier.*

"The ability, diligence, and faithfulness, with which Michaud has executed his great task, are undisputed; and it is to his well-filled volumes that the historical student must now resort for copious and authentic facts, and luminous views respecting this most romantic and wonderful period in the annals of the Old World."—*Boston Daily Courier.*

MARMADUKE WYVIL.

An Historical Romance of 1651, by HENRY W. HERBERT, author of the "Cavaliers of England," &c., &c. Fourteenth Edition. Revised and Corrected.

"This is one of the best works of the kind we have ever read—full of thrilling incidents and adventures in the stirring times of Cromwell, and in that style which has made the works of Mr. Herbert so popular."—*Christian Freeman, Boston.*

"The work is distinguished by the same historical knowledge, thrilling incident, and pictorial beauty of style, which have characterized all Mr. Herbert's fictions and imparted to them such a bewitching interest."—*Yankee Blade.*

"The author out of a simple plot and very few characters, has constructed a novel of deep interest and of considerable historical value. It will be found well worth reading."—*National Ægis, Worcester.*

DISCOVERY AND EXPLORATION

Of the Mississippi Valley. With the Original Narratives of Marquette, Allouez, Membré, Hennepin, and Anastase Douay. By John Gilmary Shea. With a fac-simile of the Original Map of Marquette. 1 vol., 8vo, ; Cloth. Antique. $2.00.

"A volume of great and curious interest to all concerned to know the early history of this great Western land."—*Cincinnati Christian Herald.*

"We believe that this is altogether the most thorough work that has appeared on the subject to which it relates. It is the result of long-continued and diligent research, and no legitimate source of information has been left unexplored. The work combines the interest of romance with the authenticity of history."—*Puritan Recorder.*

"Mr. Shea has rendered a service to the cause of historical literature worthy of all praise by the excellent manner in which he has prepared this important publication for the press."—*Boston Traveller.*

NEWMAN'S REGAL ROME.

An Introduction to Roman History. By Francis W. Newman, Professor of Latin in the University College, London. 12mo, Cloth. 63 cents.

"The book, though small in compass, is evidently the work of great research and reflection, and is a valuable acquisition to historical literature."—*Courier and Enquirer.*

"A work of great erudition and power, vividly reproducing the wonderful era of Roman history under the kings. We greet it as a work of profound scholarship, genial art, and eminent interest—a work that will attract the scholar and please the general reader."—*N. Y. Evangelist.*

"Nearly all the histories in the schools should be banished, and such as this should take their places."—*Boston Journal.*

"Professor Newman's work will be found full of interest, from the light it throws on the formation of the language, the races, and the history, of ancient Rome."—*Wall-street Journal.*

THE CHEVALIERS OF FRANCE,

From the Crusaders to the Mareschals of Louis XIV. By Henry W. Herbert, author of "The Cavaliers of England," "Cromwell," "The Brothers," &c., &c. 1 vol. 12mo. $1.25.

"Mr. Herbert is one of the best writers of historical tales and legends in this or another country."—*Christian Freeman.*

"This is a work of great power of thought and vividness of picturing. It is a moving panorama of the inner life of the French empire in the days of chivalry."—*Albany Spec*

"The series of works by this author, illustrative of the romance of history, is deservedly popular. They serve, indeed, to impart and impress on the mind a great deal of valuable information; for the facts of history are impartially exhibited, and the fiction presents a vivid picture of the manners and sentiments of the times."—*Journal of Commerce.*

"The work contains four historical tales or novelettes, marked by that vigor of style and beauty of description which have found so many admirers among the readers of the author's numerous romanaes."—*Lowell Journal.*

MOORE'S LIFE OF SHERIDAN.

Memoirs of the Life of the Rt. Hon. Richard Brinsley Sheridan, by THOMAS MOORE, with Portrait after Sir Joshua Reynolds. Two vols., 12mo, cloth, $2.00.

"One of the most brilliant biographies in English literature. It is the life of a wit written by a wit, and few of Tom Moore's most sparkling poems are more brilliant and fascinating than this biography."—*Boston Transcript.*

"This is at once a most valuable biography of the most celebrated wit of the times, and one of the most entertaining works of its gifted author."—*Springfield Republican.*

"The Life of Sheridan, the wit, contains as much food for serious thought as the best sermon that was ever penned."—*Arthur's Home Gazette.*

"The sketch of such a character and career as Sheridan's by such a hand as Moore's, can never cease to be attractive."—*N. Y. Courier and Enquirer.*

"The work is instructive and full of interest."—*Christian Intelligencer.*

"It is a gem of biography; full of incident, elegantly written, warmly appreciative, and on the whole candid and just. Sheridan was a rare and wonderful genius, and has in this work justice done to his surpassing merits."—*N. Y. Evangelist.*

BARRINGTON'S SKETCHES.

Personal Sketches of his own Time, by SIR JONAH BARRINGTON, Judge of the High Court of Admiralty in Ireland, with Illustrations by Darley. Third Edition, 12mo, cloth, $1 25.

"A more entertaining book than this is not often thrown in our way. His sketches of character are inimitable; and many of the prominent men of his time are hit off in the most striking and graceful outline."—*Albany Argus.*

"He was a very shrewd observer and eccentric writer, and his narrative of his own life, and sketches of society in Ireland during his times, are exceedingly humorous and interesting."—*N. Y. Commercial Advertiser.*

"It is one of those works which are conceived and written in so hearty a view, and brings before the reader so many palpable and amusing characters, that the entertainment and information are equally balanced."—*Boston Transcript.*

"This is one of the most entertaining books of the season."—*N. Y. Recorder.*

"It portrays in life-like colors the characters and daily habits of nearly all the English and Irish celebrities of that period."—*N. Y. Courier and Enquirer.*

JOMINI'S CAMPAIGN OF WATERLOO.

The Political and Military History of the Campaign of Waterloo, from the French of Gen. Baron Jomini, by Lieut. S. V. BENET, U. S. Ordnance, with a Map, 12mo, cloth, 75 cents.

"Of great value, both for its historical merit and its acknowledged impartiality."—*Christian Freeman, Boston.*

"It has long been regarded in Europe as a work of more than ordinary merit, while to military men his review of the tactics and manœuvres of the French Emperor during the few days which preceded his final and most disastrous defeat, is considered as instructive, as it is interesting."—*Arthur's Home Gazette.*

"It is a standard authority and illustrates a subject of permanent interest. With military students, and historical inquirers, it will be a favorite reference, and for the general reader it possesses great value and interest."—*Boston Transcript.*

"It throws much light on often mooted points respecting Napoleon's military and political genius. The translation is one of much vigor."—*Boston Commonwealth.*

"It supplies an important chapter in the most interesting and eventful period of Napoleon's military career."—*Savannah Daily News.*

"It is ably written and skilfully translated."—*Yankee Blade.*

MACAULAY'S SPEECHES.

Speeches by the Right Hon. T. B. MACAULAY, M. P., Author of "The History of England," "Lays of Ancient Rome," &c., &c. Two vols., 12mo, price $2.00.

"It is hard to say whether his poetry, his speeches in parliament, or his brilliant essays, are the most charming; each has raised him to very great eminence, and would be sufficient to constitute the reputation of any ordinary man."—*Sir Archibald Alison.*

"It may be said that Great Britain has produced no statesman since Burke, who has united in so eminent a degree as Macaulay the lofty and cultivated genius, the eloquent orator, and the sagacious and far-reaching politician."—*Albany Argus.*

"We do not know of any living English orator, whose eloquence comes so near the ancient ideal—close, rapid, powerful, *practical* reasoning, animated by an intense earnestness of feeling."—*Courier & Enquirer.*

"Mr. Macaulay has lately acquired as great a reputation as an orator, as he had formerly won as an essayist and historian. He takes in his speeches the same wide and comprehensive grasp of his subject that he does in his essays, and treats it in the same elegant style."—*Philadelphia Evening Bulletin.*

"The same elaborate finish, sparkling antithesis, full sweep and copious flow of thought, and transparency of style, which made his essays so attractive, are found in his speeches. They are so perspicuous, so brilliantly studded with ornament and illustration, and so resistless in their current, that they appear at the time to be the wisest and greatest of human compositions."—*New York Evangelist.*

TRENCH ON PROVERBS.

On the Lessons in Proverbs, by RICHARD CHENEVIX TRENCH, B. D., Professor of Divinity in King's College, London, Author of the "Study of Words." 12mo, cloth, 50 cents.

"Another charming book by the author of the "Study of Words," on a subject which is so ingeniously treated, that we wonder no one has treated it before."—*Yankee Blade.*

"It is a book at once profoundly instructive, and at the same time deprived of all approach to dryness, by the charming manner in which the subject is treated."—*Arthur's Home Gazette.*

"It is a wide field, and one which the author has well cultivated, adding not only to his own reputation, but a valuable work to our literature."—*Albany Evening Transcript.*

"The work shows an acute perception, a genial appreciation of wit, and great research. It is a very rare and agreeable production, which may be read with profit and delight."—*New York Evangelist.*

"The style of the author is terse and vigorous—almost a model in its kind."—*Portland Eclectic.*

THE LION SKIN

And the Lover Hunt; by CHARLES DE BERNARD. 12mo, $1.00.

"It is not often the novel-reader can find on his bookseller's shelf a publication so full of incidents and good humor, and at the same time so provocative of honest thought."—*National* (Worcester, Mass.) *Ægis.*

"It is full of incidents; and the reader becomes so interested in the principal personages in the work, that he is unwilling to lay the book down until he has learned their whole history."—*Boston Olive Branch.*

"It is refreshing to meet occasionally with a well-published story which is written for a story, and for nothing else—which is not tipped with the snapper of a moral, or loaded in the handle with a pound of philanthropy, or an equal quantity of leaden philosophy."—*Springfield Republican.*

A STRAY YANKEE IN TEXAS.

A Stray Yankee in Texas. By PHILIP PAXTON. With Illustrations by Darley. Second Edition, 12mo., cloth. $1 25.

"The work is a *chef d'œuvre* in a style of literature in which our country has no rival, and we commend it to all who are afflicted with the blues or *ennui*, as an effectual means of tickling their diaphragms, and giving their cheeks a holyday."—*Boston Yankee Blade.*

"We find, on a perusal of it, that Mr. Paxton has not only produced a readable, but a valuable book, as regards reliable information on Texan affairs.—*Hartford Christian Secretary.*

"The book is strange, wild, humorous, and yet truthful. It will be found admirably descriptive of a state of society which is fast losing its distinctive peculiarities in the rapid increase of population."—*Arthur's Home Gazette.*

"One of the richest, most entertaining, and, at the same time, instructive works one could well desire."—*Syracuse Daily Journal.*

"The book is a perfect picture of western manners and Texan adventures, and will occasion many a hearty laugh in the reader."—*Albany Daily State Register.*

NICK OF THE WOODS.

Nick of the Woods, or the Jibbenainosay; a Tale of Kentucky. By ROBERT M. BIRD, M. D., Author of "Calavar," "The Infidel," &c. New and Revised Edition, with Illustrations by Darley. 1 volume, 12mo., cloth, $1 25.

"One of those singular tales which impress themselves in ineradicable characters upon the memory of every imaginative reader."—*Arthur's Home Gazette.*

"Notwithstanding it takes the form of a novel, it is understood to be substantial truth in the dress of fiction; and nothing is related but which has its prototype in actual reality."—*Albany Argus.*

"It is a tale of frontier life and Indian warfare, written by a masterly pen, with its scenes so graphically depicted that they amount to a well-executed painting, at once striking and thrilling."—*Buffalo Express.*

WHITE, RED, AND BLACK.

Sketches of American Society, during the Visits of their Guests, by FRANCIS and THERESA PULSZKY. Two vols., 12mo., cloth, $2.

"Mr. Pulszky and his accomplished wife have produced an eminently candid and judicious book, which will be read with pleasure and profit on both sides of the Atlantic."—*New York Daily Times.*

"The authors have here furnished a narrative of decided interest and value. They have given us a view of the Hungarian war, a description of the Hungarian passage to this country, and a sketch of Hungarian travels over the country."—*Philad. Christian Chronicle.*

"Of all the recent books on America by foreign travellers, this is at once the most fair and the most correct."—*Philad. Saturday Gazette.*

"Unlike most foreign tourists in the United States, they speak of our institutions, manners, customs, &c., with marked candor, and at the same time evince a pretty thorough knowledge of our history."—*Hartford Christian Secretary.*

"This is a valuable book, when we consider the amount and variety of the information it contains, and when we estimate the accuracy with which the facts are detailed.
—*Worcester Spy*

POETICAL WORKS OF FITZ-GREENE HALLECK.

New and only Complete Edition, containing several New Poems, together with many now first collected. One vol., 12mo., price one dollar.

"Halleck is one of the brightest stars in our American literature, and his name is like a household word wherever the English language is spoken."—*Albany Express.*

"There are few poems to be found, in any language, that surpass, in beauty of thought and structure, some of these."—*Boston Commonwealth.*

"To the numerous admirers of Mr. Halleck, this will be a welcome book; for it is a characteristic desire in human nature to have the productions of our favorite authors in an elegant and substantial form."—*Christian Freeman.*

"Mr. Halleck never appeared in a better dress, and few poets ever deserved a better one."—*Christian Intelligencer.*

THE STUDY OF WORDS.

By Archdeacon R. C. Trench. One vol., 12mo., price 75 cts.

"He discourses in a truly learned and lively manner upon the original unity of language, the origin, derivation, and history of words, with their morality and separate spheres of meaning."—*Evening Post*

"This is a noble tribute to the divine faculty of speech. Popularly written, for use as lectures, exact in its learning, and poetic in its vision, it is a book at once for the scholar and the general reader."—*New York Evangelist.*

"It is one of the most striking and original publications of the day, with nothing of hardness, dullness, or dryness about it, but altogether fresh, lively, and entertaining." —*Boston Evening Traveller.*

BRONCHITIS, AND KINDRED DISEASES.

In language adapted to common readers. By W. W. Hall, M. D. One vol., 12 mo, price $1.00.

"It is written in a plain, direct, common-sense style, and is free from the quackery which marks many of the popular medical books of the day. It will prove useful to those who need it."—*Central Ch. Herald.*

"Those who are clergymen, or who are preparing for the sacred calling, and public speakers generally, should not fail of securing this work."—*Ch. Ambassador.*

"It is full of hints on the nature of the vital organs, and does away with much superstitious dread in regard to consumption."—*Greene County Whig.*

"This work gives some valuable instruction in regard to food and hygienic influences."—*Nashua Oasis.*

KNIGHTS OF ENGLAND, FRANCE, AND SCOTLAND.

By Henry William Herbert. One vol., 12mo., price $1.25.

"They are partly the romance of history and partly fiction, forming, when blended, portraitures, valuable from the correct drawing of the times they illustrate, and interesting from their romance."—*Albany Knickerbocker.*

"They are spirit-stirring productions, which will be read and admired by all who are pleased with historical tales written in a vigorous, bold, and dashing style."—*Boston Journal.*

"These legends of love and chivalry contain some of the finest tales which the graphic and powerful pen of Herbert has yet given to the lighter literature of the day." —*Detroit Free Press.*

LYRA, AND OTHER POEMS.

By ALICE CAREY. In one volume, 12mo, cloth, price 75 cts.

"Whether poetry be defined as the rhythmical creation of beauty, as passion or eloquence in harmonious numbers, or as thought and feeling manifested by processes of the imagination, Alice Carey is incontestably and incomparably the first living American poetess—fresh, indigenous, national—rich beyond precedent in suitable and sensuous imagery—of the finest and highest qualities of feeling, and such powers of creation as the Almighty has seen fit to bestow but rarely or in far-separated countries."—*Bost. Trans.*

"The genuine inspiration of poetic feeling, . . . replete with tenderness and beauty, earnestness and truthful simplicity, and all the attributes of a powerful imagination and vivid fancy. We know of no superior to Miss Carey among the female authors of this country."—*New York Journal of Commerce.*

"Alice Carey's book is full of beautiful thoughts; there is draught after draught of, pure pleasure for the lover of sweet, tender fancies, and imagery which captivates while it enforces truth."—*New York Courier and Inquirer.*

"'Lyra and other Poems,' just published by Redfield, attracts everywhere, a remarkable degree of attention. A dozen of the leading journals, and many eminent critics, have pronounced the authoress the greatest poetess living."—*New York Mirror.*

LILLIAN, AND OTHER POEMS.

By WINTHROP MACKWORTH PRAED. Now first Collected. One Volume 12mo. Price One Dollar.

"A timely publication is this volume. A more charming companion (in the shape of a book) can scarcely be found for the summer holydays."—*New York Tribune.*

"They are amusing sketches, gay and sprightly in their character, exhibiting great facility of composition, and considerable powers of satire."—*Hartford Courant.*

"There is a brilliant play of fancy in 'Lillian,' and a moving tenderness in 'Josephine,' for which it would be hard to find equals. We welcome, therefore, this first collected edition of his works."—*Albany Express.*

"As a writer of *vers de societe* he is pronounced to be without an equal among English authors."—*Syracuse Daily Journal.*

"The author of this volume was one of the most fluent and versatile English poets that have shone in the literary world within the last century. His versification is astonishingly easy and airy, and his imagery not less wonderfully graceful and aerial."—*Albany State Register.*

THE CAVALIERS OF ENGLAND;

Or, the Times of the Revolutions of 1642 and 1688. By HENRY WILLIAM HERBERT. One vol., 12mo., price $1.25.

"They are graphic stories, and in the highest degree attractive to the imagination as well as instructive, and can not fail to be popular."—*Commercial.*

"These tales are written in the popular author's best style, and give us a vivid and thrilling idea of the customs and influences of the chivalrous age."—*Christian Freeman.*

"His narrative is always full of great interest; his descriptive powers are of an uncommon order; the romance of history loses nothing at his hands; he paints with the power, vigor, and effect of a master."—*The Times.*

"They bring the past days of old England vividly before the reader, and impress upon the mind with indelible force, the living images of the puritans as well as the cavaliers, whose earnest character and noble deeds lend such a lively interest to the legends of the times in which they lived and fought, loved and hated, prayed and revelled."—*Newark Daily.*

CLOVERNOOK;

Or, Recollections of our Neighborhood in the West. By Alice Carey. Illustrated by Darley. One vol., 12mo., price $1.00. (Fourth edition.)

"In this volume there is a freshness which perpetually charms the reader. You seem to be made free of western homes at once."—*Old Colony Memorial.*

"They bear the true stamp of genius—simple, natural, truthful—and evince a keen sense of the humor and pathos, of the comedy and tragedy, of life in the country."—*J G Whittier.*

DREAM-LAND BY DAY-LIGHT:

A Panorama of Romance. By Caroline Chesebro'. Illustrated by Darley. One vol., 12mo., price $1.25. (Second edition.)

"These simple and beautiful stories are all highly endued with an exquisite perception of natural beauty, with which is combined an appreciative sense of its relation to the highest moral emotions."—*Albany State Register.*

"Gladly do we greet this floweret in the field of our literature, for it is fragrant with sweet and bright with hues that mark it to be of Heaven's own planting."—*Courier and Enquirer.*

"There is a depth of sentiment and feeling not ordinarily met with, and some of the noblest faculties and affections of man's nature are depicted and illustrated by the skilful pen of the authoress."—*Churchman.*

LAYS OF THE SCOTTISH CAVALIERS.

By William E. Aytoun, Professor of Literature and Belles-Lettres in the University of Edinburgh and Editor of Blackwood's Magazine. One vol., 12mo. cloth, price $1.00.

"Since Lockhart and Macaulay's ballads, we have had no metrical work to be compared in spirit, vigor, and rhythm with this. These ballads embody and embalm the chief historical incidents of Scottish history—literally in 'thoughts that breathe and words that burn.' They are full of lyric energy, graphic description, and genuine feeling."—*Home Journal.*

"The fine ballad of 'Montrose' in this collection is alone worth the price of the book.' *Boston Transcript.*

THE BOOK OF BALLADS.

By Bon Gaultier. One volume, 12mo., cloth, price 75 cents.

"Here is a book for everybody who loves classic fun. It is made up of ballads of all sorts, each a capital parody upon the style of some one of the best lyric writers of the time, from the thundering versification of Lockhart and Macaulay to the sweetest and simplest strains of Wordsworth and Tennyson. The author is one of the first scholars, and one of the most finished writers of the day, and this production is but the frolic of his genius in play-time "—*Courier and Enquirer.*

"We do not know to whom belongs this *nom de plume*, but he is certainly a humorist of no common power."—*Providence Journal.*

ISA, A PILGRIMAGE.

By CAROLINE CHESEBRO'. One vol., 12mo., cloth, price $1.00.

"The Pilgrimage is fraught throughout with scenes of thrilling interest—romantic, yet possessing a naturalness that seems to stamp them as real; the style is flowing and easy, chaste and beautiful."—*Troy Daily Times.*

"Miss Chesebro' is evidently a *thinker*—she skims not the mere surface of life, but plunges boldly into the hidden mysteries of the spirit, by which she is warranted in making her startling revelations of human passion."—*Christian Freeman.*

"There comes out in this book the evidence of an inventive mind, a cultivated taste, an exquisite sensibility, and a deep knowledge of human nature."—*Albany Argus.*

"It is a charming book, pervaded by a vein of pure ennobling thought."—*Troy Whig.*

"There is no one who will doubt that this is a courageous and able work, displaying genius and depth of feeling, and striking at a high and noble aim."—*N. Y. Evangelist.*

"There is a fine vein of tenderness running through the story, which is peculiarly one of passion and sentiment."—*Arthur's Home Gazette.*

LECTURES AND MISCELLANIES.

BY HENRY JAMES. One vol., 12mo., cloth, price $1.25.

"A series of essays by one of the most generous thinkers and sincere lovers of truth in the country. He looks at society from an independent point of view, and with the noblest and most intelligent sympathy."—*Home Journal.*

"This is the production of a mind richly endowed of a very peculiar mould. All will concede to him the merit of a vigorous and brilliant intellect."—*Albany Argus.*

"A perusal of the essays leads us to *think*, not merely because of the ideas which they contain, but more because the ideas are earnestly put forth, and the subjects discussed are interesting and important to every one."—*Worcester National Ægis.*

"They have attracted much attention both here and in Europe, where the author is considered as holding a distinctive and prominent position in the school of modern philosophy."—*Albany Atlas.*

"The writer wields a masterly and accurate pen, and his style is good."—*Boston Olive Branch.*

"It will have many readers, and almost as many admirers."—*N. Y. Times*

NAPIER'S PENINSULAR WAR.

History of the War in the Peninsula, and in the South of France, from the Year 1807 to 1814. BY W. F. P. NAPIER, C.B., Col. 43d Reg., &c. Complete in one vol., 8vo., price $3.00.

"We believe the Literature of War has not received a more valuable augmentation this century than Col. Napier's justly celebrated work. Though a gallant combatant in the field, he is an impartial historian."—*Tribune.*

"NAPIER'S History, in addition to its superior literary merits and truthful fidelity, presents strong claims upon the attention of all American citizens; because the author is a large-souled philanthropist, and an inflexible enemy to ecclesiastical tyranny and secular despots."—*Post.*

"The excellency of Napier's History results from the writer's happy talent for impetuous, straight-forward, soul-stirring narrative and picturing forth of characters The military manœuvre, march, and fiery onset, the whole whirlwind vicissitudes of the desperate fight, he describes with dramatic force —*Merchants' Magazine.*

CHARACTERS IN THE GOSPEL,

Illustrating Phases of Character at the Present Day. By Rev. E. H. CHAPIN. One vol., 12mo., price 50 cents. (Second edition.)

"As we read his pages, the reformer, the sensualist, the skeptic, the man of the world, the seeker, the sister of charity and of faith, stand out from the Scriptures, and join themselves with our own living world."—*Christian Enquirer.*

"Mr. Chapin has an easy, graceful style, neatly touching the outlines of his pictures, and giving great consistency and beauty to the whole. The reader will find admirable descriptions, some most wholesome lessons, and a fine spirit."—*N. Y. Evangelist.*

"Its brilliant vivacity of style forms an admirable combination with its soundness of thought and depth of feeling."—*Tribune.*

LADIES OF THE COVENANT:

Memoirs of Distinguished Scottish Females, embracing the Period of the Covenant and the Persecution. By Rev. JAMES ANDERSON. One vol., 12mo., price $1.25.

"It is a record which, while it confers honor on the sex, will elevate the heart, and strengthen it to the better performance of every duty."—*Religious Herald. (Va.)*

"It is a book of great attractiveness, having not only the freshness of novelty, but every element of historical interest."—*Courier and Enquirer.*

"It is written with great spirit and a hearty sympathy, and abounds in incidents of more than a romantic interest, while the type of piety it discloses is the noblest and most elevated."—*N. Y. Evangelist.*

TALES AND TRADITIONS OF HUNGARY.

By THERESA PULSZKY, with a Portrait of the Author. One vol., price $1.25.

THE above contains, in addition to the English publication, a NEW PREFACE, and TALES, now first printed from the manuscript of the Author, who has a direct interest in the publication.

"This work claims more attention than is ordinarily given to books of its class. Such is the fluency and correctness—nay, even the nicety and felicity of style—with which Madame Pulszky writes the English language, that merely in this respect the tales here collected form a curious study. But they contain also highly suggestive illustrations of national literature and character."—*London Examiner.*

"Freshness of subject is invaluable in literature—Hungary is still fresh ground. It has been trodden, but it is not yet a common highway. The tales and legends are very various, from the mere traditional anecdote to the regular legend, and they have the sort of interest which all national traditions excite."—*London Leader.*

SORCERY AND MAGIC.

Narratives of Sorcery and Magic, from the most Authentic Sources. By THOMAS WRIGHT, A.M., &c. One vol. 12mo., price $1.25.

"We have no hesitation in pronouncing this one of the most interesting works which has for a long time issued from the press."—*Albany Express.*

"The narratives are intensely interesting, and the more so, as they are evidently written by a man whose object is simply to tell the truth, and who is not himself bewitched by any favorite theory."—*N. Y. Recorder.*

THE MASTER BUILDER;

Or, Life at a Trade. By DAY KELLOGG LEE, author of "Summerfield, or Life on the Farm." One vol., 12mo, price $1.00.

"He is a powerful and graphic writer, and from what we have seen of the pages of the 'Master Builder,' it is a romance of excellent aim and success."—*State Register.*

"The 'Master Builder' is the master production. It is romance into which is instilled the reality of life: and incentives are put forth to noble exertion and virtue. The story is pleasing—almost fascinating; the moral is pure and undefiled."—*Daily Times.*

"Its descriptions are, many of them, strikingly beautiful; commingling in good proportions, the witty, the grotesque, the pathetic, and the heroic. It may be read with profit as well as pleasure."—*Argus.*

"The work before us will commend itself to the masses, depicting as it does most graphically the struggles and privations which await the unknown and uncared-for Mechanic in his journey through life. It is what might be called a romance, but not of love, jealousy and revenge order."—*Lockport Courier.*

"The whole scheme of the story is well worked up and very instructive."—*Albany Express.*

GRISCOM ON VENTILATION.

The Uses and Abuses of Air: showing its Influence in Sustaining Life, and Producing Disease, with Remarks on the Ventilation of Houses, and the best Methods of Securing a Pure and Wholesome Atmosphere inside of Dwellings, Churches, Workshops, &c. By JOHN H. GRISCOM, M. D. One vol. 12mo, $1.00.

"This comprehensive treatise should be read by all who wish to secure health, and especially by those constructing churches, lecture-rooms, school-houses, &c.—It is undoubted, that many diseases are created and spread in consequence of the little attention paid to proper ventilation. Dr. G. writes knowingly and plainly upon this all-important topic."—*Newark Advertiser.*

"The whole book is a complete manual of the subject of which it treats; and we venture to say that the builder or contriver of a dwelling, school-house, church, theatre, ship, or steamboat, who neglects to inform himself of the momentous truths it asserts, commits virtually a crime against society."—*N. Y. Metropolis.*

"When shall we learn to estimate at their proper value, pure water and pure air, which God provided for man before he made man, and a very long time before he permitted the existence of a doctor? We commend the Uses and Abuses of Air to our readers, assuring them that they will find it to contain directions for the ventilation of dwellings, which every one who values health and comfort should put in practice."—*N. Y. Dispatch.*

HAGAR, A STORY OF TO-DAY.

By ALICE CAREY, author of "Clovernook," "Lyra, and Other Poems," &c. One vol., 12mo, price $1.00.

"A story of rural and domestic life, abounding in humor, pathos, and that naturalness in character and conduct which made 'Clovernook' so great a favorite last season. Passages in 'Hagar' are written with extraordinary power, its moral is striking and just, and the book will inevitably be one of the most popular productions of the season."

"She has a fine, rich, and purely original genius. Her country stories are almost unequaled."—*Knickerbocker Magazine.*

"The Times speaks of Alice Carey as standing at the head of the living female writers of America. We go even farther in our favorable judgment, and express the opinion that among those living or dead, she has had no equal in this country; and we know of few in the annals of English literature who have exhibited superior gifts of real poetic genius."—*The (Portland, Me.) Eclectic.*

Life under an Italian Despotism!

LORENZO BENONI,

OR

PASSAGES IN THE LIFE OF AN ITALIAN

One Vol., 12mo, Cloth—Price $1.00.

OPINIONS OF THE PRESS.

"THE author of 'Lorenzo Benoni' is GIOVANNI RUFFINI, a native of Genoa, who effected his escape from his native country after the attempt at revolution in 1833. His book is, in substance, an authentic account of real persons and incidents, though the writer has chosen to adopt fictitious and fantastic designations for himself and his associates. Since 1833, Ruffini has resided chiefly (if not wholly) in England and France, where his qualities, we understand, have secured him respect and regard. In 1848, he was selected by Charles Albert to fill the responsible situation of embassador to Paris, in which city he had long been domesticated as a refugee. He ere long, however, relinquished that office, and again withdrew into private life. He appears to have employed the time of his exile in this country to such advantage as to have acquired a most uncommon mastery over the English language. The present volume (we are informed on good authority) is exclusively his own—and, if so, on the score of style alone it is a remarkable curiosity. But its matter also is curious."—*London Quarterly Review for July.*

"A tale of sorrow that has lain long in a rich mind, like a ruin in a fertile country, and is not the less gravely impressive for the grace and beauty of its coverings . . . at the same time tho most determined novel-reader could desire no work more fascinating over which to forget the flight of time. . . . No sketch of foreign oppression has ever, we believe, been submitted to the English public by a foreigner, equal or nearly equal to this volume in literary merit. It is not unworthy to be ranked among contemporary works whose season is the century in which their authors live."—*London Examiner.*

"The book should be as extensively read as 'Uncle Tom's Cabin,' inasmuch as it develops the existence of a state of slavery and degradation, worse even than that which Mrs. Beecher Stowe has elucidated with so much pathos and feeling."—*Bell's Weekly Messenger.*

"Few works of the season will be read with greater pleasure than this; there is a great charm in the quiet, natural way in which the story is told."—*London Atlas.*

"The author's great forte is character-painting. This portraiture is accomplished with remarkable skill, the traits both individual and national being marked with great nicety without obtrusiveness."—*London Spectator.*

"Under the modest guise of the biography of an imaginary 'Lorenzo Benoni,' we have here, in fact, the memoir of a man whose name could not be pronounced in certain parts of northern Italy without calling up tragic yet noble historical recollections. . . . Its merits, simply as a work of literary art, are of a very high order. The style is really beautiful—easy, sprightly, graceful, and full of the happiest and most ingenious turns of phrase and fancy."—*North British Review.*

"This has been not unjustly compared to '*Gil Blas*,' to which it is scarcely inferior in spirited delineations of human character, and in the variety of events which it relates. But as a description of actual occurrences illustrating the domestic and political condition of Italy, at a period fraught with interest to all classes of readers, it far transcends in importance any work of mere fiction."—*Dublin Evening Mail.*

"SHAKESPEARE AS HE WROTE IT."

THE WORKS OF SHAKESPEARE,

Reprinted from the newly-discovered copy of the Folio of 1632 *in the possession of J. Payne Collier, containing nearly*

Twenty Thousand Manuscript Corrections,

With a History of the Stage to the Time, an Introduction to each Play, a Life of the Poet, etc.

BY J. PAYNE COLLIER, F.S.A.

To which are added, Glossarial and other Notes, the Readings of Former Editions, a PORTRAIT *after that by Martin Droeshout, a* VIGNETTE TITLE *on Steel, and a* FACSIMILE OF THE OLD FOLIO, *with the Manuscript Corrections.* 1 vol, Imperial 8vo. Cloth $4 00.

The **WORKS OF SHAKESPEARE** the same as the above. Uniform in Size with the celebrated Chiswick Edition, 8 vols. 16mo, cloth $6 00. Half calf or moroc. extra

These are *American Copyright Editions*, the Notes being expressly prepared for the work. The English edition contains simply the text, without a single note or indication of the changes made in the text. In the present, the variations from old copies are noted by reference of all changes to former editions (abbreviated f. e.). and every indication and explanation is given essential to a clear understanding of the author. The prefatory matter, Life, &c., will be fuller than in any American edition now published.

"THIS is the only correct edition of the works of the 'Bard of Avon' ever issued, and no lover or student of Shakespeare should be without it."—*Philadelphia Argus.*

"Altogether the most correct and therefore the most valuable edition extant."—*Albany Express.*

"This edition of Shakespeare will ultimately supersede all others. It must certainly be deemed an essential acquisition by every lover of the great dramatist."—*N. Y. Commercial Advertiser.*

"This great work commends itself in the highest terms to every Shakespearian scholar and student."—*Philadelphia City Item.*

"This edition embraces all that is necessary to make a copy of Shakespeare desirable and correct."—*Niagara Democrat.*

"It must sooner or later drive all others from the market."—*N. Y. Evening Post.*

"Beyond all question, the very best edition of the great bard hitherto published."—*New England Religious Herald.*

"It must hereafter be the standard edition of Shakespeare's plays."—*National Argus.*

"It is clear from internal evidence that they are genuine restorations of the original plays."—*Detroit Daily Times.*

"This must we think supersede all other editions of Shakespeare hitherto published. Collier's corrections make it really a different work from its predecessors. Compared with it we consider them hardly worth possessing."—*Daily Georgian, Savannah.*

"One who will probably hereafter be considered as the only true authority. No one we think, will wish to purchase an edition of Shakespeare, except it shall be conformable to the amended text by Collier."—*Newark Daily Advertiser.*

"A great outcry has been made in England against this edition of the bard, by Singer and others interested in other editions; but the emendations commend **themselves** too strongly to the good sense of every reader to be dropped by the public—**the old** editions must become obsolete."—*Yankee Blade, Boston.*

www.ingramcontent.com/pod-product-compliance
Lightning Source LLC
LaVergne TN
LVHW020120110826
845151LV00001B/224
9781425541101